Scottish Place-names

For Jock Holm

Scottish Place-names

David Ross

Birlinn

First published in 2001 by
Birlinn Limited
West Newington Place
10 Newington Road
Edinburgh EH9 1QS

www.birlinn.co.uk

ISBN 1 84158 173 9

British Library Cataloguing in Publication Data
A catalogue record for this book is available from the British Library

Typesetting and origination by Brinnoven, Livingston
Printed and bound by Creative Print and Design, Wales, Ebbw Vale

Contents

Introduction   vi

Maps   xxii

Place-Names A–Z   1

Bibliography   227

List of Place-names Noted Outside
the Alphabetical Sequence   229

Introduction

What's in a Name?

Names are signs of thought, language and social organisation. They give identity to a place, or a landscape feature. Once it is named, we see it as itself, an individual entity. And names can have remarkable durability. In the introduction to his *Scottish Place-Names*, W. F. H. Nicolaisen notes how far the name Hawick has come from its origins in Old English *haga wic*, 'hedge farm', and how it now expresses an identity that is quite different and far more complex. It is typical of very many others, many of them much older.

What is the function or purpose of a place-name? The original answers to this simple question are lost in time. The oldest place-name of all is simply *home,* though for a nomadic people, home is where the tent is. We can suppose that for a dwelling-place this purpose included an affirmation of personal, family or tribal association: 'our place'; as well as the exclusivity of occupancy: 'not your place'. For the hunter and traveller a place-name might have a different kind of significance, enabling a course to be steered across an untracked landscape or along a coastline. 'The split hill' (Criffel) or 'summit ridge' (Drumochter) or 'turning point' (Cape Wrath) described features that served as location-markers for people on the move. 'Salmon firth' (Laxford) may have referred to a special quality or abundance, at a time when almost all firths were salmon-rich. The range of geographical reference was not enormous; place-names were given on a local basis without reference to other districts. Otherwise there would not be so many Ben Mores, or Carn Deargs. There was no need to be highly specific: the context of the locality, or the subject under discussion would be sufficient to make clear which 'big hill' or 'red peak' was being referred to.

But even though such simple name-forms continued to be coined, far back in prehistory some name-forms had already progressed beyond basic labelling. At an early stage, there were places which had acquired a mystical significance for humans. Certain hill summits, river confluences, coastal headlands, among other features, were chosen as places of worship or reverence. Under the auspices of religion, a name might be given to convey a numinous presence:

'black goddess river' is a name that occurs several times in Scottish toponymy (*see* Lochy). Later, the names of holy men and women would be chosen to lend their prestige and protection to selected places, as in Kilbride, 'Church of St Bride' and many more. The nature of some early settlements is indicated by such names as those beginning with Caer- and Dun-, indicative of a hill or fort situation, and often of both. Sometimes, the origin of a name is as a definition of alien space: 'their place' – Scotland itself is a name bestowed by those outside the country in order to characterise the territory of people they knew as the Scots; Dunkeld is from a Gaelic name given to a Pictish community, whose own name is not recorded. As the population grew and society developed, names began to reflect such social institutions as mills, with Balavoulin, 'place of the mill', from Gaelic *baile a' mhuillin,* and the many Miltons; or markets, as with Knockando, 'hill of trading'; and gatherings, as with Dingwall, 'parliament field'.

An important development in place-naming occurred when names took on a possessive rather than a descriptive significance. A prominent landscape feature is common to everyone; 'my place', with my name attached to it, is a different kind of proposition. 'Private' and 'Trespassers Will be Prosecuted' are already foreshadowed. Here we reach a point where place-names can tell something about the nature and structure of the society which coined them. This kind of naming was not a practice of the early Celtic inhabitants, whose use of personal names in place-names was largely confined to those of saints, in a form of dedication. (Exceptions to this such as Balmaclellan, Balornock, Ben Macdhui are usually from a later period.) Such self-effacement was not for the 'teutonic' arrivals, Anglians in the south and the later Norsemen in the north and north-west. Whether or not their naming practice reveals the insecurity of the usurper, it certainly displays a different concept of land-ownership to that of the tribally-minded Britons and Gaels, and hints at the quasi-feudal system that was to come in the twelfth and thirteenth centuries.

Some of these person-based names, like thirteenth-century Dolphinton, 'Dolfine's place', or eighteenth-century Colinsburgh, continue to emphasise an individual owner or founder centuries after the individual's death. Distinctive buildings could also define places, like Falkirk, 'vari-coloured church', or Redcastle. In a society ever-preoccupied by land ownership, very many names reflect boundaries and subdivisions, like Cree, 'boundary', and Pennyghael, 'penny (rent) land of the Gaels', as well as the Pit- names of the eastern side. Others reflect the productive capacity of the land, like the

Davoch- and Oxgangs names. The meanings of some name-forms were liable to evolve; from its former sense of 'fortified place', burgh came to indicate a community with a corporate life and trading privileges. Creative fancy was not lavished on names: a new burgh was likely to be called Newburgh. With only rare exceptions, like Beauly, 'beautiful spot', place-names remained essentially factual or functional until the seventeenth century. Earlier, even those names which seemed to imply an aesthetic judgement, like the numerous Pittendreichs, 'portion of the good aspect', probably meant the portion receiving most sunlight: a practical farming consideration. A more relaxed attitude and the perception of a wider range of possibilities later produced Biblical names, like Padanaram; complimentary ones, like Helensburgh and Arabella; and commemorative ones like Camperdown and Waterloo.

Most people know that place-names, especially ancient ones, were not given arbitrarily, or 'invented' as a string of meaningless Scottish-sounding syllables. With a population largely illiterate, few roads, no road-signs and no maps, ancient place-names very often had a functional importance that today has passed to site-descriptions like 'Household Waste Recycling Point'. A glance at the text will reveal that virtually all place-names mean something – usually something with specific reference to the actual location – and the only problem is that we don't always know, or agree, what that something is.

In Scotland, there is a close link between place-names and surnames. Along with patronymics, descriptive and occupational names, place-names form one of the four main groups of Scottish surnames. Many surnames began as place-names, and often still remain current around the same location or in the same region. This is highly noticeable among the Cursiters, Isbisters, Linklaters and others in Orkney, but is also true for Anstruther, Lauder, Stenhouse, Urquhart and many another mainland name. There is an intriguing side-issue as to why some small towns, Abernethy, Busby and Irvine for example, have relatively numerous human homonyms, while many larger places have none. Indeed, such well-known surnames as Carnegie and Cochrane have arisen from very tiny places, in Angus and Renfrewshire respectively. In both ancient and modern times, this place-personal link has on occasion also been established from the other direction in such old places as Cowal and such relatively new ones as Macduff. These connections, apart from exemplifying the close relationship between place and people, add their own interest to Scottish toponymy.

A consequence of the Scottish diaspora is that Scottish place-names occur in many parts of the world, given by settlers or developers to nameless sites, or perhaps more often usurping some already existing name (as they quite possibly had done in Scotland before). Some of these names are new coinages using individuals' names, like the Mackenzie River or the Ross Sea; most are specifically intended as tributes to or reminders of home, like Perth (Western Australia), Hamilton (Ontario) and Blantyre (Malawi). Some incorporate Scottish elements in new names and ways, like Invercargill (New Zealand: a Gaelic prefix attached to a Scots name) and the Scoto-Hindi hybrid Campbellpore. Names such as these have sometimes been criticised for their lack of roots in local history or topographical truth; but this is to ignore the fact that names take on a life of their own. The Scottish visitor to Melbourne will find a very different St Kilda to the Atlantic archipelago of the same name (with its own curious non-saintly origin), and the Canadian visitor to Mull will find a very different Calgary to that in Alberta. Such contrasts add their own touch of zest to travel, and to atlas-gazing.

Names, especially of significant places, have never been free from manipulation by interested parties, usually those in power. The history of St Andrews is an example, where ninth century politics and religion, inextricably linked, promoted the cult of the Apostle under the aegis of the MacAlpin kings at the expense of Abernethy and Dunkeld with their Columban links, and old Mucros or Kilrymont became first the town of St Rule and then St Andrews. A similar process may have assisted the anglicisation of Din Eiddyn to Queen Margaret's favoured Edinburgh. The history of Fort William is a notable example of political naming.

Recording Scotland's Place-Names

The first, sparse records of Scottish place-names, prior to the Roman invasions, are found in the writings of Latin authors. The earliest known voyager to Britain is a Carthaginian, Himilco, whose account, by then almost a thousand years old, was preserved at third-hand in a fourth century BC Latin poem and leaves us the name 'Albion', referring to Britain rather than Scotland. The classical writers' main source is Pytheas, the Greek merchant–navigator who sailed from Marseilles to the North Sea around 320 BC, and left an account (no longer extant at first hand) of his expedition. The name Orcas, 'Orkney', is traceable back to Pytheas, as is Hebudes, later 'Hebrides'. With Agricola's military campaigns, between AD 80 and 85, recorded by his son-in-law Tacitus, a few more names appear, including Clota (see Clyde) and Bodotria (see Forth), as well as the elusive Mons Graupius. Around AD 150 the pioneering Greek

geographer and astronomer Ptolemy of Alexandria supplied the best
scientific information of his time in his *Introduction to Geography*,
clearly based on research and information from those who had
actually visited the British Isles. He records almost sixty different
location names, apart from tribal names, in what is now Scotland.
A long gap in the written record follows, until the seventh-century
Ravenna Cosmography, compiled in Italy from sources that go back
to the second century, lists a number of site-names in Scotland;
from the sixth century onwards the annals and records of Irish
abbeys also become available. These church documents, concerned
primarily with religious events and royal successions, mention some
place-names. Bede's *Ecclesiastical History of the English People*
(731), necessarily includes much information relating to the Celtic
Church, and gives a number of names, including that of prior Boisil
of Melrose whose name is preserved in that of St Boswells. The oral
tradition of Gaelic and Old Welsh verse also preserved place-names,
like Din Eidynn in the 'Gododdin' poem of the sixth century, though
frequently in uncertain or baffling forms. From the twelfth century,
as landholding in Scotland began to be recorded on a documentary
basis, an increasing number of sources is available which specifically
cite place-names. The scribes of these charters, mostly speakers of
the evolving Scots tongue, and writing in Latin, frequently found
great difficulty with the Gaelic names whose meaning they even
then did not know. Some contemporary Gaelic names are found
written in the eleventh–twelfth century *Book of Deer*, a book of
Latin gospels from the monastery of Deer, which found its way to
Cambridge University Library. *Ragman's Roll* of 1296, recording
the names of most Scottish landowners, is a valuable source,
though the removal of Scottish state documents by Edward I of
England, in the same year, is a grievous loss to the modern study
of names. Many were later sent back, but the ship foundered with
its cargo. The development of literature in Scots in the thirteenth
and fourteenth centuries preserves names from the period, not
only through occasional text references but also through the long-
standing custom of calling a land-owner by the name of his property,
as in the flyting poet Hume of Polwarth. But the next great step
forward happened in the early seventeenth century, when Timothy
Pont made his topographical survey of Scotland: the maps, revised
by Robert Gordon of Straloch, made a whole volume in Blaeu's
Theatrum Orbis Terrarum of 1654, published in Amsterdam. From
then on, records become more frequent and most names have their
modern form or something close to it. The establishment of the
Ordnance Survey and the grand project of mapping the whole of

Great Britain in detail, which was completed between 1844 and 1896, left few significant locations nameless, though here too ancient names were sometimes contorted into bizarre 'English' forms, as with the rendering of Loch Sionnascaig, in Coigach, itself a Gaelic form of a Norse name, into Loch Skinaskink. The national postal system, set up in the nineteenth century, also served to confirm and stabilise the toponymy of human settlements; but despite all forces of conservation, names remain remarkably fluid, restless things, with a life of their own which the most ubiquitous bureaucracy cannot quite stamp out.

The Earliest Names

Our ancestors, whether Celtic speaking of the Brythonic (Pictish–Welsh–Cornish) type or the Goidelic (Gaelic) groups, or Norse, or Anglian, took a prosaic view of place-names. This is typical of virtually all early societies. The old names are tersely descriptive. Unsurprisingly, in a countryside then relatively undisturbed by humanity's destructions and improvements, many of the locality names mean in one form or another, 'boggy place', or refer to woods, rocks and clearings. Among the few more figurative types of older Scottish names are the many hill and mountain names which correspond to words for the female breast (the history of Lochnagar is interesting in this context). A facile visual resemblance, or the product of a deeper sense of human identification and integration with the landscape of 'Scotland, stern mother'? The answer remains an enigma. But this early, basic, naming style is most apparent, and most mysterious, in the oldest known names, those of the rivers.

In many cases, the sources of the names of Scottish rivers cannot be clearly traced. They are more ancient than the Western Celtic languages, going back far beyond the availability of written evidence in these tongues. Two and a half thousand or more years ago, the rivers were not the relatively tamed and docile streams of today. They were wilder, swifter, unembanked, unbridged – dangerous hazards for the settler or the hunter. Immediate and formidable barriers, they could also be communication routes, food sources, cult places and territorial boundaries. It may be that certain river and other names were inherited from the prehistoric, pre-Celtic inhabitants of the country, whose languages can only be guessed at (even these peoples originally came as settlers from somewhere else, presumably in Europe, after the end of the Ice Age). Such as yet unexplained names as Affric, Cheviot, Farrar, Isla and Mar have been tentatively ascribed to such a source. Many other river-names, like Avon, Averon, Awe, Don, Deveron, Esk, Teith, Teviot, appear to share their basic form, or elements such as -*on*, with Celtic or pre-Celtic river-names in Europe, reaching geographically and linguistically far back towards India. Their meaning has been elucidated as implying wetness, or flowing, or mist – that is to say, 'water'. But the resonance or full original significance is knotted too tightly into these often monosyllabic names for us to unpick it. Just as the Orcadians of two generations ago had a variety of terms for 'rain', so the early Europeans had a number of words indicating 'running water', no doubt each with special connotations. As a justification of the prosaic nature and limited range of river-names, it has been suggested that many rivers also had sacred names which were not for everyday use, and have consequently been lost. It is a tantalising thought that such names might have held the key to an important strand of early Celtic religious thought and practice. On the other hand, rivers were not the only cult places, and the naming of non-water features is neither more nor less banal than the water-names.

Names and Languages: Picts and Britons

Humans have lived continuously in Scotland for some 8000 years and from those who lived there in the greater bulk of that period, the first six millennia, a mere handful of dubious and disputable names have come down. The Celtic language speakers who inhabited the country in the latter centuries BC spoke a Brythonic form, or forms, of the 'Common Celtic' tongue. Two main linguistic groups emerge in early historical times: the Britons of Strathclyde, whose language, 'Cumbric', developed into the Old Welsh of the 'Gododdin' poem (preserving the name of the Votadini tribe); and the Picts, whose territory lay north of the Forth–Clyde line and extended to include the Hebrides and the Northern Isles. Their language, Pictish, appears to have died out between the ninth and eleventh centuries, supplanted by Gaelic. The main fortress of the Britons in historical times was Dumbarton, 'fort of the Britons', though they called it Alclut, 'rock of Clyde'. Unsurprisingly, many names from that Clyde–Annandale region, including Clyde, Lochmaben, Dumfries, are of Cumbric origin. But the Cumbric speakers once occupied a much wider area, extending across into Lothian, where the hill fort of Din Eiddyn was, and where names like Penicuik, 'hill of the cuckoo', and numerous other Pen- names, show the typical *p*- of the Brythonic languages, which had replaced *c*- in words existing prior to the time of the change (later words beginning with *c*- can also be found in the

Brythonic languages, just as there are later Gaelic words which begin with p-). The Goidelic language group had retained the *c*-. This key distinction, shown for example in Gaelic *ceann* and Cumbric *pen*, 'head, top', is a useful guide to the language of origin of many place-names. Although Strathclyde retained a separate identity until 1034, its later history is one of decline. Picts, Scots from Ulster, Angles, and later the Gall–Gael Scots–Norse, all raided it and left their mark on its place-names.

The language of the Picts has left very little by way of written record; in fact, surviving place names have been used to help establish its form, rather than the opposite process. The Pictish centre of power has been identified at different times as Inverness, Forteviot, and other places. Two key sets of place-names are especially identified with Pictish occupancy and origin: those beginning with Aber- and those beginning with Pit-. The once-intense controversy among scholars over the implications of these place-names and their locations has now subsided. They are among the few signposts available to the political and social, as well as the linguistic, history of 'Dark Age' Scotland and have been keenly scrutinised by those who seek to clarify what happened and when in the tangled history of Britons, Picts and Scots between the third and the ninth centuries. Pit-, though related to Gaulish *pett*-, is unique to east-central and north-east Scotland as a place-name prefix. It has been pointed out that the other element, in the majority of names to which Pit- is found prefixed, is Gaelic. Nevertheless, the concentration of Pit- names in certain districts is striking, and also corresponds with other evidence relating to the existence and populated zones of the Pictish kingdom. Land organisation and the demarcation of boundaries is a practice that goes a very long way back, and is still associated with annual rituals in some places; and it has been plausibly argued that the preservation, maybe even the creation, of Pit- names in a later, Gaelic-speaking, society has to do with the legal significance acquired by the prefix, indicating the precise nature of the land-holder's tenure. Aber- names, though predominantly in 'Pictland', are shared with locations in the Cumbric-speaking area, and of course also with Wales. Another name-form in the Pictish region, ascribed to Brythonic–Pictish is that incorporating the word *cardden*, 'thicket', as in Pluscarden.

Romans

The invading Romans of the first century of the Common Era (thereafter referred to AD)identified the names of some fifteen tribal groups. By around AD 180 these were loosely organised in two main confederacies, the Maeatae, just north of the Forth–Clyde lines, and the Caledonii, farther north. Both tribal names are preserved in Dumyat and Dunkeld respectively. Roman military occupancy of the Southern Uplands, which lasted through the second century AD, and sporadically to the fourth century, resulted in much building, and has left its trace in a small number of names, such as Chesters, from Latin *castrum*, 'fort', via the Old English form *ceastre*. Not far away, Bonchester preserves the same Latin element, with a Gaelic prefix grafted on. Other names relating to the Roman period may include Straiton in South Ayrshire ('place on the Roman road'), but Latin names are rare, as the Romans established no permanent civilian settlements. The Latinised forms of place-names often found in medieval documents relate to the practice of the times, when much legal business was conducted in Latin, and have nothing to do with the ultimate derivations of the names.

The Gaelic Language

There had long been communication between the peoples living in Ireland and in Scotland. From the fifth century the Gaelic-speaking Scots, from Ulster, began to settle in the west, naming their territory Argyll ('coastland of the Gael') and Dàl Riada, after the kingdom they had left behind. This importation of previous names marks a departure from the purely referential form of name, whether done for sentimental reasons or pragmatically to set the seal on a new political reality. At very much the same time, speakers of the Anglian dialect of Old English were moving into the south-eastern region. By 547 they were in control of Lothian. These were immensely important developments. The Gaelic speech of Argyll would spread to become the national language, ousting Cumbric and completely eclipsing Pictish. By the early eleventh century, Scotland, apart from the Anglian enclave and the areas conquered by the Norsemen, was a Gaelic-speaking country. Even in Lothian there was a Gaelic presence. The Anglian speech would develop into Scots and in its turn force Gaelic out of the entire south and centre, in its progression towards the form of vernacular English spoken throughout present-day Scotland.

The spread of Gaelic meant that Gaelic place-names were formed in virtually every part of the country. In many cases, the mutual resemblance of the various languages may have made only slight modification necessary for a Pictish or Cumbric name to appear as a Gaelic one; in others, as with many Pit- and Aber- names, a hybrid might emerge, showing elements from both languages. But doubtless many older names were lost. The similarities between Pictish, Cumbric and Gaelic made it easy to borrow word-elements into the 'invading' language. Kincardine, a name found in several parts of old Pictland, incorporates a Gaelix prefix, *cinn*, from *ceann*, 'at the head of' and the Pictish *cardden*. But this latter word had also acquired a Gaelic form, *chardain*, with the same sense of 'wood' or 'thicket'. The incorporation of French *-ville* as a suffix in some eighteenth-century names shows a similar process, though not necessarily the same sort of cultural causes.

Norse

The consolidation of Gaelic nomenclature was halted or seriously interrupted over a wide area by the Norse attacks and invasions beginning around 790. By around 870, Orkney and Shetland were a Viking earldom under the crown of Norway. Their Pictish identity was virtually obliterated. In Caithness and down through the Hebrides, colonists from Norway and Denmark established themselves in communities and imported their languages and their own names. Names deriving from Old Norse were given between the ninth and twelfth centuries, mostly in the Northern and Western Isles, Caithness and Sutherland, but reaching into other areas. Norse settlers from Dublin sailed up to Galloway and along the Solway Firth (itself a Norse name that ousted its predecessor). Others penetrated north from the Viking kingdom of York. To the Gaels, Caithness (a Norse suffix added to the archaic name Cat) became Gallaibh, 'land of the strangers'. There was little resemblance between Gaelic and Old Norse and many Gaelic names were replaced by Norse ones or given Norse affixes

There were many resemblances between Old Norse and Old English, both languages stemming from the same Indo–Germanic source. Thus the Scots word 'kirk' came into Scotland from both ends, Old Norse *kirkja* in Halkirk and Kirkwall, and Old English *cirice* in Kirkoswald and Muirkirk. Most of the Norse landscape names are as severely practical as those of the Celts, like Cape Wrath, or Laxford; very few suggest a touch of imaginative appreciation of the scene: Fitful Head is perhaps an example.

With the end of Viking rule, the use of Gaelic was reasserted in the Western Isles, but not in (formerly Pictish) Orkney and Shetland, which spoke their own Norn dialect evolved from Old Norse; and to only a limited degree in Caithness. Pleonastic names began to appear, where Gaelic speakers, ignorant of the meaning of a place-name, added their own element to give it sense to themselves. Thus on Mull Eass Forss is the name of a waterfall in which both parts, Gaelic and Norse respectively, mean the same thing, 'waterfall'. The Skye fiord-lochs, like Snizort and Eishort, are among many examples of the same effect.

Scots

The Anglian form of Old English, its vocabulary enriched with many contributions from Gaelic, French and Flemish, is the source of the Scots tongue which survived in vigour from the Middle Ages almost to the nineteenth century, and which itself was a prolific source of names. These are mostly for minor localities, moors, woods and fields, since the major features and most of the centres of population already had been named. Scots, however, played a substantial part in the 'corruption' of older names. This process had already begun in the form of Gaelic–Pictish and Gaelic–Norse hybrid names. With the spread of Scots, the old languages were forgotten, parish by parish, and names were often manipulated to make better 'sense', like King Edward; or had linguistically unnecessary additions made, like Ardtornish Point. Such a process has to be seen as a natural one, in a country with such a range of linguistic sources and a relatively homogeneous population. In New Zealand, English speakers' happy-go-lucky way with Maori place-names is a hot issue; in Scotland, we have long done as we please with our historic names. As long ago as the thirteenth century, names like Gordon and Huntly were arbitrarily transferred from the far south of the country to the north. More recently, such curiosities as Crossmyloof and Auchenshuggle appeared.

Modern English

The seventeenth and eighteenth centuries brought many new names, and a new, broader approach to the giving of place-names. By the eighteenth century, with the Union of the Parliaments, there was a new desire to use 'correct' English both in speech and in spelling. In its own way, this was part of the drive for 'improvement' that characterised the century far more genuinely than the episodic Jacobite risings. Hundreds of new townships and villages were developed. New names appeared, often literally outlandish, like Patna or the -heim added to Friock, brought to Scotland in a converse process to the 'diaspora' names. At this time the proprietorial name often assumed prominence, in new or remodelled communities like Fraserburgh, Grantown and Campbeltown; and sometimes a place-name became a compliment to the laird's lady, as in Helensburgh and Jemimaville. The absent and controversial monarchy of the 1690s reinforced its position in people's minds with fortress-town names like Fort Augustus. A post-Reformation Biblical element crept in, with names like Jordanhill. But despite such novelties, a Scottish sense of tradition largely prevailed. The many new villages of the eighteenth and early nineteenth centuries, pioneered by John Cockburn's Ormiston, mostly preserved the name of the farm-toun or clachan that they had supplanted. Whilst Pulteneytown, the new part of Wick, commemorated a living commissioner of fisheries, the newly laid-out Ullapool, more typically, kept the name of the otherwise long-forgotten Olaf. An interesting pamphlet on the history of Ardler, and how it failed to become Washington, published by Abertay Historical Society, gives a good example of a process that went on in dozens of other communities.

Many names are undoubtedly still evolving. Comparison of modern and nineteenth-century maps will show many local changes, such as the arrival of the *t* in Glen Moriston. In addition to such development', an element of antiquarianism has also encouraged some movement in the opposite direction – a civic decision in recent years restored St Monance in Fife to its ancient form of St Monans. The great increase in use of bilingual English and Gaelic name signs, seen even in such central Glasgow locations as Queen Street Station, whether driven by the tourist industry or a revived sense of the national heritage, is itself an acceptance that name-forms are variable, and may herald further changes. Whilst spelling has been codified by officialdom, pronunciation continues to follow its own laws. In cases like Strathaven and Milngavie, we see spoken usage and orthography failing to conform. In these cases the spoken form keeps closer to the 'original' pronunciation of these formerly Gaelic names. In modern Scots prose and verse the name Edinburgh is often written as Embro or Embra in an effort to reproduce the local pronunciation, with its tendency to compress and elide sounds and syllables; in the same way, 'Glescae' may be closer to the original pronunciation of dear old Glaschu.

The Basic Types of Place-Name

From the previous pages, it emerges that Scottish place-names fall into seven main types:

1. Referential – where or what the place is, as Coshieville, 'by the trees', or Wick, 'bay'.

2. Functional – what the place is for, as Faskally, 'stance by the ferry'.
3. Descriptive – as Monadhliath, 'grey mountains', or New Deer, indicating a new parish.
4. Devotional – indicative of a tutelary spirit, as Lochty, 'dark goddess', or Kilbride, 'St Bride's church-place'.
5. Cadastric – signifying a fixed taxable area, as Merkland, 'land at one merk's rental'.
6. Denominative – incorporating an owner's, founder's or occupants' name, as Grantown, or Dunkeld ('fort of the Caledonians').
7. Artificial – as in commemorative names like Camperdown, aspirational ones like Jordanhill, political names like Fort George, invented ones like Jarlshof or fanciful ones like Lora. This rather miscellaneous class is hardly found before the eighteenth century.

Classification is not necessarily straightforward. Dysart, 'desert', may have implied 'place of a holy hermit', from a Celtic imitator of St Anthony, rather than simply a bare or empty place. And of course, many compound names contain elements of more than one type, but the defining one is normally apparent, as in Boat of Garten.

The 'Building Blocks' of Scottish Place-Names

A little examination of place-names soon makes it clear that many share the same elements. A high proportion of Scottish place-names are prefixed by Ach-, Bal-, Kil-, Kin- and Dun-, for example. Many end in -ach or -och; -dal or -dale; -ton or -ington. If all of these elements meant only one thing each, they would be reliable guides; as it is, they can often be false friends, with two or more meanings. These forms are covered in the alphabetical section of this book, and the individual place-names themselves show the range of variant meanings.

The Present-day Pattern – Stirling

Even from the very sketchy account of Scottish place-name history given above, it will be clear that the pattern of names in almost any part of the inhabited landscape is complex in terms of chronology and language. Place-names in and around Stirling, a town described by the nineteenth century writer Alexander Smith as the brooch clasping the two parts of Scotland together, demonstrate this variety clearly. Stirling, where the Forth and Allan valleys offer ways into the hills, has always been a border place. It was very close to the Maeatae tribal confederation's fortified hill of Dumyat; and sat between the western edge of Anglian Lothian and the eastern edge of the Lennox, which was first British, then Pictish in its occupancy before becoming a Gaelic-speaking district. But in the area just round the town, Gaelic would have been very much on the wane by the thirteenth century. The 1:50,000 Ordnance Survey map shows some sixty names, including three rivers, in a five-mile square around Stirling. They fall into language-groups as follows:

Gaelic: 17
Gaelic–English compound: 6
Gaelic–Scots compound: 5
Scots: 13
Scots–English compound: 4
Modern English: 7
Cumbric: 5
Cumbric–English compound: 2
Not readily classified: 4

Gaelic forms are clearly in the majority, though the spelling of virtually all of them has been scotticised through long usage, as with Torbrex (found from 1562) from *torr breac*, 'speckled hill', or Drumbrae from *druim*, 'ridge' and *bràigh*, 'upper part'. It is possible that some Gaelic–Scots compound names incorporating an element of Gaelic origin, like Abbey *Craig*, are in fact from the Scots period, Scots having absorbed a great many Gaelic loan-words, including 'craig' in the sense of rocky crag. Craigforth is found as early as 1215 in the form Craighorth: the 'f' lost by aspiration. The Gaelic names are of several kinds, from the topographic-referential Blairlogie, 'field of the hollow', and Cultenhove, 'nooks with caves'; to the descriptive Raploch, from *rapalach*, 'noisy'; and devotional Skeoch (Skewok in 1317), indicating the site of a chapel dedicated to a once-famous Irish female saint. Devotional-seeming St Ninians is a modern area name; though the church is ancient, the old Scots name of its surrounding area was simply Kirkton. Another celebrated local Gaelic name (not on the O.S. map) is Ballengeich, 'place of the wind', or perhaps 'of the marsh' whose gude man was the night-wandering King James V. Several Gaelic or Cumbric names incorporate a later English or Scots element, like Logie Villa (though 'villa' itself has a long history) and Blair Mains, both by Blairlogie (found as Blairlogy, 1451), and of course the hybrid Bannockburn. Scots descriptive names are given to numerous farms, like Netherton and Muirton, as well as to location points like Loanhead and denominative names like Steuarthall. There is the functionally-named Coxet Hill, 'cock-shoot hill', a seventeenth-century name indicating a swathe of hillside cleared for game-bird shooting. The district's old royal associations may be responsible for Queenshaugh. 'Modern English' names, which may be as old as the eighteenth century, include Old Mills and New Mills, Riverside and King's Park. In some cases these too may be anglicised forms of older names, or translated from Gaelic. The Cumbric or pre-Cumbric names, including those of the rivers, Forth, Teith, Allan, may in fact have developed via Pictish; there is also Dumyat, and possibly the much-debated name of Stirling itself, though a Gaelic source has also been proposed.

The example of Stirling shows just how important the Gaelic-speaking period of from five- to six hundred years was in establishing Scottish place-names. Most mainland areas would reveal an even greater Gaelic dominance of the toponymy. Only in Orkney and Shetland is there an almost complete (Norse) homogeneity, and Norse names predominate in the northern isles of the Hebrides.

Apologium

This book does not come from the cutting edge of scholarship, but sets out, in default of anything of comparable range, to provide the enquiring reader with the established derivations of Scottish place-names, and also to indicate where alternative derivations exist, and where the source is still speculative or tentative. I am very grateful for the general comments and criticisms made on an early draft of the text by Dr Simon Taylor of St Andrews University, though he will find it still short of his standards in various ways. The work of the Scottish Place Names Survey, under the auspices of the School of Scottish Studies, demonstrates the intensive and scrupulous scholarship necessary to research and establish the origin of a name: there are very many discoveries still to be made. But the aim here is wider than that. To paraphrase Nicolaisen again, names have come a long way, and most of them have gathered resonances. Ben Bhraggie in Sutherland means 'speckled mountain', like Ben Vrackie, but the mind's eye cannot see it without its crowning monument, the giant statue of the third duke of Sutherland, presiding over a landscape which he and his predecessors so notably cleared of most of its human population. Some people would like to see that monument destroyed. But history will not be changed, and a certain irony would be lost. Events, institutions and individuals colour our awareness of many places. Bannockburn and Culloden generate not only historical images but distinct psychological reactions in the Scottish mind, as, in their own way, do Ibrox, Parkhead or Murrayfield. Carstairs to some means a pleasant country village, to others a railway junction, to others a high-security hospital-cum-prison. The name embraces all these associations, though none have the slightest linguistic relationship to it or to one another. Part of the purpose of the book is to indicate some at least of the aspects that give individual names their special significance. Readers who would like to pursue their interest further may like to know of the Scottish Place-Name Society, based in St Andrews (web-site: www.st-and.ac.uk/institutes/sassi/spns/index.htm).

Note on entries: in each case, after the name, the region or regions where it occurs are given, using the unitary local authorities set up in 1994; then, if necessary, the (approximate) pronunciation. I make no apology for this. Although the original pronunciation of Gaelic names is an important means of tracing their meanings, it is a specialised and tricky aspect, and can often be contentious; and not all readers will be familiar with the phonetic alphabet. In general modern usage, a non-Gaelic speaker may be more easily understood by saying 'Ben Rinnes' as it looks, rather than by attempting 'Ben Reenyaysh'. There follow the derivation of the name, earliest or significant forms, and other details of relevance or interest. Reference to languages is intended to be of a general nature: 'Brythonic' is used to represent the *p*-Celtic language spoken in Scotland which, as noted earlier in the Introduction, may have been the precursor, and certainly is a relation, of the language of the Picts and of the Cumbric speech of the Britons of Strathclyde. The question of another Pictish language, whilst touched upon in one or two places, is not one for this book, and 'Brythonic–Pictish' is used here, with an intention to clearly indicate a branch of Brythonic. 'Scottish Gaelic' is used for names that have arisen since the Scots' settling of Argyll, while 'Irish Gaelic' is used for *q*-Celtic names which clearly go back into the fifth century or earlier; in some cases, for obsolete Gaelic words, 'Old Gaelic' is resorted to. Whilst the majority of names given by the Scandinavian settlers are Norwegian, a number are Danish; I have simply identified the Norse names as 'Old Norse'.

Index: entries in the body of the book are in A–Z sequence. A number of minor location names, the derivations of which are given within individual entries on other places, and thus outside of the alphabetical sequence, are listed at the end.

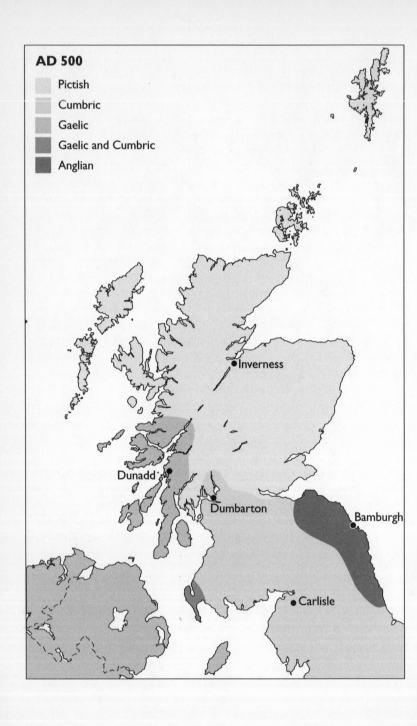

AD 500

- Pictish
- Cumbric
- Gaelic
- Gaelic and Cumbric
- Anglian

● Inverness

Dunadd ●

● Dumbarton

● Bamburgh

● Carlisle

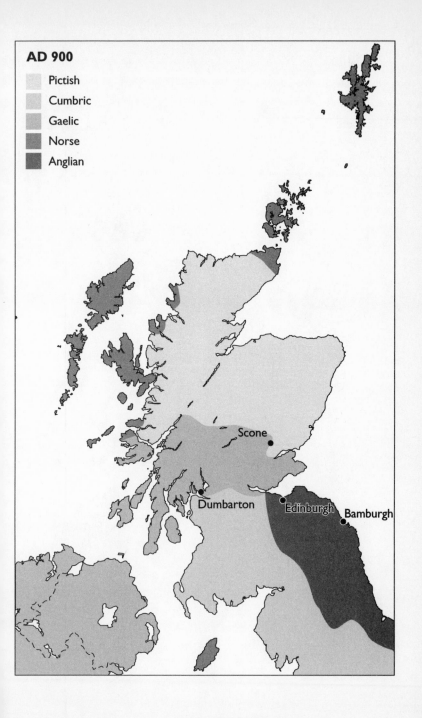

Scone

Dumbarton

Edinburgh Bamburgh

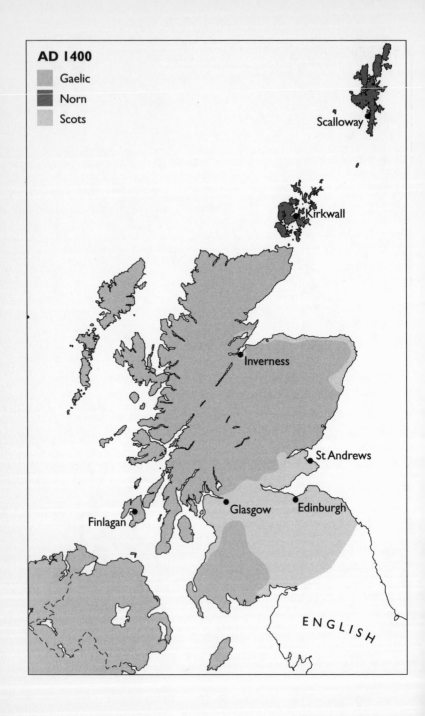

Traditional Regions

Shetland

Orkney

Caithness

Sutherland

Assynt

Lewis

Outer Hebrides

Wester Ross

Easter Ross

Moray

Buchan

Skye

Badenoch

Mar

The Mounth

Inner Hebrides

Lochaber

Atholl

Mearns

Angus

Gowrie

Morvern

Mull

Lorn

Breadalbane

Strathearn

Fife

Lennox

Cowal

Islay

Cunningham

Strathclyde

Lothian

Tweeddale

Kintyre

Bute

Kyle

Carrick

Cheviots

Antrim

Galloway

Man

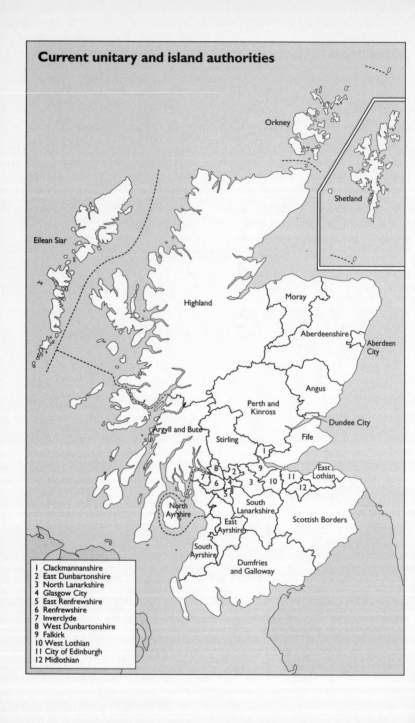

Current unitary and island authorities

Orkney

Shetland

Eilean Siar

Highland

Moray

Aberdeenshire

Aberdeen City

Angus

Perth and Kinross

Dundee City

Argyll and Bute

Stirling

Fife

East Lothian

North Ayrshire

South Lanarkshire

East Ayrshire

Scottish Borders

South Ayrshire

Dumfries and Galloway

1 Clackmannanshire
2 East Dunbartonshire
3 North Lanarkshire
4 Glasgow City
5 East Renfrewshire
6 Renfrewshire
7 Inverclyde
8 West Dunbartonshire
9 Falkirk
10 West Lothian
11 City of Edinburgh
12 Midlothian

A

Aber- This prefix normally indicates a place where two rivers join, or a river enters the sea or a loch. It is a Brythonic word, in both Cumbric and Pictish, and cognate with the Aber- names of Wales. In Scottish Gaelic it has become a loan-word as *Obair,* but the equivalent original Gaelic term is *Inbhir,* scotticised to Inver. Aber-names are most frequently found on the eastern side of the country, between Aberlady in Lothian and Abernethy on the north-western edge of the Cairngorms. North of Inverness and on the west coast they are extremely rare: Aberscross (Sutherland), Applecross and Lochaber are isolated examples. The locations of Aber- and Inver-names have been used to help ascertain the extents of Brythonic naming, of a residual Pictish-speaking population and also, where the two prefixes overlap, of the subsequent 'invasion' of Gaelic names, but this is part of a highly specialised area of study. Toponymists are still exploring the significance of Aber- names, including the possibility that they denote confluence sites of special cultic significance. It is notable that many Aber- names have Gaelic forms following the Pictish prefix, suggesting that the prefix was retained for a reason (see also Pit- names).

Aberargie (Perth & Kinross) 'Confluence of the fierce stream'. *Aber* (Brythonic–Pictish) 'confluence, river-mouth'; *feargach* (Scottish Gaelic) 'fierce, terrible'; the initial *f* has been lost through aspiration. In the *Pictish Chronicle,* c. 970, it is noted as Apurfeirt. Here the River Farg flows into the Earn. *See* Farg.

Aberbrothock See Arbroath.

Abercairney (Perth & Kinross) 'Confluence by the thicket' or 'cairns'. *Aber* (Brythonic–Pictish) 'confluence, river-mouth'; *cardden* (Brythonic–Pictish) 'thicket', with *-ach* (Scottish Gaelic suffix) indicating 'place'; or alternatively *càirneach* (Scottish Gaelic) 'place of cairns or rough rocks'. Recorded in 1218 as Abercarnich.

Aberchirder (Aberdeenshire) Aber-hirder. 'Mouth of the dark water'. *Aber* (Brythonic–Pictish) 'mouth of a river'; *chiar* (Scottish Gaelic) 'dark'; *dobhar* (Gaelic from Brythonic) 'waters'. Noted c. 1212 as Aberkerdouer, its Gaelic form is now Obair-chiardair.

Abercorn (West Lothian) Perhaps 'horned confluence'. *Aber* (Brythonic–Pictish) 'confluence'; *corniog* (Brythonic) 'horned', cognate with Latin *cornus*: a reference to the 'horn' between two joining streams (one still called the Cornie Burn). But a source for the second part in a Brythonic–Pictish word cognate with Welsh *curn,* 'heap, cone', has also been proposed, suggesting that the short stream took its name from the presence of the hill it skirts. Bede notes it (731) as Aebbercurnig. An Anglian bishopric was briefly established here in 678. This modest locality was chosen as the name of a dukedom for one of Queen Victoria's sons.

Aberdeen 'Mouth of the River Don'. *Aber* (Brythonic–Pictish) 'mouth of a river'; the second element seems to suggest the river Dee, which flows into the North Sea at the centre of modern Aberdeen, but the name was recorded as Aberdon in the twelfth century and at that time referred to the original settlement now known as Old Aberdeen, situated some distance to the north at the mouth of the River Don, with the cathedral of St Machar. By the thirteenth century the current name form, probably a conflation of the two, was emerging: Aberdoen 1178; Aberden 1214. *See also* rivers Dee and Don. Aberdeen overtook Perth to be the third city of Scotland in the Middle Ages. Its university began with King's College in 1500. The combination of a rich agricultural hinterland and its North Sea fishing enabled it to survive disasters like the collapse of its textile industry in the early nineteenth century. It became one of the main deep-sea fishing centres of the United Kingdom; and since the growth of the North Sea oil industry in the 1970s, has become a world centre of 'offshore' industrial technology and development. Scotland's third city in population, its many buildings of the local hard and shiny granite stone have given it such titles as 'the Granite City' and 'the Silver City'.

Aberdour (Fife; Aberdeenshire) 'River-mouth'. *Aber* (Brythonic–Pictish) 'mouth of a river'; *dobhar,* (Gaelic from Brythonic) 'waters', as in Dover and Andover in England: this word, common in Scottish Gaelic as well as in Welsh place-names, but not in Irish Gaelic, was probably a Scottish Gaelic borrowing from Cumbric or Pictish. A seaport on the south coast of Fife, noted in the ballad of 'Sir Patrick Spens': 'Half ower, half ower, to Aberdour, 'Tis fifty fathom deep.' The Fife name is found in 1126 as Abirdaur. There is also Aberdour parish in Buchan, noted in the *Book of Deer* c. 1100, as Abbordoboir; with the village of New Aberdour (founded 1798), near where the Dour flows out to the sea through a gap in the cliffs.

Aberfeldy (Perth & Kinross) 'The confluence of Pallidius or Paldoc'. *Aber* (Brythonic–Pictish) 'river confluence'; *phellaidh* (Old Gaelic) refers to St Paldoc, Christian missionary to the Picts in the fifth century, or alternatively, an *uruisg,* or water sprite, believed to live where the local Urlar, (Scottish Gaelic, 'land floor') Burn meets the River Tay. At the bridge here the companies of the 'Black Watch' were formed into the 42nd Regiment, the oldest of the Highland regiments.

Aberfoyle (Stirling) 'The confluence of the pool'. *Aber* (Brythonic–Pictish) 'river confluence' or 'mouth'; *phuill* (Scottish Gaelic) 'of a pool'. Found in the eleventh century as Eperpuill; 1481 as Abirfull. The main village of the Trossachs, and site of a famous fictional encounter in Sir Walter Scott's *Rob Roy* where the Glasgow bailie, Nicol Jarvie, outfaces a Highland brigand.

Abergeldie (Aberdeenshire) 'Confluence of white water'. The Geldie Burn here flows into the Dee. *Aber* (Brythonic–Pictish) 'river confluence; *geall* (Scottish Gaelic) 'white'. The -*die* suffix is from an Old Gaelic ending used to form adjectives from nouns, -*aidh* in the modern Gaelic form: Obair Gheollaidh. The full name is found in 1611 as Abiryeldie.

Aberlady (East Lothian) Possibly 'river-mouth of the lady', as in the Virgin Mary. *Aber* (Brythonic–Pictish) 'river-mouth'; *hlaedig* (Old English) 'lady' or 'loaf-kneader'. The ruins of Mary's Chapel are found here; but the form Aberleuedi, noted 1214, may show a form of Scottish Gaelic *lobh,* 'putrefy': 'river mouth of the swamp'; although the stream once bore the name Peffer, 'radiant' (*see* Strathpeffer).

Aberlemno (Angus) 'Confluence of the elm-wood'. *Aber* (Brythonic–Pictish) 'confluence, mouth'; *leamhanaich* (Scottish Gaelic) 'of the elm-wood'. Noted as Aberlevinach in 1250. Well-preserved Pictish sculptured stones are found here and in the locality.

Aberlour (Moray) 'Loud confluence'. *Aber* (Brythonic–Pictish) 'mouth, confluence', *labhar* (Gaelic) 'loud'. Its later name of Charleston of Aberlour comes from that of Charles Grant of Wester Elchies, who developed the 'new' village in 1812. *See* Lawers.

Abernethy (Perth & Kinross; Highland) 'Mouth of the bright river'. *Aber* (Brythonic–Pictish) 'confluence, mouth'; the second part has been suggested as derived from *an eitighich* (Scottish Gaelic) 'gullet', indicating water rushing through a gorge, but it is likely to be pre-Gaelic in origin. The Tayside place, Apurnethige in the *Pictish Chronicle*, c. 970, was a stronghold of Nechtan, king of the Picts around 700. The river has been identified with his name, but the reverse is more likely; the Brythonic river-name *Nedd*, which stems from a conjectured root-word *nido,* indicating 'gleaming', and which is also the root of Nidd and Nith, and Welsh Neath. Nechtan, meaning 'purified one', stems from the same root-form; Necton was a European Celtic water deity, especially of mineral and hot springs. Abernethy on Tayside, as well as having many

Pictish stone carvings, has one of Scotland's two remaining round towers from the tenth century, and has given its name to a kind of biscuit. The Highland Nethy, which joins the Spey just below Nethy Bridge, has the same derivation.

Abhainn A Gaelic word for 'river', cognate with English Avon, and pronounced awan. Found in its original form in remoter streams, and incorporated into a number of place-names; *see* Portnahaven. An archaic or localised form, *àbh*, is also found in certain place-names: *see* Afton.

Abington (South Lanarkshire) 'Albin's village', found as Albintoune, 1459. *Ael-wine* (Old English) 'noble friend'; *tun* (Old English) 'enclosure' or 'settlement'.

Aboyne (Aberdeenshire) 'White cow ford'. *Ath* (Scottish Gaelic) 'river ford'; *bó* (Scottish Gaelic) 'cow'; *fhionn* (Scottish Gaelic) 'white'. Older forms include Obyne, 1260; modern Gaelic is A-bèine. The cow may have been the incarnation of a river spirit. This is the site of a famous Highland gathering each year.

Abriachan (Highland) 'Mouth of the steep burn'. *Aber* (Brythonic–Pictish) 'confluence, mouth'; *bhritheachán* (Scottish Gaelic) 'of the steep hillside'. Noted as Abirhacyn, 1239. The stream here falls steeply into Loch Ness.

Achallader (Stirling) 'Field of the stream'. *Achadh* (Scottish Gaelic) 'field'; *chaladair* (Scottish Gaelic stream name), anglicised as 'Calder', perhaps from a conjectured Brythonic *caleto-dubron*, 'hard water'. *See* Calder.

Achanalt (Highland) 'Field by the river'. *Achadh* (Scottish Gaelic) 'field'; *an*, 'by the'; *uillt* (Scottish Gaelic) 'of the stream'.

Acharacle (Argyll & Bute) 'Torquil's ford'. *Ath* (Scottish Gaelic) 'ford'; *Torcuil* (Gaelic–Norse proper name) 'Torquil', from Thorketil, meaning 'vessel of Thor'. Thor (Old Norse Thorir) was the Norse god of thunder and warfare.

Achiltibuie (Highland) *Achilti-booey*. Possibly 'field of the yellow stream'. *Achadh* (Scottish Gaelic) 'field'; *allt* (Scottish Gaelic) 'stream'; *buidhe* (Scottish Gaelic) 'yellow'. Locally, the preferred explanation for this straggling Coigach township is 'field of the yellow(-haired) lad', derived from Achadh-a-gille-buidhe; with *gille* (Scottish Gaelic) denoting a lad or a young man.

Achmelvich (Highland) 'Field of the place of sea-bent'. *Achadh* (Scottish Gaelic) 'field'; *mealbhain* (Scottish Gaelic) 'bent grass', from Old Norse *melr*, 'bent grass, grassy dunes'. *See* Melvich.

Achmore (Highland) 'Big field'. *Achadh* (Scottish Gaelic) 'field'; *mór*, 'big'.

Achnabreck (Argyll & Bute) 'Field of the trout'. *Achadh* (Scottish

Gaelic) 'field; *na*, 'of the'; *breac* (Scottish Gaelic) 'trout' from the adjective *breac*, 'speckled'. This place near Lochgilphead is a site of many Bronze Age stone carvings.

Achnacarry (Highland) Perhaps 'Field of the fish-weir'. *Achadh* (Scottish Gaelic) 'field'; *na*, of; *caraidh* (Scottish Gaelic) 'fish-weir'. 'Field of the wrestlers', from *caraiche* (Scottish Gaelic) 'wrestlers, tumblers', has also been suggested. Noted as Auchnacarre in 1505, it is the seat of Cameron of Lochiel, chief of Clan Cameron.

Achnacloich (Highland; Argyll & Bute) 'Field of stones'. *Achadh* (Scottish Gaelic) 'field'; *na*, 'of'; and *cloich* (Scottish Gaelic) 'stones', a settlement name from Skye and Lorn.

Achnahannet (Highland) 'Field of the patron saint's church', *Achadh* (Scottish Gaelic) 'field', *na h-* 'of the'; *annait* (Scottish Gaelic) 'church of a patron saint, church with relics'. There is also Achnahanat, with the same derivation, seven miles north-west of Bonar Bridge in Sutherland. *See* Annat.

Achnasheen (Highland) 'Field of the storms'. *Achadh* (Scottish Gaelic) 'field'; *na* (Scottish Gaelic) 'of the'; *sian* (Scottish Gaelic) 'storm'. This Ross-shire village, the railhead for Gairloch and the Torridon area, is not stormier than other places but is in quite an exposed situation.

Achnashellach (Highland) 'Field of willows'. *Achadh* (Scottish Gaelic) 'field'; *na*, 'of'; *seileach* (Scottish Gaelic) 'willow trees', found as Auchnashellicht, 1543. There is also Achnashelloch near Lochgilphead in Argyll & Bute.

Achray, River and **Loch** (Stirling) Possibly 'ford of shaking'. *Ath* (Scottish Gaelic) 'ford', and *chrathaidh* (Scottish Gaelic) 'shaking' (*see* Crathie). The Gaelic name is Loch Ath-Chrathaigh. The short Achray Water cuts through a hilly pass between Loch Katrine and Loch Achray; the ford was probably near the site of the road bridge.

Ackergill (Highland) 'Ravine of the open field'. *Akr* (Old Norse) 'open field'; *gil* (Old Norse) 'cleft, ravine', found in the sixteenth century both as Acrigill and Akirgill. The reference is to the clifftop pasture of this Caithness township, which has an ancient tower.

Adder, River (Borders) 'Water'. The Blackadder and Whiteadder combine near Chirnside (Old English *cyrin,* 'churn' and *sete,* 'seat') and flow into the Tweed above Berwick. 'Black' and 'White' appear to be given as marks of identity rather than descriptive terms; there may also be some lost significance relating to how the rivers were viewed by prehistoric inhabitants. Adder itself is one of the numerous river-words that go back to the language of the European Celts; cognate with the German Oder, its original form is conjectured as Adara, indicating 'flowing water'. Found as Blacedre, c. 1098. *See* Edrom.

Addiewell (West Lothian) 'Adam's Well'. *Addie* (Scots) diminutive form of 'Adam'.

Ae, River and **Forest** (Dumfries & Galloway) 'Water'. The river-name, from Old Norse *aa,* 'water', has given its name to the huge modern forest and to the village housing the foresters and their families. *See* River E.

Affleck (Angus) 'Place of flagstones'. *Achadh* (Scottish Gaelic) 'field'; *na,* 'of the'; *leac* (Scottish Gaelic) 'flagstones'. A compressed form of Auchinleck; the same name is found in Aberdeenshire, a few miles south-east of Oldmeldrum.

Affric, River, Glen, Loch (Highland) Possibly 'speckled ford', or 'ford of the trout', or 'of the boar'. *Ath* (Scottish Gaelic) 'ford'; *breac* (Scottish Gaelic) 'speckled,' trout'; or *bhraich* (Scottish Gaelic) 'boar'. Noted as Auffrik, 1538.

Afton (East Ayrshire) 'Brown stream'. *Abh* (Scottish Gaelic) 'stream'; *donn* (Scottish Gaelic) 'brown'. This is the stream addressed by Robert Burns in his love poem 'Flow gently, sweet Afton'.

Aigas (Highland) 'Place of the abyss'. *Aigeann* (Scottish Gaelic) 'chasm'. The Beauly river flows here in a deep gorge, divided by *Eilean* (Scottish Gaelic) 'island' Aigas.

Ailort, Loch (Highland) Ay-lort. Perhaps from *él* (Old Norse) 'snow shower', and *fjordr* (Old Norse) 'sea inlet, fiord', with *loch* (Scottish Gaelic) 'lake, loch', though why this loch should be singled out in such a way is unclear.

Ailsa Craig (South Ayrshire) 'Fairy rock' has been suggested. *Aillse* (Scottish Gaelic) 'fairy'; *creag* (Scottish Gaelic) 'rock'. Also, *ail* (Old Gaelic) 'steep rock'. The oldest English form is Ailsay, 1404; there are two Gaelic names, the older is Allasan, the other is Creag Ealasaid ('Elizabeth's rock'). Perhaps more likely is an Old Norse origin, Ael's isle, from *Ael* (Old Norse proper name) and *ey* (Old Norse) 'island', with the Scots 'Craig' added after the significance of the -*ey* had been lost. This very prominent island landmark on the Firth of Clyde route from Ireland to Glasgow is known as 'Paddy's Milestone'. Its extra-hard granite is used to make curling stones.

Aird (Highland) 'The high ground'. *Airde* (Scottish Gaelic) 'height'; the name comes from the hilly district around Kirkhill and Kiltarlity in Inverness-shire. There are numerous other Airds, including a village on the Eye Peninsula in Lewis; Aird of Sleat in Skye; and many coastal features in the Western Isles and West Highlands.

Airdrie (North Lanarkshire) 'High hill slope'. *Airde* (Scottish Gaelic) 'height'; *ruighe* (Scottish Gaelic) 'slope'. Found as Airdrie, 1584. In the nineteenth century Airdrie became a densely populated industrial town. There is another Airdrie three miles west of Crail, Fife; and another in Kirkbean parish, Dumfries & Galloway.

Airth (Stirling) Erth. 'Level green place', from *àiridh* (Scottish Gaelic), which apart from 'summer pasture' has the meaning 'level green place', with the sense of being among hills.

Airthrey (Stirling) Derived in the same way as Airdrie. This locality by Bridge of Allan was famous for its mineral waters in the nineteenth century.

Aith (Shetland) 'Isthmus, neck of land'. *Eidh* (Old Norse), 'isthmus'. There are three populated Aiths in Shetland; also Aithsetter ('farm on the aith') at Dunrossness.

Alba (Scotland) *Allipa*. The Gaelic name for Scotland, originally applying to the former combined kingdoms of the Picts and Scots, but nowadays referring to the whole country. Alban and Albany are other modern forms. In the oldest texts the name refers to the whole island of Britain, and the form 'Albion', which has been traced back to Himilco, a Carthaginian voyager of c. 500 BC, is still sometimes used in that sense.

Alder, Ben (Highland) 'Mountain of falling water'. *Beinn* (Scottish Gaelic) 'mountain', *all dobhar* (Old Gaelic) respectively 'rock' and 'water'. The Alder Burn would thus appear to have given its name to the mountain (3765ft/980m), by no means an unusual process. The present Gaelic form is Beinn Eallar, giving the pronunciation *Ben Yallar*. *See also* Ben Avon.

Aldourie (Highland) 'Streams'. The name combines Scottish Gaelic *allt* and *dobhraidh*, from the stream name Dobhrag. Both forms mean 'stream'. Although the Brythonic–Pictish *dobhar*, 'water, stream', was borrowed into Gaelic, it seems that in this case it was found as a place name and had *allt* added to it in ignorance.

Ale, Water of. *See* Ancrum

Alexandria (West Dunbartonshire) This town in the Vale of Leven lying to the north of Dumbarton was named after the local member of parliament, Alexander Smollett, around 1760. *See* Renton.

Alford (Aberdeenshire) Afford. 'High ford'; the most probable derivation is from *ath* (Scottish Gaelic) 'ford'; *àrd* (Scottish Gaelic) 'high'. Noted as Afford around 1200. English Alford (Somerset) is 'Aldgyth's ford', but this derivation is most unlikely here.

Aline, Loch (Highland) 'The beautiful one'. *Aluinn* (Scottish Gaelic) 'beautiful', and *loch* (Scottish Gaelic) 'lake, loch'.

Allan (Stirling; Borders) The River Allan flowing through Strathallan, and the Allan Water, a tributary of the Teviot, have a pre- or early-Celtic root *alauna*, meaning 'flowing'; cognate probably with Welsh *Alun*. *See also* Alness.

Alligin, River and **Ben** (Highland) The original name is that of the river, Ailiginn in Gaelic, now also applied to the village and the adjacent Ben Alligin. Its origin is not clear.

Alloa (Clackmannanshire) *All-o-ah*. 'Rocky plain'. Derived from a compound word *ail-mhagh* (Scottish Gaelic) meaning 'rocky plain', apposite to the town's location on a flood plain on the north bank of the River Forth. It is noted as Alveth, 1357. This was an early industrial town, its glassworks set up by the Jacobite earl of Mar who led the 1715 Rising.

Alloway (South Ayrshire) 'Rocky plain'. This village, famous as the birthplace of Robert Burns, lies on the flat land of the Ayr Basin. Its name has the same derivation as that of Alloa; noted as Auylway, c. 1340.

Allt A Gaelic word for 'mountain stream' or 'steep-banked stream', found all over the Highlands, usually in its original form in smaller or remote streams; incorporated into a number of settlement names, sometimes in the form Ault. *See* Altnabreac, Auldgirth.

Almond (West Lothian; Perth & Kinross) *Ammond*. The river-name is from pre-Celtic *Ambona*, deriving from an Indo-European root-word meaning 'water'. The Gaelic name is Abhainn Aman.

Alness (Highland) 'Stream place'. This large village takes its name not from the river which divides it, often known as the Alness River (*see* Averon) but probably from the small stream close to the old parish church. Recorded as Alenes and Alune in the thirteenth century, it probably has the same early or pre-Celtic river-name origin, *alauna*, as Allan, the River Alun in Wales and River Aln in England. The *-ais* suffix is found as an indication of 'place' in many locations in the former Pictland. The emphasis is on the first syllable, which rules out *nes* (Norse) 'headland', as part of the formation. The Gaelic form is Alanais.

Alsh, Loch (Highland) This name has been derived from *aillse* (Scottish Gaelic) 'fairy, spectre'; an earlier spelling is Loch Ailsh, and the Gaelic name is Loch Aillse. There is another Loch Aillse inland on the Ross–Sutherland border. It is unusual for such an important sea-loch – the passage between the mainland and Skye – to have such an un-geographical name, and if the derivation is correct it suggests an archaic origin, related to a belief in a water-spirit.

Altnabreac (Highland) *Alt-na-brake*. 'Stream of the trout'. *Allt*

(Scottish Gaelic) 'river'; *na*, 'of'; *breac* (Scottish Gaelic) 'trout', linked with the adjective *breac*, 'speckled'.

Altnaharra (Highland) 'Walled or embanked stream'. *Allt* (Scottish Gaelic) 'stream'; *na*, 'of'; *earbhe* (Scottish Gaelic) 'wall'. A similar form is Altnaharrie.

Alva (Clackmannanshire) 'Rocky plain'. The derivation of this town's name is the same as that of its neighbour Alloa. There is also the Hill of Alvah, south of Banff. *See* Alloa.

Alvie (Highland) 'Rocky place'. Derived from the same root word *al* (Brythonic–Pictish) 'rock, rocky', giving Gaelic *aillbhe*, 'rock', as the prefix of Alloa. Alves in Moray also has the same derivation.

Alyth (Perth & Kinross) *Ay-lith*. 'Steep bank or rugged place'. This small Angus town derives its descriptive name from the Hill of Alyth that rises steeply on its northern edge. *Aileach* (Scottish Gaelic) 'mound' or 'bank'; alternatively, *aill* (Old Gaelic) 'steep rock'.

Amisfield (Dumfries & Galloway) *Aimsfield*. 'Amyas's field'. One Amyas de Charteris was a medieval lord of the local manor, Amyas deriving from *amatus* (Latin) 'beloved'.

Amulree (Perth & Kinross) *Ammle-ree*. 'Ford of Maelrubha'. *Ath* (Scottish Gaelic) 'ford'; the second element refers to the seventh-century missionary saint who became the local patron saint here. He may have had a special affinity with fords; *see* Applecross. The Gaelic name is Ath Maol-Ruibhe.

An Teallach (Highland) *An-challah.* 'The anvil'. *An* (Scottish Gaelic) 'the', and *teallach* (Scottish Gaelic) 'anvil, forge'. This mountain of Wester Ross, with several peaks, the highest at 3484ft/1065m, rising above Little Loch Broom, is often mist-shrouded, as if in steam. The figurative name is unusual for a major feature.

Ancrum (Borders) 'Bend on the River Ale'; older forms include Alnecrumba (twelfth century): Ale from a pre-Celtic form *alaua*, 'water'; *crum* from Cumbric *crwm*, 'bend', cognate with Gaelic *crom*, 'bent'.

Anderston (Glasgow) 'Andrew's farm'. The origin of the suffix is old English *tun*, 'farmstead', but once established as Scots *-ton*, a place-name ending, it has also been attached to modern places, like this, with no ancient links.

Angus A former county name (also known as Forfarshire), now a unitary local authority; generally taken as commemorating the eighth-century king of the Picts, *Aonghus* or *Oengus* (Pictish and Scottish Gaelic proper name) 'unique choice', a highly successful warrior-king, who died in 761. Together with the Mearns it formed one of the major divisions of Pictland, recorded in the twelfth century as Enegus. In legend Oengus was also one of the seven sons of Cruithne, founder of the Pictish people.

Annan (Dumfries & Galloway) On the basis of the latinised form *Anava*, found in the *Ravenna Cosmography*, it has been construed as a river-name, deriving from *Anu*, the Celtic goddess of prosperity; *an* is also an obsolete Gaelic term for 'water'. Medieval forms of the name have a final *t* or *d,* as in Stratanant (from Cumbric *ystrad*, 'valley') in 1152. The Old Norse form Annandale, the valley of the Annan, taking its latter part from Old Norse *dalr*, 'valley', has however prevailed. This long dale was the heartland of the territory chartered to the Bruce family of Norman immigrants by King David I.

Annat (Highland; Argyll & Bute; other areas) In Irish Gaelic *andóit* indicates 'church holding relics of its founder'. The many Annats in Scotland mostly have evidence of an ancient church or burial ground, and in Scotland the name may simply indicate the latter rather than any special church. Often the Annats also boast a clear stream, and this has also been suggested as the source of the name. It is possible, however, that the sacred place was specifically located by the stream, convenient for the important function of baptism. The Allt na' h Annait, flowing into Glen Kinglass on the south-east face of Ben Dorain, seems far from a church, but holy men often preferred remote sites; Duncan Bàn Macintyre praised its virtue, and another remote one is at the foot of Ben Lawers. The Gaelic prefix *An*, 'the', found in many Annat names, favours the burial ground or church meaning. Among numerous others, there are Càrn na h-Annaid and Clach na-h-Annaid (cairn and stone of the Annat) near Contin, Ross-shire; an Annat Bay at the seaward end of Loch Broom, and Annathill in North Lanarkshire. The form Annet is also found.

Anstruther (Fife) 'The little stream'. *An* (Scottish Gaelic) 'the'; *sruthair* (Scottish Gaelic) 'little stream'. Recorded as Anestrothir 1205, Anstrother 1231, but the current local pronunciation is *Ainster.* This old Fife fishing port has many streams flowing beneath its houses; one is tapped as a well in Scotland's national fishing museum, housed by the harbour.

Antonine Wall (West Lothian to West Dunbartonshire) A Roman fortification of the late first century AD that extended from Kinneil on the Forth to Old Kilpatrick on the Clyde. It was named after the then reigning Roman emperor Antoninus Pius (AD 86–101).

Aonach Eagach (Highland) *Ö-nach ay-gah.* 'Airy notched ridge'. *Aonach* (Scottish Gaelic) 'steep hill', normally applied to ridged mountains; *eagach* (Scottish Gaelic) 'notched'. An aptly descriptive name for this exposed mountain ridge (3173ft/951m) of rock spires and pinnacles rising above Glencoe.

Aonach Mór (Highland) *O-nach more*. 'Great steep ridge'. *Aonach* (Scottish Gaelic) 'steep hill', normally applied to ridged mountains; *mór* (Scottish Gaelic) 'big'. This mountain near Ben Nevis, now 'developed' for winter skiing, forms the peak of a two-mile open ridge that ends to the south with the slightly higher and thus curiously named Aonach Beag (4060ft/1218m) – 'little ridge'.

Appin (Argyll & Bute) 'Abbey lands'. *Apuinn* (Scottish Gaelic) 'abbey lands'. The name probably refers to the land that was owned here in medieval times by St Moluag's foundation on the nearby Isle of Lismore, across the Lynn of Lorn.

Applecross (Highland) 'Mouth of the Crosan River'. *Aber* (Brythonic–Pictish) 'mouth of a river'; *Crosan* (Brythonic–Pictish river-name of uncertain derivation). The *Annals of Tighernach* referring to c. 731 refer to it as Aporcrosan. The second element may be Gaelic *crossain*, 'crosses', associated with the monastery founded here in Wester Ross in AD 673 by St Maelrubha, but the river-name seems more likely as this saint is associated with at least two other water-features. With the exception of Lochaber, this is virtually the only Aber- name in the West Highlands. *See* Amulree, Maree.

Arbirlot (Angus) 'Confluence of the Elliot Water'. *Aber* (Brythonic–Pictish) 'mouth of a river'. *See* Elliot.

Arbroath (Angus) 'Mouth of the turbulent stream'. *Aber* (Brythonic–Pictish) 'mouth of a river'; the second element refers to the name of the local burn, the root of which is the conjectured Pictish form *brudaca,* cognate with *brothach* (Scottish Gaelic) 'filthy', but perhaps here 'boiling, turbulent', as in the related Gaelic *bruth,* 'hot', referring to its waters. The name is found as Aberbrudoc in 1189; the present name still reflects the old Gaelic pronunciation. At the abbey here the celebrated 'Declaration of Arbroath', asserting the basis of Scottish nationhood, was composed in 1320. The town is famous for its smoked haddocks, 'Arbroath smokies'.

Ardbeg (Argyll & Bute) 'Small height'. *Ard* (Scottish Gaelic) 'high'; *beag* (Scottish Gaelic) 'small'.

Ardchattan (Argyll & Bute) 'The high place of Catán'. *Ard* (Scottish Gaelic) 'high'; *Chatáin* (Old Gaelic personal name) 'Catán', a Celtic saint associated with Bute and the coast of Argyll. Noted as Ercattan, 1296.

Ardeer (North Ayrshire) 'Western headland'. *Airde* (Scottish Gaelic) 'height, headland'; *iar* (Scottish Gaelic) 'west'. The chemical works here were set up in 1873 by the Swedish inventor of dynamite, Alfred Nobel.

Ardelve (Highland) 'Height of the fallow land'. *Ard* (Scottish Gaelic) 'high'; *eilghidh* (Scottish Gaelic) 'fallow ground'. Recorded in the mid-sixteenth century as Ardillie. Ardullie on the east of Ross-shire has the same derivation.

Ardentinny (Argyll & Bute) Although suggested as 'heights of the fox': *àrd* (Scottish Gaelic) 'high'; *an t-sionnaigh* (Scottish Gaelic) 'of the fox'; with Craigentinny in Edinburgh similarly 'rock of the fox'; the latter part is more likely to be *teine* (Scottish Gaelic) 'fire, beacon', in both cases.

Ardeonaig (Perth & Kinross) 'Adamnan's point'; the name of St Columba's biographer, ninth abbot of Iona, is preserved here, from Scottish Gaelic *àirde*, 'point, height', and *Eódhnan* (Scottish Gaelic personal name), 'Adamnan's'.

Ardersier (Highland) Possibly 'high western promontory'. *Ard* (Scottish Gaelic) 'high'; *ros* (Scottish Gaelic) 'promontory'; *iar* (Scottish Gaelic) 'west'. It was noted as Ardrosser in 1227. Now an oil-platform construction site, it is on the western side of the prominent point terminating in Whiteness Head (*see* Whiten Head). Since 1623 it has had the alternative name of Campbelltown, after the Campbells of Cawdor, who were local proprietors.

Ardgay (Highland) *Ard-guy.* 'Height of the wind'. *Airde* (Scottish Gaelic) 'height'; *gaoithe* (Scottish Gaelic) 'wind'. Ardgye, four miles west of Elgin, appears to be cognate.

Ardgour (Highland) Possibly 'promontory of Gabran'. *Airde* (Scottish Gaelic) has the sense of 'promontory' as well as 'height'; the second element refers to Gabran, grandson of Fergus of Dàl Riada. Alternative derivations include 'promontory of the goat' from (Scottish Gaelic) *gobhar*; or 'sloping' or 'crooked promontory' (fitting the local topography) derived from Cumbric *gwry*, 'slope, bend'.

Ardkinglas (Argyll & Bute) 'Height of the dog-stream'. *Airde* (Scottish Gaelic) 'height'; *con* (Scottish Gaelic) 'dog, wolf'; *glas* (Scottish Gaelic) 'water'. The Gaelic form is Aird-chonghlais.

Ardlamont (Argyll & Bute) 'Height of Lamont'. *Airde* (Scottish Gaelic) 'height'; *mhicLaomuinn* (Scottish Gaelic personal name) 'Lamont', the man of law. This is in the territory historically occupied by the Clan Lamont.

Ardle, River and **Strath** (Perth & Kinross) Perhaps 'river dale'. Old Norse *aar*, 'water', *dalr*, valley, gaelicised into Srath Ardail.

Ardler (Perth & Kinross) The Strathmore village name seems unrelated to Ardle; perhaps 'height of the mares', from Scottish Gaelic *àirde*, 'height' and *làir*, 'of the mares', especially if it is the same name as Ardlair in Perthshire. Older forms include Ardlair and also Ardley. For a time between c. 1830–1860 an attempt was made to rename the locality Washington, as the site of a new 'model' village, but the replacement name failed to stick.

Ardlui (Argyll & Bute) 'Height of the calves'. *Ard* (Scottish Gaelic) 'high'; *laoigh* (Scottish Gaelic) 'calves'. A reference either to a calving place or one where calves were rounded up. *See* Lui.

Ardmair (Highland) 'Finger promontory'. *Àirde* (Scottish Gaelic) 'promontory, height'; *mheàra* (from Scottish Gaelic *meur*) 'finger'. There is a pebbled spit here, but Scottish Gaelic *meara,* 'airy', has also been suggested. Ben More Coigach looks down on this crescent-shaped beach.

Ardmeanach (Highland, Argyll & Bute) 'Middle height'. *Airde* (Scottish Gaelic) 'height'; *meadhonach* (Scottish Gaelic) 'middle, central', referring to the main ridge of the Black Isle. The same name is given to an area of West Mull.

Ardmore (Highland, Argyll & Bute) 'Big height'. *Airde* (Scottish Gaelic) 'height'; *mór* (Scottish Gaelic) 'big'. The name of numerous locations in these and other regions, mostly on the west side but including a settlement near Edderton in Easter Ross.

Ardnamurchan (Highland) Probably 'promontory of the otters'. *Airde* (Scottish Gaelic) 'promontory'; *na* (Scottish Gaelic) 'of the'; *muir-chon* (Scottish Gaelic) 'sea dogs'. Another derivation of the last two parts of this name suggests 'piracy', which may have been associated with this remote peninsula: *muir-chol* (Scottish Gaelic) 'sea villainy'. The point marks the westernmost extremity of the Scottish mainland.

Ardoch (Dumfries & Galloway; Perth & Kinross; Highland) 'High place'. *Ard* (Scottish Gaelic) 'high'; *-ach* (Old Gaelic suffix) 'land'. The Tayside locality has a well-preserved Roman camp-site, dating from the Roman campaign to subjugate Caledonia under Septimius Severus in AD 208–10.

Ardrishaig (Argyll & Bute) 'Height of bramble-bushes by the bay'. *Airde* (Scottish Gaelic) 'height'; *dris* (Scottish Gaelic) 'brambles, brier'; *aig* (Gaelic form of Old Norse *vik*) 'bay'. The name of a village on Loch Fyne, eastern terminus of the Crinan Canal, but also found in a number of other localities.

Ardross (Highland, Fife) 'Height of the promontory'. *Airde* (Scottish Gaelic) 'height'; *rois* (Scottish Gaelic) 'of the promontory'. The name refers to the highest ground between the Cromarty and Dornoch Firths, and to the rising land of the sea coast between St Monans and Elie, where the alternative Gaelic meaning of 'woodland' is equally possible.

Ardrossan (North Ayrshire) Perhaps 'height of the little cape'. *Airde*

(Scottish Gaelic) 'promontory, height'; *rois* (Scottish Gaelic) 'cape, headland'; *-an* (Scottish Gaelic suffix) 'little'. Noted in this form in 1375. The Gaelic name is however Ard Trosain, which suggests a derivation from Brythonic *tros*, 'cross-place'. This seaside and harbour town has been a resort since the late eighteenth century.

Ardtornish (Highland) 'Thori's cape'. *Airde* (Scottish Gaelic) 'promontory'; *Thori* (Old Norse personal name), *naes* (Old Norse), 'point'; Gaelic 'aird' having been prefixed when the sense of 'ness' was lost. The English 'point' adds a further superfluous word. This Morvern castle close to Loch Aline was a stronghold of the Lords of the Isles, and the place where the 'Treaty of Westminster–Ardtornish', between King Edward IV of England and the lord of the Isles, was made in 1462.

Ardvreck (Highland) 'The speckled height'. *Airde* (Scottish Gaelic) 'height'; *breac* (Scottish Gaelic) 'speckled, vari-coloured'. Ardvreck was the home of Neil Macleod of Assynt who captured the fugitive Montrose after the battle of Carbisdale in 1650; its gaunt ruins remain.

Argyll (Argyll & Bute) 'District or coastland of the Gaels'. *Airer* (Scottish Gaelic) 'coastland'; *Gaidheal* (Scottish Gaelic) 'of the Gaels'. The Gaelic-speaking Scots, originating in Ireland, colonised much of the western seaboard of Scotland during the sixth to ninth centuries. In medieval times, the coast between Kintail and Lochbroom was known as 'North Argyll'. The name was recorded as Arregaithel in the *Pictish Chronicle*, c. 970. The Scots form, Argyle, was used for many centuries and is still current in fashion terminology.

Arinagour (Argyll & Bute) 'Summer pasture of the goats'. *Airidh* (Scottish Gaelic) 'summer pasture, shieling'; *nan* 'of', *gobhair* (Scottish Gaelic) 'goats'.

Arisaig (Highland) 'River-mouth bay'. *Ar-óss* (Old Norse) 'river mouth'; *aig* (from Old Norse *vik*) 'bay'. *See also* Aros.

Arkaig, Loch (Highland) The name has been conjectured as 'dark water'. The Gaelic form, Loch Airceig, may stem from *arc* (Celtic root form) 'dusky'; *airc* (Scottish Gaelic) 'strait' has also been suggested, though its meaning is largely figurative. The *-aig* ending here is of uncertain origin. Numerous people have seen a 'monster' in this loch, which also has a legend of lost Jacobite gold.

Arkle (Highland) 'Ark mountain'. *Arkfjall* (Old Norse) 'ark-like hill', rendered into Gaelic as Arcuil. A mountain in the Reay Forest, rising to 2580ft/774m. The use of this and other nearby mountain names for race-horses is through the proprietorship of the duke of Westminster.

Arklet, Loch (Stirling) Perhaps 'dark water', of similar derivation to Arkaig, or 'steep-sloped' from *airc* (Scottish Gaelic) 'difficulty, strait', and *leathad* (Scottish Gaelic) 'slope'.

Armadale (West Lothian; Highland) Perhaps 'arm-shaped dale'. It does not directly apply to the Lothian town, named after a local landowner, lord Armadale, who took his title from the village of Armadale on the north coast of Sutherland. The name's likely meaning, 'arm-shaped valley', is Scandinavian in origin and also applies to Armadale on the Isle of Skye. *Arm-r* (Old Norse) 'arm, arm-shaped'; *dalr* (Old Norse) 'dale, valley'. The Old Norse personal name *Eorm* has also been suggested for the first part.

Arncroach (Fife) 'Place or height of the humped hill'. *Àirde* (Scottish Gaelic) 'height'; *na*, 'of'; *cruach*, 'humped hill, stack'.

Arngask (Stirling) Perhaps 'place or height of the crossings'. *Airde* (Scottish Gaelic) 'height'; *nan*, 'of'; *Chroisg*, 'crossings'. But the loss of the *r* is hard to explain. There is an Ardnagrask near Muir of Ord in Easter Ross. *Gasg* (Scottish Gaelic) 'tail' (of land) may be more likely. *See* Gask.

Arnisdale (Shetland) 'Orn's valley'. *Orn* (Old Norse personal name) 'eagle-like'; *dalr* (Old Norse) 'valley'.

Arnprior (Stirling) 'The Prior's land'. *Earann* (Scottish Gaelic) 'portion or share of land'; *na*, 'of'; with English 'prior'. A hybrid Gaelic–English combination; the priory is that of Inchmahome, in the Lake of Menteith.

Aros (Argyll & Bute) 'River mouth'; *á* (Old Norse) 'water'; *óss* (Old Norse) 'river-mouth, oyce'. As *óss* on its own implies the river, the reason for the prefix is unclear. There is also the Gaelic *àros*, 'house' or 'palace', and the name is noted as dun Aros, 1410. At Aros in Mull there is both the estuary and a castle. The name has been applied to the surrounding district of Mull looking across the northern part of the Sound of Mull to Morvern.

Arran (North Ayrshire) The name of this mountainous island, Arainn in Gaelic, may indicate 'place of peaked hills'. *Aran* (Cumbric) 'height, peaked hill'. Alternatively, the derivation may be related to that of the Irish Aran Islands where *arainn* (Irish Gaelic) 'kidney', implies an arched ridge. Arran is the oldest known form, from 1154, but thirteenth century forms include Araane, 1251; and Aran, c. 1294. Strategically placed in the Firth of Clyde, the island became an earldom closely linked with the crown.

Arrochar (Argyll & Bute) 'Ploughgate'. The 'aratrum' – an ancient Scottish square land measure of 104 acres, ploughgate in Scots, was the area of land eight oxen could plough in a year at thirteen acres each. Derived as a Gaelic form of *aratrum* (Latin) 'plough', early medieval recordings include Arathor 1248; Arachor 1350. In the nineteenth century it was often spelt Arroquhar. Alternatively, a local hill spelt as Ben Arrochar on an early map is derived from Beinn Airigh-chiarr (Scottish Gaelic) 'mount sheiling-dark'. The area round Arrochar is associated with Clan Macfarlane. *Compare* Haddo, Kirriemuir.

Arthur, Ben (Argyll & Bute) 'Arthur's Mountain', in Gaelic Beinn Artair. Arthur was the legendary hero of the Britons in their resistance to the invading Saxons, and it is not surprising to find this prominent mountain (2891ft/867m) in their old Strathclyde kingdom named after him. The modern alternative name, 'The Cobbler', known from around 1800, originally referred to the central peak, and is said to be a translation of Gaelic *an greasaiche crom*, 'the crooked shoemaker'. There is also Loch Arthur, with a prehistoric crannog dwelling, south-west of Dumfries.

Arthur's Seat (Edinburgh) Numerous location-names in Scotland refer to the legendary hero of the Britons: this one, given to the prominent Edinburgh landmark, is among Lothian's Cumbric place-names, recalling the Votadini tribe who spoke this language (their name commemorated in the 'Gododdin' poem) before the incursions of Angles and Gaels into the region. There is another Arthur's Seat in the Borders, part of the Hart Fell massif, and another in Banffshire.

Artney, Glen (Perth & Kinross) 'Pebbled'. *Artein* (Scottish Gaelic) 'pebble', presumably with reference to the valley sides or floor. The river in Glen Artney is the Water of Ruchill; the glen, unusually, does not take its name from the stream.

Askaig, River, Loch (Highland, Argyll & Bute) Perhaps 'river strip', from Old Norse *á*, 'river' and *skiki*, 'strip of land'.

Assynt (Highland) Perhaps '(land) seen from afar'. *Asynt* (Old Norse) 'visible', referring to the sight of the area's many isolated and distinctive peaks as seen from out at sea in the Minch. This is a conjectural derivation. Old Norse *àss*, 'ridge' has also been put forward for the first part of the name. The Gaelic name, Assainn, is simply a phonetic rendering. This wide crofting district of West Sutherland also holds the county's highest mountain, Ben More Assynt ('great hill of Assynt'), 3273ft/982m.

Athelstaneford (East Lothian) 'Athelstan's ford'. King Athelstan, of Mercia and Wessex, conquered Northumbria and invaded Lothian in the early tenth century. In 934 his troops were defeated near this village, which possibly commemorates his name, which means 'noble stone' (Old English). Legend has it that during another battle near here in 761, the Picts, under their king, Aengus, facing a

Northumbrian army, saw a St Andrew's cross in the sky. Inspired by it to victory, they took Andrew as their patron saint and the saltire as their national flag. It has also been suggested that the origin of this place-name has no connection at all with the Anglo-Saxon name Athelstan(e), but represents a tautology of *ath-ail-stane* (Gaelic, Scots) 'stone ford'. Nevertheless, the village flies the saltire every day in commemoration of Aengus's vision.

Atholl (Perth & Kinross) The name of this south Grampian district is much discussed: the ath- part has been connected to *ath* (Scottish Gaelic) 'next, second'; also to *àth* (Scottish Gaelic) 'ford'. The second part has been derived from *Fhodla* (Old Gaelic), a traditional name for Ireland, linked with the tutelary Irish goddess Fodla. The name could thus be either 'next or new Ireland' or 'ford of Fodla'. The distinction is important since the former would imply territorial naming by incursive Scots. In the *Annals of Tighernach*, referring to c. 739, it is noted as Athfoithle. It is notable that this Gaelic name was in any case used to apply to the area while it was still within the Pictish kingdom, indicating the eastward spread of the Scots settlers from their original base in Argyll. Atholl (formerly spelt Athole) became a medieval Scottish earldom, and is still the name of a large mountainous district. *See also* Blair Atholl

Attadale (Highland) 'Ata's valley'. *Dalr* (Old Norse) 'valley', prefixed by the Old Norse personal name *Ata*.

Attow, Ben (Highland) 'Long mountain'. *Beinn* (Scottish Gaelic) 'mountain', *fhada* (Scottish Gaelic) 'long'. This mountain (3385ft/1015m) rises in the Kintail Forest of Wester Ross, behind the 'Five Sisters'. There is another Beinn Fhada on Mull.

Auchendinny (Midlothian) 'Field of the height or fortress'. *Achadh* (Scottish Gaelic) 'field'; *denna* (Old Irish, genitive of *dind*) 'of the height'. Noted as Aghendini, 1335.

Auchenlochan (Argyll & Bute) 'Field of the little loch'. *Achadh* (Scottish Gaelic) 'field', *na*, 'of the'; *lochainn* (Scottish Gaelic) 'small loch'.

Auchenshuggle (Glasgow) 'Rye field'. This quaint-sounding Glasgow district name derives from *achadh* (Scottish Gaelic) 'field'; *na*, 'of the'; *seagal* (Scottish Gaelic) 'rye'.

Auchinleck (East Ayrshire) 'Field of the flat stones'. *Achadh* (Scottish Gaelic) 'field'; *na* (Scottish Gaelic) 'of the'; *leac* (Scottish Gaelic) 'flat stones', found as Auchinlec, 1239. This was the family estate of James Boswell (1740–1795), diarist and biographer of Samuel Johnson.

Auchmithie (Angus) 'Field of the herd'. *Achadh* (Scottish Gaelic) 'field'; *muthaidh* (Scottish Gaelic) 'herd'.

Auchnagatt (Aberdeenshire) 'Field of the wild cats'. *Achadh* (Scottish Gaelic) 'field'; *na*, 'of'; *cat*, 'cat'. *See* Cadboll, Lynchat.

Auchterarder (Perth & Kinross) 'Upland of high water'. *Uachdar* (Scottish Gaelic) 'upper' (land); *ard* (Scottish Gaelic) 'high'; *dobhar* (Brythonic) 'water'; found as Uchterardouere, c. 1200.

Auchterless (Aberdeenshire) 'Upland of the enclosed field'. *Uachdar* (Scottish Gaelic) 'upper'; *liós* (Scottish Gaelic) 'enclosure, garden'. Found as Uchterless, c. 1280.

Auchtermuchty (Fife) 'Upper pig enclosure'. *Uachdar* (Scottish Gaelic) 'upper' (land); *muc* (Scottish Gaelic) 'pig'; *garadh* (Scottish Gaelic) 'enclosure'. Early records show Huedirdmukedi 1250, Utermokerdy 1293, Utremukerty 1294.

Auchtertool (Fife) 'Athwart-lying upland'. *Uachdar* (Scottish Gaelic) 'upper' (land); *tuathal* (Scottish Gaelic) 'crosswise-set, leftwards'.

Auchtertyre (Highland) 'Upper section of land'. *Uachdar* (Scottish Gaelic) 'upper' (land) *tìr* (Scottish Gaelic) 'land'.

Auldearn (Moray) Traditionally derived as 'river of Erin'. *Allt* (Scottish Gaelic) 'river', *Eireann* (Irish Gaelic) 'of Erin'. Erin was a queen-goddess of ancient Ireland, a personification of the land itself, and brought to the Scottish landscape with the Gaelic-speaking Scots in the sixth century. But Earn as a name is likely to predate the Scots' arrival, and to be one of Scotland's many ancient river-names derived from a pre-Celtic root form, perhaps *Ar-* or *Er-*, indicating flowing water. The form Aldheren is found in 1298. *See* Earn.

Auldgirth (Dumfries & Galloway) 'Stream of the enclosure', from *allt* (Scottish Gaelic) 'stream' and *gart* (Scottish Gaelic) 'enclosure, field'.

Auldhouse (South Lanarkshire) 'Stream of the ghost'. *Allt* (Scottish Gaelic) 'stream'; *fhuathais* (Scottish Gaelic) 'spectre, apparition'. The nature of the spirit is not known; perhaps a water-kelpie.

Aultbea (Highland) 'Stream of the birches', *Allt* (Scottish Gaelic) 'stream'; *beithe* (Scottish Gaelic) 'birches'. The village on the wide, sheltered anchorage of Loch Ewe was a strategic naval depot in World War II. *See* Beith.

Aultguish (Highland) 'Stream of the pines'. *Allt* (Scottish Gaelic) stream'; *giuthais* (Scottish Gaelic) 'of the pines'.

Aultnaharra *See* Altnaharra

Averon, River (Highland) The original name for the Alness river. It has been linked with the Aveyron of southern France. Both may stem from the Celtic prefix *ab-, av-,* indicative of a stream; while the latter part seems cognate with that of Deveron.

Aviemore (Highland) 'Big pass'. *Agaidh* (Scottish Gaelic) 'pass'; *mór* (Scottish Gaelic) 'big'. This popular mountain and ski resort lies at the centre of the wide Strathspey, and at a strategic entry point into the Cairngorms. Like other places in the area, its development occurred with the building of the Highland Railway in the mid-nineteenth century, though its present 'centre' is the result of 1960s commercialism.

Avoch (Highland) *Awch.* 'Place of the stream'. *Abh* (Old Scottish Gaelic) 'water', related to *abhainn*, 'river', and stemming from the same continental celtic root *ab* or *av* as Averon; *-ach* (Scottish Gaelic) a variant on *achadh*, 'field'. Noted as Auauch, around 1333. This Black Isle fishing port was settled by Scots 'incomers' in the eighteenth century and still retains distinctive local surnames and speech forms. Auch, at the foot of Ben Dorain (Argyll), has the same derivation, as does Avochie on the Deveron.

Avon, River, Loch (Highland; Moray; West Lothian) 'Stream', from *abhainn* (Scottish Gaelic) 'stream, river'. It is cognate with Welsh *afon* and the numerous Avons of England, and stems originally from a conjectured Indo-European root form *-ab* or *-aub*, seen also in Danube and Punjab.

Avon, Ben (Aberdeenshire) *Aan.* The mountain (3843ft/1171m), a lofty eastern outlier of the Cairngorms, takes its name from the river above which it rises (*see* Avon, River, Loch).

Awe, River and **Loch** (Argyll & Bute, Highland) 'Water', from *àbh* (Scottish Gaelic, obsolete) 'water' (see Averon, Avoch). 'A far cry from Loch Awe' is a Campbell phrase meaning anywhere remote. The Argyll Loch Awe is often found in pre-twentieth century texts as Lochow.

Ayr (South Ayrshire) The former county town of Ayrshire, still an important administrative centre, market and resort town, takes its name from the river at whose mouth it stands; its Gaelic name is Inbhir-àir, 'Ayr-mouth'. Ayr has many similar forms in England (Aire; Oare) and elsewhere in Europe (Aar, Ahr, Ohre, Ore). It has been traced to a hypothetical Brythonic form, Ara, with the original sense of 'smooth-running'. Noted as Ar, 1177. It was hymned by Robert Burns as unsurpassed 'for honest men and bonny lasses'. Ayrshire has given its name to a famous breed of dairy cow.

Ayre (Orkney) 'Tongue of land', from Old Norse *eyri,* 'tongue, spit'. There are numerous instances of ayres, known to geologists as tombolos: sand or shingle spits joining two islands, or linking an island to the mainland, in the Orkney islands.

Ayton (Borders) 'Place on the river Eye'; the river-name is *éa* (Old English) 'running stream', with *-tun* (old English) 'farmstead'; recorded as Eitun, 1098. There is also an Ayton by Aberargie in Perth and Kinross.

B

Back (Western Isles) 'Hollow', from *bac* (Scottish Gaelic) 'hollow, bend in the ground'.

Badachro (Highland) 'Place of saffron'. *Bad* (Scottish Gaelic), 'particular place', *chròch* (Scottish Gaelic) 'saffron'. *Chro-chorcur* is the saffron crocus. Saffron was important in making dye for the *leine croch*, the saffron shirt worn by Highlanders.

Badbea (Highland) 'Birch clump', or 'place of birches'. *Bad* (Scottish Gaelic) 'particular place', also with the meaning 'clump'; *beith* (Scottish Gaelic) 'birch tree'. This is a cleared and utterly deserted village site on a steep slope above the sea on the Ord of Caithness; in its name the final *-th* has been lost, unlike the nearby Dunbeath (see also Aultbea).

Badcall (Highland) 'Hazel clump'. *Bad* (Scottish Gaelic) which as well as 'particular place', can have the meaning 'clump', and *call* (Scottish Gaelic) 'hazel tree'. The Gaelic name is Bada Call.

Badenoch (Highland) 'Drowned or marshy land'. *Bàithte* (Old Gaelic) 'liable to flooding', with the suffix *-ach* (Old Gaelic) 'land'. The name, found as Badenach, 1229, was given to the wide and almost level area of Strathspey between Kingussie and Granton. The 'Wolf of Badenoch' was not a local brigand but a son of King Robert II of Scotland, in theory responsible for maintaining law and order in the north.

Badentarbet (Highland) 'Place of the isthmus'. *Bad* (Scottish Gaelic) 'particular place'; *an* 'of the'; *tairbeart* 'isthmus, portage place'.

Baile Mòr (Argyll & Bute; Western Isles) 'Big village', from Scottish Gaelic *baile*, 'village', and *mòr*, 'big'. The name of the village on Iona and also of a North Uist hamlet.

Bal- The most common place-name prefix in Scotland, from Scottish Gaelic *baile*, which means 'village, home, farm' or simply 'place'. It is found throughout the country, except for the extreme south-east and the Northern Isles. Although there are no large towns with this prefix, it is found in many district and village names and in a host of farm names. In many areas in the east and north, this prefix may have supplanted the earlier Pictish Pit- prefix, though its meaning is different (*see* Pit-). The form Bally-, so common in Ireland, is rare in Scotland.

Balaclava (Renfrewshire) This modest place dates from 1856 and was named after the Crimean War battlefield; there are a number of other commemorative Balaclavas and also Waterloos as local names.

Balado (Perth & Kinross) 'Long place'. *Baile* (Scottish Gaelic) 'homestead, hamlet', and *fhada* (Scottish Gaelic) 'long'. *See also* Ben Attow. 'House at the yew-tree ford', from Scottish Gaelic *baile*; 'homestead, hamlet'; *àth*, 'ford'; *eo*, 'yew' has also been suggested.

Balblair (Highland) 'Village on the plain'. *Baile* (Scottish Gaelic) 'homestead, hamlet'; *blàr* (Scottish Gaelic) 'plain', found in four locations between Inverness and Bonar Bridge.

Baldragon (Dundee) Perhaps 'place of the hero'. *Baile* (Scottish Gaelic) 'homestead', *dreagan* (Scottish Gaelic) 'dragon', used figuratively to describe a great warrior. If so, his identity has been lost.

Balerno (West Lothian) 'Village of the sloe tree'. *Baile* (Scottish Gaelic) 'homestead, hamlet'; *airneach* (Scottish Gaelic) 'sloe tree'. The name of this western suburb of Edinburgh was first recorded in 1280 as Balhernoch and has since been further modified to its present form.

Balfour (Angus) 'Pasture place'. *Baile* (Scottish Gaelic) 'homestead'; *pór*, 'pasture' with the genitive form *phùir*, is a borrowing into Gaelic from Cumbric or Pictish, seen in modern Welsh *pawr*, 'pasture'. The same name is found in unanglicised form in Baile Phùir (Highland), and there is also a Balfour in Fife.

Balfron (Stirling) Perhaps from a personal name, prefixed by Scottish Gaelic *baile*, 'homestead'. The 'fron' part may be related to the same uncertain root as 'fruin' in Glen Fruin.

Balgie (Highland, Perth & Kinross) 'Bubbly stream', from *balg* (Scottish Gaelic) 'bag, swelling', has been suggested; also *Baile* (Scottish Gaelic) 'homestead', *gaoth* (Scottish Gaelic) 'marsh, bogland'. In older forms this is seen as *gáeth* or *góith*. The name occurs in different parts of the Highlands, sometimes as Balgy. A similar form is found in Balgay (Perth & Kinross). *See also* Bogie.

Balintore (Highland) 'Place of the bleaching ground'. *Baile* (Scottish Gaelic) 'homestead' or 'hamlet'; *an*, 'of the'; *todhair* (Scottish Gaelic) 'bleaching green', referring to the grassy parkland of this sea-salmon fishing village. Other Balintores occur as farm or field names, in the Highland and Angus regions (there is also Balintore Castle in the latter).

Balivanich (Western Isles) 'Monk's place'. *Baile* (Scottish Gaelic) 'homestead, hamlet'; *a'* 'appertaining to'; *mhanaich* (Scottish Gaelic) 'monk's'. The Gaelic name is Baile a' Mhanaich. Benbecula's airport is located on the flat ground here.

Ballachulish (Highland) 'Village of the narrows'. *Baile* (Scottish

Gaelic) 'homestead, hamlet'; _caolas_ (Scottish Gaelic) 'narrows, straits'. Noted as Ballecheles in 1552. This name is descriptive of the village's location on Loch Leven at the typical narrow fiord entrance by which it stands, and over which the main Glasgow–Fort William road now crosses by a bridge. The area was once important for slate-quarrying: the waste heaps can still be seen.

Ballantrae (South Ayrshire) 'Village on the shore'. _Baile_ (Scottish Gaelic) 'homestead, hamlet'; _an_ (Scottish Gaelic) 'of the, on the'; _traighe_ (Scottish Gaelic) 'tidal beach'. A long stretch of open sandy shore is found here where the River Stinchar (perhaps 'shallow bends', from Gaelic _staoin,_ 'shallow'; _car,_ 'bend, meander') flows into the Firth of Clyde. R. L. Stevenson uses the location in his novel _The Master of Ballantrae._

Ballater (Aberdeenshire) Possibly 'broom land'. _Bealaidh_ (Scottish Gaelic) 'broom'; _tir_ (Scottish Gaelic) 'land'. Alternatively, it could be 'pass of the water', which describes the situation of this Royal Deeside village. _Bealach_ (Scottish Gaelic) 'mountain pass'; _dobhar_ (Brythonic–Gaelic) 'water'. Certainly, eighteenth-century records would suggest the latter derivation: Balader 1704, Ballader 1716.

Ballingry (Fife) 'Village of the cave, or den'. _Baile_ (Scottish Gaelic) 'homestead'; _an,_ 'of'; _garaidh_ (Scottish Gaelic) 'cave'. Noted as Ballyngry, c. 1400. This was once a coal-mining village.

Ballinluig (Perth & Kinross) 'Township by the hollow'. _Baile_ (Scottish Gaelic) 'homestead'; _an luig_ (Scottish Gaelic) 'towards the hollow', from _lag,_ 'hollow'. The village is located in the gap where the rivers Tummel and Tay meet. The name is found in other localities, by Balquhidder, and in Strathardle, for example.

Balloch (West Dunbartonshire, Highland) 'Pass', or 'gap'. Scottish Gaelic _bealach,_ 'mountain pass', a reference here to the river-gap linking Loch Lomond to the Clyde. 'Balloch' is a frequent element in other place-names. Balloch by Inverness has however been construed as Scottish Gaelic _baile an loch,_ 'place by the loch'.

Ballochmyle (East Ayrshire) Perhaps 'Pass of the rocky brow'. _Bealach_ (Scottish Gaelic) 'mountain pass', with _maol_ (Scottish Gaelic) 'brow of a rock'. This steep valley has Scotland's highest masonry viaduct, carrying the Glasgow–Kilmarnock–Carlisle railway.

Ballygown (Argyll & Bute) 'Place of the smith'. _Baile_ (Scottish Gaelic) 'homestead, hamlet'; _ghobhainn_ (Scottish Gaelic) 'smith'. This Mull name is one of a very few Bally- place-names in Scotland, compared to the many in Ireland, all of them found in the Inner Hebrides, and indicating an early name given by the Dàl Riadan migrants around the turn of the sixth century.

Balmacaan (Highland) 'Steading of the sons of Cathan'. *Baile* (Scottish Gaelic) 'homestead'; *mac Cathain* (Scottish Gaelic personal name) 'of the sons of Cathan'.

Balmacara (Highland) 'Place of the MacAras'. *Baile* (Scottish Gaelic) 'homestead'; *mac Ara* (Scottish Gaelic personal name) 'of the MacAras'. But MacAra is not a name of the Lochalsh region. An older form from the sixteenth century is Ballimaccroy, which may be a form of Macrae, the clan of the locality.

Balmaclellan (Dumfries & Galloway) 'MacLellan's place'. *Baile* (Scottish Gaelic) 'homestead'; *mac Gille Fhaolain*, (Scottish Gaelic patronymic) 'son of the follower of (St) Fillan'. One of relatively few personal names attached to a Gaelic place-name, and probably late in formation; found in 1183 as Balmacglenin.

Balnagown (Highland) 'Place of the smith'. *Baile* (Scottish Gaelic) homestead'; *na*, 'of the'; *ghobhainn* (Scottish Gaelic) 'smith'. Balnagown Castle was the seat of the chief of Clan Ross. The names Balnagowan, Balgowan have the same derivation.

Balmaha (Stirling) '(St) Maha's place'. *Baile* (Scottish Gaelic) 'homestead'; *Mo-Thatha* (Scottish Gaelic form of Irish *Tua* 'the silent one', with the prefix *mo-* indicating 'dear'; perhaps indicating a hermit-saint). St Maha's well is nearby.

Balmerino (Fife) '(St) Merinac's place'. *Baile* (Scottish Gaelic) 'homestead'. Recorded as Balmerinach, c. 1200. St Merinac was one of the associates of St Regulus, who is said to have brought the bones of St Andrew to Scotland.

Balmoral (Aberdeenshire) Perhaps 'homestead in the big clearing'. *Baile* (Scottish Gaelic) 'homestead, settlement'; *mór* (Scottish Gaelic) 'big'; *ial* (Brythonic–Pictish) 'clearing'. *Mòrail* (Scottish Gaelic) 'majestic, splendid' has also been suggested, perhaps influenced by the castle's royal ownership. The Gaelic name is Baile Mhoreil. The estate was purchased by Prince Albert and Queen Victoria in 1853, and remains a royal holiday home.

Balmullo (Fife) 'Place on the height'. *Baile* (Scottish Gaelic) 'homestead, settlement'; *mullach* (Scottish Gaelic) 'height, summit'.

Balornock (Glasgow) 'Louernoc's place'. From Old Welsh *bod*, 'place', and *Louernoc*, a personal name meaning 'little fox'. The earliest form (twelfth century) is Budlornac. Balernock, near Garelochhead, may have the same derivation.

Balquhidder (Stirling) *Bal-whidder.* Apparently 'settlement of fodder'. *Baile* (Scottish Gaelic) 'homestead, hamlet'; *foidir* (corrupt Gaelic form of Old Norse *fothr*) 'fodder'. Its earliest known form is Buffudire (1266), indicating that the prefix was either replaced by, or for a time interchangeable with, *buth* (Scottish Gaelic) 'house, hut'. This typically long, straggling Highland township has long been associated with cattle rearing. Rob Roy MacGregor is buried here. The Braes of Balquhidder, from *bràigh* (Scottish Gaelic) 'upper part', refers to the upland grazing slopes rising above Loch Voil.

Balta (Shetland) This has been derived as 'belt island', from Old Norse *balti*, 'belt', and *ey*, 'island'.

Banavie (Highland) A stream name, perhaps 'Pig's burn'. *Banbh* (Scottish Gaelic) 'pig', an animal often met in Celtic mythology. This community at the southern end of Glen More is close to the set of locks on the Caledonian Canal known as 'Neptune's Staircase'.

Banchory (Aberdeenshire; Perth & Kinross) *Bank-ry*. 'Horns'. *Beannach* (Scottish Gaelic) 'horned, forked'. The Gaelic form of the name is Beannachar. The *-y* ending has been explained as the dative form *Beannchraigh,* 'by the bends'. The bends are on the River Dee, both at Banchory Devenick and Banchory Ternan (the names relate to churches dedicated to the Celtic saints Devinicus and Ternan); Banchory Devenick is some miles to the east. Recorded as Benchorin, 1164; Banchery Defnyk, c. 1300. Although the meaning has also been sought as 'place among mountains', from Scottish Gaelic *beinn,* 'mountain', which is is any case a related term, its original sense having been 'horn', the situation of Easter and Wester Banchory on the meandering River Isla south of Blairgowrie in Perthshire, and well away from hills, is significant. The Irish and Welsh Bangors are of similar derivation.

Banff (Aberdeenshire) The origin of this ancient royal burgh's name is uncertain. Some authorities have suggested 'land left fallow for a year': *banbh* (Scottish Gaelic). Others have made the tentative connection with a traditional Gaelic name for Ireland, *Banba*. Scottish Gaelic *banbh*, 'young pig' has also been suggested (*see* Banavie), perhaps the River Deveron was symbolised by a pig. Medieval documents record the development of the name form: Banb 1150, Banef 1160, Bamphe 1290, Banffe 1291. Formerly county town of Banffshire, Banff has many fine town houses from the seventeenth and eighteenth centuries. Bamff, north of Alyth in Perth & Kinross, would seem to share the same derivation.

Bangour (West Lothian) 'Goats' peak'. *Beinn* (Scottish Gaelic) 'mountain', *ghobhar* (Scottish Gaelic) 'goats'. Shown as Bengouer in the early fourteenth century. There is also a Bangour in Fife.

Banknock (Falkirk) 'Hill place'. *Baile* (Scottish Gaelic) 'place, settlement'; *cnoc* (Scottish Gaelic) 'hill'. The form Ballinknok is found in the early sixteenth century.

Bannockburn (Stirling) A name acquired in two stages, with the Scots 'burn' either an addition or else a replacement of an earlier

Cumbric stream-suffix. Bannock- has been related to a Cumbric form of the Old Welsh *bannauc,* 'peaked hill', found in the sixth-century 'Gododdin' poem, though the hills around are not notably peaked. Recorded as Bannokburne, 1654. This village, now a southern suburb of Stirling, stands on the banks of the Bannock Burn, which was the site of the famous battle in 1314, when the Scots, led by King Robert I, routed the English army of Edward II. Another Bannock Burn flows into the Helmsdale River, far to the north, in Sutherland: this may be a more recent name, though it is in a hilly district.

Bar- A frequently-found prefix, which may be from Scottish Gaelic or Cumbric *barr,* 'ridge, crest', indicating a location on a ridge or hill-top.

Barassie (South Ayrshire) 'Summit of the droving stance'. *Barr* (Scottish Gaelic) 'crest'; *fasadh* (Scottish Gaelic) 'stance, level place'. Also found as Barrassie.

Barbaraville (Highland) 'Barbara's town'. One of the numerous new (late eighteenth- early nineteenth-century) villages created by lairds and named in compliment to their wives; other examples are Jemimaville and Arabella, in the Black Isle and Easter Ross respectively.

Barcaldine (Argyll & Bute) 'Ridge of the hazel trees'. *Barr* (Scottish Gaelic) 'crest, clump', and *calltuin* (Scottish Gaelic) 'hazel trees'.

Barlanark (Glasgow) 'Bare hill or ridge'. *Barr* (Cumbric) 'crest', and *lanerc* (Cumbric) 'clear space, glade'.

Barlinnie (Glasgow) 'Hilltop by the pool'. *Barr* (Scottish Gaelic) 'summit, top'; *linne* (Scottish Gaelic) 'pool'. A suburb of Glasgow, it is well known for its prison, popularly referred to as 'the Bar-L'. The name refers to the location on top of one of the city's many hills and close to Hogganfield (Scots *hog, hoggan,* 'young sheep') Loch, features left after the retreat of the last Ice Age glaciers.

Barnton (East Lothian) 'Barn farm'. Old English *berne,* 'barley store'; and *tun,* 'farmstead'. In the Anglian period, barley appears to have been the main cereal crop up the Lothian coast (*see* Berwick).

Barra (Western Isles) Perhaps piously derived as 'Isle of St Barr'. Barr or Finnbarr (c. 560–615) was bishop of Cork. His name is from Irish Gaelic *fionn,* 'white', and *barr,* 'crest'; and his monastery was a vigorous mission centre. Monks trained there evangelised much of the West, and there are the ruins of a church dedicated to him here at Cille-bharra. An alternative source is Gaelic *barr,* 'hill', with the later addition of Old Norse *ey,* 'island'. The name c. 1200 was Barey; in Gaelic it is Barraidh.

Barrhead (East Renfrewshire) 'Hilltop'. *Barr* (Scottish Gaelic) 'crest, top'; *head*, 'summit, top'. The name of this industrial town, founded in the 1770s on the outer south-western edge of Glasgow, does not seem to relate to the local topography. In the south-west, Barr on the River Stinchar, and Barrhead on the River Duisk, are both close to hills.

Barrisdale (Highland) Possibly 'Valley of the peaks'. *Barr* (Scottish Gaelic) 'crest' and *dalr* (Old Norse) 'valley'. Such hybrid combinations are not uncommon where Norse and Gaelic were both spoken, and Barrisdale, on Loch Hourn, lies at the foot of very steep slopes. But the *Barr-* here may be from a Scandinavian personal name, as its genitive form suggests.

Barskimming (East Ayrshire) 'Simon's heights'. *Barr* (Scottish Gaelic) 'crest'; *Sími* (Scottish Gaelic personal name) 'Simon'. Recorded as Barskinning in 1639.

Barrock (Highland) 'Little crest'. *Barr* (Scottish Gaelic) 'crest', with *-ag* (Scottish Gaelic) diminutive suffix.

Barry (Angus) 'Barrows' has been suggested, from *beorg* (Old English) which has the sense of both 'hill' and 'grave-mound'. There was at least one battle fought here between Picts and Danes, which could have resulted in the raising of grave-mounds. But perhaps, like Barry in South Wales, it has a Brythonic source in *barr*, 'hill' with *-i,* suffix indicating 'stream'. Barry Links, to the south, was noted as a golfing site in 1527.

Bass Rock (East Lothian) 'The brow'. *An* (Scottish Gaelic) 'the'; *bathais* (Scottish Gaelic) 'brow, forehead', referring to the distinctive shape of the rock, in the Firth of Forth off North Berwick, used by the authorities as a secure prison until the nineteenth century.

Bathgate (West Lothian) 'Boar wood' or 'House in the wood'. *Baedd* (Cumbric) 'boar'; *coed* (Cumbric) 'wood'. Alternatively, the first element could be derived as *bod* (Cumbric) 'house'. Recorded around 1160 as Bathchet.

Bealach nam Bò (Highland) *Bay-alach nam Boh.* 'Pass of the Cattle'. *Bealach* (Scottish Gaelic) 'mountain pass'; *nam* (Scottish Gaelic) 'of the'; *bò* (Scottish Gaelic) 'cattle'. This scenic pass, rising steeply from sea level to 2054ft (628m) on the Applecross peninsula, was in the past one of the Highland drove roads along which cattle were driven to the market trysts. There are many other *Bealach* names, often scotticised to Balloch; another Bealach nam Bò, noted in Sir Walter Scott's *The Lady of the Lake* is above the east end of Loch Katrine.

Bearsden (East Dunbartonshire) 'Boar's valley'. *Bár* (Old English) 'boar'; *denu* (Old English) 'valley'. This satellite residential town, developed to the northwest of Glasgow in Victorian times, has no connection with bears, which, probably extinct by the first millennium AD, are not recorded in place names.

Beattock (Dumfries & Galloway) Probably 'sharp-topped (hills)'. *Biodach* (Scottish Gaelic) 'sharp-topped'. The village lies in upper Annandale, a few miles south of Beattock Summit, over which the main Glasgow to London road and rail links pass from Annandale into Upper Clydesdale.

Beauly (Highland) *Byoo-ly.* 'Beautiful Place'. *Beau* (French) 'beautiful'; *lieu* (French) 'place'. Compare Beaulieu in Hampshire. It is recorded in 1230 as Prioratus de Bello Loco (Latin) 'priory of the lovely spot', with reference to the then newly-founded Valliscaulian monastery here. One of the few older names expressing aesthetic appreciation of the landscape. In Gaelic it is A' Mhanaichann, 'the monastery'.

Beeswing (Dumfries & Galloway) This village name comes from an inn which was here, named after the nineteenth century racehorse, Beeswing.

Beinn *See* Ben

Beith (North Ayrshire) *Beeth.* 'The place of the birch tree'. *Beithe* (Scottish Gaelic) 'birch tree'. The name of a town in Renfrewshire, it is also found in local and field names in other areas. *See* Aultbea, Dunbeath.

Beley (Fife) The name of this minor East Fife locality is of interest as possibly preserving the name of the Celtic deity Bel. Its oldest form, noted in the Chartulary of St Andrews, is Ballebelin, where the prefix is *Baile* (Scottish Gaelic) 'homestead, settlement'.

Belladrum (Highland) 'Ridge of the ford-mouth'. *Beul* (Scottish Gaelic) 'mouth'; *àtha* (Scottish Gaelic) 'ford'; *druim* (Scottish Gaelic) 'ridge'.

Bellahouston (Glasgow) 'Settlement of the crucifix'. *Baile* (Scottish Gaelic) 'settlement, hamlet'; *cheusadain* (Scottish Gaelic) 'crucifix'. Noted as Ballahaustane, 1578. It is assumed that the original place manifested a holy cross in some form. In latter centuries the name has been confused with Houston.

Ben From Scottish Gaelic *Beinn,* 'mountain'. The original sense of the word was 'horn', and it was probably first applied to peaked mountains. It has become the standard word for a Scottish mountain, because of its application to the highest peaks, though apart from some thirty examples in the south-west, it is found only north of the Forth–Clyde line and in the Western Isles. It is also found in the form Bin, as in The Bin, and The Bin Forest, near Huntly in Aberdeenshire. *See also* Càrn, Meall, Sgùrr.

Benarty (Fife) 'Stony hill'. *Beinn* (Scottish Gaelic) 'mountain'; *artaich* (Scottish Gaelic) 'stony'. The two parts of the name appear to have been welded togther in common usage. A link between -*arty* and the personal name *Art* or *Artur*, has also been suggested, which would make this another 'Ben Arthur'. It has also been identified with the name Cabennartye, recorded in the Chartulary of St Andrews, with a suggested relation to Brythonic *cefn*, 'ridge', as in Giffnock; found also in the Cevennnes range in France.

Benbecula (Western Isles) 'Hill of the salt-water fords'. The Gaelic name is Beinn na Faoghla. *Beinn* (Scottish Gaelic) 'hill, mountain, peak'; *na* (Scottish Gaelic) 'of the'; *faoghail* (adapted Scottish Gaelic form of *fadhail*) 'salt-water ford'. Alternatively, the last element may have been *faoghlach* (Scottish Gaelic) 'strand, beach'. Both these possible derivations fit this low-lying island which, until the construction of causeways to the north and south, could be reached on foot only by fording the tidal sandbanks joining it to North and South Uist. The name is recorded in early documents as: Beanbeacla 1495; Benvalgha 1549; Benbicula 1660.

Ben Lomond *see* Lomond

Ben Nevis *see* Nevis

Benderloch (Argyll & Bute) 'Hill between Lochs'. The name is wholly Scottish Gaelic, *Beinn*, 'mountain'; *eadar*, 'between'; *dá*, 'two'; *loch*, 'lake, loch'. The Gaelic form is Meadarloch, with the unstressed first syllable almost lost.

Bennachie (Aberdeenshire) 'Mountain of the nipple'. *Beinn* (Scottish Gaelic) 'mountain; *na*, 'of'; *cìche* (Scottish Gaelic) 'nipple, breast'. Although not lofty, 1733ft/529m, it is a conspicuous peak. The derivation 'blessed place', from *beannaichte* (Scottish Gaelic) 'blessed', has also been suggested, but seems much less probable. This area is regarded as the most likely site for the celebrated battle of Mons Graupius between Romans and Caledonians in AD 84.

Bernera (Highland; Argyll & Bute) *See* Berneray

Berneray (Western Isles) 'Bjorn's isle'. *Bjorn* (Old Norse proper name) 'Bear-like'; *ey* (Old Norse) 'island'. The Gaelic name is Eilean Bhearnaraigh. *See also under* Glenelg.

Berriedale (Highland) Noted as Berudal in the *Orkneyinga Saga*, c. 1225; the latter part is Old Norse *dalr*, 'dale, valley'; and a possible derivation of the first part from *borgar* (Old Norse) 'fort', has been suggested, but the reason for the vowel change is not clear. It may be from Old Norse *berg*, 'hill', like The Berry on Hoy in Orkney; or perhaps a proper name, though in this locality unlikely to be the St Bearach of Kilberry in Kintyre. The valley, on the Ord of Caithness, is notably steep.

Berwick (Northumberland) *Berrik.* 'Barley farm.' *Bere* (Old English) 'barley' or 'bere'; *wic* (Old English) 'farm'. The name is found as Berwic from 1095. The town, officially known as Berwick upon Tweed, was in early medieval times Scotland's main trading centre. Since the fourteenth century it has been an English possession, but the former Scottish county of Berwickshire still bears its name. *See* North Berwick.

Bettyhill (Highland) Named after Elizabeth, countess of Sutherland, this village was set up about 1820 as an agricultural and fishing centre to provide housing and work for some of those evicted in the clearances of people from the landward glens. In Gaelic it retained its name of Am Blàran Odhar, 'the brown fields'.

Bhraggie, Ben (Highland) *Vrackie.* 'Speckled mountain', from *beinn* (Scottish Gaelic) 'mountain', and *breachaidh* (Scottish Gaelic) 'speckled'. This hill (1298ft/397m), above Golspie, is topped by a statue of the third duke of Sutherland (*see* Introduction).

Biggar (South Lanarkshire) 'Barley field'. *Bygg* (Old Norse) 'barley'; *gardr* (Old Norse) 'enclosure'. Alternatively, the latter may be the more specific *geiri* (Old Norse) 'triangular plot'. Early records include Bigir, 1170, Begart, 1524.

Birkhall (Aberdeenshire) 'Birch bank'. *Birk* (Scots) 'birch'; *haugh* (Scots) 'bank, water-meadow'. Because of the Scots practice of dropping the final *-ll* sound in words like 'hall', a confusion between this and 'haugh' has crept in; the written form makes a false assumption.

Birnam (Perth & Kinross) 'Village of the warrior'. *Beorn* (Old English) 'warrior'; *ham* (Old English) 'homestead, hamlet'. In Middle English, *beorn* had mutated to *birn*. This is unusually far into the Highlands to find a name with an Anglian source, but the district was 'feudalised' in the late twelfth century. It links oddly with that of Dunkeld, on the other side of the Tay, the two places now forming a single community.

Birsay (Orkney) 'Hunting-ground valley'. *Birgis* (Old Norse) 'hunt'; *herath* (Old Norse) 'valley'. The name is found as Birgisherad in the *Orkneyinga Saga*, c. 1225. It was the seat of the earls of Orkney until the late sixteenth century.

Bishopbriggs (East Dunbartonshire) 'Bishop's lands'. The 'bishop' is that of Glasgow; *riggs* (Scots) 'fields'. The *b* has crept in through confusion with the word *brig* (Scots) 'bridge'. Now a north-western extension of the Glasgow conurbation.

Black Isle, The (Highland) The name of this broad and fertile peninsula between the Beauly and Cromarty Firths may be an English translation of Scottish Gaelic *eilean*, 'island', *dubh*, 'dark', referrring either to black soil or dark forest cover. An alternative explanation is that the Gaelic name was Eilean Duthac, St Duthac's island, mis-translated into English as 'black isle'. St Duthac was a revered figure in the North.

Blackadder, River (Borders) *See* Adder

Blackwater, River (Highland; Perth & Kinross; Stirling) Translation of the Scottish Gaelic *Allt*, 'stream' and *dubh*, 'dark'. This is a frequently found river-name.

Blair- Found as a prefix to many local names, like Blairadam, Blairlogie, it is Scottish Gaelic *blàr*, 'plain' or 'level clearing'. Sometimes it designates a battlefield as in Blàr na Leine, 'field of the shirts', in the Great Glen, scene of a battle between Clanranald Macdonalds and Frasers in 1540

Blair Atholl (Perth & Kinross) 'Plain of the New Ireland', or 'plain of the ford of Fodla' (see Atholl). *Blàr* (Scottish Gaelic) 'plain, level clearing', often with the sense of 'battlefield'. Blair Castle, near the village, has been the seat of the earls and dukes of Atholl since 1269, and is sited on the most cultivable part of the lands.

Blairadam (Argyll & Bute) 'Plain of the oxen'. *Blàr* (Scottish Gaelic) 'plain, level clearing'; *nan* 'of the'; *damh* (Scottish Gaelic) 'oxen'.

Blairgowrie (Perth & Kinross) 'Plain of Gabran'. *Blàr* (Scottish Gaelic) 'plain, level clearing'; the second element relates to the district of Gowrie, perhaps to distinguish it from Blair Atholl, which is not far away. Noted as Blair in Gowrie, 1604. *See* Gowrie, Rattray.

Blantyre (South Lanarkshire) 'Edge-land'. *Blaen* (Gaelic, from Cumbric) 'edge'; *tìr* (Scottish Gaelic) 'land'. Noted in 1289 as Blantir. The name of this town south of Glasgow, birthplace of David Livingstone (1813–1873) and site of his memorial centre, is descriptive of its situation above the steeply incised River Clyde.

Blaven (Highland) Bla-wen. 'Yellow mountain'. *Blà* (Old Scottish Gaelic) 'yellow'; *bheinn* Scottish Gaelic) 'mountain'. It may be noted that *bla* (Old Norse) is 'blue', a more plausible-seeming colour (though *see* Suilven). This Skye mountain rises to 3034ft/928m.

Blinkbonny (Borders; Fife; Midlothian) Often used as a house name, with the intended sense of 'fine view', this name of several rural localities has also been suggested as a Scots rendering from Scottish Gaelic *baile*, 'homestead, settlement', and *bainne*, 'milk', thus Milktown.

Boat of Garten (Highland) 'Boat' as an inland name indicates the one-time existence of a ferry, in this case across the wide River Spey, close to its confluence with the tributary River Garten. The need for the ferry was ended in 1898 when a bridge was built here. The Gaelic name is Coit Ghartainn, from *coit,* 'boat'. *See* Garten.

Bochastle (Stirling) 'Hut of the castle'. *Both* (Scottish Gaelic) hut, cot', and *chaisteil* (Scottish Gaelic) 'castle'.

Boddam (Aberdeenshire; Stirling) 'Bottom place'. Old English *botm*, 'bottom'. Boddam is placed at the cliff-foot. Buddon, as in Buddon Ness (Angus), is from the same source, as is Boddin, just south of Montrose.

Bog of Gight (Aberdeenshire) 'Bog of the winds'. *Bog* (Scottish Gaelic) 'marsh', and *gaoithe* (Scottish Gaelic) 'winds'. The chief of Clan Gordon, whose castle was here, was known as the 'Gudeman of the Bog'.

Bogie, River and **Strath** (Aberdeenshire) Perhaps 'stream with the bag-like pools', from *balg* (Scottish Gaelic) 'bag'. Earlier forms include Strabolgin, 1187. *See* Balgie.

Bolton (East Lothian) 'Village with buildings', presumably big enough to be notable. From Old English *bothel,* 'house'; *tun,* 'village, homestead'.

Bonar Bridge (Highland) 'Bridge at the lowest ford'. *Bonn* (Scottish Gaelic) 'bottom, base'; *àth,* 'ford'. A bridge was first built here in the early nineteenth century to replace the frequently impassable ford across the Kyle (Scottish Gaelic *caol,* 'narrows') of Sutherland.

Bonawe (Argyll & Bute) 'Water-foot'. *Bonn* (Scottish Gaelic) 'bottom, base', and *abh* (Old Gaelic) 'water'. There is a Bonawe on both banks of Loch Etive, where the loch narrows; that on the south bank was a site of iron-smelting in the eighteenth century, and the ruins of the buildings are still to be seen. The Gaelic name is sometimes given as *Bonn-atha,* 'ford at the foot' (*see* Bonar).

Bo'ness (West Lothian) The name is a contraction of Borrow-stounness, Old English *Beornweard* (personal name) with *tun,* 'farmstead': 'Beornweard's farm', later assimilated to Borrowstoun (Scots) 'burgh town' or town with a charter; *naes* (Old English) 'promontory'. Noted as Berwardeston, c. 1335. This coastal royal burgh is situated on a headland protruding into the Firth of Forth.

Bonhill (West Dunbartonshire) 'Hut by the stream'. *Both* (Scottish Gaelic) 'hut'; *an,* 'by'; *uillt* (Scottish Gaelic) 'stream'. Now a residential area in the Leven valley.

Bonnybridge (Falkirk) 'Swift stream bridge'. *Buan* (Scottish Gaelic) 'swift'. The name originally referred to the stream, whose fame was eclipsed by the settlement which grew up round the bridge, and found itself reduced by back-formation to being the 'Bonnybridge Burn'.

Borders Since 1975 'Scottish Borders' has been the official name of the south-eastern unitary local authority, but the term has long been used to describe the area lying immediately north and south of the border with England. On each side the Border was divided into western, eastern and middle 'marches', each with its warden to organise defence or attack, until the union of the crowns in 1603 put an end to the old Border way of life, with its raids or 'reivings'.

Boreraig (Highland) 'Fort bay'. *Borgar* (Old Norse) 'fort'; *aig* (Scottish Gaelic from Old Norse *vik*) 'bay'. Here on Skye was established the celebrated piping school of the MacCrimmon family.

Borgue (Western Isles) 'Fort'. *Borgar* (Old Norse) 'fortified site'.

Borrobol (Highland) 'Fort-place'. *Borgar* (Old Norse) 'fort', *bolr* (Old Norse abbreviated form of *bolstadr*) 'settlement'.

Borrodale (Highland) 'Dale of the fort'. *Borgar* (Old Norse) 'fortified place'; *dalr* (Old Norse) 'valley'. A superfluous Glen- has been added; the *-dalr* ending never having been borrowed into Gaelic. Also found as Borradale. It was at Borradale on Loch nan Uamh that Prince Charles Edward Stewart came ashore in July 1745.

Borthwick (East Lothian) 'Home farm', or possibly 'wood farm'. *Bord* (Old English) is 'table', but as a derivation from 'plank, wood'. *Wic* (Old English) 'farm'. Noted as Borthuic, 1430.

Borve (Western Isles) 'Fort'. *Borgar* (Old Norse) 'fort'. This name, found in several of the Outer Hebrides, is related to Burgh and Brough in Shetland and Orkney.

Bothwell (South Lanarkshire) This been taken as 'Buth's pool'. *Buth* (Old English personal name); *wael* (Old English) 'pool'; the first part has also been seen as Old English *bothe,* 'hut, house'. Noted in 1242 as Botheuill. Bothwell's strategic site made it a castle and the seat of an earldom. At the nearby battle of Bothwell Brig (Scots, 'bridge'), 1678, the Covenanters were routed by the royal army.

Bower (Highland) 'House', from Old Norse *búr,* 'house'. Noted as Bouer, c. 1230.

Bowling (West Dunbartonshire) Perhaps 'the place of Bolla's people.' *Bolla* (Old English proper name); *inga* (Old English) 'of the people of'. Such names oftern terminate with *-ham* (Old English) 'village', but not in this case. A Gaelic source has also been suggested, in *Bò,* 'cow's'; *linn,* 'pool'. In 1303 it was recorded as Bolline.

Bowmore (Argyll & Bute) Place of the 'big hut'. *Both* (Scottish Gaelic – silent th) 'hut, house'; *mór* (Scottish Gaelic) 'big'. The reference is presumably to the house of a local chief on Islay; in 1767 the old clachan was laid out as a 'model town'.

Brabster (Highland) 'Wide house'; the name of this Caithness place derives from Old Norse *breidr*, 'broad', and *bolstadr*, 'house, farm'.

Braan, River and **Strath** (Perth & Kinross) The name of this Perthshire strath and its river means 'roaring'. *Freamhainn* (Scottish Gaelic) from an older root *bremava*, 'noisy, rumbling'. Noted in 1200 as Strathbranen. Brahan in Ross-shire may have the same derivation.

Bracklinn (Stirling) 'Speckled cataract'. *Breac* (Scottish Gaelic) 'speckled', *linne* (Scottish Gaelic) 'waterfall'. This waterfall in the hills above Callander is a well-known attraction for visitors.

Braco (Stirling) 'Grey place'. *Braca* (Scottish Gaelic) 'grey, greyish'; *-ach* (Scottish Gaelic) affix denoting place. The name recurs in Glen Shee, Perthshire, and in Wester Bracco, south of Caldercruix in North Lanarkshire.

Braemar (Aberdeenshire) 'The upper part of Mar'. *Bràigh* (Scottish Gaelic) 'upland'; the second element, *Mar*, is a personal name of unknown derivation. Early records include Bray of Marre 1560, Brae of Mar 1610, Breamarr 1682. In the nineteenth century it was known as Castleton of Braemar, having grown up around the castle.

Braemore (Highland) 'Big upland'. *Bràigh* (Scottish Gaelic) 'upland'; *mòr* (Scottish Gaelic) 'big'. A referential name from several localities.

Braeriach (Moray) 'The brindled or grey hill'. *Am* (Scottish Gaelic) 'the'; *bràigh* (Scottish Gaelic) 'upland', borrowed into Scots as 'brae'; *riabhach* (Scottish Gaelic) 'brindled, greyish'. This is the second-highest top of the Cairngorm Mountains (4248ft/1296m), and the River Dee rises on its stony summit plateau.

Braes (Highland and other regions) 'Uplands'. *Bràigh* (Scottish Gaelic) 'upland'. The name is found in numerous places; best known is that on Skye, where in the land disputes of 1880 a battle was fought between crofters and police.

Brahan (Highland) Possibly 'place of the quern' (hand-mill). *Brathainn* (Scottish Gaelic, genitive of *bràth*, 'quern'). This is noted as the local tradition for the name, which was recorded in 1479 as Browen (*see also* Braan). The district is strongly associated with the Mackenzie clan, whose chief resided at Brahan Castle, and Coinneach Odhar ('Brown Kenneth') the semi-legendary Brahan Seer.

Brander, Pass of (Argyll & Bute) This narrow pass now carrying road and railway by the side of Loch Awe and along the shoulder of Ben Cruachan may mean 'the pot', *Ám* (Scottish Gaelic) 'the'; *brannraidh* (Scottish Gaelic) 'pot', though older Gaelic meanings also include 'trap' or 'snare'. Here Robert Bruce avenged an earlier defeat (at Tyndrum) against MacDougall of Lorn, in 1308.

Braid (Midlothian) 'Upper slopes', or 'gullet'. *Bràghad* (Scottish Gaelic) 'upper part, neck'. The reference may be to the deeply-indented Braid Hills on the southern edge of Edinburgh.

Breadalbane (Perth & Kinross; Stirling) *Bredd-alban*. 'Upper part of Alban'. *Braghad* (Scottish Gaelic) 'higher, upper part, hill district'; *Albainn* (Scottish Gaelic) 'of Scotland'. The *Pictish Chronicle*, c. 970, refers to Brunalban, from Brythonic–Pictish *bryn,* mountain. Breadalbane, an area name applied now to a large tract of the central Highlands lying to the west of Atholl, was politically part of Atholl until its medieval earldom was created.

Breakachy (Highland) *Bray-kahy*. 'Speckled field'. *Breac* (Scottish Gaelic) 'speckled', and *achadh* (Scottish Gaelic) 'field'.

Breacleit (Western Isles) *Bray-cleet*. 'Broad cliff or hill'. *Breidhr* (Old Norse) 'broad'; *klettr* (Old Norse) 'rocky holm, cliff'. Breascleit, also in Lewis, is from Old Norse *breid-áss-klettr,* 'broad ridge cliff'.

Breich (West Lothian) '(Steading on the) bank'. *Bruaich* (Scottish Gaelic) genitive form of *bruach* 'bank, brink'.

Brechin (Angus) 'Brychan's place'. This old cathedral town may commemorate the name of a legendary character from Celtic legend, the Brythonic hero Brychan (as in modern Brecon, Wales). Old forms are found in the genitive, as in the *Pictish Chronicle*, c. 970, *civitas brechni*, 'Brychan's community'. But a minor Pictish ruler, Brachan, has been noted in the Angus region: it may be Brachan's community. In Scottish Gaelic, *brychan* may mean 'holy' or 'high' and is related to the Celtic goddess name Brigantia. Brechin has one of Scotland's two tenth-century round towers.

Bressay (Shetland) Probably 'breast-shaped island'. *Brjost* (Old Norse) 'breast'; *ey* (Old Norse) 'island'. This refers to its main conical shaped hill, the Ward of Bressay.

Bridge of Allan *See* Allan

Bridge of Don *See* Don

Bridge of Dun (Angus) 'Bridge of the brown stream'. *Donn* (Scottish Gaelic) 'brown'. The Gaelic name of the river is Abhainn Donn, but the name comes from the former railway station on the now-closed railway line through Strathmore.

Bridge of Earn *See* Earn

Bridge of Orchy *See* Orchy

Bridge of Weir (Renfrewshire) 'Bridge of Vere's stream'. *Vere* is a Norman–French proper name, imported to Lanarkshire, from *ver* (Old Norse) 'stance, station'.

Brig o' Balgownie (Aberdeenshire) 'Bridge of the smith's place'. *Brig* (Scots) 'bridge'; *baile* (Scottish Gaelic) 'place, homestead'; *gobhainn* (Scottish Gaelic) 'of the smith'. The bridge was built in 1329, when Scots was the language of the area.

Brig o' Turk (Stirling) 'Bridge of the pig'. *Brig* is the Scots translation of *droichead* (Scottish Gaelic) 'bridge'; *nan*, 'of'; *tuirc* (Scottish Gaelic) 'hog, boar'. In Gaelic it was more often known as Ceann Drochaid, 'bridge at the head'.

Brittle, Glen (Highland) 'Broad bay'. *Breithr* (Old Norse) 'broad'; *vik* (Old Norse) 'bay'. The 'Glen' is a later addition to designate the valley behind the bay.

Broadford (Highland) 'The broad ford', English translation from Scottish Gaelic *an t-àth*, 'the ford'; *leathan*, 'broad'. *An t-àth Leathann* remains the Gaelic name. This Skye village grew up around the ford and the route junction of the coastal and inland roads.

Brodick (North Ayrshire) 'Broad Bay'. *Breithr* (Old Norse) 'broad'; *vik* (Old Norse) 'bay'. Early records show: Brathwik 1306; Bradewik 1488. In Gaelic it is Breadhaig. This main Arran resort stands on what is now called Brodick Bay.

Brodie (Moray) 'Place by the ditch' or 'muddy place'. *Brothag* (Scottish Gaelic) 'ditch, hollow'. The Clan Brodie takes its name from here.

Brogar (Orkney) Perhaps 'Place by the bridge'; *Bru* (Old Norse) 'bridge'; *gardr* (Old Norse) 'enclosure, garth', but the locality name is Brodgar, which may stem from Old Norse *breith*, 'broad', and seems more apt to the site of the standing stones of the 'Ring of Brogar'.

Broom, River, Loch (Highland) 'Water, falling water'. *Braon* (Scottish Gaelic) 'water, drop'. The upper loch, which still retains its Gaelic name, Loch a' Bhraoin, and the sea-loch (with the nearby Little Loch Broom) take their name from the river linking them, which cascades, two miles above its mouth at Inverbroom, over the Falls of Measach (Scottish Gaelic *miasaich*, 'platters', referring to the pot-holes worn in the rock) and into the Corriehalloch gorge. Loch Braoin in Perthshire has the same derivation as Broom.

Broomielaw (Glasgow) 'Hill of broom'. *Law* (Middle English and Scots) hill. This highly urbanised Glasgow riverbank site, formerly a busy steamer terminal, was once in open country. Another Broomy Law overlooks the Meggat Water in Dumfriesshire.

Brora (Highland) 'Place of the bridge's river'. *Bru'r* (Old Norse) 'bridge'; *aa* (Old Norse) 'river'. Noted in 1499 as Strabroray, 'Strathbrora'. Unusually, a river has been named after a bridge here, presumably because of the general rarity of bridges. The river here is steep-banked. This little town was a pocket of industry, with one of the two coal-mines in the Highlands; and the local clay was also used in a brickworks.

Broughton (Borders) *Broch-ton*. 'Brook place'. *Bróc* (Old English) 'brook'; and *tún* (Old English) 'village, farmstead'. Noted as Broctuna, 1128.

Broughty Ferry (Dundee) *Braw-ty*. 'Tay-bank ferry'. This suburb of Dundee lies on the north bank of the Firth of Tay at its entrance narrows, across which there was a ferry crossing to Fife before the opening of the Tay Road Bridge in 1966. *Bruach-taibh* (Scottish Gaelic) 'bank of the Tay', thus provides the first part of the name, and 'ferry' (English) the second. Records show Bruchty Craig, 1541.

Broxburn (West Lothian) 'Badger's stream'. *Brocc-s* (Old English) 'badger's'; *burna* (Old English) 'stream'.

Bruar (Perth & Kinross) Perhaps 'bridge stream', referring to natural arches formed by the river. *Briva* (Old Gaelic) bridge; *ara-* (Old Gaelic) suffix denoting water or stream. It seems cognate with Brora but the location makes an Old Norse name unlikely. The modern Gaelic form is Bruthar.

Buachaille Etive (Highland) *Boo-hal Etiv*. 'The shepherd of Etive'. *Buachaille* (Scottish Gaelic) 'shepherd'. An unusually imaginative Gaelic hill-name for the two mountains looming over the eastern end of Glencoe, but in fact the older names are the descriptive Stob Dearg ('red peak') and Stob Dubh ('black peak'). There are two 'shepherds', *Mór*, 'big', and *Beag*, 'small', at 3345ft/1022m and 3029ft/926m respectively. *See also* Etive.

Buchan (Aberdeenshire) Possibly 'place of the cow'. *Buwch* (Brythonic, with the suffix *-an*) 'cow place'. An alternative derivation that produces the same meaning is through *baoghan* (Scottish Gaelic) 'calf'. The name was recorded as Buchan around 1150 in the *Book of Deer*; and Baugham 1601. Either way, the description fits the area today, which, after the great agricultural improvements of the eighteenth and nineteenth centuries, is a major beef cattle farming area, home of the Aberdeen-Angus breed.

Buchanan (Stirling) This district name may be related to Buchan, or may be from *both* (Scottish Gaelic) 'house'; *chanain* (Scottish Gaelic) 'priest'. Noted as Buchquhanane around 1240. In the latter case its adoption as a surname may have led to a wider area of reference. It is at the centre of the territory of Clan Buchanan.

Buchanty (Perth & Kinross) 'House of the cow-place'. *See* Buchan, above. The *-ty* suffix is *taigh* (Scottish Gaelic) 'house'.

Buchlyvie (Stirling) 'House or hut on the slope'. *Both* (Scottish Gaelic) 'hut'; *slèibhe* (Scottish Gaelic) 'slope'.

Buckhaven (Fife) A name dating from the mid sixteenth century, and probably of similar derivation to Buckie, 'harbour of bucks or buckies'. It forms a continuous town with Methil to the east.

Buckie (Moray) Probably 'Place of bucks'. *Bocaidh* (Scottish Gaelic) 'whelk'. However, *bucaidh* (Scottish Gaelic) 'pimple, protuberance', has also been suggested. Bucksburn, Aberdeen, would seem to suggest the latter meaning. It is recorded as Buky c. 1350. Since the late nineteenth century it has been an important fishing and boat-building town.

Bunchrew (Highland) 'Low place of trees'. *Bonn* (Scottish Gaelic) 'bottom', and *chraobh* (Scottish Gaelic) 'trees'. Recorded as Bunchrive in the sixteenth century.

Bunessan (Argyll & Bute) 'Foot of the waterfall'. *Bonn* (Scottish Gaelic) 'bottom'; *easan* (Scottish Gaelic) 'little waterfall'. There is plenty of tumbling water around this Mull village.

Bunnahabhainn (Argyll & Bute) *Bunna-awan*. 'Stream-foot'. The name of this Islay distilling village is from *bonn* (Scottish Gaelic) 'bottom'; *na, 'of'; *abhainn* (Scottish Gaelic) 'stream, river'.

Burghead (Moray) 'Headland of the fort'. *Borgar* (Old Norse) 'fort'. There were Pictish fortifications here. 'Head' may be an English translation of a lost *nes* (Old Norse) 'headland'.

Burntisland (Fife) An implausible local legend ascribes the name of this Fife harbour town, specialising in bauxite import, and once a shipbuilding centre, to fisher-huts burnt down on an island close to the present harbour. Another proposed derivation is 'Burnet's land'. *Burnet* (Old English personal name); *land* (Old English) 'estate'. Brythonic–Pictish *bryn*, 'mountain', has also been suggested for the first part; the second remains obscure, though perhaps linked with *telyn,* modern Welsh 'harp'. In 1538 it was noted as Bruntisland.

Burra (Shetland) 'Fortified isle'. *Borgar* (Old Norse) 'fort'; *ey* (Old Norse) 'island'. Burray (Orkney) has the same derivation.

Busby (East Renfrewshire) 'Bushy place'. *Busk* (Old Norse) 'bush' and *by* (Old Norse) 'farm' or 'place'. Noted c. 1300 as Busbie. This town south of Glasgow may be the place where the headpiece known as the 'busby' was first made. There is also a Busbie Muir in West Renfrewshire.

Busta (Shetland) 'Farmstead'. *Bolstadr* (Old Norse) 'farmstead', usually found as a suffix, but here on its own. Busta Voe is 'inlet of the farmstead'. Bosta in Lewis has the same origin.

Bute (Argyll & Bute) Possibly 'patch of land'. *Bót* (Old Norse) 'patch' or 'piece of land'. A derivation from *bot* (Old Irish Gaelic) 'fire', has also been suggested. Early records show Bot 1093, Bote 1204, Boot 1292. The modern Gaelic name is *Bód*.

Butt of Lewis (Western Isles) This is the only cape so designated, and its origins are unclear. Old French *buter*, 'to butt out', has been suggested, as has Danish *but*, 'stumpy', as a root, but neither seems very plausible. There may be some connection with the several Buddons/Buttons of eastern promontories. Its Gaelic name is Rudha Robhanais, *rudha*, 'point'; *raud* (Old Norse) 'red'; *nes* (Old Norse) 'point'. The anglicised form Redpoint is also found on the western tip of Torridon.

Butterstone (Perth & Kinross) This seems to be be a Gaelic–Scots hybrid, from *bothar* (Scottish Gaelic) 'road, causeway', and *-ton*, Scots suffix indicating a farmstead or settlement, from Old English *tun*, of the same meaning. Butterstone Loch takes its name from the locality. Not far away is Buttergask (*see* Gask). Butterlaw, a Berwickshire farm name, may have the English sense of 'butter', with Scots *law*, 'hill'.

C

Cabrach (Moray) In Scottish Gaelic, *cabrach* means 'stag', also 'thicket', and in adjectival form, 'antlered'. This remote community on the upper Deveron still has many deer in the vicinity. Nearby is The Buck, or Buck of the Cabrach (2358ft/721m), from Gaelic *boc*, 'roebuck', which suggests the settlement name has the 'thicket' meaning.

Cadboll (Highland) Perhaps 'place of wild cats', though the cats may be tutelary tribal symbols rather than real. Noted as Kattepoll, 1281; Cathabul, 1529. *Cat* (Scottish Gaelic) 'cat'; *ból* (Old Norse abbreviated form of *bolstadr*) 'farm'. It has been suggested that names in which *bolstadr* is reduced to its first syllable, in places on the north and western mainland, in the Inner Hebrides and in many cases in the Outer Hebrides, represent a Gaelic influence, where the stress is placed on a word's first syllable rather than the second, as in Old Norse. The Pictish carved Cadboll Stone is one of the treasures of the Museum of Scotland in Edinburgh.

Cadder (East Dunbartonshire) 'Stone fort'. *Cathair* (Scottish Gaelic) 'round fort of stone'. A common prefix in Irish place names, but less often found in Scotland (*see* Catterline). Recorded as Chaders, 1170. There is a (square) Roman fort at Cadder, now bounded by the Forth and Clyde Canal, but an earlier work may also have been built there, above the haughs of Kelvin.

Caddon Water (Borders) 'Hard hill' or 'fort' has been suggested, from Cumbric *caled,* 'hard' also found in Calder and other places, and *din*, 'hill, fort'. It was noted as Keledenelee, c. 1175 (the *lee* suffix is Old English 'meadow'). 'Water' is a common Scots word for stream, usually in translation of Gaelic *uisge* or Old English *ea*. Perhaps because Caddonlee, 'meadow by the Caddon' was the mustering-place of the Scottish army, it has also been identified with *cath* (Scottish Gaelic) 'battle'.

Cadzow (South Lanarkshire) *Cad-yow.* This older name for Hamilton may commemorate a battle, from *cath* (Scottish Gaelic) 'battle'. The latter part may be cognate with *howe* (Scots) 'hollow'. The name is recorded in 1360 as Cadyow. As in numerous other Scottish place names, the *z* is a relic of the attempt to convey the sound 'gh' in writing, and does not intend the present alphabetical 'z'.

Caerlaverock (Dumfries & Galloway) 'Fort in the elm trees'. *Cathair* (Scottish Gaelic) 'fort'; *leamh-reaich* (Scottish Gaelic) 'elm tree'.

The ruins of an impressive fourteenth-century castle, surrounded by trees, are still to be found here today. The name, its Scots form influenced by the phonic resemblance to *laverock,* 'skylark', occurs as a local one in some other districts.

Cairnbawn, Loch (Highland) 'Loch of the bright hills'. *Càrn* (Scottish Gaelic) 'humped hill'; *bán* (Scottish Gaelic) 'fair', 'bright'. The name is found as a local one in some other areas, usually spelt Cairnbaan or Cairnban.

Cairndow (Argyll & Bute) 'Dark mount'. *Càrn* (Scottish Gaelic) 'humped hill'; *dubh* (Scottish Gaelic) 'dark'.

Cairn Gorm (Moray; Highland) 'Blue humped hill'. *Càrn* (Scottish Gaelic) 'humped hill'; *gorm* (Scottish Gaelic) 'blue'. But *gorm* also means 'green'; as in many old languages, the colour words in Gaelic are notably few and imprecise. This single mountain's name, run into one as the Cairngorms, has been adopted for the whole range, and though 'blue' seems right for this granite massif that appears from afar as blue, rounded high hills, its Gaelic name is Monadh Ruadh, 'red mountains', probably because of the reddish granite of which they are formed. Cairn Gorm rises to 4084ft/1245m.

Cairnie (Moray) 'Place of thickets'. *Carden* (Brythonic–Pictish) 'thicket'; *ach* (Scottish Gaelic) locative suffix. Also Cairney. It is frequently found in other areas as a farm or field-name.

Cairnpapple (West Lothian) 'Pebble hill', a hybrid name with Scottish Gaelic *càrn,* 'humped hill' and Old English *popel,* 'pebble'. An alternative is 'hill of the priest's place', from *càrn* (Scottish Gaelic) 'humped hill', and *pabail* (Scottish Gaelic combination of *pap,* 'priest, pope', with locative ending *-ail*) 'priest's place'. Noted as Kernepopple, 1619. There is a prehistoric hill-fort on this hill, which just tops 1000ft/306m.

Cairnryan (Dumfries & Galloway) 'Fort by (Loch) Ryan'. *Caer* (Brythonic-Welsh) 'fort', and *see* Ryan.

Cairn Toul (Moray) The Gaelic name of this Cairngorm mountain, which rises to 4241ft/1293m is Càrn an t-Sabhail, from Scottish Gaelic *càrn,* 'humped hill', and *sabhal,* 'barn'; perhaps its rounded shape resembled a thatched barn (Màm Sodhail, 3862ft/1181m, at the head of Glen Affric, was originally Màm Sabhail). It has also been suggested that it may signify 'ominous' or 'thwarting' hill, from *tuathal* (Scottish Gaelic) 'athwart-placed', 'ominous'. Carrantuohil, Ireland's highest mountain, whose second part is also *tuathal,* is prefixed by *Carran* (Irish Gaelic) 'reaping-hook', and does not appear to be cognate.

Caithness (Highland) The first part is noted in the *Pictish Chronicle,* c. 970, as having been a Pictish province-name, *Cat* or *Cait;*

supposedly from a son of Cruithne, 'founder' of the Picts; perhaps the cat was a tribal emblem. It has been suggested that the Cat-people came south from Shetland, perhaps absorbing or supplanting the second century inhabitants noted by Ptolemy as the Cornavii. The suffix, added in the ninth-tenth century by Norse colonists, is *nes* (Old Norse) 'ness, headland'; amply suggested to the seaborne visitors by the coastal outline. The *Book of Deer* notes Catness, c. 1150, suggesting that the Gaelic name had not yet become Gallaibh, 'land of the strangers'.

Calder (Highland; West Lothian; Argyll & Bute) Possibly 'hard or rapid water'. *Caled* (Brythonic) 'hard'; *dobhar* (Brythonic) 'water'. Alternatively, the first part may be derived from *callaidh* (Scottish Gaelic) 'rapid, nimble'. Old Gaelic *call*, 'hazel' has also been suggested for the first part. The most frequent Gaelic form of the name is Caladar, found in Callater and Achallader, among many other examples. Noted in Lothian as Kaldor, c. 1250, Caldovere, 1293. This is a frequent local place name, often separated, as in West Lothian, into East, Mid and West Calder. However Calder in Caithness has been linked to Old Norse *kálfr*, 'calf'; *dalr*, 'dale', found as Kalfadal in the *Orkneyinga Saga*, c. 1225.

Caldercruix (North Lanarkshire) 'Bends of Calder'. *Cruix* (Scots) from Old Norse *krókr*, 'crooks, bends'. *See* Calder.

Caledonia 'Scotland'. Used by the Romans from a tribal name, it may not have a Celtic linguistic origin though it has been linked to the Brythonic–Pictish *caled*, 'hard', found in such place-names as Calder. The tribe of Caledones is first mentioned on Ptolemy's map (AD 150), and in its Latin form given by the Romans to the territory north of the Antonine wall. In more recent times it is used as a poetic or antiquarian synonym for Scotland, as in Sir Walter Scott's 'Caledonia, stern and wild' from 'The Lay of the Last Minstrel'. *See* Dunkeld.

Calgary (Argyll & Bute) 'Cali's garth'. *Kali* (Old Norse personal name); *gerdhi* (Old Norse diminutive of *gardr*) 'garth' meaning the land between the machair and the moorland, taken into Gaelic as *gearraid*.

Callander (Stirling) Probably as for Calder, the meaning of this town's name is 'hard or rapid water'; in this case from the River Teith, which is quite turbulent here. The name was recorded as Calentare 1164; Callanter 1350. The town developed in the nineteenth century as a tourist resort on the now-closed Callander and Oban Railway.

Callanish (Western Isles) 'Kali's ness'. *Kali* (Old Norse personal name); *nes* (Old Norse) 'cape, point'. At this Lewis location on

East Loch Roag (Old Norse *ró-vagr*, 'roe-deer bay') is an extensive complex of standing stones and chambered cairns, first excavated in 1857, and dating back to around 1800 BC. The name is also found as Callernish.

Callater, River, Glen (Angus) *See* Calder

Cally, Bridge of (Perth & Kinross) 'Ferry'; a translation of Scottish Gaelic *drochaid* 'bridge' and *challaigh*, 'of the ferry'. The crossing was over the River Ardle.

Calton (Edinburgh; Glasgow and other areas) 'Hazel (place)'. *Calltuinn* (Scottish Gaelic) 'hazel'. The numerous local Caldon place-names in the south-west have the same source. Some more recent post-Gaelic Caltons might be 'cold place', from Scots *cauld*, 'cold', and *toun*, 'farmstead'. Farm names are sometimes apotropaic, in order to ward off ill luck. Calton in Strathclyde was the location of a famous strike of weavers in the late eighteenth century; the 'Calton Weaver', famous in folk-song, was someone to be reckoned with.

Calvine (Perth & Kinross) Perhaps 'smooth wood', from *coille* (Scottish Gaelic) 'wood', and *mhìn* (Scottish Gaelic) 'smooth'.

Camas This prefix, also found as Camus, is Scottish Gaelic *camus*, 'bay, creek, harbour'. Mostly found on coastal locations, it is also found on a number of riverside sites, and normally refers to a place where ships or boats could be drawn up out of the water.

Cambus (Stirling) 'Place of the bay'. *Camus* (Scottish Gaelic) 'bay'. Most *camus* names have some further identifier, but not here.

Cambuskenneth (Stirling) 'Cinaed's Bay'. *Camus* (Scottish Gaelic) 'bay'; the second part may be an anglicisation of the Pictish personal name *Cinaed*, or perhaps a translation of Scottish Gaelic *Choinnich*, Kenneth. Found in this form 1147; Cambuschynoch 1527. This site by the Forth estuary had an important abbey in medieval times; Robert I held a parliament here.

Cambuslang (South Lanarkshire) 'Bay of the ship'. *Camus* (Scottish Gaelic) 'bay'; *luinge* (Scottish Gaelic) 'ship's'. Found as Cameslank, 1296. The name indicates that small oared vessels could come up the Clyde at least as far as here.

Cambus o' May (Aberdeenshire) 'Bay on the May Water'. *Camus* (Scottish Gaelic) 'bay'. May has been inferred to come from Old Irish *Miathi*, a form of Maeatae, one of the tribes identified by the Romans; but more probable is *magh* (Scottish Gaelic) 'plain'.

Camelon (Falkirk) The resemblance of the name to Arthurian Camelot or Camlann has been ascribed to a mistake in Hector Boece's *Scotorum Historiae* of 1526, where he confuses this Roman wall site with Camulodunum, an error maintained by his translator Bellenden, who rendered it as Camelon. Other Camelons or Camlings are 'crooked pool'. *Cam* (Scottish Gaelic) 'bent, crooked'; *linne* (Scottish Gaelic) 'pool'.

Cameron (Fife; Edinburgh) Suggested as 'crooked hill', from Scottish Gaelic *cam*, 'crooked', and Old Gaelic *brun*, hill, cognate with Brythonic *bryn*. Found in 1190 as Cambrun. The real origin may be Pictish, cognate with Gaulish Cambronne.

Campbeltown (Argyll & Bute) The chief town of Kintyre was named after Archibald Campbell, earl of Argyll, in 1667. Formerly it had been called Lochhead, and even earlier was known as Kilkerran. In the nineteenth century it had more distilleries than any other town in the country.

Camperdown (Dundee) This area and park in Dundee commemorates the Battle of Camperdown, 1797, off the Dutch coast, won by Admiral Lord Duncan, who was born in Dundee.

Campsie Fells (East Dunbartonshire) 'Crooked hills'. *Cam* (Scottish Gaelic) 'crooked'; *sìth* (Scottish Gaelic) 'hill'. As *sìth* also means 'fairy', the name has sometimes been taken as 'fairy hills', but it cannot be both. 'Fells', from *fjall* (Old Norse) 'hill', is a later addition; it is an unusual but not unknown hill-word in Scots. Recorded as Kamsi 1208; Camsy 1300; Campsy 1522. The *p* would appear to have crept in through a fancied connection with 'camp'.

Camster (Highland) 'Kam's steading'. *Kami* (Old Norse personal name); *bolstadr* (Old Norse) 'small farm'. Camster is famous for its 'Grey Cairns' – prehistoric chamber tombs.

Canaird, Loch and **Strath** (Highland) *Kan-yard*. At first sight it looks of similar derivation to Kinnaird, and the spelling Kanaird is also found, but it has been traced back to Old Norse *kanna*, 'can'; *fjordr*, 'firth', with the 'can' referring to the shape of the broch 'Dun Canna' at the seaward end of the loch.

Canisbay (Highland) 'Canons' farm'. Shown around 1240 as Cananesbi, with *canane* (early Scots) 'canon', and *by* (Old Norse) 'farmstead, village'.

Canna (Highland) 'Bucket island'. *Kanna* (Old Norse) 'can, bucket'; presumably from the island's shape. This is the northernmost of the 'Small Isles' lying to the south of Skye. *See* Canaird.

Canonbie (Dumfries and Galloway) 'Canons' village'. *Canon* (Middle English) refers to the Augustinian priory that was here, 1165–1542; *-by* (Old Norse, probably Danish) 'farmstead, village'. Noted as Canneby, 1290.

Canongate (Edinburgh) 'Street of the canons'. *Gata* (Old English) 'street'. This continuation of Edinburgh's High Street leads down to Holyrood Abbey. For centuries it was a separate burgh.

Cannich, River, Glen (Highland) Perhaps 'place where cotton sedge grows'. *Canach* (Scottish Gaelic) 'cotton sedge'. The Gaelic name is Canaich.

Caputh (Perth & Kinross) 'Hill, top'. *Ceap* (Scottish Gaelic) 'hilltop'; *-ag* (Scottish Gaelic) diminutive ending. The word is related to Latin *caput*, 'head', which it closely resembles.

Carberry (West Lothian) 'Palisade of branches'. *Craobh* (Scottish Gaelic) 'branch, tree', and *barrán* (Scottish Gaelic) 'hedge', suggestive of early defences. Carberry Hill was where Mary, Queen of Scots was taken prisoner after the flight of the earl of Bothwell, in 1567.

Carbost (Western Isles; Highland) 'Kari's steading'. *Kari* (Old Norse proper name); *bolstadr* (Old Norse) 'homestead'.

Cardenden (Fife) 'Den or hollow of the thicket'. *Cardain* (Scottish Gaelic from Brythonic–Pictish *cardden*) 'thicket'; *den* (Scots, from Old English *denu*) 'small steep valley'. *See* Kincardine.

Cardno (Aberdeenshire) 'Place of thickets'. *Cardain* (Scottish Gaelic from Brythonic–Pictish *cardden*) 'thicket'; *-o* is a form of *ach* (Scottish Gaelic) 'place'. An older form is Cardenauch.

Cardrona (Borders) Possibly 'fort of winds or breezes'. *Cathair* (Scottish Gaelic) 'fort'; *drothanach* (Scottish Gaelic) 'breezy'. Noted as Cardronow in 1530.

Cardross (Argyll & Bute) 'Wooded promontory'. *Cardden* (Cumbric) 'wooded'; *ros* (Cumbric) 'promontory'. Recorded in 1208 as Cardinros. Here on Clydeside King Robert I had a country house built, where he died in 1328. It is the birthplace of the novelist Tobias Smollett (1721–71).

Carlops (Borders) 'The hag's leap'. *Carline* (Scots) 'old woman'; *loups* (Scots) 'leaps'. In Wyntoun's *Chronicle* (c. 1400) it is referred to as Karlinlippis. A curious name, which was first given to the stream, the village being founded in 1784.

Carloway (Western Isles) 'Karl's Bay'. *Karla* (Old Norse personal name); *vágr* (Old Norse) 'bay', gaelicised into Càrlabagh. There is a well-preserved Pictish broch on this west Lewis site, Dun Carloway.

Carluke (South Lanarkshire) Possibly 'Fort on the marsh'. *Caer* (Cumbric) 'fort'; *lwch* (Cumbric) 'marshland'. Less likely, the first element may be derived from *carn* (Scottish Gaelic) 'cairn, humped hill'; and the latter part could be an obscure personal name. First recorded in 1320 as Carneluke.

Carmyllie (Angus) 'Warrior's fort'. *Caer* (Brythonic–Pictish) 'fort'; *milidh* (Scottish Gaelic) 'warrior'.

Càrn This Gaelic word, scotticised into 'cairn', means 'piled stones', either in an artificial heap or a rocky hill. It is a frequent prefix to mountain names.

Càrn Mòr Dearg (Highland) *Carn more jerrig.* 'Great red cairn'. *Càrn* (Scottish Gaelic) 'cairn, heaped stones'; *mòr* (Scottish Gaelic) 'great'; *dearg* (Scottish Gaelic) 'red'. This mountain (4012ft/1223m), just east of Ben Nevis, is tallest of a north–south group that includes Càrn Dearg Meadhonach ('middle') and Càrn Beag ('little') Dearg (3313ft/1010m).

Càrn Smeart (Highland) A Ross-shire hill name from the area between Strathcarron and Strathoykel, of interest as it appears to preserve the name of the Smertae tribe, recorded in this area by Ptolemy, c. AD 150; *càrn* (Scottish Gaelic) 'cairn'.

Carno (Argyll & Bute) This place, tentatively identified with the area around Tyndrum, is the site of a battle in 729 where Oengus, son of Fergus, defeated Nechtan, a rival for the Pictish kingship. In the *Annals of Ulster* it is noted as Monith Carno, the first part from Scottish Gaelic *monadh*, 'mountain', the second probably from Scottish Gaelic *càrn*, 'cairn'. There are several Càrn names in the area, though none that seems to stem from Carno. There is a Carno in Powys, Wales, suggesting a possible Brythonic origin.

Carnoch (Highland) 'Rock place'. *Càrnach* (Scottish Gaelic) 'rocky place'. The name is also found as Carnock in Fife.

Carnoustie (Angus) Possibly 'rock of the fir tree'. *Carraig* (Scottish Gaelic) *na*; (Scottish Gaelic) 'of the'; *ghiuthais* (Scottish Gaelic) 'fir tree'. A document of the late fifteenth century records this place as Carnusy. The *t* of the name was interpolated at a later date. The links here have become a championship golf course. Burnside of Carnousie, east of Aberchirder in Banffshire, preserves the original form. *See also* Kingussie for a similar derivation.

Carnwath (South Lanarkshire) Apparently 'Kaerandi's ford'. *Kaerandi* (Old Scandinavian personal name); *vath* (Old Scandinavian) 'ford'. Recorded around 1165 as Charnewid.

Carpow (Perth & Kinross) 'Fort of the pool'. *Caer* (Brythonic–Pictish) 'fort'; *pwll* (Brythonic–Pictish) 'pool'. Around AD 210, a Roman legionary fortress was set up here, linch-pin of the emperor Septimius Severus's campaign to subdue the northern tribes, and the first bridge over the Tay (a floating 'bridge of boats') was built here.

Carrbridge (Highland) 'Bridge at the rocky shelf'. *Drochaid* (Scottish Gaelic) translated to English 'bridge'; *charra* (Scottish Gaelic) 'rock shelf'. There are now several bridges, of differing periods, over the Dulnain River at this point. The Water of Charr, in the Grampians, suggests the same derivation.

Carrick (South Ayrshire) 'Rocky place'. *Carraig* (Scottish Gaelic) 'rock, crag'. This is one of the three districts of the former Ayrshire, and formerly an earldom; since Robert Bruce's time an appanage of the heir of the crown.

Carron (Falkirk; Highland; Moray; Dumfries & Galloway) 'Rough river'. The names of the rivers and straths in Ross-shire and the stream near Falkirk, as well as other Carrons, derive from the early-Celtic root *kar* 'harsh, rough', that also gives the place name Carrick, and Gaelic *càrn,* 'heap of stones'. The *-on* suffix is found in other ancient river-names, from a root-form *-ona,* indicating 'water'. The Falkirk Carron is found as Caere in 710, Carun in the ninth century. Carron on the Spey, above Aberlour, may refer to a particularly rough section of this fast river. The name was used for the Carron Ironworks, near Falkirk; Scotland's first large-scale industrial enterprise, set up in 1759; and from it came the carronade, a highly successful naval gun.

Carse This Scots word, derived from Old Norse *kerss,* means 'low-lying land by a river'. It is often found in local and farm names, sometimes in the suffix form *-kerse, -kersie.*

Carse of Gowrie *See* Gowrie

Carsphairn (Dumfries & Galloway) 'Carseland of the alder-trees'. *Carse* (Scots from Old Norse *kerss*) 'low-lying land by a river; *feàrna* (Scottish Gaelic) 'alders'. Above the village rises Cairnsmore (from Gaelic *càrn,* 'hill', and *mòr,* 'big') of Carsphairn (2614ft/799m).

Carstairs (South Lanarkshire) 'Castle Tarras'. *Caisteil* (Scottish Gaelic) 'castle'; *Tarras* is of obscure origin, probably a personal name. Recorded as Casteltarres in 1170. A railway junction where the London–Glasgow West Coast main line diverges to Edinburgh, and the site of Scotland's only high-security hospital.

Cart, River (Renfrewshire) Perhaps 'cleanser'. The resemblance of the name to Scottish Gaelic *càraid,* 'pair', has been noted, since this river is formed by the joining of the White and Black Cart streams. But many other rivers combine in a similar manner. A suggested link with an older root-form, Old Irish Gaelic *cartaim,* 'I cleanse'; or with the same pre-Celtic root-form, *kar,* 'hard, stony', as Carron, seems more probable.

Carter Bar (Borders) 'Short-horn head'. This location right on the Border, where the Corbridge–Jedburgh road crosses the Cheviots, derives from Old Norse *kort-r,* 'short-horn', and Scottish Gaelic *barr,* 'crest'. It has nothing to do with carters. Carter Fell, nearby, has a similar derivation, with Old Norse *fjall,* 'hill, fell'.

Cassillis (North Ayrshire) 'Castles', from Irish Gaelic *caiseal,* 'stone fort'. Found as Casselys, 1385. A number of similar names are also linked to the presence of brochs or forts, including Cashel Point on Loch Lomond, Cashlie in Glen Lyon, and Glen Cassley in Ross-shire.

Castlebay (Western Isles) The name of the main stettlement on Barra, referring to the MacNeil castle of Kisimul, which stands on a rock in the bay around which this town lies. The Gaelic form is Bagh a Chaisteil, though the usual name was Baile MhicNéill, 'MacNeil's place'.

Castle Douglas (Dumfries & Galloway) 'Castle of the Douglas family'. This town was acquired and developed by Sir William Douglas in 1789, having made his fortune trading with Virginia. Previously the settlement here was first known as Causewayend, then Carlingwark.

Castlecary (North Lanarkshire) 'Fort of the fortifications'. 'Castle' is late twelfth century, added when the sense of *caerydd* (Cumbric) 'forts', was lost: Castlecarris, c. 1200. There is a Roman wall fort here.

Castlemilk (Glasgow) 'Castle on the milky-white stream'. *Chaisteil* (Scottish Gaelic) 'castle'; *melg* (Old Irish Gaelic) 'milk'. This is one of the vast outer Glasgow housing development zones, often referred to simply as 'The Milk'. There is a much smaller Castlemilk just to the south of Lockerbie, in Dumfries & Galloway.

Catterline (Aberdeenshire) 'Fort by the pool'. *Cathair* (Scottish Gaelic) 'fort', from Brythonic–Pictish *cader*; *linne* (Scottish Gaelic) 'pool'. Noted in 1201 as Katerlen.

Cathcart (Glasgow) 'Wood' or perhaps 'fort' of Cart. *Coet* (Cumbric) 'wood', or *caer* (Cumbric) 'fort', with *Cert* (Cumbric river-name), see Cart. Old forms include Kerkert, 1158, and Katkert, c. 1170.

Cathkin (South Lanarkshire) 'Place of common pasture'. *Coitchionn* (Scottish Gaelic) 'common pasture'.

Catrine (East Ayrshire) 'Battle point'. *Cath* (Scottish Gaelic) 'battle'; *roinne* (Scottish Gaelic) 'point'.

Cauldcleuch (Borders) 'Cold hollow'. *Cauld* (Scots) 'cold'; *cleuch* (Scots) 'hollow, cleft'.

Cawdor (Highland) Possibly 'hard or rapid water'. The derivation of this name is probably the same as for Calder, with a form Kaledor noted in 1280. Its Gaelic form is Caladair. In this case an adapted river-name has been transferred to the village and the fourteenth-century castle, made famous for its associations with Shakespeare's *Macbeth*.

Central This unimaginative name was selected by civil servants in 1975 to define the administrative region that took in all or part of the former counties of Stirlingshire, Clackmannanshire and Dunbartonshire, until 1994.

Ceres (Fife) 'Western place'. *Siar* (Scottish Gaelic) 'western'; *-ais* (Scottish Gaelic affix) 'place'. Found as Syreis in 1199. The resemblance to the name of the Greek goddess of crops seems coincidental.

Cessford (Borders) 'Cessa's enclosure'. *Cessa* (Old English personal name); *worth* (Old English) 'enclosed fields', altered into 'ford'. Anglo-Saxon *-worth* names, so common in England, are rare in Anglian Scotland; by the time Anglians were moving in, it was obsolete, and *-tun* or *-ham* were the normal forms. *See also* Jedburgh, Polwarth.

Challoch (Dumfries & Galloway) 'Forge'. *Teallach* (Scottish Gaelic) 'anvil, forge'. Challoch Junction near Stranraer was where the railway from Glasgow to that port joined the line (now closed) from Carlisle; there is another Challoch some distance east, by Newton Stewart.

Chanonry Point (Highland) 'Point of the canons'. The adjacent village of Rosemarkie was the site of an important abbey in Pictish times.

Chatelherault (South Lanarkshire) This entirely French name is owed to the history of the Hamilton family. The Hamilton earl of Arran was made duke of Chatelherault in the early sixteenth century as a reward for giving up the regency of Scotland. The estate, outside Hamilton, is now a country park.

Chesters (Borders) 'Camps', from Latin *castrum*, 'military camp', giving Old English *ceaster*. There are a number of other Roman-related names in this region: Bonchester Bridge appears to combine *bonn* (Scottish Gaelic) 'foot', with Old English *ceaster*. The region between Hadrian's and Antonine's Walls was a Roman military district in the first and second centuries AD.

Cheviot (Borders) The source of this name is unclear; it may be linked to a pre-Celtic tribal name. Cumbric *cefn*, 'ridge' has also been suggested. It is noted as Chiuiet, 1181. Properly the name of the highest point in the range (on the English side), always known as 'The Cheviot', it has been extended to the range of hills along which the Scotland–England border runs for part of its way.

Chon, Loch (Stirling) 'Loch of the dog or wolf'. *Con* (Scottish Gaelic) 'dog, wolf'.

Clach- This frequently-found prefix is from Scottish Gaelic *clach*, 'stone'. The genitive form is *cloiche*, the dative *cloich*, hence the *-cloch* form found at the end of some place-names, indicating 'of or by a stone'.

Clachan (Highland; Argyll & Bute) 'Place of stones'. *Clachan* (Scottish Gaelic) 'stones'. A clachan is a stone-built village.

Clachnacudden (Highland) 'Stone of the tubs', from *clach* (Scottish Gaelic) 'stone'; *nan,* 'of'; *cudainn* (Scottish Gaelic) 'tubs'; said to have been a stone on which the women of Inverness rested their wash-tubs on the way to the river, which became a sort of totem for the town.

Clachtoll (Highland) 'Hollow of stones'. *Clach* (Scottish Gaelic) 'stone', and *toll* (Scottish Gaelic) 'hollow, hole'. The West Sutherland area in question is hummocky, hollowed and rocky.

Clackmannan (Clackmannanshire) 'Stone of Manau or Manan'. *Clach* (Scottish Gaelic) 'stone'; *Manau* or *Manan* is an ancient personal or divinity name given to this area at the head of the Firth of Forth. The present form of the name is found in 1221. The symbolic stone is a glacial erratic rock, set on a rock pillar by the tolbooth of the town of Clackmannan.

Clackmannanshire Once Scotland's smallest county, abolished in 1975, reinstated as a unitary authority in 1994. *See* Clackmannan.

Clash, Loch (Highland) 'Loch of the trench', from *clais* (Scottish Gaelic) 'trench, deep furrow'. Clash- in names generally has this meaning; *see also* Cleish.

Clashmore (Highland) 'Deep furrow'. *Clais* (Scottish Gaelic) 'trench, furrow'; *mòr* (Scottish Gaelic) 'big'.

Clatt *See* Clett

Cleghorn (South Lanarkshire) 'Clay house'. *Claeg* (Old English) 'clay'; *erne* (Old English) 'house'. Noted in 1230 as Clegerne.

Cleish (Perth & Kinross) 'Furrow, trench'. *Clais* (Scottish Gaelic) 'trench, furrow'. The form Kles is recorded in 1221. The township is in the valley of the Gairney (possibly from Gaelic *gearain,* 'to sigh'). Water and presumably gave its name to the Cleish Hills rising behind. There is also a Cleish in West Lothian.

Clett 'Cliffs', from Old Norse *klettr*. There are many Clett names in Shetland and Orkney. Clatt in Aberdeenshire is also derived from *clett;* the Correen Hills rise steeply to the south. *See also* Breacleit.

Cleuch, Ben (Clackmannanshire) 'Gully mountain'. *Beinn* (Scottish Gaelic) 'mountain'; *cleuch* (Scots) 'gully'. At 2364ft/723m, this is the highest point of the Ochil Hills.

Clickhimin (Shetland; other districts) 'Rock mouth', from Old Norse *klakk,* 'rock', and *minni,* 'mouth'. The Cleekhimin Burn flows into the Leader Water in the Borders.

Clinterty *See* Clynder

Clisham (Western Isles) 'Craggy hill', from Old Norse *klif-s-hamra*: *klyf,* 'crag'; *holmr,* 'hill'. At 2622ft (800m) this Harris hill is the highest point in the Outer Hebrides.

Cloch (Inverclyde) 'By the stone', from Scottish Gaelic *cloiche,* 'by the stone'. Cloch Point opposite Dunoon, known to seamen as 'The Cloch', with its lighthouse, is an important navigational mark for vessels heading towards the Clyde docks; noted in 1600 as Clochstane.

Cloich Hills (Borders) 'Stone hills', from *clach* (Scottish Gaelic) 'stone'.

Cluanie (Highland) 'Meadow'. *Cluain* (Scottish Gaelic) 'meadow', with -*ach* locative ending. Cluny in Badenoch and Clunie in Tayside have the same derivation. Clunes in Lochaber is *cluain* with the locative suffix -*ais*; its name was given by a proprietor to the Clunes near Inverness, previously Fingask (Scottish Gaelic *fionn*, 'bright'; *gasg*, 'tail or point of land').

Clyde, River, Strath, Firth (South Lanarkshire; Renfrewshire; Inverclyde) Probably 'Cleansing one'. A Cumbric river-name, traced back to a hypothetical *Clouta*; derived from the Indo-European root element *clut,* with the sense of 'washing'; and so linked in significance with other river-names, such as Nith, Nethy, which also convey a sense of purification. The Latin form was recorded in the first century AD by Tacitus as Clota. Adamnan's *Life of St Columba* refers to it as Cloithe. Bede (731) refers to Alcluith, 'rock on the Clyde'. The literary form Clutha is a poetic term for the Clyde. Industry on the Clyde began upstream of Glasgow, using its falls for water-power, then shifted downstream with the dredging of the estuary and the growth of the shipbuilding industry. *See* Strathclyde.

Clydebank (West Dunbartonshire) A modern name, given to this industrial town, lying on the north bank of the Clyde immediately to the west of Glasgow, when it was developed in the nineteenth century. It became a major shipbuilding centre, reaching its greatest fame in the 1930s with the building of the liners *Queen Mary* and *Queen Elizabeth.*

Clynder (Argyll & Bute) 'Red slope'. *Claon* (Scottish Gaelic) 'slope'; *dearg* (Scottish Gaelic) 'red'. Clinterty in Perthshire, and also near Dyce in Aberdeenshire may have the same derivation, with *taigh* (Scottish Gaelic) 'house', added.

Clyne (Highland) 'Slope'. *Claon* (Scottish Gaelic) 'slope'; the locative form is *claoin*. Clynelish, a distillery name in the same east Sutherland locality, adds Scottish Gaelic *lios*, 'garden'.

Cnoc 'Hill, knoll'. This Gaelic term is found very widely in the Northern Highlands, and Kintyre and its adjacent islands; and sporadically elsewhere. In the south-west and north-east it has been largely supplanted by the Scots form Knock.

Coaltown (Fife) This name is prefixed to a number of localities in the former Fife coalmining area, to indicate a colliery or colliers' houses, as in Coaltown of Wemyss.

Coatbridge (North Lanarkshire) 'Bridge by the cottages'. The bridge was built here only about 1800 as part of the development of the area as a coal-mining centre around the earlier small settlement of Cotts (Old English *cot*, meaning 'shelter, cottage'). It is found as Coitts in 1582.

Coatdyke (North Lanarkshire) 'Cottage by the dyke'. *Cot* (Old English) 'hut, cottage'; *dyke* (Scots) 'wall'.

Cockburnspath (Borders) *Coburnspath*. 'Colbrand's path', from Old English *Colbrand* (personal name), and path. Earlier forms include Colbrandespade (c. 1128); by 1508 Cokburnspath is found but the 'ck' has never been pronounced.

Cockenzie (East Lothian) The meaning of this name is obscure, but a personal name could be involved. Some authorities suggest 'Kenneth's nook'. *Cuil* (Scottish Gaelic) 'nook'. Recorded as Cowkany in 1590, and still pronounced today as 'Cockennie', it is dominated by a vast power station.

Cockleroy (West Lothian) The 'cockle' part of this hill name is obscure; perhaps Old English *coc*, 'hill' or *cocc*, 'hillock'. The latter part is *ruadh* (Scottish Gaelic) 'red'.

Coigach (Highland) 'The place of fifths'; *na Cóigich* (Scottish Gaelic) 'of the fifths': implying some form of land division in times past. The same derivation applies to the area known as the Coigs of Strathdearn, south of Inverness.

Coire Cas (Highland) 'Steep corrie'. *Coire* (Scottish Gaelic) 'corrie'; *cas* (Scottish Gaelic) 'steep'. The corrie is in the centre of much climbing and skiing activity.

Coldbackie (Highland) 'Cold bank', from *kald* (Old Norse) 'cold'; *bakki* (Old Norse) 'bank'.

Coldstream (Borders) Before the bridge was built (1766), the Tweed was forded here, and the name is a reference to the temperature of the river, which is a substantial stream at this point. Recorded 1128 as Kaldestrem. The Coldstream Guards regiment was founded here by General Monk in 1659, and set off for London in 1660 to bring about the restoration of King Charles II.

Coldingham (Borders) 'Village of the people of Colud'. *Colud* (Old English personal name); *inga* (Old English) affix with the sense of 'people of'; *ham* (Old English) 'village'. The site of an important early priory, it is noted around 798 as Coludesburg, with the present form found in 1098.

Colinsburgh (Fife) This small village is named after Colin Lindsay, earl of Balcarres, who founded it in 1705. A Stewart sympathiser, he is said to have established a colony of former Jacobite soldiers there.

Colinton (Edinburgh) 'Colgan's farm'. The form in 1296 was Colgyntone. Colgan is an Irish Gaelic personal name, and may have supplanted an earlier Anglian name: the suffix is from Old English *tun*, 'farmstead'.

Colintraive (Argyll & Bute) 'Swimming narrows', from Scottish Gaelic *caol*, 'strait, kyle', and *snàimh*, genitive form of *snàmh*, swimming. Here cattle were swum across from Bute to the mainland.

Collessie (Fife) 'Nook of the water', from Scottish Gaelic *cuil*, 'nook, corner', and *eas*, 'waterfall', with the locative suffic *-ach*.

Coll (Argyll & Bute) Probably 'barren place'. *Kollr* (Old Norse) 'bald head, bare top'. This description is apt for this Inner Hebridean island, which presents a bleak face of gnarled gneiss rock protruding through the heather, in contrast to its flat and fertile neighbour, Tiree.

Colonsay (Argyll & Bute) Possibly '(St) Columba's Isle'. Alternatively, some commentators suggest *Kolbein* (Old Norse) as an alternative personal name; the second part is derived from *ey* (Old Norse) 'island'. Older forms include Golwonche, 1335, Colowsay, 1376.

Coltness (North Lanarkshire) 'Wood by the water (fall)'. *Coille* (Scottish Gaelic) 'wood'; *an*, 'by the'; *eas* (Scottish Gaelic) 'waterfall'. This was a coal-mining place until the 1970s.

Comiston (Edinburgh) 'Colman's farm'. *Colmàn* (Scottish Gaelic proper name, deriving from *Colum*, 'dove') and *tun* (Old English) 'farmstead'. Found as Colmanston, 1335.

Comrie (Perth & Kinross) 'Place of the confluence'. *Comar* (Scottish Gaelic) 'river confluence'. Near here both the Water of Ruchill and the River Lednock (Gaelic Liadnaig, perhaps from *lia*, 'stone', but also 'flood, stream' in Perthshire Gaelic) meet with the River Earn in a convergence of valleys. Noted as Comry, 1268. Another Comrie is by Oakley in Fife. *See also* Cumbernauld.

Condorrat (North Lanarkshire) 'Place of the river confluence'. *Comh* (Scottish Gaelic) 'joining'; *dobhar* (Scottish Gaelic) 'water, stream'; *-ait* (Scottish Gaelic suffix indicating place). Recorded in 1553 as Cundurat.

Connel (Argyll & Bute) 'Whirlpool'. From Scottish Gaelic *coingheall*, 'whirlpool', referring to the tidal rapids here at the entrance to Loch Etive. For a long time the place was known as Connel Ferry, until the cantilever bridge was built over the rapids, originally carrying both road and the now-closed Ballachulish branch of the Callander and Oban Railway. *See* Lora.

Conon River, Strath and **Village** (Highland). 'Wolf, or dog, river'. The root form appears to be *con* (genitive form of Old Irish *cu*) 'wolf, dog'. The *-ona* (early-Celtic) 'water' suffix is frequently found in river-names. The name is frequently found in pre-twentieth century sources as Conan. The same name appears to recur in Cononsyth and Grange of Conon, in Angus, where the stream is a very modest one; and there are Conon Crofts in Snizort, Skye.

Contin (Highland) The root form appears to be, as with Conon, *con* (genitive form of Old Irish *cu*) 'wolf, dog', with *dainn* (Scottish Gaelic) 'rampart'. Perhaps 'fort of the dog'. Noted as Conten in 1226.

Convinth, Glen (Highland) 'Glen of roaring', from Scottish Gaelic *confhadh,* 'howling, rage'. The Gaelic name is Gleann Confhadhaich. The reference may be to wind or water noise in this funnel-shaped glen.

Copinsay (Orkney) 'Kolbein's isle'. From Old Norse *Kolbein* (personal name) and *-ey,* 'island'.

Cora Linn (South Lanarkshire) 'Pool or falls of the boggy place'. *Corrach* (Scottish Gaelic) 'marshy place'; *linne* (Scottish Gaelic) 'pool, falls'. A popular walking place in the gorge of the Clyde.

Cor- Found as a prefix or other element in numerous place names, it sometimes stems from Scottish Gaelic *còrr,* which in addition to 'surplus', can mean 'snout' and 'horn', derived from Irish *cor,* and related to Latin *cornus,* 'horn'. The horn-shape is often a horizontal one, of a river or loch associated with tapering or horn-shaped features. *See* Banchory.

Corgarff (Aberdeenshire) 'Rough corrie'. *Coire* (Scottish Gaelic) 'corrie, mountain hollow'; *garbh* (Scottish Gaelic) 'rough'.

Corpach (Highland) 'Corpse-place'. *Corpach* (Scottish Gaelic) 'corpses', from the fact that funerals from Fort William on their way to the church at Annat rested here. There is another Corpach on Jura.

Corran (Highland) 'Low tapering cape'. *Còrr* (Scottish Gaelic) 'tapered, drawn to a point', with *-an* diminutive ending. A derivation from Irish Gaelic *carran,* 'reaping hook', indicating a curving spit of land, is also possible. This is the ferry point across the narrows of Loch Linnhe. There is also a Corran on the Ardnamurchan peninsula, and at Glenelg.

Corrie 'Mountain hollow', from Scottish Gaelic *coire,* which originally had the sense of 'pot' or 'cauldron', and then, by association, a basin-shaped mountain hollow, normally created by glacial action. The name is found wherever such features occur; in remoter parts the Gaelic form is usually preserved.

Corrie (North Ayrshire) This Arran hamlet's name comes from its location: *see* Corrie above.

Corriehalloch (Highland) 'Foaming corrie', from Scottish Gaelic *coire*, 'mountain hollow', and *salach*, which means 'turbulent' as well as 'ugly, dirty'. The unpronounced *s* gives the usual English spelling; the Gaelic spelling has given rise to the alternative English form 'Corrieshalloch'.

Corrievreckan (Argyll & Bute) 'Whirlpool of Brecon'. *Coire* (Scottish Gaelic) 'cauldron' here also has the sense of 'whirlpool'; *Brychan* (a personal name) common in Celtic mythologies. In Gaelic legend, the hero Brychan perished with all his fifty ships in this notorious whirlpool, which lies north of the island of Jura. *See* Brechin.

Corrieyairack, Pass of (Highland) 'Rising corrie'. *Coire* (Scottish Gaelic) 'mountain hollow'; *eirich* (Scottish Gaelic) 'rising'. There is an old military road over the pass from the Great Glen to Badenoch, linking Fort Augustus to the military barracks at Ruthven.

Corrour (Highland) 'Brown hollow'. *Coire* (Scottish Gaelic) 'corrie' and *odhar* (Scottish Gaelic) 'brown'.

Corsewall Point (Dumfries & Galloway) 'Cross well'. There is an ancient well-site here dedicated to St Columba.

Corstorphine (Edinburgh) Possibly 'cross of the fair hill'. *Crois* (Scottish Gaelic) 'cross'; *torr* (Scottish Gaelic) 'hill'; *fionn* (Scottish Gaelic) 'fair'. A cross did stand here by Corstorphine Hill in what is now a western suburb of Edinburgh. Other less well-founded derivations include one from Torphin (personal name) or from the eleventh-century Norse earl Thorfinn the Mighty. Records show Crostorfin 1128; Corstorphyne 1508.

Coruisk, Loch (Highland) *Cor-ooshk*. 'Water hollow'. *Coire* (Scottish Gaelic) 'mountain hollow'; *uisge* (Scottish Gaelic) 'water'. As a definition of the Cuillin-hemmed Loch Coruisk, this is something of an understatement.

Coshieville (Perth & Kinross) 'By the trees'. *Cois* (Scottish Gaelic) 'beside'; *a*, 'the'; *bhile* (Scottish Gaelic) 'thicket'. The modern form has developed by modelling on -ville suffixes.

Coulter (South Lanarkshire) 'The back land'. *Cul* (Scottish Gaelic) 'back, rear'; *tìr* (Scottish Gaelic) 'land'. Noted as Cultyr, c. 1210. Also found as Culter.

Coupar Angus (Perth & Kinross) Named to distinguish it from Cupar, Fife, but no longer located in Angus. Perhaps derived as Cupar, from *comphairt* (Scottish Gaelic) 'common grazing'. Found as Cubert, 1169; Coupre in Anegos, 1296.

Cove (Argyll & Bute; Aberdeenshire; Borders; Highland) 'Hut', from *kofi* (Old Norse) 'hut'. Cove Bay in Cowal and south of

Aberdeen are therefore 'hut bays', not as tautologous as they look. Cove in Cockburnspath parish in the Borders may be from Old English *cófa*, 'cave, room'.

Cowal (Argyll & Bute) The name of this Highland peninsula lying between Loch Fyne and the Firth of Clyde is a corruption of *Comhgall*, the name of a grandson of Fergus of Dàl Riada.

Cowcaddens (Glasgow) 'Hazel nook'. *Cuil* (Scottish Gaelic) 'corner, nook'; *calldainn* (Scottish Gaelic) 'of hazels'. The hazels have long gone in this central Glasgow area.

Cowdenbeath (Fife) Possibly 'Cowden's (land) by the birches'. *Cowden* (personal name) suggested by the earliest available record in 1626, which refers to the place as Terris de Cowdounesbaithe (but *see* Cowdenknowes); the second element is derived from *beith* (Scottish Gaelic) 'birch'.

Cowdenknowes (Borders) 'Hazel knolls'. *Calltuin* (Scottish Gaelic) 'hazel'; *knowes* (Scots) 'knolls'. Recorded in 1559 as Coldenknollis. Cowdens is found by itself as a farm or local name in numerous places in the south.

Cowie (Stirling) 'Wood', from Scottish Gaelic *coille*, 'wood'.

Coylum (Highland) 'Gorge leap'. *Cuing* (Scottish Gaelic) 'gorge'; *leum* (Scottish Gaelic) 'leap'. The name encourages speculation as to how wayfarers got across the River Druie (Old Gaelic *dru*, 'oak', or perhaps Scottish Gaelic *druidh*, 'druid, magic-worker') before the bridge here was built.

Craigellachie (Moray) 'Rock of the stony place'. *Creag* (Scottish Gaelic) 'rock, crag'; *ealeachaidh* (Scottish Gaelic) 'stony', from Irish *ailech*, 'rock'. 'Stand fast, Craigellachie', was the war-cry of Clan Grant.

Craigendoran (Argyll & Bute) 'Rock of the waters'. *Creag* (Scottish Gaelic) 'rock'; *an t-*, 'of the'; *dobhráinn* (Scottish Gaelic) 'waters'.

Craigentinny (Edinburgh) 'Rock of the fire', from Scottish Gaelic *creag*, 'rock'; *an*, 'of'; *teine*, 'fire', indicating a signal point. 'Fox's rock', *an t-Sionnaich* (Scottish Gaelic) 'of the fox', has been suggested, but the Gaelic form is Creag an Teine. *See* Ardentinny.

Craiglockhart (Edinburgh) 'Rock of the ship-station', or 'camp place'. *Creag* (Scottish Gaelic) 'rock'; *luing* (Scottish Gaelic) 'ship'; *phort* (Scottish Gaelic) 'landing-place'. *See* Longart.

Craigmillar (Edinburgh) 'Rock of the bare height'. *Creag* (Scottish Gaelic) 'rock'; *maol* (Scottish Gaelic) 'bare, bald'; *ard* (Scottish Gaelic) 'height'.

Craignure (Argyll & Bute) 'Yew tree rock'. *Creag* (Scottish Gaelic) 'rock'; *an*, 'of'; *iubhair* (Scottish Gaelic) 'yew tree'. The mention of the yew trees may indicate an old burial ground at this Mull ferry-port.

Craigroyston (Argyll & Bute) This has been derived as 'Drostan's rock'. *Creag* (Scottish Gaelic) 'rock'; *Drostan* (Scottish Gaelic personal name, from Pictish *Drust*). Drostan was reputed to be a seventh century holy man. The Gaelic name is Creag Trostain, and *trostan* (Scottish Gaelic) 'foot-stool, pillar', is an alternative possibility. There is a hill in Antrim simply called Trostan. The 'roy' element appears to have been interpolated by popular etymology linking the name with the local hero, Rob Roy MacGregor.

Crail (Fife) 'Boulder rock'. *Carr* (Old Gaelic) 'boulder'; *ail* (Old Gaelic) 'rock'. This ancient port of the East Neuk of Fife was recorded as Caraile in 1153, showing the two elements of this apparent tautology. The dangerous Carr Rocks lie three miles offshore to the east in the Firth of Forth.

Cramond (Edinburgh) 'Fort on the river Almond'. *Caer* (Brythonic) 'fort'; and *see* Almond. Recorded as Caramonth, 1178. There was a Roman fort here, and evidence of a port town has been discovered, including the famous 'Cramond lion'.

Crarae (Argyll & Bute) Perhaps 'Boggy place'. *Cràthrach* (Scottish Gaelic) 'boggy place', but the Gaelic form of the name is Carr-eibhe, suggesting *carr* (Old Gaelic) 'boulder', and perhaps *eighe*, 'file'. The quarries here were a famous source of hard granite.

Crathie (Aberdeenshire) Perhaps 'shaking place', a reference to boggy ground. The Gaelic form is Craichidh, but an older Crathaigh has been postulated, cognate with Cray in Glen Shee and with Achray.

Crawford (South Lanarkshire) 'Crow ford', from Old English *crawe,* 'crow', and ford as in modern English. Found as Crauford, c. 1150. 'Crooked ford' has also been proposed.

Crawfordjohn (South Lanarkshire) 'Crow's ford of John'. Recorded as Craufurd Johnne in 1275. John was the son-in-law of Baldwin, sheriff of Lanark.

Cree, River (Dumfries & Galloway) Cree is from *crìoch* (Scottish Gaelic) 'boundary'; found as Crethe, 1301. Creetown is modern, 'town on the Cree'.

Creich (Highland; Fife; Argyll; Dumfries & Galloway) 'Boundary place', from Scottish Gaelic *crioch,* 'boundary'; or possibly 'tree place'. The Gaelic form is *Craoich*, which could derive from *craobh* (Scottish Gaelic) 'tree'; *critheach* (Scottish Gaelic) 'aspen' is also possible. Creich in Fife is noted as Creyh, 1250.

Crewe (Edinburgh) 'Animal pen, hut', from Cumbric *creu,* 'hovel, sty', though as it was a toll place, a link with Scottish Gaelic *crioch,* 'boundary', might seem possible. Crewe in England has been related to Cumbric *cryw,* 'stepping-stones'.

Crianlarich (Stirling) Possibly 'little pass'. *Crion* (Scottish Gaelic) 'little'; *lairig* (Scottish Gaelic) 'pass'. This could describe the situation of the village at the rise out of Glen Dochart that goes over into Glen Falloch, forming a strategic road and railway junction on the Fort William and Oban routes from Glasgow and Perth. An alternative derivation is Scottish Gaelic *critheann* 'aspen tree'; *laraich* 'house-site'. It is noted as Creinlarach, 1603.

Crichton (Midlothian) 'Boundary farm'. *Crioch* (Scottish Gaelic) 'boundary'; *tun* (Old English) 'farmstead'. Found c. 1145 as Crechtune.

Crieff (Perth & Kinross) 'Place among the trees'. *Craobh* (Scottish Gaelic locative) 'tree'. Recorded as Creffe in 1178. Until the eighteenth century this was the scene of a great annual cattle tryst, when cattle were brought from all over the Highlands for sale and onward driving to England. Nowadays it is a pleasant residential town and tourist centre.

Criffel (Dumfries & Galloway) 'Split fell'. *Kryfja* (Old Norse) 'to split'; *fjalr* (Old Norse) 'hill, fell'. The name of this distinctive granite hill (1868ft, 569m) near Dalbeattie was recorded in 1330 as Crefel.

Crimond (Aberdeenshire) 'Hill-mound'. *Crech* (Old Gaelic) 'hilltop'; *monadh* (Scottish Gaelic) 'hill, mountain'. Older forms are Creymund, 1250; Crichmound 1550. The name has been given to a famous psalm tune.

Crinan (Argyll & Bute) The derivation 'place of the Creones' has been tentatively suggested. This was one of the western tribes identified by Ptolemy around AD 150. The pre-Celtic root form is *cre-* and the Gaelic form of the name is Crìanan. 'Crinan' was also in use as a personal name in the eleventh century, when it was borne by a lay abbot of Dunkeld. The canal across the narrow peninsula between here and Ardrishaig was begun in 1793.

Cromalt (Highland) 'Crooked river'. *Crom* (Scottish Gaelic) 'bending, crooked', and *allt* (Scottish Gaelic) 'river'. The Cromalt flows into Loch Urigill (Old Norse *úttar,* 'outer'; *gill,* 'cleft') and gives its name to the surrounding rugged hills.

Cromarty (Highland) Originally 'crooked bay'. *Crom* (Scottish Gaelic) 'crooked'; *bàgh* (Scottish Gaelic) 'bay', an apt description for this former county town lying in the hook-shaped bay formed by the South Sutor at the tip of the Black Isle peninsula. The modern Gaelic form is Crombà. Records show its earlier forms as Crumbathyn in 1257 and Crombathie (1296). Perhaps because of the existence of an alternative form incorporating *ard* (Scottish Gaelic) 'height', the name altered to Cromardy in 1398, and Cromarte in 1565.

Crombie (Aberdeenshire; Fife) 'Crooked stream', from Scottish Gaelic *crom*, 'bent, crooked', with -*aidh* adjectival suffix.

Cromdale (Moray) 'Bent haugh'. *Crom* (Scottish Gaelic) 'bent'; *dail* (Scottish Gaelic) 'meadow, haugh'.

Crook of Devon (Perth & Kinross) 'Bend of Devon'. *Krókr* (Old Norse) 'crook, bend'. The River Devon here takes a sharp turn westwards into Glen Devon. Crook of Alves in Moray has the same meaning. *See also* Caldercruix.

Crossmyloof (Glasgow) Though scotticised into 'Cross my palm' (*loof*, 'palm') this Glasgow district name means 'Cross of Malduff', from *crois* (Scottish Gaelic) 'cross', and *Maolduibh* (Scottish Gaelic personal name) 'Malduff' (literally 'bald dark one').

Crossraguel (South Ayrshire) 'Cross of the bare fort.' 'Bare' probably means 'without a tower'. *Crois* (Scottish Gaelic) 'cross'; *rathaig* (Scottish Gaelic) 'small fort'; *maol* (Scottish Gaelic) 'bare'. The now ruined abbey here was founded in 1244. Noted c. 1200 as Cosragmol, 1225 Crosragmol.

Croy (North Lanarkshire; Highland; South Ayrshire) 'Hard place'. *Cruadh* (Scottish Gaelic) 'hard'. Found as Croy in 1369. Croy Brae, south of Ayr, is known as the 'Electric Brae' because of the optical illusion that its slope goes in a contrary direction to the actual lie of the land.

Cruachan, Ben (Argyll & Bute) 'The heaped or haunched mountain'. *Cruach* (Scottish Gaelic) 'pile, stack'. *Cruachann* (Scottish Gaelic) 'thigh, haunch'. Recorded as Crechanben c. 1375. This steep mountain (3695ft/1129m) rises above the Pass of Brander. Its name is often used without the prefix 'Ben', especially in Gaelic. A hydro-electric power station has been installed in a vast man-made cavern under the mountain.

Cuillin (Highland) Possibly 'high rocks'. *Kiolen* (Old Norse) 'high rocks, ridge'. Traditionally this Skye mountain range, a favourite among rock-climbers, was thought to have been named after the Celtic hero Cuchulainn, and nineteenth-century texts refer to the Cuchulin Hills, but this is probably through late association of similar-looking names, even though the young Cuchulainn was said to have learned the art of war from the female warrior Scathach on Skye. The Gaelic form is An Cuilfhionn or An Culthionn. But a Norse origin is much more likely, as with most other Hebridean mountains. The Rum mountains are also referred to as Cuillins. The River and Loch Coulin, near Kinlochewe in Wester Ross, Gaelic *Cùlainn*, seem to have a different derivation, perhaps from Gaelic *con*, 'together', and *lann*, 'enclosure'. There were shielings here at one time.

Culbin (Moray) 'Back of the hill'. *Cul* (Scottish Gaelic) 'back'; *bheinne* (Scottish Gaelic) 'of the mountain'. Noted as Coulbin, c. 1270. Culbin is known for its extensive sand dunes which cover a once-flourishing village.

Cullen (Moray) 'Holly'. *Culeann* (Scottish Gaelic) 'holly'. Noted as Inverculan, 1190; indicating that it was originally the stream name. This Banffshire fishing port is the source of the fish soup known as 'Cullen skink'.

Culloden (Highland) Possibly, at the 'back of the little pool.' *Cul* (Scottish Gaelic) 'back, ridge'; *lodair* (Scottish Gaelic) 'little pool'. A document of 1238 records the name as Cullodyn. The moor here (also known as Drumossie) was the site of the last full-scale battle fought in Scotland, in April 1746, in which the Jacobite army of Prince Charles Edward Stewart was defeated by Hanoverian Government troops under the duke of Cumberland.

Culross (Fife) *Koo-ross*. Possibly, 'holly wood'. *Culeann* (Scottish Gaelic) 'holly'; *ros* (Scottish Gaelic) 'wood'. Records show Culenros in 1110. Once a flourishing commercial town, its well-preserved seventeenth- and eighteenth-century houses, in Scottish vernacular style, are now a tourist attraction.

Culter *See* Coulter

Cults (Aberdeen) It has been derived as 'the nooks', from Scottish Gaelic *cùiltean*, 'nooks', plural of *cùilt*. *Coillte* (Scottish Gaelic) 'woods', has also been suggested. The terminal -*s* has been added in the Scots form to maintain the plural. There is another Cults in Aberdeenshire, near Gartly, and others in Dumfries & Galloway and Fife.

Culzean (South Ayrshire) *Cull-ane*. 'Nook of birds'. *Cuil* (Scottish Gaelic) 'nook, corner'; *ean* (Scottish Gaelic) 'of birds'. Found in 1636 as Cullen. At this seaside location the birds were presumably seabirds. The castle here, rebuilt by James Adam in the eighteenth century, was the seat of the Kennedys.

Cumbernauld (North Lanarkshire) The 'meeting of the burns'. *Comar* (Scottish Gaelic) 'river confluence'; *na* (Scottish Gaelic) 'of the'; *allt* (Scottish Gaelic) 'stream, burn'. Recorded as Cumyrnald in 1417. Vastly enlarged as a New Town since 1955, the original village here still has a burn flowing through it, to join another nearby.

Cumbrae (North Ayrshire) Apparently 'island of the Cumbrians'. *Cymry* (Cumbric) tribal name of the Cumbrian people who inhabited southern Scotland in early times; *ey* (Old Norse) 'island'. Recorded as Kumbrey 1270; Cumbraye 1330.

Cuminestown (Aberdeenshire) 'Town of the Comyns or Cummings', a reminder of the powerful Comyns of medieval times, earls of Buchan and at times *de facto* rulers of the country. There is also Cummingstown close to Burghead in Moray.

Cumlodden (Argyll & Bute) 'Crooked pool', from Scottish Gaelic *cam*, 'bent', and *lodan*, 'little pool'. Cumloden in Minnigaff parish, Dumfries & Galloway, has the same derivation.

Cumnock (East Ayrshire) Perhaps 'crooked hill'. *Cam* (Scottish Gaelic) 'crooked, sloping'; *cnoc* (Scottish Gaelic) 'hill'. It was recorded as Comnocke 1297; Cunnok 1461; Canknok 1548.

Cunningham (North Ayrshire) This old Ayrshire district name is of obscure but probably Celtic origin; attempts have been made to identify *cuinneag* (Scottish Gaelic) 'milk pail' (see Quinag) in it. In 1153 it was recorded as Cunegan. It is also found in the form Cunninghame.

Cupar (Fife) Possibly, 'the common-(land)'. *Comhpairt* (Scottish Gaelic) 'common pasture'. Some authorities believe that this ancient market town's name has a pre-Celtic derivation. Recorded as Cupre 1183. It has come into Scottish proverb, in 'He that will to Cupar, maun to Cupar.'

Curly Wee (Dumfries & Galloway) The odd-looking name of this hill (2405ft/729m) has been derived as 'windy bend', from *cuir* (Scottish Gaelic) 'bend'; *le*, 'in the'; *gaoith* (Scottish Gaelic) 'wind', though the Old Irish *cor*, 'hill', has also been suggested.

Currie (Edinburgh) 'Boggy land'. *Currach* (Scottish Gaelic) 'bogland, marshy area'. Now a south-western suburb of Edinburgh; the site of the original settlement was on lowlying land by the Water of Leith.

Cursetter (Orkney) 'Cow pasture'. *Ky-r* (Old Norse) 'cows'; *saetr* (Old Norse) 'farm, pasture land'.

Cushnie (Aberdeenshire) 'Cold, frosty', from *cuisneach* (Scottish Gaelic) 'frosty, freezing'. This may be an example of an apotropaic place-name; the name deliberately given to ward off the quality it describes. There are several Cushnies in the north-east, one near the coast at Gamrie. The Annals of Tighernach record a Pictish shipwreck in 729 off Ross Cuissini, perhaps an earlier name of the nearby Troup Head (Troup, of unresolved meaning, appears Old Norse in origin). Another Cushnie is inland, south-west of Alford, with the helpful alternative name of 'Frosty Hill'; and another south of Rhynie. A similar Scots name is Frostineb ('frosty nose') a farm-toun by Fala in Midlothian.

D

Daer, River (South Lanarkshire) The name has been conjectured as coming from Scottish Gaelic *deifir*, 'speed', which would certainly fit this hill stream. Although the infant Clydes Burn, which joins it, is less substantial, the river from there on bears the name of Clyde.

Dailly (South Ayrshire) 'Thorny place', from Scottish Gaelic *dealg*, 'thorn', with locative suffix *-ach*. Noted as Daylie, 1625. *See* Delny.

Dairsie (Fife) The first part of the name appears to be 'oak', whether from Gaelic *dair* or Brythonic *derw*. The second part is uncertain; it has been tentatively identified with Gaelic *beus*, which among other things means 'fornication'. If correct, it may refer to oak-grove rites. The name is recorded as Dersey, 1629. This is one of the few locations with an alternative name, here Osnaburgh, from an Old Norse personal name, with *burgh* (Scots, from Old Norse *borgr*, 'fort'). The survival of both identities is interesting.

Dal- An extremely common place-name prefix throughout the mainland and also found in the Western Isles, from Scottish Gaelic *dail*, 'field, dale, meadow, plain.' There is also the obsolete Irish Gaelic *dál*, 'portion, tribe', and some ancient Dal- names, like Dàl Riada (*Dàl Riata*, 'Riata's portion'), stem from this. But there is also a Brythonic form *dol*, of the same meaning, as in the Breton Dol de Bretagne, giving a number of names in the former Pictland (*see* Dallas). Dal- names need to be investigated carefully to identify the linguistic source and period of origin.

Dalbeattie (Dumfries & Galloway) 'Meadow of the birch trees'. *Dail* (Scottish Gaelic) 'meadow', *beitheach* (Scottish Gaelic) 'birch tree'. Recorded as Dalbaty in 1469.

Dalcross (Highland) 'Spit of the promontory'. *Dealg* (Scottish Gaelic) 'point'; *an*, 'of the'; *rois* (Scottish Gaelic) 'promontory'. An earlier form is Dalginross, and there is a Dalginross in the Teith valley.

Dalgetty (Fife) 'Windy field'. *Dail* (Scottish Gaelic) 'field'; *gaoithe* (Scottish Gaelic) 'of the winds', suitable for the exposed coastal setting of this Edinburgh dormitory town, recorded as Dalgathyn, 1168.

Dalguise (Perth & Kinross) 'Haugh of fir'. *Dail* (Scottish Gaelic) 'haugh, meadow', *giuthas* (Scottish Gaelic) 'fir'.

Dalhousie (Midlothian) Recorded in the thirteenth century as Dalwussy; the prefix is Scottish Gaelic *dail*, or Brythonic *dol*, 'field'; the suffix is unclear.

Dalkeith (Midlothian) 'Field by the wood'. *Dol* (Cumbric) 'field';

coed (Cumbric) 'wood'. Early documents show Dalkied 1140; Dolchet 1144; Dalketh 1145. Dalkeith Palace is a residence of the dukes of Buccleuch; an earlier house on the site was occupied by the sixteenth century Regent Morton, who was reputed to have hidden his extorted treasures there.

Dallas (Moray; Highland) 'Field by the waterfall'. *Dail* (Scottish Gaelic) 'field'; *eas* (Scottish Gaelic) 'waterfall'. Noted 1306 as Dolays. The less well-known Dallas near Edderton in Ross-shire, Gaelic *Dalais*, has been derived from *dol* (Brythonic–Pictish) 'plain', and *-ais*, a Brythonic–Pictish suffix denoting place.

Dalmally (Argyll & Bute) 'Site of Màillidh's church'. *Dail* (Scottish Gaelic) 'field', in this case specifically belonging to the church, from Old Gaelic *dol*, *Màillidh* (Old Gaelic personal name). Màillidh appears to have been a holy man whose name is commemorated in a number of places. *See* Kilmallie.

Dalmarnock (Glasgow; Perth & Kinross) 'Site of Marnock's church'. *Dail* (Scottish Gaelic) 'field', in this case one specifically belonging to the church, from Old Gaelic *dol*; *Mernóc* (Old Gaelic personal name). *See* Kilmarnock.

Dalmellington (South Ayrshire) Of uncertain meaning, though Scottish Gaelic *dail*, 'plain, meadow', is assumed to be the prefix; but *-mellington* has not been explained. Found in 1275 as Dalmellingtoun.

Dalmeny (Edinburgh) Perhaps 'My Ethne's meadow'. *Dail* (Scottish Gaelic) 'meadow', *mo*, 'my', *Eithne* (Old Gaelic personal name). As the mother of St Columba, Ethne was a revered figure, though other saintly women also bore the name. *See* Kilmany. But older forms include Dumanie (c. 1180) and Dunmany (1296), suggesting Scottish Gaelic *dùn*, 'fort', from Cumbric *din*, perhaps with Cumbric *meini*, 'stones'.

Dalmore (Highland) 'The big field'. *Dail* (Scottish Gaelic) 'field'; *mòr* (Scottish Gaelic) 'big'. A distillery and farm name.

Dalmuir (West Dunbartonshire) 'The big field'. *Dail* (Scottish Gaelic) 'field'; *mòr* (Scottish Gaelic) 'big'. Noted c. 1200 as Dalmore, but the suffix later became confused with *muir* (Scots) 'moor'; found as Dalmuire in 1680.

Dalnacardoch (Highland) 'The tinker's field'. *Dail* (Scottish Gaelic) 'field'; *na*, 'of the'; *ceard* (Scottish Gaelic) 'tinker', 'tinsmith'; *-ach* (Scottish Gaelic suffix denoting place).

Dalnaspidal (Perth & Kinross) 'Field of the refuge'. *Dail* (Scottish Gaelic) 'field'; *nan*, 'of'; *spideal* (Scottish Gaelic) 'refuge, hospice'. The place is located just south of the Pass of Drumochter, a natural site for a travellers' refuge.

Dalry (Edinburgh; Dumfries & Galloway; Argyll & Bute) The derivation is not clear; it may be 'field of the heather'. *Dail* (Scottish Gaelic) 'field'; *fhraoich* (Scottish Gaelic) 'heather', or the latter part may be from Gaelic *righ*, 'slope', as in Portree. It has also been suggested that the Dumfriesshire village, known in full as St John's Town of Dalry, had associations with King James IV, and could be derived as 'the king's meadow': *righ* (Scottish Gaelic) 'king'. It was recorded as Dalrye in 1497.

Dalserf (South Lanarkshire) 'Place of St Serf's church'. *Dail* (Scottish Gaelic) 'field', in this case specifically belonging to the church, from Old Gaelic *dol*; *Serf* (personal name from Latin *servus*, 'slave'). St Serf is mostly associated with Fife towns.

Dalrymple (South Ayrshire) 'Field of the winding pool'. *Dail* (Scottish Gaelic) 'field'; *crom* (Scottish Gaelic) 'bent, winding'; *poll* (Scottish Gaelic) 'pool'. The *c* of *crom* has been lost. Found in 1300 as Dalrimpill.

Dalswinton (Dumfries & Galloway) The elements add up to 'Field of the pig-farm', but they are anachronistic. *Dail* (Scottish Gaelic) 'field'; *swin* (Old English) 'pig'; *tun* (Old English) 'farmstead'. Noted in 1292 as Dalsuyntone, and in 1295 as Baleswyntoun; but prior to these Gaelic prefixes it must just have been 'Swynton'. There was a large Roman fort here. On the loch one of the earliest steam boats was tried out, with Robert Burns on board.

Dalwhinnie (Highland) Apparently the 'field of the champion'. *Dail* (Scottish Gaelic) 'field'; *cuingid* (Scottish Gaelic) 'champion'. This may refer to some historic or legendary contest.

Dalziel (North Lanarkshire) *Dal-yell*. 'White meadow'. *Dail* (Scottish Gaelic) 'field, meadow', *gheal* (Scottish Gaelic) 'white'. There are numerous Dalziels and Dalzells throughout the country. The *z*, as in many other cases, is actually a form of written *gh*. Recorded in 1200 as Dalyell.

Darvel (East Ayrshire) Perhaps 'stream by the township'. *Dobhar* (Brythonic–Scottish Gaelic) 'water'; *bhaile* (Scottish Gaelic) 'of the township'. Noted on Blaeu's map of Scotland as Darnevaill.

Dava (Highland) 'Ford of the stags, or oxen'. *An* (Scottish Gaelic) 'the'; *damh* (Scottish Gaelic) 'ox, stag'; *àth* (Scottish Gaelic) 'ford'. The old drove and military road here crossed the Dorback Burn (Scottish Gaelic *dorbàg*, 'tadpole') flowing from Loch an Dorb ('tadpole loch').

Davaar (Argyll & Bute) 'St Barr's (isle)', in Gaelic *Eilean da Bharr*. With its hermit's cave, this island guarding access to Campbeltown Loch was a mission station of St Barr or Finbarr of Barra.

Daviot (Highland; Aberdeenshire) *Day-veeot*. This appears to be from an ancient tribal name, latinised as *Demetae*. Its Gaelic form is Deimhidh, from a conjectured root form *dem* (Brythonic–Pictish) 'fixed, sure'. It is cognate with Welsh Dyfed. Noted as Dauyot, 1136. The two Daviots are small communities, one south of Inverness, the other in Formartine, north-west of Aberdeen.

Davoch This Scottish Gaelic land-measure term occurs in numerous place-names. An anglicised form of Scottish Gaelic *dabhach*, 'vat', it indicated an area of land whose annual produce would fill a vat of standard size. It is found in pristine form in Davoch of Grange, on the River Isla near Keith (Moray). *See also* Dochfour.

Dean, River (Midlothian) 'Valley, den'. *Denu* (Old English) 'dene': a name which corresponds to the steep-banked Dean River in Edinburgh, and found c. 1145 as Dene.

Dearg, Ben (Highland; Aberdeenshire) *Ben Jerrig.* 'Red mountain'. *Beinn* (Scottish Gaelic) 'mountain'; *dearg* (Scottish Gaelic) 'red'. There are numerous mountains of this name throughout the Highlands, and also Càrn Deargs.

Dee, River and **Strath** (Aberdeenshire; Dumfries & Galloway) This ancient river-name has a complex history, not yet fully explored. Its Gaelic name *Dé* has been related to *Dia*, 'god', though the river's gender is feminine. Its early-Celtic root is *Deua*, meaning a female divinity; it shares this with the Don. The Galloway Dee is also known as the Black Water of Dee.

Deer (Aberdeenshire; Dumfries & Galloway) 'Forest grove'. *Doire* (Scottish Gaelic) 'grove', normally of oaks, from Old Irish Gaelic *daur*, 'oak', and noted in the eponymous Book of Deer as Dear, c. 1150. In Aberdeenshire there is still today the Forest of Deer, and Aikiehill (Scots 'oak hill'), beside the remains of the twelfth-century Deer Abbey, whose *Book of Deer*, preserved at Cambridge University, contains some of the oldest Scottish Gaelic writing.

Delny (Highland) 'Place of thorns'. *Dealgan* (Scottish Gaelic) 'thorn'; with -*ach* (Scottish Gaelic suffix indicating place). Recorded as Dalgeny, 1356. Delnies in other place-names, like the Carse of Delnies, west of Nairn, has the same derivation.

Denhead (Aberdeenshire; Angus; Dundee; Fife) 'Valley head', from *denu* (Old English) 'valley' giving Scots *den, dean;* and English 'head'.

Denholm (Borders, Dumfries & Galloway) 'Island in the valley'. *Denu* (Old English) 'valley'; *holmr* (Old English) 'river island'.

Denny (Falkirk) Presumably 'valley'. *Denu* (Old English) 'valley'. Noted as Litill Dany in 1510. This industrial town lies in the Carron Valley near the site of the famous iron works. Nearby is Dennyloanhead, 'valley at the head of the lane'. *See* Loanhead.

Deveron (Aberdeenshire) 'Black Earn'. This river was originally called *Eron*, perhaps from Old Irish *Erin*, like several others; or more probably from an older pre-Celtic source (see Earn). *Dubh* (Scottish Gaelic) 'dark' is a later prefix, perhaps to distinguish this river from the Findhorn, as with the Adder rivers in the borders, and the various Esks. It was recorded as Douern in 1273.

Devon, River and **Glen** (Perth & Kinross) 'Black stream'. *Dub* (Old Irish) 'black'; -*ona* (pre-Celtic) suffix indicating 'water', 'river'. It has also been suggested that it may stem from an inferred Brythonic word *domnona*, 'deep one, mysterious one', cognate with -*dovan* names like Baldovan. Its valley was recorded as Glendovan around 1210. English Devon is from the tribal name Dumnonii, via Old English *Defnas;* the similarly-named Damnonii were also recorded in second century Scotland, but in Clydesdale rather than here.

Diabaig (Highland) 'Deep bay', from *djúp* (Old Norse) 'deep', and *vik* (Old Norse) 'bay'.

Dingwall (Highland) 'Parliament field'. *Thing* (Old Norse) 'parliament, assembly'; *vollr* (Old Norse) 'field, open space'. This indicates the site of an annual meeting to make laws and administer justice in the days of Viking occupation. Exact parallels to the name are found in other areas of Norse influence (e.g. Tynwald Hill on the Isle of Man, Tingwall on Shetland, and Tinwald in Dumfries & Galloway). This market town, recorded as Dingwell, 1227, was formerly county town of Ross and Cromarty; its castle, now vanished, was a stronghold of Pictish kings and, in the fifteenth century, of the lords of the Isles.

Dinnet (Aberdeenshire) 'Place of refuge'. *Dìon* (Scottish Gaelic) 'shelter'; *ait* (Scottish Gaelic) 'place'.

Dirie Mór (Highland) *Jeerie More*. 'The big climb'. *Direadh* (Scottish Gaelic) 'climbing', *mòr* (Scottish Gaelic) 'big'. The reference is to the Garve–Ullapool road on the rise towards the Droma (Gaelic *druim*, 'ridge') watershed.

Divie, River (Moray) 'Dark water'. The Gaelic name is *Duibhe*, 'dark'. *See* Eassie.

Doch- This element in Scottish Gaelic place-names often stems from the land-measurement term *dabhach* (see Davoch).

Dochart, River and **Glen** (Stirling) 'Evil scourer'; the river-name, from *do-* (Scottish Gaelic prefix) 'evil', and *cartaim,* 'I cleanse, scour'. Noted c. 1200 as Glendochard.

Docharty, Glen (Highland) This may have the same derivation as Dochart; its Gaelic form is Gleann Dochartaich. *Dochair* in current Gaelic means 'hurt, misery, pain'; and *dochairt* means 'sick' – possible but unlikely name sources.

Dochfour (Highland) 'Pasture area'. *Dabhach* (Scottish Gaelic field measure), *phùir* (Scottish Gaelic) 'pasture'.

Dod (Borders; Dumfries & Galloway) 'Rounded hill'. 'Dod' is a frequent hill name in the Lowther Hills, occasionally on its own, but also in such names as Windy Dod, or the tautologous Dod Law in the Cheviots. It comes from the Middle English verb *dodden*, 'to clip, or poll', indicating a bald or rounded hill. There is a Dodd Hill both to east and west of Merrick in Ayrshire. The same element is found as the suffix -doddy in some local place-names.

Doll, Glen (Angus) 'Glen of the meadows', from Old Gaelic *dol*, 'meadow, valley'.

Dollar (Clackmannanshire) Place by the 'ploughed field'. Dol (Cumbric) 'field'; *ar* (Cumbric) 'arable, ploughed'. Noted in the *Pictish Chronicle*, c. 970, as Dolair and little changed by 1461, Doler. The name applies to the fertile lands here by the River Devon at the foot of the Ochil Hills. There is a local legend relating to the nearby Castle Campbell as 'Castle Gloom', between the burns of 'Dolour' and 'Grief'; but with no etymological backing; 'Gloom' is Scottish Gaelic *glòm; see* Glomach.

Dolphinton (Midlothian) 'Dolfin's place'. A charter of 1253 records this as Dolfinston; Dolfin was the brother of the first earl of Dunbar.

Don, River (Aberdeenshire) The Gaelic name is Deathan, from the same root source as its neighbour the Dee: *deua* (pre-Celtic) 'god', with suffix -*ona* indicating 'water, river'. The form Don is found from 1170. The belief in a river-spirit is indicated. *See* Dee.

Donibristle (Fife) 'Breasal's fort'. *Dùnadh* (Scottish Gaelic) 'camp'. *Breasail* (Old Irish personal name). Noted as Donibrysell, c. 1165.

Doon, River, Loch (South Ayrshire) The same name as Don, from the same root, *deuona* (pre-Celtic) 'river goddess'; noted as Don, 1197. This river is invoked in one of Robert Burns's most beautiful songs.

Dorain, Ben (Argyll & Bute) 'Hill of the streamlets'. *Dobhráinn* (Scottish Gaelic) 'of streams', linked with Brythonic *dobhar*, 'water, stream'. The mountain (3524ft/1077m) rising above Glen Orchy, is celebrated in the Gaelic verses of Duncan Bàn MacIntyre. There is also Beinn Dhorain above Strath Kildonan, in Sutherland, though this has also been derived from *dòbhran* (Scottish Gaelic) 'otters'.

Dores (Highland) 'Black woods'. *Dubh* (Scottish Gaelic) 'black'; and *ros* (Old Gaelic) 'wood'. Recorded as Durris, 1263 (*see* Durrisdeer).

Dorlinn (Argyll & Bute; Highland) 'Tidal isthmus' or 'tombolo', from Scottish Gaelic *doirlinn*, 'piece of land submerged by the tide'. Among the dorlinns are those joining Oronsay to Morvern, and Erraid to the Ross of Mull (used by R. L. Stevenson in *Kidnapped*).

Dornie (Highland) 'Place of pebbles'. *Dornach* (Scottish Gaelic) 'with pebbles'. There is a pebbly spit here where Loch Long and Loch Duich join with Loch Alsh.

Dornoch (Highland) 'Place of pebbles'. *Dornach* (Scottish Gaelic) 'with pebbles' or 'fist-size stones'. The root-word *dorn* means 'fist'. Today, the beach here on the Dornoch Firth is mainly sandy. The name was recorded as Durnach in 1150. Nowadays a golf and holiday town, this was also a cathedral city, and the much-restored medieval cathedral still stands in the centre. Scotland's last witch-burning was here, in 1727. Dornock on the Solway coast east of Annan is likely to derive from a related Cumbric form.

Douglas (Dumfries & Galloway; South Lanarkshire) 'Dark water'. *Dubh* (Scottish Gaelic) 'black'; *glas* (Scottish Gaelic) 'water'. The Lanarkshire town was recorded as Duuelglas around 1150. The name is also found in other localities in Argyll and Angus; some, like Castle Douglas and Douglastown, are later creations taken from the family name rather than any topographical water feature.

Doune (Stirling) *Doon*. 'Castle, fortified place'. *Dùn* (Scottish Gaelic) 'fortress'. This town, lying on the River Teith north-west of Stirling, is dominated by the fourteenth-century Doune Castle, although earlier fortifications also existed here. The local names Dounie, Downie, in various districts, have the same derivation.

Dounby (Orkney) 'Township by the fort'. *Dùn* (Scottish Gaelic) 'fort'; *by* (Old Norse) 'township'.

Dounreay (Highland) Possibly 'fortified rath'. *Dùn* (Scottish Gaelic) 'fortified place'; *rath* (Scottish Gaelic) 'circular fort' or 'broch'. Britain's first experimental fast nuclear reactor, now decommissioned, is located here.

Dowally (Perth & Kinross) 'Black cliff'. *Dubh* (Scottish Gaelic) 'black', *àille* (Scottish Gaelic) 'cliff'. Noted as Dowalye in 1505. Also found as a field or farm name in related forms, like Dowald.

Dreghorn (Edinburgh; North Ayrshire) 'Dry house'. *Dryge* (Old English) 'dry'; *erne* (Old English) 'house'. This Edinburgh district is now the site of a large barracks. There is another Dreghorn close to Irvine in North Ayrshire, recorded as Dregerne c. 1240.

Drem (East Lothian) 'Ridge'. *Druim* (Scottish Gaelic) 'ridge', 'hump'.

Dron (Perth & Kinross) 'Ridge, hump', from Scottish Gaelic *dron*. Numerous names incorporate Dron- as an element, sometimes in the form Drongan (East Ayrshire) and Drungan (Dumfries &

Galloway) from Scottish Gaelic *dronnan,* 'little ridge'. See also Drunkie.

Dronach, Glen (Aberdeenshire) 'Glen of the ridge', from *dron* (Scottish Gaelic) 'ridge, hump', and *-ach,* Scottish Gaelic suffix indicating 'place'. There is however an obsolete Scottish Gaelic word *dronnach,* 'white-backed cow', or 'white-rumped' as an adjective.

Drum 'Ridge' from Scottish Gaelic *druim,* originally meaning 'back' and related to Latin *dorsum,* 'back', is found as a local place-name in many parts, as well as a prefix to many hill-names.

Drumalban 'The ridge of Scotland'. This is the name of the great spinal watershed that runs up from central to northern Scotland, from *druim* (Scottish Gaelic) 'ridge'; and *Albainn* 'of Scotland', from *Alba* (Scottish Gaelic name for Scotland north of the Forth).

Drumchapel (Glasgow) 'Ridge of the horse'. *Druim* (Scottish Gaelic) 'ridge'; *chapuill* (Scottish Gaelic) 'of the horse'. This large housing estate was built in the 1950s on the western edge of Glasgow as part of the city's post-war 'overspill' programme to relieve overcrowding in the inner areas.

Drumbeg (Highland) 'Little ridge'. *Druim* (Scottish Gaelic) 'ridge, hump'; *beag* (Scottish Gaelic) 'small'.

Drumbuie (Highland) 'Yellow ridge'. *Druim* (Scottish Gaelic) 'ridge, hump'; *buidhe* (Scottish Gaelic) 'yellow'.

Drumclog (South Lanarkshire) 'Ridge of the rock' or of 'the bell'. *Druim* (Scottish Gaelic) 'ridge, hump'; *clog* may be either Brythonic, 'rock, crag', or Scottish Gaelic, 'bell'. This was the site of a Covenanters' victory over Claverhouse's dragoons in 1679.

Drumlanrig (Dumfries & Galloway) 'Clear space on the ridge'. *Druim* (Scottish Gaelic) 'ridge, hump'; *llanerch* (Cumbric) 'clear space'.

Drummond (Perth & Kinross; Highland) 'Humped mount'. *Druim* (Scottish Gaelic) 'ridge, hump'; *monadh* (Scottish Gaelic) 'mountain'. Drummond near Crieff is recorded as Droman, 1296.

Drumnadrochit (Highland) 'Ridge by the bridge'. *Druim* (Scottish Gaelic) 'ridge'; *na* (Scottish Gaelic) 'of the'; *drochaid* (Scottish Gaelic) 'bridge'. At this place there is a bridge over the River Enrick beneath a very steep ridge on the western bank of Loch Ness.

Drumochter (Highland; Perth & Kinross) 'Top of the ridge'. *Druim* (Scottish Gaelic) 'ridge'; *uachdar* (Scottish Gaelic) 'the top of, the upper part'. The name of the mountain pass carrying the main road and railway line from the south to Inverness, and the highest point of a main-line railway in Britain (1484ft/454m). The two mountains overlooking it to the west are the Boar of Badenoch and the Sow of Atholl.

Drumpellier (North Lanarkshire) 'Fort of spears'. Noted in 1203 as Dunpeleder, from *din* (Cumbric) 'fort'; *peledyr* (Cumbric) 'of spears'. The transformation of *din* to *drum* was presumably through association with other Gaelic or gaelicised names. The area is now a country park.

Drunkie, Loch (Stirling) 'Loch of the litle ridge'. *Loch* (Scottish Gaelic) 'lake, loch'; *dronnaig* (Scottish Gaelic) 'little ridge', 'knoll'.

Dryburgh (Borders) 'Fort town'. *Dryge* (Old English) 'fort'; *burh* (Old English) 'town, borough, burgh'. Early records show Drieburh 1160, Dryburg 1211. Old English *dryge,* 'dry' has also been suggested, though it does not seem particularly appropriate. The abbey here was founded in 1140.

Dryhope (Borders) Perhaps 'fortified hollow' or 'dry hollow'. Old English *dryge* can mean both 'fort' and 'dry'. *Hop* (Old English) is 'hollow, land enclosed by hills'. Dryhope was a nest of Border Reivers.

Drymen (Stirling) Drimmin. 'On the ridge'. *Drumein* (Scottish Gaelic dative/locative of *druim*) 'on the ridge'. Noted in 1238 as Drumyn. An apt description of the situation of this village to the north-west of Glasgow.

Duart (Argyll & Bute) 'Black point'. *Dubh* (Scottish Gaelic) 'black'; *àird* (Scottish Gaelic) 'point, height'. This is the promontory site of Duart Castle, the Maclean stronghold on Mull.

Duddingston (Edinburgh) 'Dodin's farmstead'. *Dodin* (Old English personal name), *tun* (Old English) 'farm, village', noted as Dodinestun, 1150. Some time prior to that it had a Cumbric name, Trauerlen, from *tref,* 'place, settlement'; *yr,* 'of the'; *llin,* 'lake'. The loch is still there.

Dufftown (Moray) Town founded and laid out in 1817 by James Duff (from Gaelic *dubh,* 'black') the fourth earl of Fife, after whom it is named. Today it is famous for its whisky distilleries.

Duffus (Moray) 'Black stance'. *Dubh* (Scottish Gaelic) 'black'; *fas* (Scottish Gaelic) 'stance, station'. Noted in 1274 as Duffhus. A place where a drover might rest his herd overnight.

Duich, Loch (Highland) 'Duthac's loch'. *Loch* (Scottish Gaelic) 'lake, loch'; *Dubhthaich* (Scottish Gaelic personal name) 'of Duthac'. St Duthac was a venerated figure; *see* Black Isle, Tain.

Duirinish (Highland) 'Deer's ness'. *Dyr* (Old Norse) 'deer'; *nes* (Old Norse) 'point, headland'; recorded in 1567 as Durynthas. *See* Durness.

Duisk, River (South Ayrshire) 'Black water', from Scottish Gaelic *dubh,* 'black'; *uisge,* 'water'.

Dull (Perth & Kinross) 'Field, haugh'. *Dail* (Scottish Gaelic)

'meadow'. A very common prefix, usually found as Dal- but it
rarely appears on its own.

Dullatur (North Lanarkshire) 'Dark slopes'. *Dubh* (Scottish Gaelic)
'black'; *leitir* (Scottish Gaelic) 'hillside'. It is noted on Blaeu's map
as Dulettyr. There is also Dullater, by Callander.

Dulnain, River (Highland) 'Flood stream'. *Tuil* (Scottish Gaelic)
'flood', with *-ean* suffix indicating a stream. The Gaelic name is
Abhainn Tuilnean. Rising in the Monadhliath Mountains, this
swift river is liable to sudden floods.

Dumbarton (West Dunbartonshire) 'Stronghold of the Britons'. *Dùn*
(Scottish Gaelic) 'fortified stronghold'; *Breatainn* (Scottish Gaelic)
'Britons'. Records show Dunbretane from 1300. The Britons
themselves called it Alcluith, 'rock of Clyde'. This fort on a steep
rock was the capital of the ancient kingdom of Strathclyde, between
the fifth and eleventh centuries, and played an important part in
medieval Scottish history. The name of its county, Dunbartonshire,
shows a more 'correct' form, though the change back from *m* to *n*
was made in modern times.

Dumfries (Dumfries & Galloway) 'Fortress of the woodland'. *Dùn*
(Scottish Gaelic) 'fortified stronghold'; *phris* (Scottish Gaelic
genitive of *preas*) 'of the woodland copse'. Found as Dunfres,
c. 1183. This bridging-point and market centre, the 'Queen of
the South', has long been the most important town in south-west
Scotland. *See* Nithsdale.

Dumfries & Galloway Official name of the south-western administrative region of the country, formed in 1975, covering the former
counties of Dumfries, Kirkcudbright and Wigtown.

Dumyat (Stirling) 'Hill of the Maeatae'. *Dùn* (Scottish Gaelic)
originally indicated a hill, but so many hilltop sites were fortified
that it acquired the sense of 'hill-fort'. The name also incorporates
that of one of the tribal groups identified by the Romans in
AD 208; their territory was close to the eventual line of Antonine's
Wall. This hill, 1366ft/418m, rises steeply above Bridge of Allan,
controlling access north and east. Myot Hill, not far away, also
appears to preserve the name of the Maeatae.

Dun- A common prefix throughout the country, but not always with
the same derivation. Scottish Gaelic *dùn* means 'heap, hill, fortified
house or hill, fortress'. The original sense was that of heap or hill,
with the other meanings following by association. *Dùn* is cognate
with Brythonic *din,* with a similar set of meanings, and in some
locations has replaced *din*.

Dunadd (Argyll & Bute) 'Fortress of the Add'. *Dùn* (Scottish Gaelic)
'fort'. The etymology of *Add* is unclear, though it presumably is

from the name of the adjacent River Add, and may be pre-Celtic. The oldest recorded spelling is Duin Att, 683. This rock outcrop was an important centre of the Dalriadic Scots, perhaps their coronation-site, with ritual stone carvings still to be seen on its summit.

Dunbar (East Lothian) 'Fort on the height'. *Din* (Cumbric) 'fort'; *barr* (Cumbric) 'height'. Recorded 709 as Dynbaer: the later *dun*-form of the prefix has been ascribed to Anglian or Gaelic influence. A castle was built on the high rocks above the port's natural harbour but was ruined in 1650 by Cromwell's army following their victory in battle here. As the outer defence of Edinburgh, numerous battles were fought in the vicinity of Dunbar.

Dunbeath (Highland) 'Hill of birches'. *Dùn* (Scottish Gaelic) 'hill, mound'; *beith* (Scottish Gaelic) 'birch tree'. Noted in this form 1450.

Dunblane (Stirling) 'Fort of St Blane'. *Dùn* (Scottish Gaelic) 'fort'; *Bláán* (Old Irish personal name) Blane. Recorded c. 1200 as Dumblann. This was said to be St Blane's chief monastery; perhaps for that reason it is awarded the designation Dun- rather than the more usual Kil-. Kilblanes have been identified elsewhere in southern and western Scotland. This was the seat of a bishop from early times, and retains its cathedral as the parish kirk.

Duncansby Head (Highland) 'Cape of Dungal's place'. *Dungal* (Gaelic personal name); *by* (Old Norse) 'village, place'. Noted in the *Orkneyinga Saga*, c. 1225, as Dungalsbaer. Dungal, a Pictish chief, clearly made himself memorable to the Norsemen, for his name to be preserved. This cliff with its sea-stacks is at the north-east tip of Scotland.

Dundee Commonly derived as the 'fort of Daig'. *Dùn* (Scottish Gaelic) 'fortified place'; *Daig* (personal name) of unknown connection. The fort presumably would have been on the high ground of Dundee Law where the thirteenth-century Dundee Castle, long since destroyed, once stood. Other possible derivations include *Dun-dubh* (Scottish Gaelic) 'dark hill', or *Dun-Dè* (Scottish Gaelic genitive of *Dia*) 'hill of God'. In early records there are various renderings: Donde 1177; Dunde 1199; Dundho, Dundo 1200. Dundee, Scotland's fourth city in population, has long been an important place, and for a time in the late nineteenth century was the world's main jute manufacturing town; 'jam, jute and journalism' were said to be its specialities, and its name is still linked with fruit cake and marmalade. It was also an important whaling port, and Captain Scott's vessel *Discovery*, built in 1901 on the lines of a Dundee whaler, is preserved in dock here.

Dundonnell (Highland) 'Donald's fort'. *Dùn* (Scottish Gaelic) 'fort'; *Domhnuill* (Scottish Gaelic personal name, with the sense of 'world chief') 'Donald'.

Dundurn (Perth & Kinross) 'Fort of the fist'. *Dùn* (Scottish Gaelic) 'fort'; *dorn* (Scottish Gaelic) 'fist'. Noted in 603 as Duin Duirn, it was a Pictish stronghold.

Dunedin *See* Edinburgh

Dunfermline (Fife). The first part is *dùn* (Scottish Gaelic) 'hill' or 'fort', the latter part is of uncertain derivation, and may be a version of a Pictish proper name. Records show Dumfermelyn 1100; Dumferlin 1124; Dunferlyne 1375. The Gaelic name is Dun Pharlain, perhaps by association with the personal name Parlain, as in MacFarlane. The town became the capital of Malcolm Canmore's dynasty; its abbey, founded in 1072, is a royal burial place. The Stuarts had a palace here whose ruins are still to be seen. Charles I was born in it in 1600.

Dungeon (Dumfries & Galloway) There are two Dungeons, separated by the Rhinn of Kells, and both are steep enclosed corries with lochs.

Dunino (Fife) 'Hill on the open moor', from Scottish Gaelic *dùn,* 'hill' and *aonach,* 'ridge, open moor'; noted as Duneynach, 1250.

Dunipace (Falkirk) 'Hill of the pass'. *Din* (Cumbric) 'hill', rendered into Gaelic *dùn, y* (Cumbric) 'of the'; *pás* (Cumbric) 'hill pass'. Found in 1183 as Dunipast.

Dunkeld (Perth & Kinross) 'Fort of the Caledonians'. *Dùn* (Scottish Gaelic) 'fort'; *Chailleainn* (Scottish Gaelic) 'Caledonians' – referring to the tribe of Picts who had a stronghold here in the first millennium AD. Early records reveal the name as Duincaillen 865; Dun-calden and Dunicallenn c. 1000. The town was in the ninth century the religious centre of the country, between the abandoning of Iona and the ascendance of St Andrews, and it retains its cathedral, now the parish church. Its most notable bishop was Gavin Douglas (c. 1474–1522), poet and translator of *The Aeneid.*

Dunlop (Dumfries & Galloway) 'Fort of the bend'. *Dùn* (Scottish Gaelic) 'fort'; *luib* (Scottish Gaelic) 'bend'. This small town gives its name both to a well-known kind of cheese and (through the surname of a locally-born inventor) a famous tyre company.

Dunnet (Highland) 'Fort on the headland'. *Dùn* (Scottish Gaelic) 'fort'; *hofudr* (Old Norse) 'headland'. Dunnet Head is the most northerly point on the Scottish mainland.

Dunnichen (Angus) 'Nechtan's fort'. *Dùn* (Scottish Gaelic) 'fort'; perhaps replacing a Brythonic–Pictish *din* of the same meaning;

Nechtan (gaelicised form of a Pictish personal name, Nehton). Probably named for the early seventh century Pictish King Nechtan, and noted as Duin Nechtain in the *Annals of Tighernach*. Close to here in 686 the army of Bridei macBili, the Pictish king, defeated the invading Angles under Ecgfrith.

Dunollie (Argyll & Bute) 'Ollach's Fort'. *Dùn* (Scottish Gaelic) 'fort'; *Ollaig* (Old Irish personal name). In the *Annals of Tighernach*, from an eighth-century source, it is Duin Ollaigh. Strategically placed to control the Firth of Lorn and the Sound of Mull, and a major fortress of the Scots, it remained an important castle until relatively modern times.

Dunoon (Argyll & Bute) 'Fort (on) the river'. *Dùn* (Scottish Gaelic) 'fort'; *obhainn* (Scottish Gaelic adjectival variant of *abh*) 'river'. Recorded as Dunhoven 1270; Dunnovane 1476. Traces of a twelfth-century castle, and an even earlier fort, can be found on a rock above the pier of this resort on the Clyde, commercial centre of the Cowal district.

Dunottar (Aberdeenshire) 'Fort on the shelving ground'. *Dùn* (Scottish Gaelic) 'fort'; *faithir* (Scottish Gaelic) 'shelved or terraced slope'. The reference is to the slope on the landward side towards the castle on its rocky outcrop. The oldest reference is Duin-foither, 681. The crown and other 'honours' of Scotland were kept here during the Cromwellian war, but removed and hidden in the nearby church of Kinneff before the castle was taken.

Dunphail (Moray) 'Fort with the palisade'. *Dùn* (Scottish Gaelic) 'fort'; *fàl* (Scottish Gaelic) 'hedge, palisade'. Noted c. 1250 as Dunfel. The reference is to an early fortification of wood rather than of stone.

Dunragit (Dumfries & Galloway) 'Fort of Rheged'. *Dùn* (Scottish Gaelic) 'fort'. This was a centre of the one-time Cumbric kingdom of Rheged, for a time part of the kingdom of Strathclyde which stretched from Dumbarton to Westmorland. The mote of Dunragit shows the site of the fort.

Dunrobin (Highland) 'Robert's fort'. *Dùn* (Scottish Gaelic) 'fort'. Recorded in 1401 as Dunrobyn. The Robert in question is the third earl of Sutherland. Dunrobin was their stronghold, but there is the remnant of a broch close by which long antedates the castle.

Dunrossness (Shetland) 'Cape of the roaring whirlpool'. *Dynr* (Old Norse) 'loud noise'; *röst* (Old Norse) 'whirlpool'; *nes* (Old Norse) 'cape, point'. There are numerous tidal races called Roosts in the Northern Isles.

Duns (Borders) 'Fortified hill'. *Dùn* (Scottish Gaelic) 'hill', came to acquire the sense of 'fortified hill'; the *s* is a later addition, possibly meant as a plural; it is found in this form in 1296. The former main town of Berwickshire, it lies at the foot of a hill called Duns Law. An older town, on the hill itself, was razed in 1542. The medieval scholar Duns Scotus (c. 1265–1308), whose name gives the word 'dunce', is reputed to have been born here.

Dunsinane (Perth & Kinross) Perhaps 'hill of the paps, or nipples'. *Dùn* (Scottish Gaelic) 'hill'; *sine* (Scottish Gaelic, plural *sineachan*) 'nipple'. Recorded in the *Pictish Chronicle* c. 970, as Dunsinoen. This was one of the favourites among the relatively few figurative names given to hills by the Gaels: compare Maiden Pap in Caithness. The name is well-known from Shakespeare's *Macbeth*.

Dunstaffnage (Argyll & Bute) 'Fort of the pillared cape'. *Dùn* (Scottish Gaelic) 'fort'; *stafr* (Old Norse) 'staff, column'; *nes* (Old Norse) 'cape, point'. It is first found noted in 1322 as Ardstofniche. This was the main fortress of the Dalriadic Scots and, like the nearby Dunollie, always a strategic castle.

Duntocher (West Dunbartonshire) 'Causeway fort'. *Dùn* (Scottish Gaelic) 'fort'; *tóchar* (Scottish Gaelic) 'causeway, road'. It was a Roman road here, by the end of the Antonine Wall. A Perthshire and Aberdeenshire township name, Kintocher ('head of the road') has the same source.

Dunvegan (Highland) Possibly 'fort of the few'. *Dùn* (Scottish Gaelic) 'fort'; *beagain* (Scottish Gaelic) 'few in number, small.' The significance is far from apparent. It may refer to an early siege. But an Old Norse personal name, *Began*, is more likely. Recorded as Dunbegane 1498, Dunveggane 1517, Dunnevegane 1553. This castle in northwest Skye is the ancestral home of the Macleods.

Durness (Highland) 'Headland of the deer'. *Dyr* (Old Norse) 'deer'; *nes* (Old Norse) 'headland'. Noted c. 1230 as Dyrnes. This village is the most northwesterly on mainland Britain, situated on a remote headland where the deer still roam.

Durno (Aberdeenshire) 'Pebbly place'. *Dornach* (Scottish Gaelic) 'pebbly'. The remains of a very large Roman camp here suggest that this was Agricola's base for the battle of Mons Graupius (AD 84). *See* Dornie, Dornoch.

Duror (Highland) 'Hard water'. The name is that of the river in Glen Duror, from *dur,* (Scottish Gaelic) 'hard' and *dobhar* (Scottish Gaelic) 'water'.

Durrisdeer (Aberdeenshire) 'Entrance to the forest'. *Dorus* (Scottish Gaelic) 'entrance'; *doire* (Scottish Gaelic) 'forest'. Noted in 1275 as Durisdeir. But the south Deeside location and forest of Durris is likely to be from *dubh* (Scottish Gaelic) 'black' and *ros* (Old Gaelic) 'wood'.

Duthil (Highland) 'North side', from *tuathail* (Scottish Gaelic) 'north'. Noted as Dothol, c. 1230.

Dyce (Aberdeenshire) Possibly 'southwards'. *Deis* (Scottish Gaelic locative of *deas*) 'to the south'. This may have been a reference to the location of the settlement here, on a south-facing slope. Alternatively, the meaning may be *dys* (Old Norse) 'cairn'.

Dysart (Fife) 'Desert place, hermit's place'. *Diseart* (Scottish Gaelic) 'hermit's place'. Recorded as Disard, c. 1210. The hermit was St Serf who lived here in a cave for a time, and had a conversation with the Devil. Once a separate town in its own right, now an eastern suburb of Kirkcaldy. The name is also found as a farm name near Montrose in Angus, and in other localities.

E

E, River (Highland) A candidate for the shortest name in Britain, this mountain stream joins the Fechlin (Scottish Gaelic *fiach*, 'worthy', *linne*, 'waterfall, pool'), above Foyers on the east side of Loch Ness. It stems from Old Norse *àa*, 'water', cognate with Old English *ea*, as in Eye.

Eaglesham (East Renfrewshire) Possibly 'church village'. *Eaglais* (Scottish Gaelic) 'church'; *ham* (Old English) 'village'. Recorded as Egilshame 1158, Eglishame 1309.

Earlsferry (Fife) This tiny royal burgh, now a single community with adjacent Elie, was established in the twelfth century as a ferry point to North Berwick, across the Firth of Forth, by the Macduff earls of Fife. Its name suggests that by the later 1100s Gaelic names were no longer being given in Fife.

Earlston (Borders) Possibly 'Earcil's hill'. *Earcil* (personal name); *dun* (Old English) 'hill'. Early records show Ercheldon 1144; Ercildune 1180. This was the home of 'True Thomas', the Rhymer.

Earlstoun (Dumfries & Galloway) 'Earl's place'. This locality, with its loch, at the southern end of the Glenkens, takes its name from the earls of Galloway.

Earn, River, Strath and **Loch** (Perth & Kinross) Traditionally derived as 'Erin'. This name *Eireann* (Old Irish Gaelic) 'of Erin', has been taken to demonstrate the eastward expansion of the Scots from Dàl Riada in the sixth and seventh centuries, awarding familiar names to new landscapes. *Erin* is an ancient Gaelic name linking a mythical goddess-queen with the land itself. But the Earn is a significant river, and most rivers bear names from a much earlier date. It is more probable that it is an early- or pre-Celtic river-name, from a root-form *ar-* indicating flowing water, found in other river-names such as Deveron, and common in parts of France. There is also an Earn Water in East Renfrewshire (*see* Mearns). The Irish River Erne and its lough have been derived from an Irish Gaelic tribal name *Erni* or *Ernai*, but the original name may again have been that of the river.

Eas Coul Aulin (Highland) 'The fine cataract of the cleft'. *Eas* (Scottish Gaelic) 'water, waterfall'; *cùil* (Scottish Gaelic) 'niche, cleft'; *aluinn* (Scottish Gaelic) 'beautiful'. This is one of Scotland's highest waterfalls, falling almost vertically down a mountainside in Assynt.

Eassie (Angus; other regions) 'Water'. *Eas* (Scottish Gaelic) 'water, waterfall'; the *-ie* ending, corresponding to Scottish Gaelic *-aidh,* is often found in river-names in regions where Pictish was spoken. A frequent local place name, sometimes found as Essie or Essy. But Essich, near Inverness, appears to show the Gaelic locative suffix *-ach:* 'place by the water'.

East Kilbride (South Lanarkshire) 'Church of (St) Bride'. *Cill* (Scottish Gaelic) 'church'; *Brigid* name of a saint who took on many of the attributes of Brid, the legendary Celtic goddess of fire and poetry. Although East Kilbride was designated as Scotland's first New Town in 1947, the old village here was recorded as Kellebride in 1180. The 'East' was added later to distinguish it from West Kilbride, thirty miles away, near to the Ayrshire coast.

East Linton (East Lothian) 'Flax enclosure'. *Lin* (Old English) 'flax' (compare 'linen'); *tun* (Old English) 'enclosure, village'. It was recorded as Lintun in 1127. The 'East' was added later to distinguish it from West Linton, thirty miles south-west, by the Pentland Hills.

East Wemyss *See* Wemyss.

Easter This typically Scottish form of 'east' is from Old Norse *austarr,* 'to eastward', and is found in many area and local names, in contraposition with 'Wester'. In some locations, however, the two forms indicate 'upstream' or 'downstream' rather than a geographical orientation.

Eathie (Highland) 'Ford' or 'ford stream', from *àth* (Scottish Gaelic) 'ford'. The Gaelic name is *Athaidh,* the *-aidh* suffix is common on stream names in the Pictish parts of the country. Ethie in Angus is cognate with this, and there are numerous local examples elsewhere.

Ecclefechan (Dumfries & Galloway) 'Fechin's church' from *eaglais* (Scottish Gaelic) 'church'; *Fechin* (Irish Gaelic personal name), the saintly seventh-century Irish abbot from Meath, whose followers helped in the evangelisation of Scotland. An alternative derivation is the Cumbric *egles-bychan,* 'little church'. Noted as Eglesfeghan, 1303. The birthplace of the writer Thomas Carlyle (1795–1881), whose home can still be visited.

Eccles (Dumfries & Galloway) 'Church', from Cumbric *egles,* derived from Latin *ecclesia.* This tiny location near Thornhill in Nithsdale was an early church site. There is another Eccles near Coldstream in the Borders district.

Eck, Loch (Argyll & Bute) 'Horse loch'. *Loch* (Scottish Gaelic) lake, loch'; *each* (Scottish Gaelic) 'horse'. The animal in question may have been a water kelpie, or *each uisge.*

Eday (Orkney) 'Island of the isthmus'. *Eidh* (Old Norse) 'isthmus'; and *ey* (Old Norse) 'island'.

Edderton (Highland) 'Place between mounds'. *Eadar* (Scottish Gaelic) 'between'; *dùn* (Scottish Gaelic) mound, hillock', referring to the glacial drumlin hills of the area. Recorded as Ederthayn in 1225.

Eddleston (Borders) 'Edulf's place', from the late twelfth century. *Edulf* (Old English personal name) and *tun* (Old English) 'farmstead'. But it is previously recorded as first Penteiacob (Cumbric) 'Headland of James's town'; then Gillemorestun, from *Gillemor* (Scottish Gaelic) 'Gilmour' (follower of Mary) and *tun* – indicating three proprietors from three different language groups before the name became fixed, with Edoluestone found c. 1200.

Eddrachillis (Highland) 'Place between two kyles'. *Eadar* (Scottish Gaelic) 'between'; *da*, 'two'; *chaolais* (Scottish Gaelic) 'kyles, narrows'.

Eden, River (Fife; Borders) This river-name, also found in Cumberland and Kent in England, is of uncertain origin. The Cumbrian Eden is *Ituna* on Ptolemy's map, and has been traced back to a conjectural Primitive Welsh *idon*. There may be more than one source.

Edin- This prefix comes from Scottish Gaelic *aodann*, 'face, forehead', both human and topographical. It is normally found in places where there is a steep or rocky hill-face, as in Edinbanchory Hill, near Kildrummy in Aberdeenshire, named after the farm at its foot, 'hill face among mountains'.

Edinample (Highland) 'Face of the cauldron'. *Aodann* (Scottish Gaelic) 'face'; *ambuill* (Scottish Gaelic) 'of the cauldron, or vat': a reference to the waterfall at this location.

Edinburgh 'Fort of the rock face'. *Eiddyn* (Cumbric) 'rock face', cognate with Gaelic *aodann*; and *burh* (Old English) 'stronghold'. The latter element was a replacement for the original prefix *din* (Cumbric) 'stronghold' or 'fort'. Prior to the Angles' arrival, it was a stronghold of the Britons, recorded by the bard Taliesin as Dineiddyn. Dùn Eideann remains the Gaelic name for the city, preserved also in Dunedin, New Zealand. The castle early became a royal stronghold and by the early Middle Ages Edinburgh was the largest town in Scotland, and remained so until overtaken by Glasgow at the start of the nineteenth century. Long the *de facto* capital, its status was confirmed by the establishment of the Court of Session in 1532 and the building of Parliament House in 1632. From 1999 it has been again the seat of the Scottish Parliament.

Ednam (Borders) 'Place on the Eden', recorded as Aedenaham, c. 1105; Hedenham, 1316. *See* Eden.

Edradour (Perth & Kinross) 'Between two waters'. *Eadar* (Scottish Gaelic) 'between'; *dà*, 'two'; *dhobhar* (Brythonic–Scottish Gaelic) 'waters'.

Edrom (Borders) 'Township on the Adder'. This is one of the few Scottish places with the Old English *-ham* suffix, which seems to have become obsolete around the time the Anglians were establishing themselves in the south-east. The prefix is the river-name Adder.

Edzell (Angus) This has been tentatively recognised as 'running water dale,' from *áa* (Old Norse) 'running water'; and *dalr* (Old Norse) 'valley'; like Edale in the English Peak District, though this is an odd location to find a Norse name. It is found in 1250 as Adel. An agricultural centre, it has given its name to a potato variety, the 'Edzell Blue'.

Egilsay (Orkney; Shetland) Possibly 'church island'. *Eaglais* (Scottish Gaelic) 'church'; *ey* (Old Norse) 'island'. Noted as Egilsey in the *Orkneyinga Saga*, c. 1225. The Orkney isle still has the ruins of St Magnus Church, but the hybrid formation is unusual, especially here, and Egil's (Old Norse personal name) isle has also been suggested for both islands.

Eglinton (North Ayrshire) Farm of Aegel's folk. *Aegel* (Old English personal name); *ing*, 'of the people'; *tun* (Old English) 'farmstead'. Noted as Eglunstone, 1205.

Eigg (Highland) *Egg*. Probably '(island with) the notch'. *Eag* (Scottish Gaelic) 'notch, nick, gap'. On this Inner Hebridean isle, a wide rift or notch runs through from southeast to northwest separating its northern plateau from the An Sgurr ridge in the south. Recorded as Egge 1292, Egg 1654.

Eighe, Beinn (Highland) In Scottish Gaelic, *eighe* means both 'ice' and 'file', or 'notch'; either could fit this prominent Torridon mountain (2898ft/1010m), though its long ridge makes 'file' more likely, as with Càrn Eige on the Ross–Inverness border.

Eilean Donan (Highland) *Aylan Donnan*. 'Donnan's isle'. *Eilean* (Scottish Gaelic) 'island'; *Donnan* (Old Gaelic personal name). Found as Elandonan, c. 1425. St Donnàn of Eigg is commemorated in numerous places, mostly called Kildonan, from Kintyre to Sutherland. The castle of Eilean Donan played an important part in West Highland history until its destruction in the Jacobite Rising of 1719.

Eildon (Borders) This famous triple set of peaks, called Trimontium by the Romans, and of volcanic origin, may have a hybrid name, from *àill* (Scottish Gaelic) 'rock', and *dún* (Old English) 'hill'. The form Aeldona is found around 1120. The impressiveness of the Eildons is greater than their height (1330ft/407m) might suggest; the view of them from the south was Sir Walter Scott's favourite. Many legends have grown up around them. The fairy kingdom, whose queen spirited Thomas the Rhymer away, was believed to lie underneath. There is a Bronze Age hill-fort here, and a large Roman camp below at Newstead, many artefacts from which are now in the Museum of Scotland, in Edinburgh.

Eishort, Loch (Highland) 'Isthmus firth', from *eidh* (Old Norse) 'isthmus', and *fjordr* (Old Norse) 'firth', with the addition of Scottish Gaelic *loch.*

Elcho (Aberdeenshire) 'Place of rocks'. *Aileach* (Scottish Gaelic) 'rocky'. Recorded as Elyoch in the thirteenth century.

Elderslie (Renfrewshire) 'Alder lea'. *Elloern* (Old English) 'alder'; *lí* (Old English) 'meadow'. Found in 1398 as Eldersly. This was the estate of William Wallace's father, and lays claim to being the hero's birthplace.

'Electric Brae' *See* Croy

Elgin (Moray) Perhaps 'Little Ireland'. *Ealg* (Scottish Gaelic) early name for Ireland, but also, perhaps by extension, 'noble, excellent'; *-in* (Scottish Gaelic diminutive suffix) 'little'. The name is found in its present form in 1140. Such a name may have been given by descendants of the original Scots settlers from Ireland to remind themselves of the mother country. It may simply mean 'worthy place', but it is likely that Scots from Dàl Riada established themselves in Moray in the tenth century, via the Great Glen. Eilginn is the Gaelic name. Compare Blair Atholl and Glenelg. The county town of Moray, it has many fine buildings including the ruins of its cathedral, once 'the lantern of the North'.

Elgol (Highland) 'Fold of the Stranger', has been put forward as the source of this Skye name: *Fàl* (Scottish Gaelic) 'fold'; *a' ghoill* (Scottish Gaelic) 'of the Gall, or stranger'.

Elie (Fife) The form seems close to *eilean* (Scottish Gaelic) 'island', and the present harbour was an island until the late eighteenth century; but 'place of the tomb' has also been proposed, from *ealadh* (Scottish Gaelic) 'tomb'; or *ayle* (Scots) 'covered cemetery'. There was once such a cemetery here. It is recorded as Elye 1491, The Alie c. 1600.

Elliot (Angus) 'Mound'. This stream-name seems to stem from Scottish Gaelic *eileach,* 'mill-dam, weir, mound'; and to be cognate with Elliock near Sanquhar in Dumfries & Galloway.

Ellon (Aberdeenshire) Possibly 'green plain or meadow', from *àilean*

(Scottish Gaelic) 'green place, meadow'. This derivation suits the location in the Ythan valley; though, as there are islands in the river here, *eilean* (Scottish Gaelic) 'island', is just as appropriate. It was recorded in the *Book of Deer*, c. 1150, as Helian and Eilan, which suggest the latter form.

Elphin (Highland) 'Rocky peak'. *Ailbhinn* (Scottish Gaelic) 'rock peak'.

Elphinstone (East Lothian) Perhaps 'Alpin's fort'; from Scottish Gaelic *Alpin* (personal name) and *dún*, 'fort'. Found as Elfyngston, around 1320. Perhaps under Anglian influence, a number of names in the south-east have been converted from -dun to -ton. See Earlston. Port Elphinstone in Aberdeenshire is a modern name, from the landowner Sir Robert Elphinstone.

Elrick (Highland; Aberdeenshire) This name is found in a number of localities. It is cognate with Elrig (Dumfries & Galloway) and is also found as Eldrick. A derivation has been proposed from Scottish Gaelic *eilerg,* derived by metathesis of *r* and *l* from Old Irish Gaelic *erelc,* 'ambush', with the sense here of 'deer trap': a cul de sac into which hunted deer were driven for slaughter.

Elvan Water (South Lanarkshire) 'Bright stream', from Cumbric *al-gwen,* 'very white'. Noted c. 1170 as Elwan, Alewyn. It joins the Clyde at Elvanfoot.

Embo (Highland) 'Eyvind's steading'. *Eyvin* (Old Norse personal name); *bol* (Old Norse, shortened form of *bolstadr*) 'farmstead'. Noted as Ethenboll, c. 1230.

Enard Bay (Highland) 'Eyvind's bay'. *Eyvind* (Old Norse personal name); *fjordr* (Old Norse) 'fiord, bay'. In 1632 it is found as Eynort. The English 'bay' is a later addition.

Enzie (Dumfries & Galloway; Aberdeenshire) *Ing-ie.* 'Angled nook'. *Eang* (Scottish Gaelic) 'point of land, gusset'. The northern Enzie is found as l'Annoy, 1295, Aynye, 1497.

Eoropaidh (Western Isles) 'Beach village'. The name of this most northerly village on Lewis is a gaelicised form of Old Norse *eyrar-by,* 'shore settlement'.

Erbusaig (Highland) 'Erp's bay'. *Erp* (Old Norse personal name, originally Pictish and related to Old Gaelic *Erc*) *-aig* a Gaelic form of *vik* (Old Norse) 'bay'.

Erchless (Highland) 'Place on the Glass'. *Air* (Scottish Gaelic) 'on the'; *glais* (Scottish Gaelic river-name). Found as Herkele, c. 1220. The castle here is the seat of Clan Chisholm. See Glass.

Eriboll (Highland) 'Farm on the ridge'. *Eyri* (Old Norse) 'tongue of land'; *ból* (from Old Norse *bolstadr*) 'farm, steading'. In 1499 it is noted as Erribull. It has been suggested that names in which *bolstadr* is reduced to its first syllable, in places on the north and western mainland, in the Inner Hebrides and in many cases in the Outer Hebrides, represent a Gaelic influence, where the stress is placed on a word's first syllable rather than the second, as in Old Norse. The name has been linked with Scottish Gaelic *earball*, 'tail' but with a toponymic sense of 'ridge'. The Gaelic name is Euraboll, however.

Ericht, River and **Loch** (Highland; Perth & Kinross) Perhaps 'beauteous', from *eireachdas* (Scottish Gaelic) 'beauteous', which can refer to landscape. Apart from the Badenoch Ericht, another River Ericht flows into the Isla above Coupar Angus. The Erichdie Water in Atholl may be related though it has also been linked to *eireachda* (Scottish Gaelic) 'assembly'.

Eriskay (Western Isles) 'Eric's island'. *Erik* (Old Norse personal name), and *ey* (Old Norse) 'island'. Noted as Yriskay, 1558. The Gaelic form is Eiriosgaigh.

Erisort, Loch (Western Isles) 'Eric's firth,' from *Erik* (Old Norse personal name), and *fjord,* 'firth'.

Errol (Perth & Kinross) This name remains of indefinite derivation, though it has been tentatively associated with Airlie, as from *ar ole* (Brythonic–Pictish) 'on the ravine', but there is no ravine here on the Carse of Gowrie. It is noted as Erolyn, c. 1190. The Hay family, hereditary constables of Scotland, take their title of earls of Errol from here. Port Errol on Cruden Bay, Aberdeenshire, is a modern name.

Erskine (Renfrewshire) Possibly 'high marsh', from *ard* (Scottish Gaelic) 'high', and *sescenn* (Scottish Gaelic) 'marsh'; but a derivation from Cumbric *ir ysgyn*, 'green ascent' has also been put forward. Noted as Erskin, 1225. This is the site of the last bridge over the Clyde as it widens into the firth.

Esk, River (Angus; Dumfries & Galloway; East Lothian) 'Water'. A basic river-name. *Uisge* (Scottish Gaelic) 'water'; the numerous Esks testify to its currency. From a pre- or early-Celtic root *esc*; Welsh Usk is related. Noted as Esce (Lothian), 800; Esche (Angus), 1369. It appears to be a preferred name for rivers reaching the sea close to each other, like the North and South Esks which flow into the Montrose basin, and those which flow between the Pentland and Moorfoot Hills to reach the sea at Musselburgh.

Eskdalemuir (Dumfries & Galloway) 'Moor of the Esk valley'. *Dalr* (Old Norse) 'valley, dale'; *muir* (Scots, from Old English *mor)* 'moor'. This community, high up in the valley of the White Esk, holds a weather-recording station which often notes very low temperatures, and a most authentic-looking Thai-style Buddhist monastery.

Esslemont (Aberdeenshire) 'Hill of spells'. *Eoisle* (Scottish Gaelic) 'spells, charms'; *monadh* (Scottish Gaelic) 'mountain, hill'. Noted as Essilmontht, pre-1600. The name has alternatively been derived from a Brythonic word cognate with Welsh *iselfynnydd,* 'low hill'. *See* Tullynessle.

Etive, River and **Loch** (Argyll & Bute) The Gaelic name is Eitche, which has been taken to be from *Eitig* (Old Irish feminine proper name) 'foul one', indicating a malevolent tutelary spirit, inspired perhaps by the turbulent Falls of Lora at the entrance to the loch. A connection with *èite* (Scottish Gaelic) 'white pebble' has also been suggested. A pre-tenth-century manuscript source has Loch-n-Eite.

Ettrick (Borders; Argyll & Bute) The name of the Border village is taken from the river on which it stands, the Ettrick Water. This also applies to other nearby places: Ettrick Forest, Ettrick Pen (the latter a Cumbric word) Ettrickbridge, etc. The first part may be related to *eadar* (Scottish Gaelic) 'between' (see Edradour), and a resemblance to Etteridge in Glen Truim (Gaelic 'between two waters') has been noted, but the suffixes are not related. There is also Ettrick Bay on the west coast of Bute. Another suggestion is *atre* (Cumbric) 'playful', as a description of the river here. However, the origin for this name is unattested, and it may be from a pre-Celtic root. The forms Ethric and Etryk are recorded from around 1235. The Border name is associated with James Hogg (1770–1835), 'The Ettrick Shepherd', one of Scotland's finest imaginative writers, who spent his life here.

Evanton (Highland) 'Evan's town'. This village on the shore of the Cromarty Firth was founded around 1810 by the landowner Evan Fraser of Balconie (Scottish Gaelic *bailcnidh,* 'strong place') in the old parish of Kiltearn.

Evie (Orkney) This Orkney parish name, found as Efju in the *Orkneyinga Saga* (c. 1225) has been suggested as 'eddy' from Old Norse *efja,* 'backwater, eddy'.

Ewe *See* Kinlochewe

Eye, Loch (Highland) 'Loch of the isthmus'. *Eidh* (Old Norse) 'isthmus', giving Scottish Gaelic *uidh;* the Gaelic name is Loch na h-uidhe. The name of this small loch on the Tarbat peninsula is of interest partly for its different derivation from the River Eye (*see* Eyemouth). The Eye peninsula in Lewis also has the 'isthmus' sense.

Eyemouth (Borders) 'At the mouth of the Eye Water'. The river-name is tautologically derived from *éa* (Old English) 'river'; 'water' was added when the old meaning was lost.

Eynhallow (Orkney) 'Holy isle'. In the *Orkneyinga Saga* of c. 1225, it is recorded as Eyin Helga, from Old Norse *ey,* 'island', and *heilag-r,* 'saint'.

F

Fair Isle (Shetland) 'Sheep Island'. *Faer* (Old Norse) 'sheep'; isle (probably English translation of Old Norse *ey*) 'island'. A record of 1529 shows Faray. The remote Fair Isle, lying midway between Shetland and Orkney, was settled by the Vikings as a staging post to which they brought sheep. A place-name exactly parallel to it is found in that of the Faeroe Islands, and for the same reasons. Its distinctive knitwear patterns are said to have been influenced by shipwrecked sailors of the Spanish Armada in 1588.

Fala (Borders) 'Sheepfold'. *Fàl* (Scottish Gaelic) 'pen' (for strayed sheep or cattle), 'wall', with -*ach* (Scottish Gaelic) 'field' ending.

Falkirk 'Speckled church'. *Fawe* (Scots) 'speckled'; *kirke* (Scots) 'church' from Old English *cirice*. Most Gaelic names were maintained in an approximation of their original form, with a Scots pronunciation, but this is a Scots translation of the original form, Egglesbreth, from *eaglais*, (Scottish Gaelic) 'church', *breac*, (Scottish Gaelic) 'speckled', first recorded in the early twelfth century. It is presumed that a settlement here, predating the industrial town by more than 600 years, had a church that was built of variegated stone. It was recorded as Faukirke in 1298, Falkirk from 1458. Close to here the Highland army of Prince Charles Edward Stuart won its last victory in 1745 before the final defeat at Culloden; in 1298 the forces of Edward I defeated the Scots under Wallace. In the eighteenth century the Falkirk Tryst was the country's main market for black Highland cattle. The town is now centre of a unitary local authority.

Falkland (Fife) The origin of the name of this burgh with its Renaissance royal palace remains uncertain. Possible associations with falconry have been made from *falca* (Old English) 'falcon'. One authority has drawn a connection with the town's regal status in proposing the derivation *folc* (Old English) 'people's, *land*' (English), i.e. Crown property. (Faulkland in Somerset derives from these sources). Early records show Falleland 1128, Falkland 1150, Falecklen 1165. The palace has strong associations with the Stewarts: here the duke of Rothesay was starved to death (by some accounts) in 1402; from here James V escaped the 'tutelage' of the earl of Angus in 1528.

Falloch, Glen (Stirling) Possibly 'Glen of hiding'. *Gleann* (Scottish Gaelic) 'valley', *Falach* (Scottish Gaelic) 'place of concealment', though a connection with Irish Gaelic *fail*, 'ring', has also been suggested.

Fannich, River, Loch and **mountain massif** (Highland) *Fàn* (Scottish Gaelic) indicates a gentle slope, and the Gaelic name *Fanaich* may be derived from this; though the frontal slopes are formidable, the dip slopes, more important for summer grazing, are fairly gentle. It has also been surmised that it may be a Brythonic–Pictish water-name, cognate with the Welsh verb *gwanegu*, 'to rise in waves', and perhaps with an older, continental Celtic root-form *ven* or *van*, as in Lacus Venetus, the latinised Gaulish name of Lake Constance.

Fare, Hill of (Aberdeenshire) 'Watch hill'. *Faire* (Scottish Gaelic) 'watchfulness, sentinel', with 'hill' substituted for Gaelic *cnoc* in the post-Gaelic era. This prominent Midmar hill rises 1545ft/487m above Strath Dee.

Farg, Glen (Perth & Kinross) 'Ferocious glen'. *Gleann* (Scottish Gaelic) 'valley, glen'; *fearg* (Scottish Gaelic) 'anger'. This is a notably steep and winding glen.

Farigaig *See* Farr

Farr (Highland) Most likely 'upper ground'. *For* (Scottish Gaelic) 'superior'; though an Old Gaelic prefix *far*, 'lower', has also been suggested for such Farr- names as Farigaig, from *far* (Scottish Gaelic) 'below', and *gàg* (Scottish Gaelic) 'cleft, ravine'. The local topography is the best guide.

Farrar, River and **Strath** (Highland) First recorded on Ptolemy's map of Scotland, c. AD 150, as *Varar*, this much-discussed name of uncertain derivation has been taken to indicate a non-Celtic but Indo-European language spoken in the territory of the Picts. Oddly, the upper reaches of the river have become called Glen Strathfarrar, perhaps indicating uncertainty as to how the valley should be classed.

Faskally (Perth & Kinross; Highland) 'Stance by the ferry'. *Fas* (Scottish Gaelic) is an obsolete term for 'house, dwelling', but in place-names it has the sense of 'stance' (see Duffus); *calaidh* (Scottish Gaelic) 'ferry'. Noted in 1611 as Faschailye. The location of a former ferry across the Tummel; the modern dam at Pitlochry has created Loch Faskally here. There is also a Faskally in Strath Kildonan, Sutherland. The *Fas-* element in many local place-names indicates the extent of sheep and cattle-droving across the countryside; not only to the market 'trysts' but in the seasonal process of transhumance: moving herds between higher and lower grazing grounds.

Faslane (Argyll & Bute) 'Stance on the enclosed land'. *Fas* (Scottish Gaelic) 'stance', *lainne* (Scottish Gaelic locative form of *lann*) 'enclosed ground, field'. Found in this form in 1531.

Fasnakyle (Highland) 'Stance in the wood'. *Fas* (Scottish Gaelic) 'stance'; *na,* of'; *coille* (Scottish Gaelic) 'wood'. The old cattle-stance is now the site of a hydro-electric power-station.

Fassifern (Highland) 'Stance of the alder trees'. *Fas* (Scottish Gaelic) 'stance'; *fearna* (Scottish Gaelic) 'of the alders'. Also found as Fassfern. Noted as Faschefarne, 1553.

Fauldhouse (West Lothian) 'House on the fallow land'. *Falh* (Old English) 'fallow land'; 'house' from Old English *hus.*

Fearn (Highland) 'Place of the alders'. *Feàrna* (Scottish Gaelic) 'alder', but the name was transferred to this location when the original monastery at West Fearn, near Edderton, was refounded here as an abbey in 1227. Noted in 762 as Ferna; 1529 as Ferne. In Gaelic it was known as Manachainn Rois, 'monastery of Ross'. Fearnan by Loch Tay has the same derivation.

Fenwick (South Ayrshire) 'Dwelling in the fen', from Old English *fen,* 'marsh, fen', and *wic,* dwelling, farm. An Old English name in this district is unusual.

Ferintosh (Highland) 'The chief's holding'. *Fearann* (Scottish Gaelic) 'land, estate'; *toisich* (Scottish Gaelic) 'chief'. Noted as Ferintosky, 1499. This place, by Dingwall, was the principal whisky-distilling centre in the Highlands up to the eighteenth century.

Ferniehirst (Aberdeenshire) 'Alder wood'. *Feàrna* (Scottish Gaelic) 'alder tree', with *hirst* (Old English) 'wood'.

Ferryport-on-Craig (Fife) There were several ferries across the Firth of Tay from Fife to Dundee and its environs, and this name appears to have been current from around the sixteenth century. The 'Craig' (Scottish Gaelic *carraig,* 'rock') affirms the steep cliff-bound aspect of the Fife side.

Feshie, River and **Glen** (Highland) 'Boggy meadowland'. *Féith* (Scottish Gaelic) 'boggy place'; *-isidh* (Scottish Gaelic) suffix denoting pasture-land, derived from *innse* (Scottish Gaelic) meaning 'meadow' as well as 'island'.

Fetlar (Shetland) The derivation of the island's name has been suggested as coming from Old Norse *fetill,* 'belt'.

Fetter- 'Terraced slope, gradient', from *faithir* (Scottish Gaelic) 'slope'. Frequently found as a prefix to names in the north-east, the oddest being Fetterletter on the upper Ythan, which seems tautologous, with the latter part being *leitir* (Scottish Gaelic) 'hillside'. It may refer to the specific local topography.

Fettercairn (Aberdeenshire) 'Wooded slope'. *Faithir* (Scottish Gaelic) 'terraced slope, gradient'; *cardden* (Brythonic–Pictish) 'wood, copse'. Recorded in the *Pictish Chronicle* around 970 as Fotherkern.

Fetteresso (Aberdeenshire) 'Watery slope'. *Faithir* (Scottish Gaelic) 'terraced slope, gradient', *easach* (Scottish Gaelic) 'water-logged, watery'. Recorded as Fodresach in the *Pictish Chronicle*.

Feus This term, attached to a number of place-names, like Kedlock Feus in Fife, relates to land-ownership and describes a property held on a *feu* (Scots law term cognate with English 'fee'), by which the occupier paid an annual fee in cash or kind to the landlord.

Fiddich, River and **Glen** (Moray) Fidach was one of the ancient province names of Pictland and it seems likely that it is preserved in this name. The root element *fid* is likely to be from a personal name. The glen lies at the heart of the Speyside whisky-distilling area.

Fife The name of this ancient Pictish province, former county and present administrative region, has been attributed in legend to the personal name Fib, a legendary precursor of the Picts, one of the seven sons of Cruithne who gave their names to the provinces of Pictland. Recorded as Fib 1150, Fif 1165. The Gaelic form is Fiobha. *See* Fyvie.

Findhorn (Moray) 'White water'. *Fionn* (Scottish Gaelic) 'white'; *eren* (pre-Celtic river-name, *see* Earn). In Gaelic it is Uisge Eire. This name, with others, has sometimes been seen as a form of Irish Gaelic *Erin*. Noted in 1595 as Fyndorn. The village, famous for its 'New Age' community and its horticultural prodigies, derives its name from the river, at whose mouth it stands.

Findochty (Moray) 'House on the fair or bright land-measure'. *Fionn* (Scottish Gaelic) 'fair, bright'; *dabhach* (Scottish Gaelic 'land measure'), *taigh* (Scottish Gaelic) 'house'. Noted in 1440 as Fyndectifeilde; the 'field', expressing the land-measure sense in Scots, has not survived. The local pronunciation is *Finnechtie*.

Findon (Aberdeenshire; Highland) 'Fair hill', from Scottish Gaelic *fionn,* 'fair, bright', and *dùn,* 'hill'.

Fingal's Cave (Argyll & Bute) A fanciful name from the eighteenth century; the famous cave on the isle of Staffa does not feature in Fingalian legend. The Gaels called it the Cave of Music, aptly in view of Mendelssohn's overture composed following a visit here in 1829. *See* Staffa.

Finlaggan (Argyll & Bute) 'Fair hollow'; Scottish Gaelic *fionn,* 'fair, bright', and *lagan,* 'hollow'. Found as Finlagan, 1427. This Islay site, headquarters of the lords of the Isles in the fifteenth century, has also been identified with the sixth-century St Findlugan, whose name incorporates that of Old Irish *Lugh,* the Celtic sun-god.

Finnan, River and **Glen** (Highland) 'Fingon's Glen'. *Gleann* (Scottish Gaelic) 'glen'; *Fhionghuin* (Scottish Gaelic personal name). The clan name MacKinnon derives from Fingon. Here the Stewart standard was raised in August 1745, signalling the start of the last Jacobite Rising; a monumental tower capped by the statue of a Highlander commemorates the event.

Finnart (Argyll & Bute) 'Bright height'. *Fionn* (Scottish Gaelic) 'fair, bright'; *àird* (Scottish Gaelic) 'height'. The site of a tanker terminal, on Loch Long. There is also a Finnart on the east shore of Loch Ryan, in Galloway.

Finnieston (Glasgow) This name was given to the Glasgow district in 1768, for John Finnie, tutor to the landowner, Matthew Orr.

Finstown (Orkney) 'Finn's place'. *Finn* (Old Norse personal name); *ton* (Scots from Old English tun) 'settlement, place'. It has been suggested that David Phin, an Irish drummer, set up an inn here in 1811; but inns tend to be started where there is already a settlement, and therefore a name.

Fintaig, River and **Glen** (Highland) 'White river'. *Fionn* (Scottish Gaelic) 'white'; *t-àg* (Scottish Gaelic) diminutive suffix indicating a stream.

Fintry (Stirling; Aberdeenshire) 'White house'. *Fionn* (Scottish Gaelic) 'white'; *tref* (Brythonic–Pictish) 'house, homestead'. Noted pre-1225 as Fyntryf. Fintry, north-east of Turriff, and Fintray, near Kintore in Aberdeenshire, have the same derivation.

Fionnphort (Argyll & Bute) 'White harbour'. *Fionn* (Scottish Gaelic) 'white'; *phort* (Scottish Gaelic) 'harbour, beaching place'. This is the ferry-port for Iona, and one of the few unanglicised Gaelic place-names in regular use.

Firth 'Sea inlet' or 'wide estuary'. *Fjordr* (Old Norse) 'sea inlet, fiord'. It was never borrowed into Gaelic and many fiord-names have been concealed by later gaelicisation and have had 'loch' added, *see* Inchard; but the Scots form *firth*, usually metathesised to 'frith' until the late nineteenth century, survives in the ten great Firths of the mainland coast as well in an Orkney place-name of the same derivation.

Fishnish (Argyll & Bute) 'Fish point'. *Fisk* (Old Norse) 'fish'; *nes* (Old Norse) 'point'. The unnecessary English 'Point' has been added to this Mull name in modern times, in ignorance of the original meaning.

Fitful Head (Shetland) 'Cape of the web-footed birds' (i.e. seabirds). *Fit* (Old Norse) 'foot'; *fugl* (Old Norse) 'bird'. 'Head' is an English translation of Old Norse *hofud*, 'headland'. An older suggested etymology is Old Norse *hvit-fjell*, 'white hill'.

Fiunary (Highland) 'Fair shieling, or hill-pasture'. *Fionn* (Scottish Gaelic) 'bright, fair'; *airidh* (Scottish Gaelic) 'shieling, hill pasture'.

Five Sisters of Kintail (Highland) A modern English name given to the mountain group at the head of Loch Duich. In Gaelic it is Beinn Mhòr, 'big mountain', though the peaks are also individually named.

Fladda (Western Isles) 'Flat island'. The numerous Fladdas, and Fladday, are from *flat-ey* (Old Norse) 'flat island'.

Flanders Moss (Stirling) This large, level, once-marshy area west of Stirling is presumably named after the low-lying country of Flanders, translated from Gaelic a' Mhòine Fhlanrasach, or after the seventeenth-century Flemings who brought the techniques to drain it.

Flannan Isles (Western Isles) 'St Flannan's isles'; in Gaelic, na h-Eileanan Flannach, from the seventh-century St Flannan. All three lighthouse-keepers here vanished mysteriously in 1900.

Fleet, River (Dumfries & Galloway) 'Estuary'. *Fleot* (Old English) 'estuary'.

Fleet, River and **Loch** (Highland) 'Flooding stream'. *Fljotr* (Old Norse) 'fleet, flood'.

Flemington (South Lanarkshire) 'Town of the Flemings'. Flemish immigrants entered Scotland from the twelfth century to the seventeenth. The several Flemingtons may denote places where Flemings (often weavers) settled, or in some cases may be back-named from the Scots surname Fleming assumed by the incomers.

Flodda (Western Isles) Also found as Floday, Flodday, and likely to be cognate with Fladda.

Flodigarry (Highland) 'Fleet garth'. *Flotr* (Old Norse) 'fleet'; *gearraidh* (Scottish Gaelic) 'land between machair and moor', describes this coastal Skye location.

Flotta (Orkney) 'Fleet island', from *flotr* (Old Norse) 'fleet'; *-ey* (Old Norse) 'island'. Flotta lies in the vast natural harbour of Scapa Flow.

Fochabers (Moray) This name has been suggested as 'lake-marsh', from *fothach* (Brythonic–Pictish) 'lake'; *aber* (Brythonic–Pictish) 'confluence', with the sense of 'marsh'. The village is close to the flood-plain of the Spey and has a small loch nearby. The terminal -*s,* found in 1514, Fochabris, appeared after 1325, when Fochabre is noted.

Foinaven (Highland) *Fonn-yaven.* This has been derived as 'wart mountain', from *foinne* (Scottish Gaelic) 'warts'; *bheinn* (Scottish Gaelic) 'mountain'. In some sources it is shown as *fionn,* 'white', but whether or not 'wart' is correct, 'white' is definitely wrong. This stark mountain (2980ft/911m) of the far north-west is, like Arkle, associated with a famous racehorse.

Fonab (Highland) 'Abbot's land'. *Fonn* (Scottish Gaelic) 'land'; *aba* (Scottish Gaelic) 'abbot'. At one time an abbey estate, it became a Campbell holding.

Footdee (Aberdeen; Fife) *Fittie*. 'Peaty place'. *Fòid* (Scottish Gaelic) 'peat'; *ait* (Scottish Gaelic locative suffix). Noted as Foty, 1337, and as Futismire, 1583. Despite its harbour-side location, the Aberdeen district name has nothing to do with the River Dee. Loch Fitty in Fife is in a peaty area, and a little to the north is Foodie Hill, with the same derivation.

Fordun (Aberdeenshire) 'On the hill above the fort'. *Faithir* (Scottish Gaelic) 'shelved or terraced slope'; *dùn* (Scottish Gaelic) 'fort'. Noted as Fothardun, pre-1100. The pre-twentieth century spelling is Fordoun. John Fordun (mid fourteenth century), one of the country's early chroniclers, is associated with this place.

Fordyce (Aberdeenshire) 'South-facing slope'. *Faithir* (Scottish Gaelic) 'shelved or terraced slope'; *deas* (Scottish Gaelic) 'south'. A favoured place.

Forfar (Angus) Possibly 'watching hill'. *Faithir* (Scottish Gaelic) 'terraced slope'; *faire* (Scottish Gaelic) 'watchfulness, sentinel'. The nearby Hill of Finhaven would have been a suitable place for such a lookout. It was recorded as Forfare c. 1200. The county town of Angus, which was also known as Forfarshire, once an important weaving centre, and still a market and textile town. The 'Forfar bridie' is Scotland's equivalent of the Cornish pasty.

Formartine (Aberdeenshire) 'Martin's land'. *Fearann* (Scottish Gaelic) 'holding, estate', *Mhartainn* (Scottish Gaelic personal name), 'Martin's'. This district of central Aberdeenshire was recorded in 1433 as Fermartyn.

Forres (Moray) 'Below the bushes'. *Far* (Scottish Gaelic) 'below, under'; *ras* (Scottish Gaelic) 'shrubs, underwood'. Recorded as Fores 1187; Forais 1283. The Gaelic name is Farrais. The name is likely to be a reference to the town's situation at the foot of thickly-wooded hills. A connection with the local tribe of the Boresti, mentioned in AD 84 by Tacitus, has sometimes been suggested. 'Sueno's Stone', tallest of all Pictish carved monoliths, is still preserved here.

Forsinard (Highland) 'Waterfall on the height'. *Fors* (Old Norse) 'waterfall'; *an* (Scottish Gaelic) 'of the'; *àird* (Scottish Gaelic) 'height'.

Forss (Highland) 'Waterfall'. *Fors* (Old Norse) 'waterfall'. The River Forss has a waterfall here.

Fort Augustus (Highland) Formerly known as Kilchomain (Scottish Gaelic *cille Chumainn*, 'St Colman's church'), the place was renamed after the 1715 Jacobite Rising in commemoration of William Augustus, duke of Cumberland, when the old fortification was rebuilt. The fort is now the site of a Benedictine abbey.

Fort George (Highland) Fort and village named after King George II. The fort is one of the best preserved eighteenth-century military installations in Europe.

Fort William (Highland) The town at the foot of Ben Nevis was originally the settlement of Inverlochy (*see* Lochy). A fort was established here by General Monk in 1655, at which time the place was called Gordonsburgh, after the duke of Gordon on whose land it had been built. Shortly afterwards, its name changed briefly to Maryburgh, after Queen Mary II, co-sovereign with King William II. Finally, in 1690 the fort was rebuilt as a major garrison, and renamed Fort William, after the king. After the building of the West Highland Railway to here (1894), it became an industrial centre, with an aluminium works powered by hydro-electricity.

Forteviot (Perth & Kinross) This ancient royal centre overlooking the Earn appears to have as its first element *fathair* (Scottish Gaelic) 'terraced or shelved slope'; the second part is of unclear derivation, perhaps a personal name. In the *Pictish Chronicle*, c. 970, it is recorded as Fothuir-tabaicht, and is not related to the Border Teviot.

Forth (Stirling; North Lanarkshire) Tacitus's first-century account of Caledonia calls the Forth Bodotria, which is not the source of the present name. A possible source has been traced to Brythonic *voritia*, 'slow-running', giving an Old Gaelic form Foirthe, though there is no clear evidence that this name was a river-name. The form 'Forth' is recorded from the twelfth century. It has not been preserved in Gaelic; the modern Gaelic river-name is Abhainn Dubh, 'black water'. The Vikings called the firth 'dark fiord', Myrkvifjord, and an alternative source has been suggested in *fjord* (Old Norse) 'sea-loch, firth', though it seems unlikely that a name would not have been fixed well before the Viking period. The North Lanarkshire village of Forth, well inland, may have a different origin, perhaps from a Cumbric word related to Welsh *fford*, 'road'. The Firth of Forth, and the river, are significant topographical features; until the building of the medieval bridge at Stirling, all overland north–south traffic on the east side of the country had to go via the Fords of Frew.

Fortingall (Perth & Kinross) 'Fortified church'. *Fartair* (Old Gaelic) 'fortress' derives from the same Celtic root as Welsh *gwerthyr*; *cill* (Scottish Gaelic) 'church'. Noted as Forterkil, c. 1240. The yew tree here is of great age, and there is a local legend that Pontius Pilate spent his last years in this place.

Fortrose (Highland) Perhaps 'Beneath the headland'. *Fo* (Scottish Gaelic) 'beneath'; *ros* (Scottish Gaelic) 'headland. The first part may be cognate with Forres; the second part is also present in the neighbour-village of Rosemarkie. The form Forterose is found in 1455. The medieval cathedral ruins here testify to its one-time status as seat of the bishop of Ross. Despite the Gaelic derivation, the latter-day Gaelic name is A' Chananaich, 'town of the canons' (*see* Chanonry Point).

Foss (Perth & Kinross) 'Stance, cattle station'. *Fas* (Scottish Gaelic) 'stance'.

Foubister (Orkney) 'Fua's farm'. *Fua* (Old Norse proper name); *bolstadr* (Old Norse) 'farmstead'.

Foula (Shetland) 'Bird Island'. *Fugl* (Old Norse) 'fowl, bird'; *ey* (Old Norse) 'island'. This remote and isolated small island, lying fourteen miles (23km) due west of the Shetland Mainland, is famed for its very high and sheer cliffs, still teeming with sea-birds.

Foulis (Highland; Perth & Kinross) 'Small stream'. *Foghlais* (Scottish Gaelic) 'lesser stream'. Foulis Castle is the seat of the chief of Clan Munro. The same derivation applies to Easter and Wester Fowlis, in Perthshire, noted as Foulis, 1147. The name is found in other formations, as in Powfowlis, 'stream pools', on the south side of the Forth estuary.

Foyers (Highland) 'Terraced slope'. *Fothair* (Scottish Gaelic) 'terraced slope, stepped gradient'. This name describes the situation of this village on the steeply terraced east side of Loch Ness. There is a famous cataract here, the Falls of Foyers, harnessed for hydro-electric production.

Fraserburgh (Aberdeenshire) 'Fraser's town'. This major fishing port on the north coast of Buchan, originally called Faithlie, was renamed in 1592 to honour Sir Alexander Fraser, the then new landowner and developer of the town. The second element is derived from *burh* (Old English and adapted Scots *burgh*) 'town'. It is known to locals as 'the Broch' (Scottish Gaelic *bruach*, 'edge, bank').

Frendraught (Aberdeenshire) *Fren-drocht*. 'Land by the bridge'. *Fearann* (Scottish Gaelic) 'land, estate'; *drochaid* (Scottish Gaelic) 'bridge'. Noted in 1282 as Fferinderahe.

Freuchie (Fife) *Froo-chie* (with 'ch' as in loch) 'Heathery place'. *Fraochach* (Scottish Gaelic) 'heathery'; noted as Fruchy, 1508. Loch Freuchie, near Amulree in Perth & Kinross, is similarly 'heathery loch'.

Frew, Fords of (Stirling) 'Current', or 'swift current', from Cumbric *friú,* 'current'. This lowest fording point on the River Forth was strategically important until modern times. The Gaelic name is na Friùthachan, a gaelicised rendering of the original. *See* Forth.

Friockheim (Angus) *Freekim.* Originally known simply as Friock Feus (*see* Feu); apparently after a bailie from Forfar by the name of Freke; *heim* (German) 'home, village', was added in 1830 by the landowner, John Anderson, who had spent some time in Germany.

Fruin, River and **Glen** (Argyll & Bute) Possibly 'raging (stream)'. *Freoine* (Scottish Gaelic) 'rage'. Recorded as Glenfrone in the thirteenth century.

Fuar Tholl (Highland) *Fooar howl.* 'Cold hollow or hole'. *Fuar* (Scottish Gaelic) 'cold'; *toll* (Scottish Gaelic) 'hole, hollow'. The expressive name of one of the peaks of Sgùrr Ruadh (Scottish Gaelic, 'red peak') in Glen Carron.

Furnace (Argyll & Bute) Kilns were set up here on Loch Fyneside for iron-smelting in the eighteenth century, using local wood fuel, hence the name. In Gaelic it is An Fhùirneis.

Fyne, River, Glen and **Loch** (Argyll & Bute) 'Stream of wine, or virtue'. *Fìne* (Scottish Gaelic) 'wine'. The name, probably first given to the river, is found in its present form from 1555. The reference may be to an ancient holy site, perhaps Kilmorich at the foot of Glen Fyne, but the complimentary description of water as wine is not uncommon in Gaelic usage. The loch was once a rich herring-fishing area, a source of wealth to the earls and dukes of Argyll.

Fyvie (Aberdeenshire) Possibly a 'path'. *Fiamh* (Scottish Gaelic) 'path'. Noted pre-1300 as Fyvyn. This has also been suggested as the source of Fife.

G

Gairloch (Highland) 'Short loch'. *Gearr* (Scottish Gaelic) 'short'; *loch* (Scottish Gaelic) 'lake, loch'. The village situated at the head of this short sea-loch has usurped the name, without being called Kingairloch as might be expected, and the loch is often called Loch Gairloch. Gareloch on the Firth of Clyde has the same derivation.

Gairsay (Orkney) 'Garek's isle', from *Garek* (Old Norse personal name) and *ey,* (Old Norse) 'island'.

Galashiels (Borders) 'Shielings by the Gala Water'. The latter part of the name comes from *skali-s* (Old Norse) 'sheilings', sheds, or huts used by shepherds as temporary shelters on summer pastures. The source of Gala has been suggested as *galga* (Old English) 'gallows', but river-names are generally older than place names, and the origin may be Cumbric *gal gwy,* 'clear stream'. The name was recorded as Galuschel 1237, Gallowschel 1416. This town has long been the main centre for the Borders woollen trade, and its technical college specialises in the processing of wool and tweed manufacture.

Galloway (Dumfries & Galloway) 'Land of the stranger Gaels'. *Gall* (Scottish Gaelic) 'stranger'; *Ghaidhil* (Scottish Gaelic) 'Gaels'. Noted in the *Pictish Chronicle,* c. 970, as Galweya. This tribal name was given by the Scots to the extreme south-west part of Scotland, which was once settled by Gaels of mixed Irish and Norse origins, who were thus regarded as 'foreigners'.

Galston (East Ayrshire) 'Village of the strangers'. *Gall* (Scottish Gaelic) 'stranger'; *tun* (Old English) 'village'. Recorded as Gauston, 1260. As in the case of Galloway, the reference here to strangers would have been to settlers of a tribe different from the Gaelic-speaking Scots.

Gamrie (Aberdeenshire) *Game-ree.* Possibly 'cold place'. *Geamhradh* (Scottish Gaelic) 'winter'. Noted as Gameryn, c. 1190. A number of place-names in the area seem to refer to cold or exposure. *See* Cushnie.

Garbost (Western Isles) 'Geirr's farm'. *Geira* (Old Norse personal name); *bolstadr* (Old Norse) 'farmstead'.

Gardenstown (Aberdeenshire) 'Garden's town'. This fishing port on the Banffshire coast was set up in 1720 by Alexander Garden of Troup, who gave it his family name.

Garelochhead (Argyll & Bute) 'At the head of the short loch'. *Gearr* (Scottish Gaelic) 'short'; *loch* (Scottish Gaelic) 'lake, loch'. The

English suffix suggests a modern name, but Keangerloch, with the Scottish Gaelic prefix *ceann*, 'head', is found in the early fourteenth century. This village is situated on the Gareloch, a short fiord-like indentation off the Firth of Clyde, at present Britain's nuclear submarine base. *See* Gairloch.

Gargunnock (Stirling) Possibly 'rounded hill'. *Garradh* (Scottish Gaelic) 'enclosure, place'; *cnuic* or *duin-ock* (Scottish Gaelic) 'rounded hill' or 'mound'. The village of this name lies at the base of the Gargunnock Hills.

Garioch (Aberdeen) *Gairy.* 'Rough ground'. *Garbh* (Scottish Gaelic) 'roughness', *-ach* (Scottish Gaelic suffix) 'field, place'. Recorded as Gariauche, around 1170.

Garmouth (Moray) 'Short plain'. *Gearr* (Scottish Gaelic) 'short', here in the sense of narrow; *magh* (Scottish Gaelic) 'plain'.

Garnkirk (North Lanarkshire) A twelfth-century form Leyngartheyn suggests the present name has been rendered from *lann* (Cumbric) 'church', become Scots *kirk,* and *gartan* (Scottish Gaelic) 'little field'. An alternative suggestion was 'hen run', from *gart* (Scottish Gaelic) 'enclosure, field'; *cearc* (Scottish Gaelic) 'hen', but in 1515 it was noted as Gartynkirk. Garnkirk was an early centre of industry, and Scotland's first effective steam railway was the Glasgow and Garnkirk in 1831.

Garnock, River (Renfrewshire; North Ayrshire) 'Little noisy stream', from Gaelic *gair*, 'cry', with the diminutive suffix *-ag.*

Garrowhill (North Lanarkshire) 'Rough hill'. *Garbh* (Scottish Gaelic) 'rough', with the later addition of English *-hill*. The first part of the name is cognate with Garioch and Garvock.

Garry, River, Loch and **Glen** (Highland; Perth & Kinross) 'Rough river'. The name comes from a Celtic root *garu*, as does *garbh* (Scottish Gaelic) 'rough'. There are two Glen Garrys, in Perthshire and Inverness-shire respectively; the latter, noted as Glengarach in 1307, being the ancient territory of the MacDonnells, from whom we have the distinctive 'Glengarry' bonnet. The Border river-name Yarrow is also derived from the same root.

Garscadden (Glasgow) 'Herring yard'. *Gart* (Scottish Gaelic) 'enclosure'; *sgadain* (Scottish Gaelic) 'herring'. Noted as Gartscadane in 1373.

Garscube (Glasgow) 'Corn-yard or field'. *Gart* (Scottish Gaelic) 'enclosure, field', *sguab* (Scottish Gaelic) 'sheaf'. Noted as Gartskube in 1457.

Gartcosh (Glasgow) 'Field with the hollow, or cave'. *Gart* (Scottish Gaelic) 'enclosure, field'; *còs* (Scottish Gaelic) 'hollow, cavern'. Found as Gartgois, 1520.

Garten, River (Highland) 'River of thickets'. *Cardden* (Cumbric) 'thicket'. *See* Boat of Garten, *also* Pluscarden.

Garth (Perth & Kinross) 'Corn field'. *Gart* (Scottish Gaelic) 'enclosure, field', can have the specific sense of 'standing corn, cornfield'. Gart-, Garty- are common prefixes for local and field names, with the sense of 'field', especially 'cornfield'. But *see* Gartocharn.

Gartmore (Stirling) 'Big cornfield'. *Gart* (Scottish Gaelic) 'standing corn, cornfield'; *mòr* (Scottish Gaelic) 'big'.

Gartnavel (Glasgow) 'Apple field'. *Gart* (Scottish Gaelic) 'enclosure, field'; *n'*, 'of the'; *abhal* (Scottish Gaelic) 'apples'.

Gartness (Stirling) 'Field (probably cornfield) by the water, or stream'. *Gart* (Scottish Gaelic) 'standing corn, cornfield'; *nan*, 'of the'; *eas* (Scottish Gaelic) 'water'.

Gartney, Strath (Stirling) 'Gartan's strath'. *Gartán* (Scottish Gaelic personal name, perhaps related to Pictish Gartnait), *srath* (Scottish Gaelic) 'wide valley'. The use of *srath* here, by the side of Loch Katrine, is more akin to the Irish Gaelic sense of lakeside meadowland, than the typical Scottish Gaelic sense of a wide river valley, and suggests an early (sixth-century) name.

Gartocharn (West Dunbartonshire) 'Place of the humped hill'. *Garradh* (Scottish Gaelic) 'enclosure, place'; *chairn* (Scottish Gaelic *carn*) 'humped hill'. Recorded as Gartcarne in 1485. This village is situated beneath the isolated dumpling-shaped Duncryne Hill ('hill of the aspen tree', from Gaelic *crithionn,* 'aspen') on the southern shore of Loch Lomond.

Gartsherrie (North Lanarkshire) 'Colt field'. *Gart* (Scottish Gaelic) 'enclosure, field'; *searraigh* (Scottish Gaelic) 'colts'. Recorded as Gartsharie, 1593.

Garve (Highland) 'Rough ground'. *Garbh* (Scottish Gaelic) 'rough'. This village is situated in a rocky, hummocky valley, at the end of the loch of the same name.

Garvelloch Isles (Argyll & Bute) 'Rough or rocky isles'. *Garbh* (Scottish Gaelic) 'rough'; *eileach* (Scottish Gaelic) 'rock'. Noted 1390 as Garbealeach.

Garvock (Aberdeenshire) 'Rough place', from Scottish Gaelic *garbh,* 'rough', and the termination *-ach,* indicating 'place, field'. The same name as Garioch.

Gask (Aberdeenshire; Highland; Perth & Kinross) 'Tongue or tail of land'. *Gasg* (Scottish Gaelic) 'tail'; and *gasgan,* 'point of land extending from a plateau'. Gask is also found as an element in numerous place-names.

Gatehouse of Fleet (Dumfries & Galloway) 'Roadhouse on the

(Water of) Fleet'. *Geata-hus* (Old English) 'roadhouse'; Fleet (Old English river-name *fleot*), 'stream, estuary'. The town was founded in 1790, but such travellers' hospices were monastic in origin and thus pre-Reformation.

Gateside (Angus; other areas) 'Roadside place or area', from Scots *gait*, 'road'. Scots 'side' can have the sense of 'area' or 'district' as well as the usual meaning. Numerous farms and hamlets have this name, mostly south of the Highland line, as might be expected, though there is a Gateside Farm by Alves in Moray.

Gattonside (Borders) 'Seat or district of the strangers', from *gall* (Scottish Gaelic) 'stranger' and *tun* (Old English) 'settlement'. The -*side* element has been related to Scottish Gaelic *suidhe*, 'seat' and also to Scots *side*, 'district'. Some Border -*side* names have however been linked to Old English *heafod*, 'head', in the locative form -*s heafod*. The form Galtuneside is found around 1143.

Gauldry (Fife) 'Wood of the Galls'. *Gall* (Scottish Gaelic) 'strangers, foreigners'; *doire* (Scottish Gaelic) 'grove, wood'.

Gaur, River (Perth & Kinross) 'Winter river'. *Geamradh* (Scottish Gaelic) 'winter'; this river flowing from Loch Eigheach (Scottish Gaelic, 'shouting') into Loch Rannoch is at its height with the melting of winter snow.

Geo 'Inlet'. Normally a steep narrow sea inlet among cliffs, from Old Norse *gjá*. Frequently found in place names in the Northern Isles and Caithness.

Georgemas (Highland) There was an annual cattle market here on St George's Day, April 23, and the name simply means 'St George's mass, or feast'. It is the most northerly railway junction in the country, where the Thurso branch joins the Highland line to Wick.

Ghlo, Beinn a' (Perth & Kinross) 'Veiled or cloudy mountain', from *beinn* (Scottish Gaelic) 'mountain', and *glo* (Scottish Gaelic, now archaic) 'veil'. A small mountain range in its own right, rising to the south side of Glen Tilt, its highest peak 3677ft/1131m, and with two others over 3000ft/1000m.

Giffnock (East Renfrewshire) 'Little ridge'. *Cefn* (Cumbric) 'ridge'; *oc* (Cumbric diminutive suffix) 'little'.

Gifford (East Lothian) The name of the locality appears to come from the Norman family name Gyffard, noted 1580 as Giffordiensis, 'of the Giffards'. The present village was established in the eighteenth century.

Gigha (Argyll & Bute) Possibly 'God's Isle'. *Gud* (Old Norse) 'God'; *ey* (Old Norse) 'island'. A derivation from Old Norse *gjá* 'gape, rift', has also been proposed, relating either to features of the

island or to the sound separating it from Kintyre. Recorded as
Gudey 1263, Geday 1343, Gya 1400, Giga 1516.

Gilmerton (Edinburgh; other areas) 'Gilmour's farm'. *Gille Moire*
(Scottish Gaelic personal name) 'servant of Mary'; with *tun* (Old
English) 'farm'. Shown as Gillmuristona c. 1200, this name is
of interest as revealing a Gaelic revival in the Lothian area,
with Gaelic personal names attached to what had been Anglian
settlements. There are numerous farms with this name, which may
not always have such a long history: Scots Gilmour's toun, from
the personal name Gilmour, derived from Gaelic.

Girnigoe (Highland) 'Gaping geo'. *Gjá* (Old Norse) 'gape'; *geo* (Old
Norse) 'sea cleft'. The site of two adjacent clifftop castle ruins,
north of Wick.

Girvan (South Ayrshire) This name is much debated. It has been
related to a Cumbric word *gerw*, 'rough', and *afon*, 'river'. An
origin as 'white thicket' has also been proposed. The first syllable
has been associated with Scottish Gaelic *gar*, 'thicket' and the
second with *fionn*, 'white', corresponding to the Ptolemaic name
Vindo-gara, c. AD 150. The derivation from *gearr* (Scottish Gaelic)
'short'; and *abhainn* (Scottish Gaelic) 'river' is no longer accepted
as likely. It was recorded as Girven in 1275.

Glamis (Angus) Glams. 'Wide gap'. *Glamhus* (Scottish Gaelic) 'wide
gap, vale'. Records show Glammes 1187, Glammis 1251. The name
describes the situation of this village, with its famous fourteenth-
century castle, seat of the earl of Strathmore, lying in the centre of
the broad vale of Strathmore between the Sidlaw Hills and the edge
of the Highlands.

Glas Maol (Perth & Kinross) Glas Mile. 'Grey bare top'. *Glas*
(Scottish Gaelic) 'grey', *maol* (Scottish Gaelic) 'bare summit'. A
mountain (3502ft/1070m) well-known to walkers and skiers.

Glasgow 'Place of the green hollow', or 'green place'. *Glas* (Cumbric)
'green'; *cau* (Cumbric) 'hollow'. The Gaelic form is Glaschu. Some
authorities consider that there is a 'familiarative' sense implied in
the derivation, hence the popular rendering 'dear green place'. The
name was recorded as Glasgu in 1116. An ecclesiastical centre,
founded by St Kentigern in the sixth century, Glasgow remained a
small, pretty cathedral city until well into the eighteenth century.
Its growth as a factory town and port began in the seventeenth
century, and by 1840 it had become one of the worst slum areas
in Europe. Its population peaked at over a million in 1901 but
it remains Scotland's largest city. Since the 1960s a process of
cultural and commercial regeneration has made radical changes to
the city.

Glass, River, Glen, Loch (Highland; Dumfries & Galloway) The noun *Glas* in Scottish Gaelic has the primary meanings of 'lock, green surface'; but also 'water'; as an adjective it means 'grey, green, pale'. There are numerous Glass rivers, and it is an element in many other names; *see* Douglas, Kinglass, etc.

Glassary (Argyll & Bute) 'Green shieling'. *Glas* (Scottish Gaelic) 'green'; *airidh* (Scottish Gaelic) 'shieling, summer grazing ground'.

Glassford (South Lanarkshire) 'Green wood'. *Glas* (Cumbric) 'green'; *ffridd* (Cumbric) 'wood'. Around 1210 the form Glasfruth is recorded.

Glasterlaw (Angus) 'Green land hill'. A hybrid name; *glas* (Scottish Gaelic) 'green'; *tìr* (Scottish Gaelic) 'land'; *law* (Scots) 'hill'. The last part is an addition from the post-Gaelic period.

Glen An anglicised form of Scottish Gaelic *gleann*, the conventional term for a river valley in mountain or hill country. It is cognate with Welsh *glyn*. Glens are generally steeper and narrower than straths: the difference is well seen in the course of the Perth & Kinross River Isla, which passes from Glen Isla into Strath Isla. See glens under defining name, e.g. More, except when the two are normally combined.

Glenalmond (Perth & Kinross) 'Glen of the river'. *Gleann* (Scottish Gaelic) 'glen, valley'; and *see* Almond.

Glenborrodale *See* Borrodale

Glenbrittle *See* Brittle, Glen

Glencoe (Highland) Probably 'the narrow glen'. *Gleann* (Scottish Gaelic) 'glen, valley'; *comhann* (Scottish Gaelic) 'narrow'. Noted as Glencole, 1494, probably based on Scottish Gaelic *caol*, 'narrow'; but in 1343 Glenchomure, from Scottish Gaelic *comar*, 'confluence'. The modern Gaelic name is Gleann Comhann. This deep, glaciated valley with its many sheer rock faces is famed for mountain climbing and notorious for the massacre of the Macdonalds that took place here in 1692. At that time they lived in numerous settlements in the glen. The modern village of Glencoe lies at the western end near where the River Coe flows into Loch Leven.

Glendaruel (Argyll & Bute) There are differing explanations for this name. It may be that the original form has become too distorted to be recognisable. The elements *Gleann* (Scottish Gaelic) 'glen'; and *dà*, 'two', are clear, but the latter part has been variously derived from Scottish Gaelic *ruadhail*, 'red spots', and *ruadha*, 'points, headlands'. In 1238 it was recorded as Glen Da Rua. This is the glen hymned by the Gaelic heroine Deirdre, in the 'Ulster Cycle' of Old Gaelic legends.

Gleneagles (Perth & Kinross) 'Glen of the church'. *Gleann* (Scottish

Gaelic) 'glen'; *eaglais* (Scottish Gaelic) 'church'. It was recorded as Gleninglese around 1165. Famous for the luxury hotel and golf courses at its open end, this narrow Ochil glen still has the remains of an old chapel and a 'St Mungo's Farm' indicating its past history as a church property.

Glenelg (Highland) This has been taken for 'glen of Ireland'. *Gleann* (Scottish Gaelic) 'glen'; *Ealg* (Scottish Gaelic) early name for Ireland. Like Elgin and Blair Atholl the reference here to Ireland would be one of commemoration of the motherland by early Gaelic-speaking settlers to this place on the west coast of Scotland. It has also been derived from *eilg* (Old Gaelic) 'noble' (compare Wyvis). But *Eilg* and *Ealg* may go back to the same root. Recorded as Glenhelk in 1282. Glenelg is notable for the remains of two Pictish brochs, as well as the ruins of Bernera Barracks, built in the eighteenth century to keep the local clans under surveillance.

Glenfinnan (Highland) Possibly 'glen of (St) Finan'. *Gleann* (Scottish Gaelic) 'glen'; *Finan* (Irish Gaelic personal name, from *fionn*, 'fair') a seventh-century abbot from Iona and contemporary of St Columba.

Glenkens, The (Dumfries & Galloway) 'Glen of the white river'. *See* Ken. The plural ending has been ascribed to the four medieval parishes forming the district; in 1181 it was noted as Glenkan.

Glenlivet (Moray) Apparently 'glen of the slippery smooth place'. *Gleann* (Scottish Gaelic) 'glen'; *liobh* (Scottish Gaelic) 'slimy, slippery, smooth'; *ait* (Scottish Gaelic) 'place'. A fierce battle took place here in 1594 between the forces of the earls of Argyll and Huntly. Whisky distilling has long been important here.

Glenrothes (Fife) A modern name created when this new town was established in 1948 as a mining centre. The mines have now closed down. There is no glen; the second part acknowledges the earls of Rothes as local landowners, and their former Rothes Colliery.

Glomach (Highland) 'Place of the chasm'. *Glòm* (Scottish Gaelic) 'abyss, chasm'; *-ach* (Scottish Gaelic suffix) 'place'. The Falls of Glomach (370ft/113m) here in Kintail, are the highest in the country.

Goat Fell (North Ayrshire) 'Goats' hill'. This is the highest peak on Arran, at 2868ft/874m, and its name stems from Old Norse *Geitar*, 'goats', and *fjall*, 'hill'. On Blaeu's map it is shown as Keadefell Hil. The Gaelic name is Gaoda-bheinn.

Goil, Loch (Argyll & Bute) Perhaps 'loch of the gall, or stranger'. *Loch* (Scottish Gaelic) 'lake, loch'; *goill* (Scottish Gaelic) 'of the stranger'. Glen Gyle would seem to have the same origin.

Golspie (Highland) Apparently 'Gulli's farm'. *Gulli* (Old Norse personal name); *by* (Old Norse) 'farmstead'. Common in the English 'Danelaw', the suffix is rare in Scotland. Recorded as Goldespy 1330; Golspi 1448. This small town shares administration of the district and former county of Sutherland with Dornoch.

Gometra (Argyll & Bute) 'Godmund's isle'. *Godmundr* (Old Norse personal name); *ey* (Old Norse) 'island'. Noted as Godmadray, 1390. The island lies immediately west of Ulva, from which it is separated by a narrow sound.

Gorbals (Glasgow) The meaning of the name of this former slum area of Glasgow remains uncertain. One authority has suggested a derivation with reference to *gorr balk-r* (Old Norse) 'built walls'. It is recorded in a document of 1521 as Gorbaldis.

Gordon (Borders; Aberdeenshire) 'Great fort'. *Gor* (Cumbric prefix to intensify the meaning of what follows); *din* (Cumbric) 'fort'. The name originated in the south and was transferred northwards by the family of Gordon in the thirteenth century. Gourdon on the coast by Inverbervie is probably the same name.

Gordonstoun (Moray) 'Gordon's town'. Renamed in 1638 after Sir Robert Gordon, the estate, now a boarding school, had previously been called the Bog of Plewlands.

Gorebridge (Midlothian) Possibly the 'bridge at the wedge-shaped land'. *Gora* (Middle English) 'triangular piece of land'; 'bridge' (English). For a Scots form *see* Gushetfaulds.

Gorgie (Edinburgh) Probably 'big field'. *Gor* (Cumbric intensifying prefix); 'big', *cyn* (Cumbric) 'field'. Now part of urban Edinburgh.

Gourock (Inverclyde) *Goo-rock*. Probably the 'place of the hillocks'. *Guirec* (Scottish Gaelic) 'pimple, hillock'. The local terrain here is made up of steep hillocks plunging straight into the Firth of Clyde. Gourock is the ferryport for Dunoon and Kilcreggan on their respective peninsulas across the Firth of Clyde.

Govan (Glasgow) *Guv-an*. 'Ridge', from *cefn* (Cumbric) 'ridge. See Giffnock. Alternative derivations include 'dear rock'. *Cu* (Cumbric) 'dear'; *faen* (Cumbric mutated form of *maen*) 'stone'; or '(place of the) smith', from *gobhainn* (Scottish Gaelic) 'blacksmith'. Names indicating a smithy are not unusual, though most have the place prefix Bal- in front, which never seems to have been the case here. It was recorded as Guven 1147, Gvuan 1150, Gwuan 1518. For about 100 years, 1860–1960, this was the world's busiest shipbuilding centre.

Gowrie (Perth & Kinross) Perhaps 'Gabran's carseland'. *Gabràin* (Old Gaelic personal name) 'of Gabràn'. The name is found as Gowrin, 1120. Gabràn was a sixth-century king of Dàl Riada, reigning from about 537, but it is probable that he had close connections with this more easterly district. Other districts, like Cowal and Lorn, are named after kings of this period. A derivation from *gabhar* (Scottish Gaelic) 'goat', is also suggested; though *Gabràn* and *gabhar* may both be from the same root. The name is most often found today as Carse of Gowrie; *carse* (Scots from Old Norse *kerss*) 'low-lying land by a river'. Gowrie with Atholl formed one of the seven major divisions of Pictland.

Graemsay (Orkney) 'Grim's isle'. *Grim* (Old Norse personal name), and *ey* (Old Norse) 'island'.

Grahamston (Falkirk) A relatively modern name following urbanisation of the area, close to Falkirk, and using the well-established suffix *-ton*; indicating a township. The previous name was Graham's Muir, after Sir John Graham, killed in the Wars of Independence, 1298.

Grampian Mountains (Highland; Moray; Perth & Kinross) The name seems to be a mis-rendered version of Graupius (Mons Graupius, site of a battle between Romans and Caledonians in AD 84, recorded by Tacitus) first written by Hector Boece in his *History of Scotland*, 1526. The derivation of 'Graupius' is unknown. The normal historic name of this mountain massif is The Mounth, from Scottish Gaelic *monadh*, 'mountain'. *See* Monadhliath.

Grandtully (Perth & Kinross) 'Thicket on the hill'. *Cardden* (Cumbric) 'thicket'; *tulach* (Scottish Gaelic) 'hill'. Noted prior to 1400 as Garintully.

Grange (Fife; other districts) This name indicates the presence of a pre-Reformation grange or barn, used for storing produce belonging to an abbey. Many parishes in Scotland were chartered to abbeys, and *-grange* occurs as an element in many names.

Grangemouth (Stirling) 'Mouth of the Grange Burn'. This industrial port on the south side of the Firth of Forth, founded in 1777, stands at the mouth of the Grange Burn, itself named after the nearby grange for Newbattle Abbey.

Grantown-on-Spey (Highland) 'Grant's town by the River Spey'. This town beside the River Spey was originally built in 1766 as a model planned village for the then local landowner Sir James Grant, after whom it is named. *See also* Spey.

Granton (Edinburgh) 'Green hill'. *Gren* (Old English) 'green'; *dún* (Old English) 'hill, rise'. Noted around 1200 as Grendun. Names like Grendon in England are cognate. Once a coastal fishing village outside Edinburgh, now incorporated into the city.

Grantshouse (Borders) A modern name, used for a former North British Railway station adjacent to an inn kept by one Tammy Grant.

Great Glen, The *See* More, Glen

Greenan (Argyll & Bute) 'Sunny place'. *Grianán* (Scottish Gaelic) 'sunny place', from *grian,* 'sun'. A frequent local name for a sun-facing slope. Grenan in Bute has the same source, as do Grennan and Bargrennan in Dumfries & Galloway.

Greenlaw (Borders) 'Green hill'. *Gren* (Old English) 'green', and *hláew* (Old English) 'hill', giving Scots 'law'. Noted as Grenlawe, 1250.

Greenock (Inverclyde) 'Sunny hillock'. *Grianàig* (Scottish Gaelic) 'at the sunny knoll'. Noted in 1400 as Grenok. The town rose to prosperity on the Atlantic trade, especially in the refining of West Indian sugar. The name is also found as a local one near Callander (Stirling) and Muirkirk (East Ayrshire).

Gretna (Dumfries & Galloway) Possibly place of the 'gravelly haugh'. *Greoten* (Old English) 'gravelly'; *halth* (Old English) 'haugh' or 'fertile land enclosed by the bend of a river', Records show Gretenho 1223; Gretenhowe 1376; Gretnay 1576. The adjacent village, Gretna Green, 'first and last' in Scotland, was the wedding place of many eloping couples, taking advantage of Scotland's relaxed marriage laws.

Grey Mare's Tail (Dumfries & Galloway) The descriptive name of a picturesque waterfall of 200ft/61m) on the stream falling from Loch Skeen to the Moffat Water.

Grimshader (Western Isles) 'Grim's farm'. *Grimr* (Old Norse proper name); *seadair* (Scottish Gaelic from Old Norse *saetr*) 'farm'.

Gruinard (Highland) *Green-yard.* This has been taken as 'Split firth', *grein* (Old Norse) 'split, divided'; *fjordr* (Old Norse) 'firth'. Now known as Gruinard Bay, and divided by Isle Gruinard in the centre. But, like Gruinart in Islay, it may be 'shallow firth', from *grunna* (Old Norse) 'shallow', which also fits the location. The 'fiord' element seems less appropriate for Gruinards or Greenyards on the Easter Ross River Carron, noted as Croinzeneorth, 1450.

Guard Bridge (Fife) 'Bridge by the enclosure'. *Gart* (Scottish Gaelic) 'enclosure, field'. The bridge was erected by Bishop Wardlaw of St Andrews, early in the fifteenth century.

Guay (Perth & Kinross) 'Boggy plain'. *Gaoth* (Scottish Gaelic) 'marsh'; *magh* (Scottish Gaelic) 'plain'. Found in this form in 1457.

Guildtown (Perth & Kinross) This 'new' township on the left bank of the Tay, north of Perth, was founded in 1818, on land owned by the Perth Guildry.

Gullane (East Lothian) *Gull-an.* The name of this Lothian resort west of North Berwick has been derived from *guallan* (Scottish Gaelic) 'shoulder', perhaps with the local hill, Gullane Law, in

mind. The emphasis on the first syllable makes a *-linn*, 'lake'
ending unlikely. Noted as Golin, c. 1200.

Gushetfaulds (Glasgow) 'Cattle or sheep-folds in the gore'. *Gushet*
(Scots) 'triangular corner, gusset, gore'; *fauld* (Scots) 'fold'.

Guthrie (Angus) 'Windy slope', from Scottish Gaelic *gaoth*, 'wind',
and *ruigh*, 'slope'. Noted in 1359 as Gutherie.

Gyle (Edinburgh) Perhaps 'place of the gall, or strangers'; from
Scottish Gaelic *goill*, 'of the stranger', as in Loch Goil.

Gyle, Glen *See* Goil

H

Haddington (East Lothian) 'Hada's people's farm'. *Hada* (personal name); *inga* (Old English) 'people's'; *tun* (Old English) 'farm'. Recorded as Hadynton 1098; Hadintun and Hadingtoun 1150. The former county town of East Lothian, and busy market centre, with many fine buildings by the Adam family and others, lies at the heart of a rich agrarian district.

Haddo (Aberdeenshire) 'Half-davoch', an agricultural measure of land. The name is derived as 'half' (Old English); *dabhach* (Scottish Gaelic) 'land measure'. Noted in 1382 as Haldawach. Apart from Haddo House, there is another Haddo near Rattray Head. Many names, especially field and farm names, come from land-measurement terms; *see* Arrochar, Kirriemuir.

Hailes (Edinburgh) 'Hall'. Here this name is likely to derive from *heal* (Old English) 'hall'; Newhall in the Black Isle is more probably from the cognate Old Norse *höll*, 'hall'. In both cases a place of assembly is implied. Recorded as Hala, c. 1150.

Halbeath (Fife) 'Wood of birches'. *Coille* (Scottish Gaelic) 'wood'; *beath* (Scottish Gaelic) 'of birches'.

Halkirk (Highland) 'High church'. *Há* (Old Norse) 'high'; *kirkju* (Old Norse) 'church'. Noted in 1222 as Hakirk, metathesised by 1621 to Halkrig; the process has also affected the Gaelic form *Hacraig*. Early bishops of Caithness had their seat here.

Halladale, River and **Strath** (Highland) Either 'holy dale' from *helg* (Old Norse) 'hallowed', and *dalr* (Old Norse) 'valley'; or 'Helgi's dale' from an Old Norse personal name. Recorded in 1222 as Helgadall; the Gaelic form Healadal suggests the latter interpretation.

Hamilton (South Lanarkshire) From the Norman–French name de Hameldon. Originally a village by the name of Cadzow, which was renamed by the first Lord Hamilton who moved here from England in the fifteenth century. It rapidly became an industrial town when the process of smelting the 'black-band' mixture of coal and low-grade iron ore was developed in the 1830s. *See* Cadzow.

Hamar (Shetland) This name is found in a number of steep locations, like Hamars Field on the north-west of the Mainland; from Old Norse *hamar-r*, meaning 'hammer, crag'. It is also found as Haamer.

Hamnavoe (Shetland) 'Harbour of the bay'. *Hamn* (Old Norse) 'harbour'; *vagr* (Old Norse) 'bay'. Recorded in Old Norse writings as Hafnarvag. There are two fishing villages of this name on Shetland, one on West Burra, the other on Yell. *See* Stromness.

Handa (Highland) 'Sand island'. *Handr* (Old Norse) 'sand'; *ey* (Old Norse) 'island'. The island, off the Sutherland coast, is nowadays a bird sanctuary.

Handwick (Shetland) 'Sand bay'. *Handr* (Old Norse) 'sand'; *vik* (Old Norse) 'bay'.

Hare Law (Dumfries & Galloway; Borders) 'Hares' hill' could be the derivation, from the animal, *hara* in Old English, *heri* in Old Norse, with *law* (Scots, 'hill' from Old English *hlaw*). An alternative possibility is from Old English *hára,* with a similar form in Old Norse, meaning 'old, hoary', and used normally in conjunction with *stan,* 'stone', indicating a boundary-stone. There is a Harstane near Biggar, and the township of Harlaw near Balerno (where the adjacent hill is Hare Hill).

Hare Ness (Aberdeenshire) 'Higher ness', from Scots *har,* 'higher', from Old English *hiera;* and Old Norse *nes,* 'cape'. There is also Hare Moss just inland from here.

Harlaw (Aberdeenshire) 'Hare hill'. This Scots name, with *law* (Scots) 'hill', from Old English *hlaw,* may be a translated version of a Gaelic name, since prior to Robert Bruce's 'herschip' of Buchan in 1307, names in this region would have been Pictish, Gaelic or Norse. Noted as Hayrlaw, 1549. *See* Hare Law and Hare Ness for alternative possibilities. In 1411 the armies of the lord of the Isles and the earl of Buchan met in the fierce but inconclusive battle of 'red Harlaw' here.

Harray (Orkney) 'High island'. *Hár* (Old Norse) 'high'; *ey* (old Norse) 'island'.

Harris (Western Isles) 'Higher island'. *Haerri* (Old Norse) 'higher', from *hár,* seems the likeliest derivation, though the -s ending is not explained. The Gaelic rendering is Na h-Earra, with the definite article. It does seem probable that the name refers to a topography of high hills, especially as compared with the lower-lying Lewis. Recorded as Heradh 1500; The Harrey 1542; Harreis 1588. Harris is not a separate island but the southerly and more mountainous part of the island which also forms Lewis. The cloth traditionally woven by the islanders and known as 'Harris Tweed' (*see* Tweed) is now mostly made on Lewis.

Hartfell (Dumfries & Galloway, Borders) 'Stag's hill'. *Hart* (Old English) 'stag'; *fell* (Old English) 'hill'.

Hasker (Western Isles) 'Deep sea skerry'. *Hafr* (Old Norse) 'open sea'; *sker* (Old Norse) 'reef, skerry'. Heisker has the same derivation.

Hatton (Aberdeenshire; other districts) 'Hall farm'. *Hall* (Old

English) 'manor house'; *tun* (Old English) 'farmstead', giving Scots 'toun'. This was a common name in the sixteenth and seventeenth centuries for the large farmhouse in which the laird lived. As with many Scottish words ending in *-all*, the *-l* sound has been lost, in this case in spelling as well as pronunciation.

Hawick (Borders) *Hoick*. 'Hedge-enclosed settlement'. *Haga* (Old English) 'hedge'; *wic* (Old English) 'settlement, farm'. It was recorded as Hawic in the twelfth century. Its civic war-cry 'Teribus' is a remnant of the Cumbric speech used in these parts a thousand years ago.

Hawthornden (Borders) 'Hawthorn dale', from Old English *denu*, 'valley'. Recorded as Hauthorndene in 1296, this was the estate of William Drummond, one of the leading Scottish poets of the seventeenth century.

Head The most frequently found word to denote a headland or promontory on the north and east coasts. The most northerly is the Head of Bratta, on Yell in Shetland; the most southerly Burrow Head in Wigtownshire. In northern areas it is likely to derive from Old Norse *hofud*, 'head', as in Duncansby Head; but St Abb's Head on the Berwick coast is from Old English *heafod*. In many cases it is likely to be a Scots or English addition to an older name which already has the same meaning, as in Kinnaird Head and Whiteness Head. It is much less frequent on the west side of the country, where 'Point' predominates. *See also* Mull; Ness; Rubha; Point.

Hebrides (Western Isles) Noted by the Roman Pliny in AD 77 as *Haebudes*, this name was given to the Inner Hebrides by the Romans, but has also been applied to the 'Long Island' or Outer Hebrides. The present name is also the product of a misreading of *ri* for *u* in the transcription of ancient manuscripts, at some point before the sixteenth century. The derivation is unknown. The Gaelic name is Innse Gall, 'isles of the strangers', given when they were under Norse occupation. The Old Norse name was Sudreyar, 'southern islands'.

Hecla (Western Isles) This mountain in South Uist (2000ft/612m) shares its name with a famous volcano in Iceland; from Old Norse *hekla*, 'cowl, hooded cloak'.

Helensburgh (Argyll & Bute) 'Helen's town'. This carefully-planned residential town of 1776 on the north shore of the Firth of Clyde was named in honour of Lady Helen Sutherland, wife of Sir James Colquhoun of Luss, who in 1752 bought land here, including the former small fishing village of Millig (from Scottish Gaelic *maolaig*, 'little round-shaped hill'; but *see* Mallaig), still used to define a district of the town.

Hell's Glen (Argyll & Bute) English translation of *Gleann* (Scottish Gaelic) 'valley, glen'; *Ifrinn* (Scottish Gaelic) 'Hell'. But it is likely that the true meaning is the complete opposite, with the original Gaelic form really *aifrionn* 'chapel, place of offerings', as in numerous other place names. *See* Inchaffray, Orrin.

Helmsdale (Highland) 'Hjalmund's dale'. *Hjalmund* (Old Norse personal name) connected with *hjalmr,* 'helmet'; *dalr* (Old Norse) 'valley, dale'. Recorded in the *Orkneyinga Saga* of c. 1225 as Hjalmunddal; in 1290 noted as Holmesdale. The fishing village is situated at the seaward end of the dale, whose river, in Gaelic Ilidh, anglicised as Ullie and cognate with Isla, has also acquired the name of Helmsdale, while its upper strath is usually known as the Strath of Kildonan.

Heriot (Borders) Perhaps 'strategic pass'. *Here* (Old English) 'army'; *geat* (Old English) 'hill-pass', indicating a pass through which an army could march abreast (as with the 'ford' at Hereford, England). An alternative is *here-geatu,* 'army equipment', perhaps a form of service required from the tenant. It was noted around 1200 as Heryt.

Hermiston (Edinburgh) 'Herd's place'. *Hirdmannis* (Old English) 'Herdsman's'; *tun* (Old English) 'settlement, place'. Recorded as Hirdmannistoun in 1233, the name was borrowed for literary use in Robert Louis Stevenson's unfinished novel *Weir of Hermiston.*

Highland Since 1975 this word, properly an adjective and not a noun, has been the name of the northernmost administrative region of mainland Scotland. First recorded in 'Hielandman', in fifteenth-century writings. The Gaelic equivalent, Gaeltachd, referring to language and race rather than topography, is also used, probably as a borrowing from Irish practice. The Highlands, as traditionally referred to, cover a larger area, all the mainland north of a line from Dumbarton to Stonehaven, but excluding the eastern coastal lowlands.

Highlandman (Perth & Kinross) The road here was known as Highlandman's Loan, since it was the route south for Highland cattle drovers, coming from the Crieff cattle tryst.

Hilton (Highland; other regions) 'Village on or by the hill'. Sometimes given an additional locative designation, as with Hilton of Cadboll in Easter Ross, translated from Scottish Gaelic Bail' a' Chnuic; Hilton in Urray, found as Hiltoun, 1456, is an early English name in Ross.

Hirta (Western Isles) This, as Hirt or Hiort, is the Scottish Gaelic name of the St Kilda islands; in English it has become the name of the main island. Its derivation has been variously explained as

Old Norse *hirtir*, 'stags', recorded from 1202 and presumably a reference to the horn-like peaks of the islands; or as Old Norse *hjorth-ey*, 'herd island'; or as Old Irish *hirt*, death, with the sense that this remote archipelago was the gateway to the western underworld, and in this form cognate with the lighthouse rock Dhu Heartach, 'black deadly place'. *See also* St Kilda.

Hobkirk (Borders) 'Church in the valley'. *Hop* (Old Norse) 'shelter, valley'; *kirkja* (Old Norse) 'church'. Formerly known as Hopekirk. Recorded as Hopechirke 1220; Hopeskirk 1586; Hoppkirck c. 1610. *See* Kirkhope.

Holburn Head (Highland; Aberdeenshire) Probably 'beacon cape', from *holl* (Old Norse) 'hill'; and *bruni* (Old Norse) 'burning'; the Caithness location was noted in 1536 as Howbrown.

Holm (Orkney) 'Island', from Old Norse *hólm-r*, 'island, water-meadow'. It is found as an element in numerous place-names, though sometimes hard to distinguish from *-ham* endings.

Holy Loch (Argyll & Bute) English form of Scottish Gaelic An Loch Seunnta. Apparently so called from its association with St Mund, follower of St Columba, and an early Christian missionary at work in this area of the Cowal peninsula. *See* Kilmun.

Holyrood (Edinburgh) 'Holy cross'. *Halig* (Old English) 'holy'; *rod* (Old English) 'cross'. Noted as Holyrud, 1392. This name, associated with the royal palace of Holyroodhouse in Edinburgh, was originally that of the twelfth-century abbey founded by King David I and containing the 'black rood', said to hold part of the True Cross, brought by his mother, St Margaret, to Scotland.

Holywood (Dumfries & Galloway) Originally Darcongall: 'wood of St Congal' (Scottish Gaelic *doire*, 'copse') and rendered into English as 'holy wood'. An abbey was founded here in the twelfth century.

Hope, Ben and **Loch** (Highland) 'Bay'. *Hop* (Old Norse) 'bay, shelter place'. The mountain (3040ft/929m) takes its name from the loch, as does the township of Hope. *See also* Oban, Obbe, St Margaret's Hope.

Hopeman (Moray) This relatively recent (1805) fishing village seems to derive its name from Haudmont, a local estate name, from *haut* (French) 'high'; and *mont* (French) 'hill'.

Hourn, Loch (Highland) 'Furnace' or 'gully'. *Sòrn* (Scottish Gaelic) 'snout, furnace, concavity'; the Gaelic name is Loch Shuirn. The latter meaning seems most apt to this deeply incised mountain sea-loch.

Houston (Renfrewshire) 'Hugo's farmstead'. *Hugo* (Old English personal name); *tun* (Old English) 'farmstead'. This residential village has grown up around the twelfth-century farmstead property of Hugo de Paduinan, noted around 1200 as Villa Hugonis.

Howe o' the Mearns (Aberdeenshire) This district, between Laurencekirk and Stonehaven, is literally the 'hollow of the Mearns', from Scots *howe,* 'hollow'. It is a direct translation of Gaelic Lag na Maoirne. *See* Mearns.

Howgate (Midlothian) Perhaps 'road in the howe'. *Howe* (Scots) 'hollow'; *gait* (Scots) 'road'. The village lies in a steep dip.

Hoy (Orkney) 'High island'. *Hár* (Old Norse) 'high'; *ey* (Old Norse) 'island'. It was recorded as Haey in the *Orkneyinga Saga*, c. 1225, Hoye, 1492. Hoy is much higher than than any of the other Orkney islands, and has lofty cliffs and a celebrated 450ft/138m rock stack (*see* Old Man of Hoy). There is also Hoy near Halkirk in Caithness, close to an island in the Thurso River. *See* Harray.

Humbie (Fife; East Lothian) 'Dog's town'. *Hund* (Old English) 'dog', probably used as a nickname, and *by* (Old Norse) 'settlement, place'. There are at least five Humbies in Southern Scotland.

Huntly (Aberdeenshire, Perthshire) 'Huntsman's wood'. *Hunta* (Old English) 'huntsman'; *leah* (Old English) 'wood'. Noted as Huntlie in 1482. Originally a Borders place-name (there is still a Huntlywood to be found near Earlston), it was transferred north in the thirteenth century by the Gordon family who became landholders here. The earl of Huntly was the principal magnate of north-east Scotland from the fifteenth to the eighteenth centuries. Alexander Gordon, fourth duke of Gordon and Earl of Huntly, founded the present town in 1769 at the confluence of the Deveron and Bogie rivers. It has grown to be an important agricultural market town. Huntly and Huntly Castle, near Longforgan, acquired their names in the same way.

Hutchesontown (Glasgow) The land in this Glasgow area was purchased by the Hutcheson brothers, founders of Hutcheson's Hospital (1639) and developed in the 1790s.

Hyndland (Glasgow) 'Back land'. A direct Scots translation of the Gaelic form *cul tir,* 'back land'. Noted as 'the hynde lande', 1538. *See* Culter.

I

Ibrox (Glasgow) 'Ford of the badger'. *Ath* (Scottish Gaelic) 'ford'; *bruic* (Scottish Gaelic) 'badger's'. *See* Broxburn. Ibrox Park is the home ground of Glasgow Rangers FC.

Inch In most but not all cases, this word, meaning 'island' or 'water-meadow', comes from Scottish Gaelic *innis*. It normally refers to small islands, often in lochs; though there are several Inches in the Firth of Forth. It is unusual among the Western Isles, where Scottish Gaelic *eilean* is the standard word for 'island', though there is Inch Kenneth between Ulva and Mull. Perhaps the best known inch is the North Inch, on the Tay in Perth, where a bloody tournament was fought between Clans Kay and Chattan in 1396. It is also found spelt Insh, Insch.

Inchaffray (Perth & Kinross) 'Isle, or water-meadow, of the chapel'. *Innis* (Scottish Gaelic) 'island, water-meadow'; *aifrionn* (Scottish Gaelic) 'chapel, place of offering'. Noted c. 1190 as Incheaffren. Situated on the Pow (Scots, 'sluggish stream') Water, east of Crieff, this was an important monastery in medieval times.

Inchard, Loch (Highland) 'Meadow-fjord'. *Engi* (Old Norse) 'meadow'; and *fjordr* (Old Norse) 'firth'. As in many other cases, *see* Laxford, 'Loch' is a superfluous later addition, made when the sense of the Norse suffix was lost.

Inch Cailleach (Argyll & Bute) 'Isle of the old woman'. *Innis* (Scottish Gaelic) 'island'; *cailleach* (Scottish Gaelic) 'old woman'. Recorded as Innischallach, 1411. One of the islands in Loch Lomond, and the site of a nunnery.

Inchcape (Highland; Angus) 'Isle, or water-meadow, of the block or head'. *Innis* (Scottish Gaelic) 'island'; *ceap* (Scottish Gaelic) 'block, head'. Old Norse *skeppa,* 'basket', has also been suggested. The Inchcape Rock off Arbroath definitely partakes of the 'isle' meaning.

Inchcolm (Fife) 'Island of (St) Columba'. *Innis* (Scottish Gaelic) 'island'; *Columba* (Latin 'dove' giving Gaelic *Colum*). This small island in the Firth of Forth is the site of the now ruined abbey dedicated to St Columba, founded in 1123 by King Alexander I, when it is noted as 'insula Sancti Columbae'.

Inchinnan (Renfrewshire) 'Isle of St Finnan'. *Innis* (Scottish Gaelic) 'island'; *Finnén* (Old Gaelic proper name). Noted as Inchenan in 1158. St Finnan is remembered in numerous place-names. *See* Kilwinning.

Inchkeith (Midlothian) The latter part of this island name from the Firth of Forth is not thought to be connected with Cumbric *coed*, 'wood'. Bede's *Ecclesiastical History of the English People*, of 731, refers to 'Giudi', which may be a personal or tribal name. The first part is *innis* (Scottish Gaelic) 'island'. Noted as Ynchkeyth, 1461.

Inchmahome (Stirling) 'Isle of St Colman'. *Innis* (Scottish Gaelic) 'island'; *mo*, 'my'; *Colmóc* (Old Irish personal name, form of Colmán). Noted in 1238 as Inchmaquhomok (*see* Portmahomack). This island in the Lake of Menteith still has the ruins of its monastery, used as the burial-place of the Grahams. Bishop Elphinstone's sixteenth-century 'Aberdeen Breviary' notes June 7 as the day of St Colmoc of Inchmahome.

Inchmarnock (Argyll & Bute) 'Island of dear little St Ernan'. *Innis* (Scottish Gaelic) 'island'; *mo*, 'my'; *Iarnan*, (Irish Gaelic personal name) 'Ernan'; with *-oc* Gaelic diminutive suffix. St Ernan, said to be St Columba's uncle, is commemorated in several different parts of the country; *see* Kilmarnock, Killearnan. This island lies to the west of Bute.

Inchmurrin (Argyll & Bute) 'Island of St Mirin'. *Innis* (Scottish Gaelic) 'island'; *Mirin* (personal name) a seventh-century Irish abbot who founded a monastery at Paisley where his name is also commemorated in that of the local football team, St Mirren. Recorded as Inchmuryne, 1395. On Inchmurrin, the largest island in Loch Lomond, there are the ruins of his chapel.

Inchnadamph (Highland) 'Isle, or water meadow of the oxen'. *Innis* (Scottish Gaelic) 'water meadow'; *na* (Scottish Gaelic) 'of the'; *daimh* (Scottish Gaelic) 'stag' or 'oxen'. The 'isle' sense here could refer to its being an area of arable limestone soil in the midst of a vast wilderness of older rocks.

Inchture (Perth & Kinross) Possibly 'hunting meads'. *Innis* (Scottish Gaelic) 'water meadow'; *a* 'of the'; *thòire* (Scottish Gaelic) 'pursuit, chase'.

Inchtuthil (Perth & Kinross) 'Thwart-lying meadow'. *Innis* (Scottish Gaelic) 'water meadow, island'; *tuathal* (Scottish Gaelic) 'thwart-placed, leftwards-bending'. This is the site of one of the largest Roman camps in Scotland: a legionary fortress begun but never completed during Agricola's expedition, around AD 83.

Inchyra (Perth & Kinross) 'Western meads'. *Innis* (Scottish Gaelic) 'water meadow, island'; *iar* (Scottish Gaelic) 'west'; *-ait* (Scottish Gaelic suffix indicating place).

Ingliston (Edinburgh) 'Ingialdr's farm'. *Ingialdr* (Old Norse personal name); *tun* (Old English) 'farm', though Scots *Inglis,* 'of the English(man)' is equally possible. This area to the west of

Edinburgh is now the permanent site of the Royal Highland Show. Kirkliston, not far away, recorded in 1230 as Lyston, and at the end of the thirteenth century as Templum de Lystone, is the site of a Templars' church, and is derived from *kirk* (Scots from Old English *cirice*), 'church', *Lisa* (Old English male personal name) and *ton* (Scots, 'village, farmstead', from Old English *tun).*

Inkster (Orkney) 'Ing's farm'. *Inga* (Old Norse proper name); *saetr* (Old Norse) 'farmstead'. Ingsetter has exactly the same derivation.

Inneans, The (Perth & Kinross) 'Anvils'. These summit-points of the Cleish Hills appeare to derive from Scottish Gaelic *innean*, 'anvil'.

Innellan (Argyll & Bute) 'Place of islands'. *An-eilean* (Scottish Gaelic) 'island place'. Noted 1571 as Inellane.

Innerleithen (Borders) 'Confluence of the River Leithen'. *Inbhir* (Scottish Gaelic); Leithen (Scottish Gaelic) river-name related to *leathann*, 'broad', with the sense of broad surrounding slopes. Recorded as Innerlethan around 1160. This Borders woollen-manufacturing town is sited where the River Leithen meets the River Tweed.

Insch, also **Insh** (Aberdeenshire; Highland) 'Meadow'. *Innis* (Scottish Gaelic) can mean 'water-meadow' as well as 'island'. Sometimes the local topography is the best guide; here 'meadows' is more likely.

Inver- This very common prefix indicates a place where two rivers converge, or where a river enters a loch or the sea. The Scottish Gaelic form *Inbhir* is derived from an early Celtic root *eni-beron*, 'in-bring'. 'Inver' names are most commonly found in the north (except Caithness) and the west, as far south as Inverkip on the Renfrewshire coast. On the east side they are less frequent, occurring sparingly among Aber- names, in a manner that suggests a degree of linguistic conflict, from Inverallochy to Inveresk. The south-west lacks both Inver- and Aber- names, as does modern Ireland. *See also* Aber-.

Inver (Highland; Perth & Kinross) 'River mouth, confluence', as where a small river flows into a larger, or into a loch or the sea. *Inbhir* (Scottish Gaelic) 'river mouth, confluence'. In these villages of Ross-shire and Perthshire, the name is used on its own (though the former was once Inverlochslin), but in hundreds of other places, it is a prefix to a river-name or some other designatory term.

Inveramsay (Aberdeenshire) 'Confluence of the nasty rock'. *Inbhir* (Scottish Gaelic) 'confluence', *àil* (Scottish Gaelic) 'of the rock', *musaich* (Scottish Gaelic) 'dirty, nasty'. Noted as Inveralmeslei, 1260.

Inveraray (Argyll & Bute) 'Mouth of the River Aray'. *Inbhir* (Scottish

Gaelic) 'river mouth'; *Aray* (pre-Celtic river-name) probably means 'smooth-running'. This river-name is widely found throughout Europe in many variant forms: Aar, Ahr, Aire, Ara, Ayr, Oare, Ore, etc. Rebuilt in the later eighteenth century, this attractive small town was the administrative centre of the powerful earls and dukes of Argyll, whose seat remains Inveraray Castle.

Inverbervie (Aberdeenshire) 'Mouth of the Bervie Water'. *Inbhir* (Scottish Gaelic) 'river mouth'; Bervie (probably Celtic river-name similar to Welsh *berw*) 'boiling, seething'. The original settlement here was Aberbervie, the Brythonic *aber-* form reflecting the strong Brythonic–Pictish influence on the place-names of the northeast part of Scotland (Haberberui, 1294). Locally it is known simply as Bervie.

Inverewe (Highland) 'Mouth of the River Ewe'. The site of a celebrated garden of temperate and 'sub-tropical' plants. *See* Kinlochewe.

Invergarry (Highland) 'Mouth of the River Garry'. *Inbhir* (Scottish Gaelic) 'river mouth'; Garry (Scottish Gaelic river-name derived from *garbh*) 'rough'. The village is sited where the river tumbles into Loch Oich, cutting through the steep-sided Great Glen. Iron-smelting was done here in the eighteenth century, and by some accounts the present form of the philabeg, or kilt, was developed here out of the old 'great plaid', to facilitate the work of the Highlanders employed in the works.

Invergordon (Highland) A fabricated name given around 1760 to honour the town's founder, Sir Alexander Gordon, who was the landowner at the time. Previously, the name of the small village here, at the mouth of the local Breckie (from Gaelic *breac,* 'speckled') Burn, was Inverbreckie. Invergordon was an important naval base in the two twentieth-century world wars; today it services oil rigs.

Invergowrie (Perth & Kinross) There is no Gowrie river; the name, though much older, seems to be formed on the same basis as Invergordon; Gowrie on the Tay estuary. Recorded in 1124 as Invergourin. *See* Gowrie.

Inverkeilor (Angus) 'Mouth of the clay stream'. *Inbhir* (Scottish Gaelic) 'river mouth'; *cil* (Scottish Gaelic) 'red clay'; *dobhar* (Scottish Gaelic borrowed from Brythonic) 'stream'. Recorded as Innerkeledur, c. 1200. *See* Rankeilour.

Inverkeithing (Fife) 'Mouth of the Keithing Burn'. *Inbhir* (Scottish Gaelic) 'river mouth'; *Keithing* (Cumbric) river-name derived from *coed*, 'wood'. Early records show Hinhirkethy c. 1050; Innerkethyin 1114. Cromwellian troops defeated a Highland army here in 1651. More recently a shipbreaking centre; many famous vessels have come to their last end here.

Inverkip (Inverclyde) 'River mouth by the crag'. *Inbhir* (Scottish Gaelic) 'river mouth'; *ceap* (Scottish Gaelic) 'block, head'. Noted as Innyrkyp, c. 1170.

Inverkirkaig (Highland) 'Mouth of the kirk-bay stream.' *Inbhir* (Scottish Gaelic) 'river mouth' added to *kirkja* (Old Norse) 'church'; and *vik* (Old Norse) 'bay'. In this case the settlement has untypically given its name to the river.

Invermoriston *See* Moriston, River and Glen.

Inverness (Highland) 'Mouth of the River Ness'. *Inbhir* (Scottish Gaelic) 'river mouth'; *Nis* (pre-Celtic river-name of undetermined origin). Recorded as Inuernis in 1171. Situated where the relatively short River Ness, having flowed out of the nearby Loch Ness, discharges into the Moray Firth. Always the largest in the Highlands, this town was the site of a royal castle and is the main commercial and administrative centre for a vast region of northern and north-west Scotland. *See* Ness.

Inveroran (Highland) 'Mouth of the stream'. *Inbhir* (Scottish Gaelic) 'mouth, confluence'; *dobhran* (Brythonic–Scottish Gaelic) 'water, stream'.

Inversnaid (Stirling) 'Mouth of the needle-stream'. The Snaid burn, flowing into Loch Lomond, immortalised in Gerard Manley Hopkins's poem 'Inversnaid', appears to be connected with *snàthad* (Scottish Gaelic) 'needle'.

Inveruglas (Argyll & Bute) 'Mouth of the dark stream'. *Inbhir* (Scottish Gaelic) 'mouth, confluence'; with *dubh* (Scottish Gaelic) 'dark'; and *glais* (Scottish Gaelic) 'water'. After the *r* the *d* of *dubh* is lost.

Inverurie (Aberdeenshire) 'Confluence of the River Urie'. *Inbhir* (Scottish Gaelic) 'river mouth, confluence'; Urie (Scottish Gaelic river-name), *see* Urie. Noted in 1175 as Enneroury. Here the Urie flows into the River Don. The Great North of Scotland Railway built its locomotives here until 1923, and the works remained active until the 1960s.

Iona (Argyll & Bute) This small island off the south-west coast of Mull was probably a sacred site long before its association with the Celtic church. There is no doubt that the original form was Ioua, and manuscript writers supplanted the *u* with the *n*. The most probable derivation is from Old Irish *eo*, 'yew'. The yew has always been associated with holy places. From the late sixth century, the island was closely associated with the name and fame of St Columcille (Columba). When the area passed into Norse control, the name appears to have undergone some confusion with Norse -*ey*, 'island'. A document of around 1100 records the name of Hiona-Columcille, and until around 1800 the island was known as Icolmkill: *ey* (Old Norse) 'isle'; *Columcille* (Irish Gaelic personal name) 'dove of the church'. The abbey, ruinous since the 1560s, was restored in the nineteenth and twentieth centuries and is the home of the ecumenical 'Iona Community'.

Irongray (Dumfries & Galloway) 'Land portion of the horse stud'. *Earran* (Scottish Gaelic) 'portion'; *na*, 'of'; *greigh* (Scottish Gaelic) 'horse herd, stud'. The oldest known record, Drungray, 1298, is taken as a scribe's mistake; it is Yrnegray when found in 1468.

Irvine (North Ayrshire) Possibly place of 'the white (river)'. *Yr* (Brythonic) 'the'; *(g)wyn* (Cumbric) 'white'. Early records show Yrewyn c. 1140, Irvin 1230.

Isbister (Orkney) 'Ine's farm'. *Ine* (Old Norse personal name), *bolstadr* (Old Norse) 'farmstead'.

Isla, River and **Strath** (Perth & Kinross; Moray) A river-name whose derivation has been tentatively traced back to a pre-Celtic root form *il* or *eil*, with the meaning of 'rapid-moving'. The southerly Isla is noted in 1187 as Strathylaf.

Islay (Argyll & Bute) Possibly 'Ile's island'. *Ile* (personal name); *ey* (Old Norse) 'island'. The name of this large island, most southerly of the Inner Hebrides, has at least in part a Norse origin, in common with most of the major islands off the west coast of Scotland. The interpolation of the *s*, modelled on English 'isle', is relatively recent. Recorded as Ilea c. 690, Ile 800.

J

Jarlshof (Shetland) 'Earl's court'. *Jarl* (Old Norse), 'earl'; *hof* (Old Norse) 'court'. The name of this important archaeological site at the southern tip of Shetland's mainland was given to the adjacent house in Sir Walter Scott's *The Pirate,* in 1816, and was later transferred to the whole site. Its original name is not known.

Jeantown (Highland) A former name for the Wester Ross village of Lochcarron, also found as Janetown. Before that it was Gaelic *Torr nan Clár,* 'hill of staves'.

Jedburgh (Borders) 'Town by the Jed Water'. The first element of the name is that of its river, the Jed, probably derived from a form of *gweden* (Cumbric) 'winding, twisting' (as of a river meander). The second element has its origins as *burh* (Old English) 'town'. Prior to its establishment as a burgh, the settlement name was Jed-worth, signifying 'enclosure by the Jed water' and still found in Bonjedward, a three-language hybrid of *bonn* (Scottish Gaelic) 'foot', *Jed*, and *worth* (Old English) 'enclosure', presumably referring to the meadowland below the steep valley slopes. Jedworth is also preserved in the adjectival form 'Jeddart'. The 'Jeddart axe' was a long-handled weapon for foot-soldiers. Records confirm Gedwearde c. 800, Jaddeuurd c. 1145, Jeddeburgh 1160. The name is oddly replicated in Daljedburgh Hill above the River Stinchar in the Carrick area of Ayrshire.

Jemimaville (Highland) One of the numerous Easter Ross 'new' eighteenth- or early nineteenth-century villages, usually named after the laird's wife, in this case that of Sir George Munro, c. 1830. The *-ville* termination, from French practice, is an effort towards something more sophisticated than the old *-ton*.

John o' Groats (Highland) Wrongly supposed by many to be the most northerly place in mainland Britain (actually Dunnet Head). It was named after John de Groot, a Dutchman who came to live in Caithness in the late fifteenth century under the patronage of King James IV. The final *-s* of the name is a reminder that the original form was 'John o' Groat's House', still preserved in a children's nursery rhyme. The shell beach here is famous for its 'groatie buckies'.

Johnstone (Renfrewshire; Dumfries & Galloway) 'John's settlement'. *John* (personal name); *tun* (Old English) 'farm, settlement'. The names go back to the thirteenth and twelfth centuries respectively.

Since 1781, when a large cotton mill was built there, the Renfrewshire Johnstone has been a substantial town.

Joppa (Edinburgh) Biblical names are not uncommon in Scotland, from the sixteenth century on, though usually applied to farms or even fields rather than larger communities. The name of this district of Edinburgh, on the shore of the Firth of Forth, came in the 1780s from that of a farm here, called after the Biblical Joppa (now Jaffa). The name itself is thought to be derived as *yapho* (Hebrew) 'beautiful'.

Jordanhill (Edinburgh; Glasgow) For these sixteenth- and seventeenth-century Edinburgh and Glasgow names, and for Edinburgh's Jordan Burn, a landowner's religious feeling seems the most likely explanation.

Juniper Green (Edinburgh) A nineteenth-century name. This south-west residential district of Edinburgh was formerly a small isolated settlement having the name of Curriemuirend, the next place to the west being the village of Currie. First recorded in 1812, the name is probably an accurate description of the locality at the time.

Jura (Argyll & Bute) Apparently 'Doirad's island'. *Doirad* (Scottish Gaelic personal name), *ey* (Old Norse) 'island'. The latter Old Norse ending may have substituted the earlier Gaelic form, recorded as Doirad Eilinn in a document of 678.

K

Kames (Inverclyde; Orkney; other regions) The Kameses in Inverclyde and in the Northern Isles have separate derivations. That in the south is *camas* (Scottish Gaelic) 'landing creek, bay', in the north from *kambr* (Old Norse) 'crest'. Thus the Kames of Hoy is a hill. But there is also a Kaim Hill in Renfrewshire. There are many other Kameses in localities throughout the country, sometimes spelt Kaimes, as in south-east Edinburgh, their location the best guide to the linguistic source.

Katrine, Loch (Stirling) *Katt-rin*. Although the river flowing out of Loch Katrine is the Achray Water, the name may nevertheless be a river-name, from *cet* (Brythonic) 'wood', giving Cumbric *coit* and Welsh *coed*, with the same archaic river-name as may be found in 'Earn'. Recorded as Ketyerne, 1463. Since the 1850s this loch has been the prime source of Glasgow's water supply, via a pipeline; hence the one-time name of 'gravity water'.

Keil (Argyll & Bute) *Keel*. 'Church (place)'. *Cill* (Scottish Gaelic) 'church'; *see* Kells.

Keiss (Highland) 'Jutting place'. *Keisa* (Old Norse) 'protrude'. Tang (from Old Norse *tange*, 'tongue') Head does protrude into the sea by this Caithness village.

Keith (Moray) *Keeth*. The etymology is unclear; it has been associated with the Pictish proper name Cait, but may more probably be from *coit* (Cumbric and Old Gaelic) 'wood', cognate with Welsh *coed*, as in Dalkeith. Recorded in 1203 as Ket. Fife Keith, beside the old town, laid out in 1817, commemorates James Duff, fourth earl of Fife. In earlier times the town was sometimes referred to as Kethmalruf ('of St Maelrubha', 1220) and Ketmariscalli ('of the marischal', 1250), the latter noting its association with the Keiths, hereditary earls marischal of Scotland – commanders of the royal cavalry. Keith Mains in Midlothian also has connections with the same family.

Kellas (Moray; Angus) 'Church place'. Though close to Dallas, the Moray location does not have the same suffix root; it has been linked to Scottish Gaelic *cill*, 'church', with the suffix *-ais*, found only in the former Pictish districts, and indicating 'place'.

Kellie (Aberdeenshire; Angus; Fife) Perhaps 'Holly'. *Celyn* (Cumbric) 'holly'; old forms include Chellin (Angus) 1140; Kellin (Buchan) 1183. Welsh Celynog comes from the same source.

Kells (Dumfries & Galloway) Perhaps 'wells' or 'springs', from Old

Norse *kell*, 'spring'. The several Kells of Ireland are from Irish Gaelic *Na Cealla*, 'the (monastic) cells', and such a derivation here is also a possibility.

Kelso (Borders) Place of the 'chalk hill'. *Calc* (Old English) 'chalk'; *how* (Old English) 'hill'. There is still a part of the town known as 'the chalkheugh'. The 'Gododdin' text mentions Calchvynnd, 'chalk hill', probably referring to here. Early records show Calkou 1126; Kelcou 1158; Kelsowe 1420. This Tweedside town, with its French-looking main square, preserves the remnant of a fine Romanesque abbey, founded in 1128.

Kelty (Fife) 'Woods'. *Coilltean* (Scottish Gaelic) 'woods'. A record of 1250 shows Quilte. See Keith.

Kelvinside (Glasgow) 'Narrow river'. This leafy district of the west end of Glasgow takes its name from the River Kelvin, a north-bank tributary of the River Clyde, *caol abhainn* (Scottish Gaelic) 'narrow river'; found as Kelvin c. 1200. The name may refer to the deep gorge that the Kelvin cuts through this area of the city. 'Kelvinside' has also become the somewhat derogatory descriptive name of an affectedly 'posh' accent once associated with this residential district.

Kemback (Fife) 'Head of the hollow', from Scottish Gaelic *ceann*, 'head', and *bac,* 'hollow'; the oldest form of this Fife locality, in rolling terrain, is Kenbak (1250).

Kemnay (Aberdeenshire) 'Head of the plain'. *Ceann* (Scottish Gaelic) 'head'; *a,* of the'; *maigh* (Scottish Gaelic) 'plain'. The transposing of the *n* and *m* goes back at least to the fourteenth century, in the early years of which the region was forcibly 'scotticised' by Robert Bruce. Found as Camnay, 1348.

Ken, River and **Loch** (Dumfries & Galloway) Suggested as 'white (stream)', from *càin* (Scottish Gaelic) 'white'; here in untranslated form but in some other streams it has been scotticised to 'Whitewater'. But there are Ken rivers in south-west England, from a Brittonic root, and this is more likely to be Cumbric, from a conjectured *Cen't* form, still with the sense of 'white, 'shining'. See Glenkens.

Kenmore (Perth & Kinross) 'Great head'. *Ceann* (Scottish Gaelic) 'head'; *mòr* (Scottish Gaelic) 'big'. Found in this form 1258.

Kenmure (Dumfries & Galloway) 'Moor of the Ken'. See Ken.

Kennethmont (Aberdeenshire) 'St Alcmund's church'. Alcmund was an early bishop of Hexham, Northumberland, and this name is recorded from the twelfth century as Kylalcmund, with *cill* (Scottish Gaelic) 'church'. Kynalcmund is also an old form. As memories of Alcmund faded, the name was misinterpreted and modelled with a false etymology on the more familiar name 'Kenneth'.

Kennoway (Fife) 'Head field'. *Ceann* (Scottish Gaelic) 'head'; *achadh* (Scottish Gaelic) 'field'. A small agricultural town, lying a few miles inland from the coastal plain, recorded as Kennachyn in 1250.

Kentallen (Argyll & Bute) 'Head of the inlet'. *Ceann* (Scottish Gaelic) 'head'; *an t* 'of the'; *saileinn* (Scottish Gaelic) 'small inlet'.

Keoldale (Highland) 'Church dale'. *Cill* (Scottish Gaelic) 'church'; *dalr* (Old Norse) 'valley'.

Keppoch (Highland) 'Block,' or 'top'. *Ceap* (Scottish Gaelic) 'block, top'; with *-ach* (Scottish Gaelic suffix) indicating 'field'. There are several locations of this name, the best known being that in Lochaber, associated with the Macdonalds of Keppoch. There is also a Keppochhill in Glasgow.

Kerrera (Argyll & Bute) Perhaps 'copse island'. *Kjarbr* (Old Norse) 'copse'; *ey* (Old Norse) 'island'. Noted in 1461 as Carbery. This island in Oban Bay is where Alexander II died suddenly on his campaign to reclaim the Hebrides from the Norwegians.

Kerry (Argyll & Bute; Highland) A name of different meanings. 'Fourth part'. *Ceathraimh* (Scottish Gaelic) 'quarter', relating to early land divisions. Kerry in Wester Ross is from Old Norse *kjarr*, 'copse', with *á*, 'river'. Neither is cognate with Kerry in Ireland (from Irish Gaelic *ciar*, 'dark').

Kershopefoot (Borders) 'Foot of Kerr's hollow'. *Kerr* (personal name derived from Scottish Gaelic *càrr*, 'marsh') and *hop* (Old English) 'hollow'. Scots *Kerse*, 'carse', has been suggested as an alternative for Kerr, making 'foot of the marshy hollow'. Noted as Kirsopfoote in 1595.

Kessock (Highland) 'St Kessoc's place'. Found as Kessok, 1437. Kessoc was a Pictish saint of whom little is known. North and South Kessock mark the former ferry points across from Inverness to the Black Isle, where there is now a bridge. At one time a tall wooden cross was erected on a rock in the waterway. In Gaelic it is Aiseag ('ferry') Cheiseig.

Kettins (Perth & Kinross) 'Soldiers' place'. *Cath* (Scottish Gaelic) 'battle, company of soldiers'; plural form *cathan;* with *-ach* suffix indicating 'place'. Recorded in 1264 as Kathenes.

Kil- This place-name prefix, found throughout the mainland and Western Isles, does not always have the same derivation. Most often it is from *cill* (Scottish Gaelic) 'church', and denotes the site of a particular church, generally with the name of its founder or patron. But other possible sources include the Scottish Gaelic words *caol,* 'narrow'; *cùl,* 'back'; and *coille,* 'wood'.

Kilbarchan (Renfrewshire) Probably 'the place of St Berchan's church'. *Cill* (Scottish Gaelic) 'church'; *Berchan* (personal name) of a seventh-century Irish saint. Found in this form 1246.

Kilbirnie (North Ayrshire) Probably 'the place of St Brendan's church'. *Cill* (Scottish Gaelic) 'church'; *Brénaind* (Irish Gaelic personal name) of either of two sixth-century Irish saints of this name, both with genuine Scottish links. It is recorded as Kilbyrny in 1413.

Kilbowie (Renfrewshire) 'Yellow back'. *Cùl* (Scottish Gaelic) 'back', perhaps here implying the hill slope; and *buidhe* (Scottish Gaelic) 'yellow'. Thirteenth-century forms of the name show the *cul-* prefix, e.g. Cullbuthe, 1233

Kilbrandon (Argyll & Bute) 'Church of St Brandon'. This was Brendan the Voyager, who founded a church on the isle of Hinba (not now identifiable), off Mull. *Cill* (Scottish Gaelic) 'church'; *Brénaind* (Irish Gaelic personal name).

Kilbrannan (Argyll & Bute) 'Strait of Brandon'. *Caol* (Scottish Gaelic) 'strait, kyle'; *Brénaind* (Irish Gaelic personal name). Noted as Culibrenin, 1549. Ignorance of the Gaelic meaning has prompted the later addition of 'Sound' to the name of this sea channel between Arran and Kintyre.

Kilbride (Argyll & Bute) 'St Bride's church'. Fifteen saints bore the name of Brìd, formerly that of a pagan goddess; and the name is found all across Scotland. *Cill* (Scottish Gaelic) 'church'; *Brìd* (Irish Gaelic personal name) 'Bride, Bridget'. *See also* East Kilbride.

Kilchoan (Highland) 'St Comgan's church'. Comgan was a holy man of the eighth century. *Cill* (Scottish Gaelic) 'church'; *Chomhghain* (Scottish Gaelic personal name, giving modern Cowan).

Kilchomain *See* Fort Augustus

Kilchurn (Argyll & Bute) 'Strait of the cairn'. *Caol* (Scottish Gaelic) 'strait, kyle'; *chùirn* (Scottish Gaelic) 'of the cairn'. Recorded as Kylquhurne, 1432. This castle-island is dramatically situated in Loch Awe.

Kilconquhar (Fife) Kin-yuchar. 'Church of Conchobar'. *Cill* (Scottish Gaelic) 'church'; *Conchubair* (Old Irish personal name). This name later became compressed to Conchar; noted as Kilconcath, 1228. Somewhat later the name was spelled Kinneuchar, 1699, which suggests *ceann* (Scottish Gaelic) 'head'; and *uachdair* (Scottish Gaelic) 'of the upper ground', and implies a false assumption as to the Gaelic etymology. The Kil- form has prevailed, though not in pronunciation. The church here is very close to the small loch, suggesting a pre-Christian sacred site relating to a water-spirit.

Kilcoy (Highland) 'Corner of the wood'. *Cùil* (Scottish Gaelic) 'corner, niche'; *coille* (Scottish Gaelic) 'wood'. Noted as Culcowy, 1557.

Kilcreggan (Argyll & Bute) 'Church on the little crag'. *Cill* (Scottish Gaelic) 'church'; *creag* (Scottish Gaelic) 'rock, crag'; *an* (Scottish Gaelic diminutive suffix).

Kildalton (Argyll & Bute) 'The daughter church'. *Cill* (Scottish Gaelic) 'church'; *daltain* (Scottish Gaelic) 'of the foster child'. Found as Kildaltane, 1548, the name implies a church set up by a mother foundation. The Kildalton Cross is one of the finest carved Celtic crosses.

Kildary (Highland) The Kil- of this Easter Ross village is *caol* (Scottish Gaelic) 'narrow'; prefixed to *daire* (Scottish Gaelic) 'oak wood', cognate with Kildare in Ireland.

Kildonan (Highland; Argyll & Bute; Western Isles) 'Church of St Donnan'. *Cill* (Scottish Gaelic) 'church'; *Donnán* (Irish Gaelic personal name). Little is known of St Donnan, murdered by Picts on Eigg in 617; legend gives him the sobriquet of 'the Great'. The district of Sutherland, noted as Kelduninach c. 1230, was the scene of a 'gold rush' in the 1880s when gold was found in the stream. For a long time afterwards it bore a Gaelic name on a signboard, Baile an Or, 'place of gold'. The name is also found on Bute, Skye and South Uist.

Kildrummy (Aberdeenshire) 'Head of the ridge'. *Ceann* (Scottish Gaelic) 'head'; *druim* (Scottish Gaelic) 'ridge'. Recorded as Keldrumin, 1238. Known in the nineteenth century and probably before as Kindrummie, the village and the ruined thirteenth-century keep are on the edge of the Correen (probably from Old Gaelic *corra*, 'round') Hills.

Kilkerran (Argyll & Bute) 'Church of St Ciaran'. *Cill* (Scottish Gaelic) 'church'; *Chiaráin* (Old Irish personal name). This is probably St Ciaran of Clonmacnoise in Ireland, who died in 549. Noted pre-1250 as Kilchiaran. Kilkerran was also a former name of present-day Campbeltown. There is also a Kilkerran near Maybole, in South Ayrshire.

Killearn (Stirling) This name appears to have undergone a change similar to Kilconquhar, from an earlier form based on Scottish Gaelic *cinn*, 'at the head of', and *earrain*, 'of the land-portion'. The form Kynerine is found from c. 1250, but by c. 1430 it was Killerne, with Scottish Gaelic *cill*, 'church', replacing the *cinn* form.

Killearnan (Highland) 'Church of St Earnan'. *Cill* (Scottish Gaelic) 'church'; *Iurnáin* (Scottish Gaelic form of Irish Gaelic personal name). Found as Kyllarnane, 1569.

Killiecrankie (Perth & Kinross) 'Wood of aspen trees'. *Coille* (Scottish Gaelic) 'wood'; *creitheannich* (Scottish Gaelic) 'of aspens'. Road and railway thread their way through this still-wooded defile, the latter by tunnel and viaduct; the modern highway is carried on stilts high on the hillside. Just south of the village is the still heavily wooded Pass of Killiecrankie, where in 1689 the troops of King William III were defeated by the Jacobites led by Graham of Claverhouse.

Killin (Stirling) Probably 'place of the white church'. *Cill* (Scottish Gaelic) 'church'; *fionn* (Scottish Gaelic) 'white'. Noted as Kyllyn, 1318. According to one story Fingal (Fionn) is buried here; the picturesque village is a tourist centre for Loch Tay.

Kilmacolm (Inverclyde) *Kil-ma-comb*. 'Church of my Columba'. *Cill* (Scottish Gaelic) 'church'; *mo* (Scottish Gaelic) 'of my'; *Coluim* (personal name) referring to the most famous early Irish–Scots saint. The addition of *mo* here denotes dedication. Kilmacolme is recorded in 1205.

Kilmahog (Stirling) *Kilmoag*. 'Church of Cùg'. *Cill* (Scottish Gaelic) 'church'; *mo*, 'of my'; *Chùg* (Scottish Gaelic personal name from Islay, anglicised to Cook).

Kilmallie (Highland) 'Church of Màillidh'. *Cill* (Scottish Gaelic) 'church', *Màillidh* (Old Gaelic personal name). Màillidh is one of the many early holy men about whom little is known. The parish of Kilmallie is the largest in extent in the country.

Kilmaluag (Argyll & Bute) 'Church of Mo-Luoc'. *Cill* (Scottish Gaelic) 'church'; *mo*, 'of my'; *Lugaidh* (Old Irish personal name). He was one of the pioneer missionary saints; his name often given wrongly as Moluag; the *mo* element not being part of it.

Kilmannan (West Dunbartonshire) The name of a reservoir in the Kilpatrick Hills, just north of Old Kilpatrick, seems to preserve the name Manau, Brythonic name of the region at the head of the Firth of Forth (*see also* Slammannan). *Kil* here may be a form of Gaelic *cùl*, 'back', as in Kilbowie, and indicate the westernmost extent of the territory.

Kilmany (Fife) 'Eithne's Church'. *Cill* (Scottish Gaelic) 'church'; *m'*, abbreviated form of *mo*, 'my'; *Eithne* (Irish Gaelic feminine personal name). Noted as Kylmanyn, 1250. This was the name of Columba's mother, but there is no definite indication that she is the dedicatee. The name is cognate with Kilmeny in Islay.

Kilmarnock (East Ayrshire) 'Church of my little St Ernan'. *Cill* (Scottish Gaelic) 'church'; *mo* (Scottish Gaelic) 'of my'; *Iarnan* (personal name) reputedly priest and uncle of St Columba; *-oc* (diminutive suffix). The name was recorded as Kelmernoke in

1299. This Ayrshire market town was where Robert Burns got the first edition of his *Poems* printed, in 1786. Development of the local coalfields turned it into an industrial town. Its name was once synonymous with the blue bonnet worn by the Scottish countryman.

Kilmaronock (East Dunbartonshire) 'Church of my little St Ronan'. Apart from the different personal name, the derivation is the same as that of Kilmarnock. Noted as Kilmerannok, c. 1325.

Kilmartin (Argyll & Bute; Highland) 'Church of St Martin'. *Cill* (Scottish Gaelic) 'church'; *Mhàrtuinn* (Gaelic form of 'Martin'). St Martin of Tours, who may have taught St Ninian, was widely venerated in Gaelic Scotland. Kilmartin in Argyll is in a district remarkably rich in prehistoric monuments.

Kilmaurs (East Ayrshire) 'Church of St Maurice'. *Cill* (Scottish Gaelic) 'church'; *Mauruis* (Scottish Gaelic form of 'Maurice'). Noted in 1413 as Sancte Maure.

Kilmelfort (Argyll & Bute) 'Church of the sandy firth'. *Cill* (Scottish Gaelic) 'church'; *melr* (Old Norse) 'sand'; *fjordr* (Old Norse) 'firth, loch'.

Kilmorack (Highland) 'Church of St Barr'. *Cill* (Scottish Gaelic) 'church'; *mo*, 'of my'; *Bharróc* (Irish Gaelic personal name of the saint most often met as Finbarr, from *fionn-barr*, 'white head'). Noted as Kilmorok, 1437. The once-famous waterfall here on the Beauly River is now under the artificial loch behind the dam.

Kilmore (Highland; Argyll & Bute) 'Great church'. *Cill* (Scottish Gaelic) 'church'; *mòr* (Scottish Gaelic) 'big'. The Argyll district is found as Kylmoor, 1304.

Kilmuir (Highland) 'Mary's church'. *Cill* (Scottish Gaelic) 'church'; *Mhuire* (Scottish Gaelic proper name) 'Mary's'. Noted as Kilmor, 1296. Kilmory has the same derivation.

Kilmun (Argyll & Bute) 'Church of St Mund'. *Cill* (Scottish Gaelic) 'church'; *Mundu* (Irish Gaelic personal name) a disciple and friend of St Columba. Recorded as Kilmun 1240; Kilmond 1410. *See* Holy Loch.

Kilninver (Argyll & Bute) 'Church at the confluence'. *Cill* (Scottish Gaelic) 'church'; *an*, 'of the'; *inbhir* (Scottish Gaelic) 'confluence, river-mouth'. Noted 1250 as Kyllivinor.

Kilpatrick *see* Old Kilpatrick.

Kilravock (Highland) *Kil-ra'ag*. 'Church on the fort-place'. *Cill* (Scottish Gaelic) 'church'; *ràth* (Scottish Gaelic) 'ring-fort'; *-aig* (Scottish Gaelic suffix denoting place). Found as Kilrevoc, 1225. The castle here is the seat of the chief of Clan Rose.

Kilrenny (Fife) 'Church of the bracken'. *Cill* (Scottish Gaelic) 'church'; *reithneach* (Scottish Gaelic) 'bracken'. Found as Kilrinny, c. 1160.

Kilsyth (North Lanarkshire) Possibly 'church of St Syth'. *Cill* (Scottish Gaelic) 'church'; Syth (personal name). However, there is no recorded saint of such a name. An alternative derivation has been suggested in *saighde* (Scottish Gaelic) 'arrows'. The place was recorded as Kelvesyth in 1210 and Kelnasythe in 1217, possibly suggesting some connection with the River Kelvin whose source is nearby at Kelvinhead. The -*syth* form is also found at Cononsyth in Angus: another river-related name. Near here Montrose defeated a Covenanting army in his brilliant campaign of 1645; the first recorded curling club had already been established here for 135 years.

Kiltarlity (Highland) 'Church of Talorcan'. *Cill* (Scottish Gaelic) 'church'; *Taraghlain* (Scottish Gaelic form of Pictish personal name) 'Talorcan's'. The name was recorded around 1225 as Kyltalargy. Talorcan may mean 'fair-browed'.

Kiltearn (Highland) 'Church of the Lord (God)'. *Cill* (Scottish Gaelic) 'church'; *Tighearna* (Scottish Gaelic) 'Lord'. Noted as Keltierny, 1226. The 'Black Rock' gorge here is a deep narrow chasm cut by the Allt Grannda, 'ugly stream'.

Kilwinning (North Ayrshire) 'Church of St Finnian'. *Cill* (Scottish Gaelic) 'church'; *Finnian* (Irish Gaelic personal name). St Finian or Finnian learned under St Ninian, and in turn taught St Columba. Recorded in 1202 as Kilvinnin. His name turns up again in Kirkgunzeon (pronounced 'Kirkgunnion'), from Old English *cirice*, 'church', giving Scots 'kirk', and *Guinneain*, (Scottish Gaelic personal name), 'Finnian's'.

Kin- This place-name prefix, most common north of the Forth–Clyde line on the mainland, usually comes from Scottish Gaelic *ceann*, 'head' or the same word in the locative case, *cinn*, 'at the head of'.

Kinbrace (Highland) 'Seat of the chief (literally, of the brooch)'. *Ceann* (Scottish Gaelic) 'head, head place'; *na*, 'of'; *bhraiste* (Scottish Gaelic) 'brooch'. A reference to the chief of Clan Gunn and his possession of a distinctive heirloom.

Kincardine (Fife; Aberdeenshire; Highland; Tayside) 'At the head of the wood'. *Cinn* (Scottish Gaelic locative of *ceann*) 'at the head of'; *cardden* (Brythonic–Pictish) 'wood, thicket'. It has also been argued that *cardden* indicated 'fort, enclosure', related to Welsh *gardden*, 'fort-site'; and seen also in the local name Cardean, north of Meigle (though its riverbank site would have been wooded then as now). This descriptive place-name was adopted as that of the former county and present district of Kincardine in the Mearns area, recorded as Kynge Carden, 1295. Here the administrative units were named after the twelfth-century Kincardine Castle. The largest village of the name is that in Fife, recorded as Kincardin, 1195; famous for its bridge, which was the lowest road bridging-point of the Forth until the building of the Forth Road Bridge.

Kincardine O' Neil (Aberdeenshire) 'Kincardine of the O'Neils'. *See* Kincardine, above; the latter part of the name is to distinguish it from Kincardine in the Mearns, and refers to the monastery of Banchory–Ternan, founded by descendants of the Ui Néill clan of Ulster, and of which this parish was a property. Noted as Kincardyn Onele, c. 1200.

Kincraig (Highland) 'End of the crag'. *Ceann* (Scottish Gaelic) 'head, end'; *na*, 'of'; *chreige* (Scottish Gaelic) 'crag, rock'. Recorded in the seventeenth century as Kyncragye, but the *-ie* ending has been lost.

Kinfauns (Perth & Kinross) 'Head of the coltsfoot'. *Ceann* (Scottish Gaelic) 'head'; *fathan* (Scottish Gaelic) 'coltsfoot'. The termination *-ais*, indicative of place, is found only in the formerly Pictish area. Noted as Kinfathenes, c. 1200.

King Edward (Aberdeenshire) 'End of the (land) division'. *Cinn* (Scottish Gaelic) 'at the head of', *eadaradh* (Scottish Gaelic) 'division'. Recorded as Kinedward, pre-1300. Although the English kings Edward I and III ventured far into Scotland, the origin of the name has no connection with them, and shows an attempt, when Gaelic was forgotten, to relate the Gaelic sound to something apparently meaningful. The locality has also given its name to a species of potato, a major crop in the region.

Kinghorn (Fife) 'At the head of the muddy ground'. *Cinn* (Scottish Gaelic) 'at the head of'; *gronn* (Scottish Gaelic) 'muddy land, marshland'. The 'king' associations made by some, since it was from the cliffs near here that King Alexander III fell from his horse in 1286, are incorrect. It was recorded as Kingorn as early as 1140.

Kinglass, Glen (Stirling) 'Glen of the dog stream'. The Gaelic form is Conghlais, from *con*, 'dog, wolf', and *glas*, 'water'. There is a Conglass stream in Banffshire. Ardkinglas at the head of Loch Fyne, though it has also been construed as 'height of the grey dog', is perhaps more likely to have the 'water' meaning of *glas,* as 'height of the dog-stream'. Kinglassie in Fife is from Scottish Gaelic *ceann*, 'head, end' and *glas,* 'water': 'head of the water, or stream'. Noted as Kinglassin, 1224, it also developed a Kil- form, resulting for a time in the cult of a wholly imaginary St Glass.

Kingoldrum (Angus) 'At the head of the wooded ridge'. *Cinn* (Scottish Gaelic) 'at the head of'; *coille* (Scottish Gaelic) 'wood'; *druim* (Scottish Gaelic) 'ridge'. Recorded 1454 as Kyncaldrum.

Kingshouse (Highland; Stirling) These remote settlements in the Moor of Rannoch and Strathy were established in the seventeenth century as government staging-posts. In Gaelic it is Taigh 'n Righ.

Kingskettle (Fife) The second part has been associated with a Pictish or Cumbric personal name, Catel; also with a Pictish word cognate with Welsh *cuddial,* 'place of retreat'. Old forms include Cathel, 1183 and Kettil, 1558. The first part may be *ceann* (Scottish Gaelic) 'head', added later; or perhaps English 'king's', associated with the nearby royal palace of Falkland. On the other side of the Firth of Forth is Kirkettle, *caer Catel* (Cumbric) 'Catel's fort'.

Kingston (Moray) Originally Kingston-upon-Spey, this village at the mouth of the Spey was named after their English home-city of Kingston-upon-Hull by two expatriate timber merchants who set up their establishment here in 1784.

Kingussie (Highland) *King-yoossie.* 'At the head of the pine wood'. *Cinn* (Scottish Gaelic) 'at the head of'; *ghiuthasaich* (Scottish Gaelic) 'abounding in pine trees'. Records show Kinguscy 1210, Kyngucy 1380. Forests of fir trees, and outcrops of the Scots Pine from the old Caledonian Forest, are still very much a feature of the Strathspey landscape. This resort village shares the Highland Folk Museum with Newtonmore.

Kinkell (Fife; Highland; other districts) 'Head of the wood', from Scottish Gaelic *ceann,* 'head'; *na,* 'of'; *coille,* 'wood'. The Fife name is found as Kinnakelle, 1199.

Kinlochbervie (Highland) 'Head of Loch Bervie'. *Ceann* (Scottish Gaelic) 'head, end'; Loch Biorbhaidh (Scottish Gaelic) 'boiling or stormy loch'. As the only pier in the far north-west, it is an important landing-place for deep-sea fishing vessels. *See* Inverbervie.

Kinlochewe (Highland) 'Head of Loch Ewe'. *Ceann* (Scottish Gaelic) 'head, end'; *Loch Iù* (Scottish Gaelic) possibly 'loch of the yew trees', or 'loch of the isthmus'; this latter part being from Old Norse *eidh,* 'isthmus', which fits the short level stretch through which the River Ewe flows to the sea, but seems etymologically less likely. The apparently odd thing is that Kinlochewe is situated at the head of Loch Maree. Loch Ewe is a sea-loch, whose name comes from the short river Ewe, which flows from the inland loch now known as Loch Maree, but which formerly bore the name Loch Ewe, noted as Loch Ew in Blaeu's *Atlas,* 1654. Kinlochewe remained as a 'fossil' name after the loch's change of name. *See* Maree.

Kinlochleven (Highland) 'Head of Loch Leven'. *Ceann* (Scottish Gaelic) 'head'; *loch* (Scottish Gaelic) 'lake, loch'; *léan* (Scottish Gaelic) 'swampy place'. *See* Leven, Lomond. The availability of hydro-electric power led to the establishment of the aluminium works here in this remote spot.

Kinloss (Moray) Possibly 'head of the garden'. *Ceann* (Scottish Gaelic) 'head'; *lios* (Scottish Gaelic) 'garden'. Noted in 1187 as Kynloss. This may have some reference to the abbey founded here in 1151, probably on an earlier religious site. It is now the site of an important military airfield, and a centre for air-sea rescue operations.

Kinnaber (Angus) 'Head of the estuary'. *Ceann* (Scottish Gaelic) 'head'; *aber* (Brythonic–Pictish) 'mouth of a river'. Recorded as Kinabyre, c. 1200. This refers to the location near Montrose, above the estuaries of the North and South Esk rivers. The former railway junction here, where the east and west coast routes from London to Aberdeen merged, marked the winning post of the 'Race to the North' of the 1890s. There is also Kinnaber on Islay; one of the rare western *aber* names.

Kinnaird (Perth & Kinross; Aberdeenshire) 'Hill head'. *Ceann* (Scottish Gaelic) 'head'; *àird* (Scottish Gaelic) 'height'. Noted as Kinard, 1183. At Kinnairds Head, by Fraserburgh, the first lighthouse of the Commissioners for Northern Lights was erected in 1787; it is now a lighthouse museum.

Kinneff (Aberdeenshire) *Ceann* (Scottish Gaelic) 'head', but the suffix of this clifftop location is of uncertain origin. Gaelic *éibhe*, or *éighe*, 'cry, death-cry', is a possibility, but it may be from a Pictish word of lost meaning. Found in this form 1361. The crown, sceptre and sword of state were hidden under the floorboards of the church here during the Cromwellian interregnum.

Kinneil (West Lothian) 'Wall's end'. *Ceann* (Scottish Gaelic) 'head, end'; *fhaill* (Scottish Gaelic) 'wall's'. The location, site of both a Hamilton mansion and a former colliery, is close to the eastern end of the Antonine Wall. It is notable as having its Pictish form given by Bede in 731, *Peanfahel;* the *p*-Celtic form of this was subsequently ousted by the Gaelic *Kin-* prefix.

Kinnoul (Perth & Kinross) 'Head of the crag'. *Cinn* (Scottish Gaelic) 'at the head of'; *aille* (Scottish Gaelic) 'crag'. Kinnell near Killin has a similar meaning.

Kinross (Perth & Kinross) 'Head of the promontory'. *Ceann* (Scottish Gaelic) 'head'; *ros* (Scottish Gaelic) 'promontory'. The name was recorded as Kynros around 1144. This historic former county town stands on a promontory that protrudes into Loch Leven.

Kintail (Highland) 'Head of the sea-water'. *Ceann* (Scottish Gaelic) 'head'; *an t-saille* (Scottish Gaelic) 'of the salt-water inlet'. This mountainous area of the north-west Highlands, once Clan

Mackenzie territory, which includes the peaks known as the 'Five Sisters of Kintail', lies at the upper end end of the long sea-loch, Loch Duich. *See* Five Sisters of Kintail, Kentallen.

Kintore (Aberdeenshire) 'At the head of the hill'. *Cinn* (Scottish Gaelic) 'at the head of', *torr* (Scottish Gaelic) 'steep hill'. Noted 1190 as Kynthor.

Kintyre (Argyll & Bute) 'Head of the land'. *Ceann* (Scottish Gaelic) 'head'; *tire* (Scottish Gaelic) 'of land'. An early record of 807 indicates Ciuntire, eighteenth century Cantire. The termination of this long, and in places fertile peninsula, the Mull of Kintyre, is from *maol* (Scottish Gaelic) 'headland'. Boldly claimed by the Norwegian king Magnus 'Barelegs' in 1098, Kintyre became the territory of the MacRanalds and later of the Campbells.

Kippen (Stirling) Place of 'the little stump'. *Ceap* (Scottish Gaelic) 'stump, block'; *-an* (Scottish Gaelic diminutive suffix). This village sits up on an elevated stump of the Gargunnock Hills overlooking Flanders Moss. Kippen is found as a prefix in some names, like Kippendavie, near Dunblane, with the suffix *dabhach* (Scottish Gaelic), a unit of land measurement.

Kirk- This place-name prefix generally indicates the location of a church, with the patron's name or some other designation, and may be from Old Norse *kirkja* or from Old English *cirice,* both giving Scots *kirk*. 'Kirk' names occur mostly in the Northern Isles, Caithness, the eastern mainland and the south-west: areas where Kil- names are rare or non-existent. Many 'Kirk' names, especially Kirktons, are relatively late, post-1400.

Kirkbister (Shetland) 'Church farm'. *Kirkja* (Old Norse) 'church'; *bolstadr* (Old Norse) 'farm'. Kirbister in Orkney has the same derivation.

Kirkcaldy (Fife) *Ker-cawdy.* 'Fort on the hard hill'. *Caer* (Brythonic) 'fort'; *caled* (Brythonic) 'hard'; *din* (Brythonic) 'hill'. The fort here presumably was on the elevated site of the present Ravenscraig Castle, above the town. Records show Kirkaladunt from around 1050. This was the world's main centre of linoleum manufacture in the late nineteenth and early twentieth centuries. Like a number of other Scottish towns, it is known as 'the lang toun', because of its straggling form along the coastal road. Adam Smith (1723–1790), the author of *The Wealth of Nations*, was born here.

Kirkconnel (Dumfries & Galloway) 'Connal's church'. *Kirk* (Scots from Old English *cirice* or Old Norse *kirkja*) 'church'; *Conall* (Old Irish proper name). Recorded as Kyrkconwelle, 1347. Conall was a pupil of St Mungo.

Kirkcudbright (Dumfries & Galloway) *Kirk-oobrie.* 'Church of St

Cuthbert'. *Kirk* (Scots, derived from the Old English *cirice*, or the Old Norse *kirkja*) 'church'; *Cudberct* (Old English personal name meaning 'famous-bright'), the great seventh-century ascetic St Cuthbert, born in the Borders, prior of Melrose and later bishop of Lindisfarne. Recorded as Kirkcutbrithe in 1291. It was county town of the former Kirkcudbrightshire.

Kirkhope (Borders) 'Church in the valley'. *Kirk* (Scots, derived from Old Norse *kirkja*) 'church'; *hop* (Old Norse) 'shelter, valley'. Noted as Kyrchope, c. 1340. *See* Hobkirk.

Kirkintilloch (East Dunbartonshire) 'Fort at the head of the hill'. *Caer* (Cumbric) 'fort'; *cinn* (Scottish Gaelic) 'at the head of'; *tulaich* (Scottish Gaelic) 'hill'. The name is found in the tenth century as Caerpentaloch, with two Cumbric elements intact; by around 1200 *pen* has given way to *cinn*, with Kirkintulach. It can be conjectured that the suffix form was originally also Cumbric. The town began as a second-century Roman fort, built as part of the Antonine Wall defences.

Kirkmichael (South Ayrshire; Perth & Kinross) 'Church of St Michael'; *kirk* (Scots) 'church', from Old English *cirice*. The name is found in a number of places; the church usually built on a hill or high place.

Kirkness (Orkney) 'Church on the headland'. *Kirkja* (Old Norse) 'church'; *nes* (Old Norse) 'headland'.

Kirk o' Shotts (North Lanarkshire) 'Church on the steep slopes'. *Kirk* (Scots, from the Old English *cirice*, or the Old Norse *kirkja*) 'church'; *sceots* (Old English) 'steep slopes'. *See* Shotts.

Kirkoswald (South Ayrshire) 'Church of St Oswald'. *Kirk* (Scots, derived from the Old English *cirice*, or Old Norse *kirkja*) 'church'; *Oswald* (Old English personal name) of the seventh-century missionary King Oswald of Northumbria, who had links with this part of ancient Strathclyde.

Kirkpatrick (Dumfries & Galloway) 'Church of St Patrick'. There are several places of this name. By the time a village had been established, an additional name was sometimes supplied to make its identity clear, as in Kirkpatrick Fleming, 'Patrick's church of the Fleming(s)'. The 'Fleming' was added in the thirteenth century at a time when much land was being granted to incomers from Flanders. Kirkpatrick Durham, the latter part shown as *Dureant* around 1280, indicates a landowner's name: a form more commonly found in England than in Scotland.

Kirkwall (Orkney) 'Church on the bay'. *Kirkja* (Old Norse) 'church'; *vagr* (Old Norse) 'bay'. The Orkney capital is situated at the head of a small sheltered bay, off the Wide Firth. The name was recorded

in the *Orkneyinga Saga*, around 1225, as Kirkiuvagr, and later as
Kirkvaw in a text of 1400. The kirk has, since its founding in 1138,
been the great cathedral of St Magnus. The Viking and Sinclair
earls of Orkney had their seat at Birsay, but Kirkwall retains the
ruins of the palace of the Stewart earls, who ruled like petty kings
until 1615, when Earl Patrick was executed for his oppression and
excessive independence.

Kirk Yetholm *see* Yetholm

Kirriemuir (Angus) 'The great quarter'. *Ceathramh* (Scottish Gaelic)
a land measure that was a fourth of a *dabhach,* or 192 Scots
acres; *mòr* (Scottish Gaelic) 'great, big'. Noted as Kerimure,
1229. Compare Arrochar; Haddo. This Angus town, birthplace
of J. M. Barrie, is the 'Thrums' of his stories; it has also gained
unwanted notoriety from the bawdy ballad 'The Ball o' Kirriemuir',
possibly composed in local farm bothies.

Kishorn (Highland) 'Protruding cape'. *Keisa* (Old Norse) 'protrude';
horn (Old Norse) 'cape'. Recorded as Kischernis, 1464. *See* Keiss.

Kitchen (Midlothian) This name, found in Kitchen Moss and the
Kitchen Burn, may be from Scottish Gaelic *cèide,* an obsolete word
meaning 'green' or 'hillock', in the form *cèideann;* or may be from
the same source, Scottish Gaelic *coitchinn,* 'common grazing', as
Cathkin.

Kittybrewster (Aberdeen) 'Brewing green'. *Cèide* (Scottish Gaelic)
'green, hillock'; *browster* (Scots) 'brewing'. Noted as Browster
Lands, 1376.

Knapp (Angus; other districts) 'Lump, hill', from *knappr* (Old
Norse) 'knob, lump' indicating a low but distinctive hill. The name
is often found as a particle, as in Knap of Trowglen ('hill of the
trolls' glen').

Knapdale (Argyll & Bute) 'Hill and dale country'. *Knappr* (Old
Norse) 'knob, lump', a protuberant, knob-like small hill; *dalr* (Old
Norse) 'dale, valley'. Noted as Knapedal, 1292. The name suits this
northern part of the Kintyre peninsula, where hills rise and fall in
parallel folds.

Knock (Moray) 'Hill, hillock'. *Cnoc* (Scottish Gaelic) 'hill'. Both in
its scotticised and Gaelic forms it occurs in very many hill and
local names, employed for lesser hills, usually under 1000ft/300m.
The Knock- form is very common in the Galloway area, but is
found throughout the country.

Knockan (Highland) 'Little hill'. *Cnocan* (Scottish Gaelic) 'small
hill' from *cnoc* with diminutive *-an* suffix. This cliff site north of
Ullapool is a celebrated one in geological history, where it was first
demonstrated that old rock formations can lie on top of newer
ones.

Knockando (Moray) 'Hill of the market'. *Cnoc* (Scottish Gaelic) 'hill'; *cheannachd* (Scottish Gaelic) 'of the market'. Found as Knockandoch, 1685.

Knowe An element in many local names south of the Highland line, the Scots word *knowe,* 'hill, hillock', derives from Old English *cnol,* 'knoll'.

Knoydart (Highland) This has been derived as 'Cnut's fiord'. *Cnut* (Old Norse personal name); *fjordr* (Old Norse) 'firth, sea-loch'. Recorded as Knodworath, 1309; it is a remote area of mountain wilderness situated on the west coast, between Loch Nevis and Loch Hourn, both fiord-lochs in appearance. Its Gaelic name is *Cnoideart*.

Kyle As a coastal term, it derives from Scottish Gaelic *caol*, 'strait', and is frequently found on the west coast, and also as the Gaelic name of the Pentland Firth, An Caol Arcach, 'strait of Orkney'.

Kyle (South Ayrshire; East Ayrshire) The old central division of Ayrshire. Although the name has been linked to the Brittonic king Coel (Coel Hen, 'old King Cole', c. 400), the source may alternatively be from the Water of Coyle, which flows to join the Ayr, and whose name probably derives from Gaelic *caol,* 'narrow' (*see* Kelvin). Recorded as Cyil by Bede, 731. The offshore sound separating Arran from the mainland here is too wide to be a kyle, and never has borne such a name.

Kyleakin (Highland) 'Narrows of Haakon'. *Caol* (Scottish Gaelic) 'straits, narrows'; *Haakon* (Old Norse personal name). Several kings of Norway bore this name, though it may alternatively be called after a local magnate. Most people take the source as Haakon IV, who ravaged this stretch of coast before his rebuff at the battle of Largs in 1263. There was a ferry crossing here until the Skye bridge was built in the 1990s.

Kyle of Lochalsh (Highland) 'Narrows of Loch Alsh'. *Caol* (Scottish Gaelic) 'narrows'. This village, the railhead and former ferry terminal for Skye, is situated at the narrow sea entrance into Loch Alsh, and opposite Kyleakin. *See* Alsh, Loch.

Kylerhea (Highland) 'Reith's strait'. *Caol* (Scottish Gaelic) 'strait, kyle'; *Réithainn* (Old Gaelic personal name) perhaps stemming from *reidh* (Scottish Gaelic) 'smooth', in legend a warrior of giant size who jumped across the kyle.

Kylesku (Highland) 'The narrow strait'. *Caolas* (Scottish Gaelic) 'narrows, strait'; *cumhann* (Scottish Gaelic) 'narrow, thin'. The name describes the narrow sea entrance where Loch Cairnbawn ('white rock') meets the junction of Loch Glendhu ('dark glen') and Loch Glencoul ('glen of the nook'). There was formerly a ferry crossing here, but the narrows have now been bridged.

L

Ladder Hills (Aberdeenshire) 'Hills of the slopes'. *Leitir* (Scottish Gaelic) 'hill slope'. 'Hills' is a later addition.

Ladybank (Fife) 'Boggy slope'. *Leathad* (Scottish Gaelic) 'slope'; *bog* (Scottish Gaelic) 'moist'.

Ladywell (West Lothian) 'Our Lady's Well', site of a well dedicated to the Virgin Mary. There are numerous other local Lady- names throughout the country, like Ladykirk in Berwickshire, dating back to before the Reformation of 1560, mostly but not all with the same derivation (*see* Ladybank); some, as with some Bride- names, may indicate a pre-Christian site originally dedicated to a female deity.

Lagavulin (Argyll & Bute) 'Hollow by the mill', from *lag* (Scottish Gaelic) 'hollow'; *a'mhuilinn* (Scottish Gaelic) 'by the mill'.

Laggan (Highland) 'Little hollows'. *Lag* (Scottish Gaelic) 'hollow', with the diminutive ending *-an*. Laggan and the relatively close Loch Laggan are not geographically connected, being on opposite sides of the east–west Grampian watershed. Lagg in Argyll and in North and South Ayrshire are also derived from *lag*.

Laich of Moray (Moray) 'Lowland of Moray', from Scots *laich*, 'lowland', borrowed from Gaelic *leachd*, 'sloping ground'. This is the fertile zone of Moray, north of the mountains. For a similar derivation, *see under* Menteith. *See also* Moray.

Laide (Highland) 'Slopes'. *Leathad* (Scottish Gaelic) 'slope'.

Lairg (Highland) 'The pass'. *Lairig* (Scottish Gaelic) 'pass, beaten path'. Noted as Larg, c. 1230. Routes from West and North Sutherland converge here; it is still the site of great annual lamb sales.

Lairig Ghru (Highland, Moray) 'The gloomy pass'. *Lairig* (Scottish Gaelic) 'pass'; *ghru* (Scottish Gaelic) 'gloomy'. The glacially-formed pass cuts a deep gash through the Cairngorms, at a maximum height of 2750ft/840m, and is a popular though tough hill-walking route.

Lake of Menteith *see* Menteith, Lake of

Lamancha (Borders) A Spanish name given to the locality by the proprietor, Admiral Cochrane, in the 1730s; formerly Grange of Romanno, from Scottish Gaelic *rath*, 'ring fort', and *manaich*, 'of the monk'.

Lamberton (Borders) 'Lambert's farm'. *Lambert* (Norman French personal name); *tun* (Old English) 'farmstead'. Noted as Lambertun, c. 1098. Lamberton Toll, north of Berwick, now marks the border with England.

Lamlash (North Ayrshire) 'Isle of Mo-Laise'. *Eilean* (Scottish Gaelic) 'island'; *Malaise* (Scottish Gaelic proper name, incorporating *mo*, 'my', or 'my dear', and *Las*, 'Flame'). Found as Almelasche, 1329. The seventh-century saint Mo-Laise had a cave on Holy Island in Lamlash Bay.

Lammermuir (Borders; East Lothian) Possibly 'lambs' moor'. *Lombor, lambre* (Old English) 'lamb'; *muir* (Scots version of Old English *mor*) 'moorland'. Nowadays known as the Lammermuir Hills, rising to 1755ft/535m. A number of hills within the range have sheep-related names, including Lamb Hill, Lammer Law, Wedder Law and Hog Law. In an early ninth-century document the area was called Lombormore, and in a later text as Lambremor. The conversion of Sir Walter Scott's novel *The Bride of Lammermoor* into Donizetti's *Lucia di Lammermoor* has made the name famous to opera-goers.

Lan- This word may stem from either Cumbric or Gaelic forms. The Gaelic word *lann* has the meanings 'enclosure, house, church'. In earlier times it indicated either a church or a piece of land that was the property of a church. In modern name-forms it is sometimes found as Len-, Lin-, or Long- , but all these prefixes also have other possible derivations.

Lanark (South Lanarkshire) 'The glade'. *Llanerc* (Cumbric) 'forest glade'. The name is recorded as Lannarc 1188, Lanerch 1430. This historic market and former county town is located on an early forest clearing settlement site at the top of the steep east bank of the River Clyde. Lanark has associations with William Wallace, who opened his campaign in the War of Independence by killing the English sheriff here. New Lanark, a model mill town set up by Robert Owen and David Dale in 1784, lies below Lanark in the river valley, near the Falls of Clyde, and was so named to distinguish it from the older settlement. Its well-preserved industrial and domestic buildings are a 'world heritage' site.

Lane (Dumfries & Galloway) 'River', from Scottish Gaelic *linne*, 'pool, stream'. The term is found in a number of stream-names, notably in Carrick around Loch Doon, into which the Carrick Lane flows. Old English *lane* can have the sense of 'slow-moving river', but this derivation seems unlikely.

Langbank (Renfrewshire) Presumably 'long bank'. *Lang* (Scots) 'long'; 'bank' (English). The name is apt for this straggling village on the raised banks of the Firth of Clyde.

Langholm (Dumfries & Galloway) 'Long water meadow'. *Lang* (Scots) 'long'; *holm* (Scots elided form of Old Norse *holmr*) 'water meadow, haugh'. Located on level ground by the meandering River Esk, this name, recorded in 1376 as it is spelt now, describes the situation of this Border woollen-manufacturing town. Hugh MacDiarmid (1892–1978), Scotland's greatest twentieth-century poet, was born and grew up here, but his relations with the town were always stormy.

Lanrick (Stirling) 'The glade' or 'clearing'. The derivation is the same as that of Lanark, with metathesis of the *r*. *See also* Lendrick.

Laphroaig (Argyll & Bute) *Laff-royg*. 'Hollow by the big bay'. *Lag* (Scottish Gaelic) 'hollow'; *a'mhor* (Scottish Gaelic) 'by the big'; *aig* (Scottish Gaelic) 'bay', from Old Norse *vik*. 'Loud bay' has also been suggested, from Scottish Gaelic *labhar,* 'loud'.

Larbert (Falkirk) Possibly 'half wood'. *Lled* (Cumbric) 'half, part'; *pert* (Cumbric) 'wood'. Recorded as Lethberth 1195, Larbert 1251.

Largo (Fife) 'Steep place'. *Leargach* (Scottish Gaelic) 'steep slope'. The name may first have been applied to the hill of Largo Law. Recorded as Largaugh 1250, Largaw 1279, Largo 1595. This town, made famous as the birthplace of Alexander Selkirk, the model for Defoe's *Robinson Crusoe*, is set on a hillside and divided into two parts: Lower Largo on the shore of the Firth of Forth, and Upper Largo situated above on the post-glacial raised beach. Largoward, some way off from the other Largo names, seems to combine *leargach* with *ward* as in Ward Hill, 'hill of watch', from an Old English or Old Norse source.

Largs (North Ayrshire) 'Hillside'. *Learg* (Scottish Gaelic) 'hillside'. This resort town on the Firth of Clyde sits on the shore under the immediate slopes of the Renfrewshire hills. The *-s* ending of the name would appear to have been a later addition as part of the anglicisation process. It was documented Larghes around 1140. A famous battle was fought here in 1263 between the Norsemen and the Scots. There is another Largs in Kintyre.

Lasswade (Midlothian) Probably 'the ford by the meadow'. *Leas* (Old English) 'meadow'; *gewaed* (Old English) 'ford'. The town, southwest of Dalkeith, lies on the North Esk river. A record of 1150 shows the name as Leswade. Lasswade now forms a single urban unit with Bonnyrigg.

Latheron (Highland) 'Miry place'. *Làthach* (Scottish Gaelic) 'miry', has been authoritatively suggested, although the -ron ending is of unclear origin. In 1274 it was noted as Lagheryn. There is also Lathro just north of Kinross

Latheronwheel (Highland) 'Miry place of the pool'. *Latharn* (Scottish Gaelic, from *làthach*, 'miry') *a' Phuill* (Scottish Gaelic) 'of the pool, or hole'.

Lauder (Borders) This small town lies on the Leader Water and presumably takes its name from this river, which may be derived as *lou* (Cumbric) 'wash'; *dobhar* (Cumbric) 'water'. *Lòthur* (Old Irish) means 'trench'. The name is recorded as Louueder 1208, Lawedir 1250, Loweder 1298. *See also* Lowther.

Laurencekirk (Aberdeenshire) 'St Laurence's kirk'. This small market town was founded by Lord Gardenstone in 1770 and at first was named Kirkton of St Laurence, the latter being a reference to the patron saint of its church, St Laurence of Canterbury. Previously it was called Conveth, from Old Irish *coindmed*, 'billetting', indicating a place where the warriors of a chief were lodged with the people.

Laurieston (Falkirk) This small town to the east of Falkirk was originally known as Langtoune, a name recorded in 1393, which still aptly describes its straggling form along the old Edinburgh road. In 1774 it was briefly called Merchistown before being renamed after its owner, Sir Lawrence Dundas of Kerse, then taking the form Laurenceton, before finally assuming its current form.

Lawers (Perth & Kinross) Probably 'Loud, resounding stream'. *Labhar* (Scottish Gaelic) 'loud'. The name was extended from the stream to Ben Lawers (3984ft/1214m) and to the surrounding area, which is divided into three (hence the plural form): Labhar Síos, 'East Lawers'; Labhar Suas, 'West Lawers', and Labhar na Craoibhe, 'Lawers of the Trees'. The Gaelic name is Beinn Labhair. Although this derivation has been contested, it remains the most probable. Not far away, just east of Comrie, there is another Lawers, with a waterfall. Further north, the Uisge Labhar, 'loud water', flows from the Ben Alder Forest into Loch Ossian.

Laxford, Loch (Highland) 'Salmon fiord'. *Laks* (Old Norse) 'salmon'; *fjord* (adaptation of Old Norse *fjordr*) 'sea-loch, firth'. The Gaelic 'loch' was added in the post-Norse period. The River Laxford, flowing from Loch Stack, has been named from the sea-loch. An interesting double example of a Lax- name is found in the Lewis hybrids Loch Laxavat Ard (Scottish Gaelic *loch,* Old Norse *laks,* with *vatn,* 'water' and Scottish Gaelic *ard,* 'high'; and Loch Laxavat Larach (perhaps Scottish Gaelic *làireach,* 'abounding in mares', but more likely *làrach,* 'building place').

Leader, River *See* Lauder.

Leadburn (Midlothian) 'Bernard's stone'. *Leac* (Scottish Gaelic) 'stone', *Bernard* (Old English personal name). The name is found as Lecbernard around 1200. There is a Leadburn stream in South Lanarkshire, close to Leadhills, flowing into the Elvan Water, where the Lead- element may be related to Leader/Lauder.

Leadhills (South Lanarkshire) The Scots name reflects that this former mining village, high in the Lowther Hills, was once an important site for the extraction of lead, as well as gold and silver. It was said that when there were only two paved roads from Edinburgh, one was to Leadhills.

Lecht, The (Moray) 'The declivity'. *Leachd* (Scottish Gaelic) 'declivity', a downward hillslope as in a mountain pass. The derivation is certainly descriptive of this high pass in the Cairngorms, where the old eighteenth-century military road (now a modern highway) rises to over 2000ft/635m and is frequently mentioned in the winter road reports as being 'blocked by snow'. In recent years a ski centre has been developed here.

Ledi, Ben (Stirling) The name has traditionally been taken as 'mountain of God'. *Beinn* (Scottish Gaelic) 'mountain'; *le*, 'in possession of'; *Dia* (Scottish Gaelic) 'God'. The principal meaning of the prefix *le* is 'with', though a possessive sense may have been stronger in earlier times. The significance of the name probably goes back to a pre-Christian holy site on the mountain (2882ft/881m). A more prosaic alternative has been suggested in *leathad* (Scottish Gaelic) 'slope': 'hill of the sloping sides'.

Ledmore (Highland) 'Big slope'. *Leathad* (Scottish Gaelic) 'slope'; *mòr* (Scottish Gaelic) 'big'. Ledbeg similarly means 'small slope', from *beag* (Scottish Gaelic) 'small'.

Leith (Edinburgh) Possibly 'wet place'. *Lleith* (Cumbric) 'moist'. The Gaelic form is Líte. Records show Inverlet 1145, Leth 1570. Inverleith, with Scottish Gaelic *inbhir*, 'river mouth', is still used as a local district name. Leith Hill in Surrey, England, has been derived from Old English *hlith*, 'slope', with a cognate form in Old Norse, *hlíth*, found in compound place-names in Yorkshire and elsewhere; but the Cumbric source is more probable here. This long-time port of Edinburgh, which was an independent burgh until 1920, lies at the mouth of the Water of Leith on the Firth of Forth, and is the new home of the Scottish Civil Service. The harbour is still a busy one; it also houses the former royal yacht *Britannia*.

Lendrick (Stirling) 'Clear space, glade'. *Llanerc* (Cumbric) 'forest glade'. The process of metathesis has transposed the latter part of the name, as with Lanrick. *See also* Lanark.

Lennox (Stirling, East & West Dunbarton) This ancient district encompassed the former county of Dumbartonshire and parts of Stirlingshire. Known as The Lennox, Gaelic Na Leamhanaich, the origin lies in the Cumbric name of the River Leven, meaning 'river of elms' and rendered into Gaelic as *leamhann*. The suffix, from *leamhnach,* gives it the sense of (place of) 'the men of Lennox'. Lennox was the domain of a Pictish mormaer, or provincial ruler.

Lennoxtown (East Dunbartonshire) This small town to the north of Glasgow, established in the 1780s with the introduction of calico printing, was named after the local family of dukes and earls of Lennox, who took their title in turn from the ancient territory of Lennox.

Leny, River and **Pass** (Stirling) 'Narrow cattle path'. *Lànaig* (Scottish Gaelic) 'narrow cattle path', still the Gaelic name, describes the winding traverse between Kilmahog and Loch Lubnaig. It was noted as Lani in 1237.

Lenzie (East Dunbartonshire) *Len-zee.* Has the same derivation as Leny. The *z*, as very often in Scottish names, is actually intended to convey the sound 'gh', a confusion caused by old writing style, but modern usage sounds the *z* in this case. Noted as Lenneth, c. 1230, and Lenye 1451.

Lerwick (Shetland) *Ler-wick.* 'Mud bay'. *Leir* (Old Norse) 'mud'; *vik* (Old Norse) 'bay'. The name of the bay is Old Norse, but there was no town here until about 1600, long after the end of the Viking era. Previously, the capital of the islands was Scalloway.

Leslie (Fife; Aberdeenshire) Possibly 'garden by the pool'. *Lios* (Scottish Gaelic) 'enclosure, garden'; *linn* (Scottish Gaelic) 'pool'. Both these Leslies are located by streams. An alternative derivation of *llys* (Brythonic–Pictish) 'court'; *celyn* (Brythonic–Pictish) 'holly' has also been advanced. The Aberdeenshire name was recorded around 1180 as Lesslyn, in 1232 as Lescelin.

Lesmahagow (South Lanarkshire) *Lez-ma-hay-go.* The name is found in virtually this form, Lesmhagu, in 1138, suggesting the first part to be from Scottish Gaelic *lios,* 'garden'. The form Ecclesia Machuti, 'church of Mahagow' occurs in 1148, suggesting *eaglais* (Scottish Gaelic form of Latin *ecclesia*) 'church'; but no other *eaglais* names have declined to a *les-* prefix. Mahagow has been surmised as possibly the Breton *Maclovius* or *Malo*; perhaps Gaelic *Mo-Fhegu* ('my Fechin').

Letham (Angus; Fife; Stirling) This has been derived as 'village of the barns' from *hlatha* (Old English) 'barns', and *ham* (Old English) 'village'. There are no English villages of this name, however.

Letterewe (Highland) *Letter-you.* 'Hillside above the river Ewe'. *Leitir* (Scottish Gaelic) 'hillside'; *Iù* (Scottish Gaelic river-name). See Kinlochewe.

Letterfinlay (Highland) 'Hill of the fair warrior'. *Leitir* (Scottish

Gaelic) 'hillside'; *fionn* (Scottish Gaelic) 'fair'; *laoich* (Scottish Gaelic) 'warriors', soldier's'. Noted as Lettirfinlay, 1553.

Letters (Highland) 'Hill slopes'. *Leitir* (Scottish Gaelic) 'hillside'.

Leuchars (Fife) *Loocherrs* (with 'ch' as in loch). Probably 'place of the rushes'. *Luachair* (Scottish Gaelic) 'rushes'. Noted pre-1300 as Locres. The village, with a modern military airfield, is situated in north-east Fife close to the estuary of the river Eden. One of the country's finest romanesque churches is here. Leuchars Moss, similarly derived, is to be found west of Aberdeen.

Leven (Fife; West Dunbartonshire; Argyll & Bute) Probably 'elm river'. The Fife town and loch, noted as Lochleuine around 955, take their names from the River Leven, which flows from Levenmouth on the loch to the sea at Innerleven (Scottish Gaelic *inbhir*, 'river-mouth') by Methil. The river-name derives from *leamhain* (Scottish Gaelic) 'elm'. In the case of the River Leven – noted as Lemn by the ninth-century Welsh chronicler Nennius – flowing from Balloch on Loch Lomond to Dumbarton on the Firth of Clyde, however, the indication by Ptolemy, c. AD 150, of a Lemannonios Kolpos, or Gulf, on the west coast, shows the name to pre-date Gaelic names in Scotland: a Brythonic term for 'elm river'. Although the given siting of Lemannonios Kolpos corresponds better with Loch Long, the correspondence of the names seems certain. *See* Lennox, Lomond.

Leven, Loch (Highland) The West Highland Loch Leven also takes its name from its river, perhaps with the same derivation as above, though in this case Scottish Gaelic *lèan*, 'swampy place', has also been suggested. Noted as Glen Lemnae, 704.

Leverburgh (Western Isles) A modern hybrid name joining the family name of Lord Leverhulme, proprietor of Lewis in the 1920s, with *burgh* (Scots) 'town' (properly a town with a charter). The village, formerly Obbe (Scottish Gaelic, 'bay'), was developed as a fishing port and processing station.

Lewis (Western Isles) 'Homes of the people'. *Ljod* (Old Norse) 'people'; also 'music'; *hus* (Old Norse) 'house, home'. In Scottish Gaelic it became *Leòdhas*, and has been confused with *leoghuis* (Scottish Gaelic) 'marshiness'. It was recorded as Leodus and Lyodus c. 1100, Liodhus in the *Orkneyinga Saga* c. 1225, Leoghuis 1449. This northern and larger part of the largest of the Outer Hebrides is a vast tract of mainly low-lying peat and bog with many streams and hundreds of lochs and lochans.

Leys (Highland) 'Garden', from Scottish Gaelic *lios*, 'garden'. This word has a number of archaic meanings, including 'fortified place', which is also possible here.

Lhanbryde (Moray) 'Church-place of St Bride'. The form of the prefix is most unusual and perhaps unique in Scotland, though *làn* is attested as an obsolete Gaelic word for 'church', related to Welsh Llan-; its later meaning of 'field' often meant a field belonging to a church. Older forms include Lamanbride in 1215, Lambride, late fourteenth century.

Liathach (Highland) 'The grey one'. *Liath* (Scottish Gaelic) 'grey'; with -*ach* (Scottish Gaelic suffix denoting place). A distinctive, steep-faced mountain (3456ft/1056m) in the Torridon range.

Liberton (Edinburgh) Once thought to be 'Lepers' place': *Liber* (Old English) 'leper', *tun* (Old English) 'place', referring to a location beyond the town wall, where lepers were segregated. More probably it is 'hillside barley farm' from Old English *hlith,* 'hill'; *bere,* 'barley'; and *tun,* 'farmstead'. Found as Liberton in 1128. Libberton, south-west of Edinburgh, is likely to have the same derivation.

Liddesdale (Borders) 'Dale of the Liddel Water'. A tautological name, as Liddel incorporates both Old Norse *hlyde,* 'noisy', and *dalr,* 'dale'. Recorded as Lidelesdale, 1179. This was the territory of the Armstrongs, among the most ferocious of the 'Border reivers'.

Liff (Angus) Perhaps '(place of) herbs'. *Luibh* (Scottish Gaelic) 'plant, herb'. Recorded in this form c. 1120. *See* Luce, Luss.

Lincluden (Dumfries & Galloway) 'Pool on the Cluden stream'. *llyn* (Cumbric) 'pool, fall'; *Cluden* (Cumbric) river-name, etymologically linked to *Cluaidh,* 'Clyde'. Noted as Lyncludene, 1452.

Lindifferon (Fife) This has been derived as 'field by the water', from Scottish Gaelic *lann,* 'field'; and a Pictish or Cumbric word cognate with Old Welsh *dyffryn,* 'watercourse, valley'. If the prefix has the same sense as is likely in Lhanbryde, it may be the same name as Welsh Llandovery, 'church among the waters'. It is found as Landifferoun in 1540.

Lindores (Fife) 'Field of the black wood'; or 'lake of the black wood'. Either *lann* (Scottish Gaelic) 'field', or *llyn* (Cumbric) 'lake'; with *dubh* (Scottish Gaelic) 'black'; and *ros* (Scottish Gaelic) 'wood'. 'Lann' normally had the sense of 'belonging to the church' and there was a well-known monastery here. Noted c. 1182 as Lundors.

Linlithgow (West Lothian) Place by 'the lake in the moist hollow'. *Llyn* (Cumbric) 'lake'; *lleith* (Cumbric) 'moist'; *cau* (Cumbric) 'hollow'. Recorded in 1124 as Linlitcu. This historic royal burgh takes its name from Linlithgow Loch, which lies in a post-glacial hollow in front of the ruins of the sixteenth-century palace, where Mary, Queen of Scots, was born in 1542.

Linnhe, Loch (Highland) 'The pool'. *Linne* (Scottish Gaelic) 'pool'.

The seaward end, past the Corran narrows, is known in Gaelic as An Linne Sealach, *sealach* (Scottish Gaelic) explained variously as 'salty', and 'of the willows'. The inner loch is An Linne Dubh, *dubh* (Scottish Gaelic) 'black'.

Linton, East and **West** (East Lothian) 'Flax-farm'. *Lín* (Scottish Gaelic) 'lint, flax'; *tun* (Old English) 'farmstead'. Noted in 1127 as Lintun. There is also Linton in the Borders, near Morebattle.

Lintrathen (Angus) Perhaps 'pool of the sandbank', from conjectured Brythonic–Pictish forms *llyn*, 'pool'; *traethen*, 'sandbank', cognate with later Welsh *llyn* and *traeth*, strand'. Noted c. 1250 as Lumtrethyn and Luntrethyn.

Linwood (Renfrewshire) Hybrid name meaning 'wood by the pool'. *Llyn* (Cumbric) 'pool'; *wudu* (Old English) 'wood'.

Lionel (Lewis) 'Flax hill'. *Lín* (Scottish Gaelic) 'flax'; *hóll* (Old Norse) 'hill'. In the era before industrial production of clothes, flax was a widely grown crop.

Lismore (Argyll & Bute) 'Big garden'. *Lios* (Scottish Gaelic) 'garden, enclosure'; *mòr* (Scottish Gaelic) 'big'. This fertile island in Loch Linnhe had a flourishing monastic community set up by St Moluag in the sixth century, and for a time in the thirteenth century it was the seat of the see of Argyll.

Livingston (West Lothian) Place of 'Leving's village'. *Leving* (Old English personal name) an early Saxon landowner; *tun* (Old English) 'village'. Recorded as Uilla Leuing, 1124, Leuinistun 1250. The old village is now incorporated in Livingston New Town, created in 1962.

Lix (Highland; Angus; Perth & Kinross) 'Place of flagstones'. *Lic* (Scottish Gaelic *leac* in the locative form) 'flagstone'. The English form represents the (English) plural.

Loanhead (Midlothian) 'At the top of the lane'. *Loan* (Scots) 'lane'; 'head' (English) 'at the top of'. Recorded as Loneheid in 1618. This former coal-mining town south-east of Edinburgh, by the attractive North Esk glen, was for long a summer retreat for inhabitants of the city. The original loan here would have been one that climbed up from the river. But Loan, a few miles west of Linlithgow, may be from Scottish Gaelic *lòn*, 'meadow, marshy place', as is Lonbain in Wester Ross (*lòn bàn*, 'fair meadow').

Loch See under specific names, Achray, etc., except where the names have been run into one. There is a Loch Loch below Beinn a'Ghlo in Perthshire; here the first part is Scottish Gaelic *loch*, 'lake', and the second Old Gaelic *lòch*, 'dark'.

Lochaber (Highland) Probably 'area of the loch confluence'. *Loch* (Scottish Gaelic) 'sea-loch, lake'; *aber* (Brythonic–Pictish) 'at the confluence of'. This is a region where several lochs join, like Loch Eil and Loch Linnhe; or almost join, like Loch Arkaig and Loch Lochy. Noted c. 700 as Stagnum Aporum, 'swamp of the confluences'; in 1297 as Lochabor. The suffix position of -aber is unusual but not unique (*see* Kinnaber), but the word itself, as with other demonstrably Pictish names, is very rare on the west coast. The warlike past of this district, home to Camerons and Macdonalds, is exemplified by the Lochaber axe, a long-handled battle-axe.

Lochaline (Highland) 'Beautiful loch'. *Loch* (Scottish Gaelic) 'lake, loch'; *alainn* (Scottish Gaelic) 'beautiful'.

Locharbriggs (Dumfries & Galloway) Lochar is from *luachar* (Scottish Gaelic) 'rushes', presumably referring to the reedy moss through which the Lochar river runs. A few miles further west there is Glenlochar at the foot of Loch Ken. Briggs has been assumed to be Scots brig, 'bridge', but the plural form is odd, and it is perhaps more likely to reflect the plural of *brig* (Scottish Gaelic) 'heap, pile', referring to gathered rushes, piled to dry, for use in thatching.

Lochay, Glen *See* Lochy.

Lochboisdale (Western Isles) The Scottish Gaelic *loch* has been added to a name already indicative of a coastal feature; *bug* (Old Norse) 'bay', indicating something less indented than a *vik*. The termination is *dalr* (Old Norse) 'dale'.

Lochcarron (Highland) Formerly known as Jeantown, this village takes its name from the loch on which it is situated. *See* Carron.

Lochearnhead (Stirling) Anglicised version of Kinlochearn, the place at the head of Loch Earn. *See* Earn.

Lochee (Dundee) 'Corn loch'. *Loch* (Scottish Gaelic) 'lake, loch'; *iodh* (Scottish Gaelic) 'corn'.

Lochgelly (Fife) Place of 'the shining loch'. *Loch* (Scottish Gaelic) 'loch, lake'; *geal* (Scottish Gaelic) 'bright, shining'. This former coal-mining town near Cowdenbeath takes its name from the small loch to the south-east of it. It used to be notorious to Scottish schoolchildren as the place where the punishment 'tawses' were made.

Lochgilphead (Argyll & Bute) 'Head of Loch Gilp'. 'Head' with the sense of 'at the top-end of'; *loch* (Scottish Gaelic) 'sea-loch'; *gilb* (Scottish Gaelic) 'chisel'. The name of the loch, noted as Louchgilp, c. 1246, comes from its shape. The English formation of the town-name indicates its relatively modern growth as an administrative centre.

Lochinvar (Dumfries & Galloway) 'Loch of the height'. *Loch*

(Scottish Gaelic) 'lake, loch'; *an* 'of the'; *bharra* (Scottish Gaelic) 'height'. Found in this form 1540. The name was borrowed by Sir Walter Scott for his famous poem, 'Young Lochinvar'.

Lochinver (Highland) 'Loch at the river mouth'. *Loch* (Scottish Gaelic) 'lake, loch'; *inbhir* (Scottish Gaelic) 'river mouth'. This West Sutherland sea-loch, fed by several streams from the surrounding mountains, has also given its name to the fishing port at its head, which one might expect to be called Kinlochinver.

Loch Lomond *see* Lomond

Lochmaben (Dumfries & Galloway) Mapon was a Celtic deity, associated with youth and the sun, and 'Mapon's loch' has been suggested. An alternative derivation is 'loch by the bare-topped hill'. *Loch* (Scottish Gaelic) 'loch, lake'; *maol* (Scottish Gaelic) 'bare top'; *beinn* (Scottish Gaelic) 'hill'. The Latin form was Locus Maponis. Noted as Locmaban, 1166. The now-ruined castle on the loch-side was one of the great strongholds of the south. The Lochmaben Stone, a one-time Border meeting-place, some way from here, may be a version of Clochmaben Stone, from Scottish Gaelic *clach*, stone: 'Mapon's stone'; the English 'stone' added when the sense of *clach* was lost.

Lochmaddy (Western Isles) 'Loch of the Dog'. *Loch* (Scottish Gaelic) 'lake, loch'; *nam*, 'of the'; *mhadaidh* (Scottish Gaelic) 'dog'. *See also* Portavadie.

Lochnagar (Aberdeenshire) 'Loch of the noise or laughter'. *Loch* (Scottish Gaelic) 'loch, lake'; *na* (Scottish Gaelic) 'of the'; *gàire* (Scottish Gaelic) 'noise, laughter'. The mountain (3791ft/1155m) took its name from the loch at the foot, noted as Loch Garr in 1640. It was also known as Beinn nan Ciochan (Scottish Gaelic) 'the mountain of the paps, or breasts'. Prudishness may have encouraged the alternative name. Lord Byron's poems 'Dark Lochnagar' and 'Lachin y Gair' helped to give it currency.

Loch Ness *see* Ness.

Lochore (Fife) Possibly 'brown loch'. *Loch* (Scottish Gaelic) 'lake, loch'; *odhar* (Scottish Gaelic) 'brown'; a reference to the peaty soil of the area. But, as the name comes from the River Ore, it may have a different and older derivation, cognate with that of the River Ayr and the English Ore and Oare, from a conjectural pre-Celtic root-form *ora*, indicating 'flowing'. Found as Lochor, 1241.

Lochty (Fife; Perthshire; Angus; Moray) 'Stream of the black goddess'. *Loch* here seems to be from *lòch* (Old Gaelic) 'black'; with *dae* (Irish Gaelic) 'goddess', related to Scottish Gaelic *dia*. The reference is to a 'black goddess' river spirit, and is intriguingly suggestive of the nature worship of the pre-Christian inhabitants.

Other Lochtys are near Almondbank outside Perth, in Menmuir parish near Brechin, and there is the Lochty Burn in Moray. *See also* Lochy, Munlochy.

Lochtyloch (West Lothian) 'Dark hill'. This locality in the neighbourhood of Bathgate stems from *lòch* (Old Gaelic) 'dark', and *tulach* (Scottish Gaelic) 'hill'.

Lochwinnoch (Renfrewshire) Loch of St Wynnin or Finnian. Noted as Lochynoc, 1158. *See* Kilwinning.

Lochy, River, Loch, Glen (Highland; Argyll & Bute; Moray) 'Stream of the black goddess'. *Lòch* (Old Gaelic) 'black'; *dae* (Irish Gaelic) 'goddess', related to Scottish Gaelic *dia*. The name is not a doublet of Loch; it comes originally from the river in each case. The River Lochy in the Great Glen is referred to as *dea nigra,* 'black goddess', and its loch as Lacus Lochdiae by Adamnan, c. 700. Glen Lochy through which the Oban road and railway descend from Tyndrum, the River and Glen Lochay in Perthshire, and the Glen and Burn of Lochy in Moray are of the same derivation. *See also* Lochty, Munlochy.

Lockerbie (Dumfries & Galloway) 'Lokard's village'. *Lokard* (Old Norse personal name); *by* (Old Norse) 'village, farmstead'. It was recorded as Lokardebi in a document of 1306. In December 1988, a Pan American jumbo jet was blown up in mid-air above the town, killing all 259 on board and 11 of the townspeople.

Logie (Highland; elsewhere) 'Place in the hollow'. *Lagaigh* (Scottish Gaelic) 'in the hollow'. Found as Logyne, 1184; the terminal -*n* explained as 'a scribe's flourish'.

Logierait (Perth & Kinross) 'My-Coeddi's hollow'. *Lagaigh* (Scottish Gaelic) 'in the hollow'; *mo,* 'my'; *Choid* (Irish Gaelic proper name). Coeddi was a bishop of Iona (died 712).

Lomond (Stirling; Fife) A name with a confusing history, perhaps caused by different sources for the hill and water names. One possible source is Cumbric *llumon,* 'beacon', as in the Welsh mountain Pumlumon. This suits Ben Lomond (Stirling, 3194ft/977m), Beinn Laomuinn in Scottish Gaelic, and the twin Lomond Hills (Fife) whose prominent positions make them all eminently suitable as beacon hills. Another possible source is *leamhan* (Scottish Gaelic) 'elm'. This accounts for the name of the River Leven which flows out of Loch Lomond to the Firth of Clyde. The ninth-century writer Nennius wrote in Latin of 'the great lake Lummonu, which in English is called Lochleven, in the region of the Picts'; and it is documented in a text of 1535 as Levin. It may be that for a long period the loch was referred to as both Lomond and Leven. The Gaelic form is Loch Laomuinn, and it may be

that – if the mountain name Beinn Laomuinn is from *llumon* –
the similarity of the names caused the loch name to be altered
from its river's name to that of the beacon-mountain which rises
so commandingly above its southern reach. It is of interest that the
Fife Lomonds also rise above a Loch Leven. Loch Lomond, broad
and shallow at the south end, deep and narrow to the north, is the
largest inland stretch of water in Britain. *See* Lennox, Leven.

Long, Loch (Argyll & Bute; Highland) 'Loch of ships'. *Loch*
(Scottish Gaelic) 'lake, loch', *luing* (Scottish Gaelic) 'of ships'.
Noted as Loch Long 1225, but it has been identified with Ptolemy's
Lemannonios Kolpos (see Leven).

Longannet (Fife) 'Field of the patron saint's church'. *Lann* (Scottish
Gaelic) 'field'; *annat* (Scottish Gaelic) 'patron saint's church', or
'church with relics' (*see* Annat). It is now the site of a vast power
station.

Longart (Highland) 'Camping place'. The source of the name of this
forest area is of interest as it ostensibly should mean 'ship station',
yet there is nowhere in the locality suitable for ships. *Long* (Irish
Gaelic) 'ship', came also to mean 'dwelling'; and *port* (Irish Gaelic)
'harbour', came also to mean 'encampment'. Luncarty near Perth,
noted as Lumphortyn, 1250, and north of Turriff have the 'camp'
meaning, as does Loch Lungard in Kintail. Camaslongart on
Loch Long in Kintail preserves the 'ship-station' meaning. The
topography helps clarify matters in each case.

Longforgan (Perth & Kinross) 'Field, or church, over the boggy
place'. *Lann* (Scottish Gaelic) can mean both 'field' and 'church';
for, 'over, above'; *gronn* (Old Gaelic) 'marsh'. It appears as
Langforgrunde in the fourteenth century. The boggy place itself
is perpetuated in Monorgan by the shore of the Firth of Tay;
originally Scottish Gaelic *mòine*, 'moss', and *gronn*. When the
sense of *gronn* became lost, it was rendered in Gaelic as Mòine
Fhorgainn, 'Forgan's moss'.

Longformacus (Borders) Apparently 'church on the land of Maccus'.
Long (Cumbric *lann*, cognate with Welsh *llan*, 'church'), *fothir*
(Cumbric) 'land, meadow'; *Maccus* (Irish-Scandinavian form of
personal name Magnus), seen also in Maxwell, Maxwelton.
Recorded as Langeford Makhous, c. 1340, but this doublet of place
and personal name, so frequent in England, is rare in Scotland,
where the two tend to be run into one.

Longhope (Orkney) 'Long sheltered bay'. *Hop* (Old Norse) 'sheltered
bay'.

Longmorn (Moray) 'Morgan's church, or field'. The likeliest
derivation is from *lann* (Scottish Gaelic) 'field', or 'church's field'

and earlier 'church'; and *Morgan* (Brythonic personal name) also found in Tillymorgan ('Morgan's hill') in Aberdeenshire.

Longniddry (East Lothian) 'Church of the new hamlet'. *Long* (Cumbric *lann*) 'church'; *nuadh* (Cumbric) 'new'; *tref* (Cumbric) 'hamlet'. Recorded as Langnedre in 1595.

Lora, Falls of (Argyll & Bute) A poetic name bestowed on the site, where, at low tide, the water from Loch Etive spills over a rock barrier towards the sea, taken from the eighteenth-century 'Ossian' poems; in the mind of the author, James Macpherson, it may have had some relation to *labhra* (Scottish Gaelic) 'noisy'.

Lorn(e) (Argyll & Bute) This area of the west coast of Scotland (Lathurna in Scottish Gaelic), centred on present-day Oban, together with the firth of the same name, was named after Loarn, brother of Fergus of Ulster, and by tradition one of the leaders of the Scots' colonisation from Ireland in the late fifth century. Noted as Lorne in 1304. Larne in Ulster has the same derivation.

Lossie, River (Moray). The river-name has been linked to the name Loxa on Ptolemy's second-century map, from a Greek root *loxos*, 'crooked'. A derivation from *lus* (Scottish Gaelic) 'herbs, plants,' has also been suggested. The town of Lossiemouth takes its name from its position at the river-mouth. The modern English *-mouth* is an indication that the town was only developed in the late seventeenth century, when a harbour was built here. The section of the town called Branderburgh is named after Mr Brander, laird of Pitgavenny, some way inland, who developed it in 1830. Ramsay Macdonald (1866–1937), Britain's first Labour prime minister, was born here.

Loth (Highland) 'Muddy place'. *Loth* (Scottish Gaelic) 'mud'.

Lothian This area, once a kingdom of the Britons, later part of the Anglian kingdom of Bernicia, and since then always the most 'English' part of Scotland, is believed to have been named after its historical founder, one Leudonus (Brythonic or pre-Celtic personal name) of uncertain origin. Early records show Loonia c. 970, Lothene 1091, Louthion c. 1200, Laodinia 1245. For a time it was one of the nine administrative regions of the mainland, now divided into four districts corresponding to former counties: Midlothian, East Lothian, West Lothian and the City of Edinburgh.

Loudoun (East Ayrshire) 'Beacon hill'. *Lowe* (Scots 'fire' from Old Norse *logr*) and *dún* (Old English) 'hill'. An association with the Celtic god Lug has also been suggested, making the name *Lugdunon*, cognate with Lyons in France (*Lugdunum*). Found in its present form c. 1140.

Lovat (Highland) 'Swampy area'. The name, perhaps Pictish from an early Celtic form *lu-vo*, 'muddy' (*see* Loth) was superseded by A Mhorfhaich (Scottish Gaelic) 'carse' or 'seaside plain'; a name found in other similar locations, like the Morrich More ('great carse') near Tain, but is retained in the title of Lord Lovat. There are two Lovat rivers in England, which are likely to derive from the same root-form.

Lowther Hills (Borders) *See* Lauder.

Loyal, Ben and **Loch** (Highland) This is an anglicised version of the Gaelic rendering Beinn Laoghal, from *beinn* (Scottish Gaelic) 'mountain'; *laga* (Old Norse) 'law'; *fjall* (Old Norse) 'hill'. This would indicate a meeting-place for the discussion and ratification of laws. But *leidh* (Old Norse) 'levy' or 'mustering-place' has also been suggested. The 'Ben' is in both cases, strictly speaking, unnecessary. The adjacent Loch Loyal has been named after the mountain (2506ft/766m), noted as Ben Lyoll, 1601.

Lubnaig, Loch (Stirling) 'Loch of the bend'. *Lùb* (Scottish Gaelic) 'bend', with a double Scottish Gaelic suffix, *-an*, and *-aig*, both of which indicate 'small'; although the loch is not specially small, it is narrow, and bends.

Luce (Dumfries & Galloway) 'Place of herbs or plants'. *Lus* (Scottish Gaelic) 'herbs, plants'. Noted as Glenlus, 1220. *See* Luss. Herb gardens were vital for providing the elements of medicines as well as food flavourings and preservatives, and were found all over the country; here probably in association with the abbey of Glenluce.

Lugar, River (East Ayrshire) 'Bright stream'. The Cumbric name is conjectured from the early Celtic root form *loucos*, 'white', with the typical Celtic termination *-ar*, indicating a river. The name of the Celtic god Lugh comes from the same source, and the name could be 'stream of Lugh'. Found in this form c. 1200. It has given its name to Lugar village.

Luggie, River (North Lanarkshire) 'Bright stream'. As with Lugar, the name is conjectured from the Celtic root form *loucos*, 'white'; cognate with the River Lugg in Herefordshire, England. Found as Luggy, c. 1300. This tributary of the Kelvin is pleasantly described in David Gray's nineteenth-century poem 'The Luggie'.

Lui, Ben (Stirling) 'Mountain of calves'. *Beinn* (Scottish Gaelic) 'mountain'; *laoigh* (Scottish Gaelic) 'of calves'. The reference is to the summer grazing slopes on the mountain (3708ft/1134m). There is also the Lui Water and Glen Lui on the southern flank of the Cairngorms. *See* Ardlui.

Luib (Stirling, Highland) 'Bend'. *Lùb* (Scottish Gaelic) 'bend, winding', used of a valley with a bend.

Luichart, Loch (Highland) 'Place of encampment'. *Long* (Irish Gaelic) 'dwelling, ship'; *phort* (Irish Gaelic) 'harbour, camp ground'. Longphort is compressed into Luichart. *See* Longart. The Gaelic *lùchairt*, 'palace' has also been suggested as the origin of the name, but this seems much less likely.

Luing (Argyll & Bute) 'Ship island'. *Luing* (Scottish Gaelic) 'ship's.'

Lumphanan (Aberdeenshire) 'Finnan's field'. *Lann* (Scottish Gaelic) 'field, enclosure'. *Fhìonain* (Scottish Gaelic proper name) 'Finnan's.' The site of a property belonging to a church dedicated to St Finnan. Lumphinnans in Fife is likely to have the same derivation.

Lunan Bay (Angus) This has been derived as 'Wave bay', from *lunnan* (Scottish Gaelic) 'waves'; if so, the name would appear to have worked its way back up the Lunan Burn from the estuary, noted as Innirlunan, 1189, all the way to Lunanhead, beyond Forfar. There is another Lunan Burn flowing through Loch Clunie and into the River Isla, far from the sea, and it seems more likely to stem from the same pre-Celtic root as the English Lune. This has been taken as cognate with Old Irish *slán*, 'health' (Scottish Gaelic *sláinte*), meaning 'health-giving stream'.

Luncarty *See* Longart.

Lundin Links (Fife) Perhaps 'boggy site'. A Pictish name which may be associated with *lodan* (Scottish Gaelic) 'marsh'. Noted as Lundin around 1200. The addition of Links in the post-Gaelic period is from *hlinc* (Old English) 'rising ground, bank', which came to be used in Scots to describe grassy dunes by the sea, and by association, golf courses.

Lurgainn, Loch (Highland) 'Shin loch'. *Lurgan* (Scottish Gaelic) 'shin, unshapely leg', probably in reference to the boomerang shape of the loch, lying in the hollow between Stac Pollaidh and Ben More Coigach.

Luss (Argyll & Bute) 'Place of herbs or plants'. *Lus* (Scottish Gaelic) 'herbs, plants'. Recorded as Lus, 1225. *See* Luce.

Lybster (Highland) 'Settlement in the lee'. *Hlie* (Old Norse) 'leeward'; *bolstadr* (Old Norse) 'farmstead', settlement'. This Caithness fishing village is set in a deep sheltered voe.

Lynchat (Highland) 'Wild cats' field'. *Lann* (Scottish Gaelic) 'field'; *chait* (Scottish Gaelic) 'cat'.

Lyne Water (Fife; Borders) The two Lynes have different derivations; that in Fife is from *lleith* (Cumbric) 'moist, wet', cognate with Leith, and noted as aqua de Letheni, 'Leithen water', 1227; that near Peebles is Scottish Gaelic *linne*, 'pool, channel, waterfall', noted as Lyn, c. 1190.

Lynwilg (Highland) 'Land of the bag or bulge'. *Lann* (Scottish

Gaelic) 'field'; *bhuilge* (Scottish Gaelic) 'bulge, bag'. Noted 1603 as Lambulge.

Lyon, River, Glen, Loch (Perth & Kinross) Apparently 'grinding river'. The Gaelic name is *Lìobhunn*, deriving from a pre-Celtic root *lim*, 'file', presumably with reference to the erosive action of the river. This is one of the longest glens in Scotland, reaching far west into the Grampians, and meeting Strath Tay at Appin of Dull.

M

Macdui, Ben (Moray) 'Hill of the sons of Dubh or Duff'. *Beinn* (Scottish Gaelic) 'mountain'; *mac Duibh* (Scottish Gaelic) 'sons of Duff'. The MacDuffs have ancient associations with the region. This mountain in the Cairngorms, 4296ft/1309m, was believed to be highest in Scotland until the superior height of Ben Nevis was established. The spelling Macdhui is also found. *See* Macduff.

Macduff (Aberdeenshire) This Banffshire fishing port was named in 1783 by James Duff, second earl of Fife, who redeveloped the settlement, previously known as Down (Scottish Gaelic *dùn*, 'fort'). Macduff, as in the surname, simply means 'son of *Dubh*, the black-haired one)'.

Machars, The (Dumfries & Galloway) 'Plains'. *Machair* (Scottish Gaelic) 'low-lying fertile plain'. The Wigtown peninsula is not exactly a plain, reaching 646ft/197m in Mochrum Fell (itself from Gaelic *magh*, 'plain', and *crom*, 'crooked') but it is much less hilly than the inland Galloway country.

Machrihanish (Argyll & Bute) 'Coastal plain of Sanas'. *Machair* (Scottish Gaelic) 'low-lying fertile plain'. Most familiarly, a *machair* is the herbaceous strip lying just inland from a beach, and there are many such in the West Highlands and the islands. The latter part of the name is unclear, perhaps a personal or district name. It has also been linked to *sean-innse* (Scottish Gaelic) 'old haugh or water-meadow', which does not seem appropriate to here. This, with Brora in Sutherland, was one of the two places in Highlands where coal was mined until the twentieth century.

Macmerry (East Lothian) The first part is 'plain', from *màgh* (Scottish Gaelic) 'plain'; the second part is unclear, perhaps related to the Gaelic root *mear-*, indicating 'exposed'.

Maddiston (West Lothian) 'Mandred's place'. A reference of 1366 has Mandredestone; *Mandred* (Old English personal name) *tun* (Old English) 'settlement, place'.

Maggieknockater (Aberdeenshire) 'The fuller's plain'. *Màgh* (Scottish Gaelic) 'plain'; *an* 'of the'; *fhucadair* (Scottish Gaelic) 'fuller': a reference to cloth-making in the area.

Magus Muir (Fife) 'Plain with the point of land'. *Màgh* (Scottish Gaelic) 'plain'; *gasg* (Scottish Gaelic) 'tail, point of land'. This accurately describes the location; *muir* (Scots) 'moor' is a post-Gaelic addition. This is where Archbishop Sharp was assassinated by Covenanters in 1679.

Mainland (Orkney; Shetland) This name for the largest island of both groups is of some antiquity, from Old Norse *megin*, 'principal', *land*, 'land'; found as Meginland c. 1150.

Mains (All regions) Very often found attached to a farm name, this indicates the main or home farm of an estate. It is an aphetic form (losing the unstressed first sound) of the word 'domain', noted from 1479. Davidson's Mains, once a farm, is now a suburb of Edinburgh. It is also found in the form 'Mains of', as in Mains of Forthar.

Mallaig (Highland) Possibly 'headland bay'. *Muli* (Old Norse) 'headland'; *aig* (Scottish Gaelic version of original Old Norse *vagr*) 'bay'. This derivation fits the topography. An alternative derivation of the first part is from *mol* (Old Norse) 'shingle'. Mallaig is the terminus of the West Highland Railway, completed to here in 1903, and the ferry-port for South Skye.

Màm 'Breast-shaped hill, rounded hill'. Many mountain names are prefixed by Màm, sometimes shown as Maam. A number have been anglicised as 'Maiden Pap', from the Ord of Caithness to Dumfries.

Mamore (Highland) 'Big round hills'. *Màm* (Scottish Gaelic) 'rounded hill', *mòr* (Scottish Gaelic) 'big'. The converse form of Mambeg (from Scottish Gaelic *beag*, 'small') is found in several places. The name has also been less probably explained as 'great plain' from *magh* (Scottish Gaelic) 'plain', and *mòr* (Scottish Gaelic) 'big'. This region, adjacent to Ben Nevis, is one of the highest parts of the country; although its summit areas form a kind of plateau, it is a much-dissected one and hard to see as a plain.

Manuel (West Lothian) Probably 'rock of the view'. *Maen* (Cumbric) 'rock', *gwel* (Cumbric) 'view, outlook'. Noted as Manuell, c. 1190.

Maol 'Great bare round hill'. This Gaelic term, always found with some defining word, and derived from an Indo-European root-form *mai*, 'to cut', is common on Mull and Islay, and less common in other parts of the Highlands and Islands.

Mar (Aberdeenshire) Mar with Buchan was one of the seven divisions of ancient Pictland. It appears to have been an Indo-European personal name from the pre-Celtic period, becoming identified with the territory, and eventually forming an earldom. The Gaelic form is Marr, noted in the *Book of Deer*, c. 1150.

Marchmont (Edinburgh) 'Horse hill'. *Marc* (Scottish Gaelic) 'horse'; *monadh* (Scottish Gaelic) 'hill', now a residential district of Edinburgh, on a ridge south of the castle.

Maree, Loch (Highland) 'Maelrubha's loch'. Until the seventeenth century this Wester Ross loch was known as Loch Ewe, from the river flowing from its western end. Maree, found as Loch Maroy, 1638, comes from the name Maelrubha, the saint who founded the abbey at Applecross. One of the islands in the loch was the location of a pre-Christian cult which was transferred to Maelrubha, and became known as Eilean Ma-ruibhe. In time this name was extended to the loch itself. The name Loch Feadhal feas also seems to have been used locally; *feadhal* has been construed as 'shallow water'; the meaning of *feas* is uncertain. *See* Kinlochewe.

Markinch (Fife) 'Isle or water meadow of the horse'. *Marc* (Scottish Gaelic) 'horse'; *innse* (Scottish Gaelic) 'water meadow, island'. This place, reputedly built originally on an island in a lake that has since been drained, was recorded as Marcinche around 1200.

Marwick (Orkney; Shetland) 'Seagull bay'. *Má* (Old Norse) 'seagull'; *vik* (Old Norse) 'bay'.

Maryburgh (Highland) Earlier name of Fort William, after Queen Mary II; Maryburgh in Easter Ross is of similar date (c. 1690).

Maryculter (Aberdeen) 'Back land of the (church of) Mary'. *See* Peterculter. There was a Templar church established here and dedicated to the Virgin in 1487.

Maryhill (Glasgow) This northern suburb of Glasgow was named in 1760 after the local landowner, Mary Hill of Gairbraid.

Mauchline (East Ayrshire) *Mochlin* (with a 'ch' as in loch). 'Plain with a pool'. *Magh* (Scottish Gaelic) 'plain'; *linne* (Scottish Gaelic) 'pool'. Noted c. 1000 as Machlind I Cuil, 'Mauchline of the nook'. This small town, much associated with Robert Burns, lies on a fertile plain between the River Ayr and the Cessnock Water.

Maud (Aberdeenshire) 'Dog's, or wolf's place'. *Madadh* (Scottish Gaelic) 'dog, wolf'. Apart from the Buchan village, once a railway junction on the defunct Fraserburgh and Peterhead lines, there is a Hill of Maud just south of Buckie in Moray.

Mawcarse (Perth & Kinross) 'Plain of the carse'. *Magh* (Scottish Gaelic) 'plain'; *carse* (Scots, from Old Norse *kerss*) 'low-lying river bank'.

May, Isle of (Midlothian) 'Isle of seagulls'. *Má* (Old Norse) 'seagull'; *ey* (Old Norse) 'island'. In the *Orkneyinga Saga* (c. 1225) it is referred to as Maeyar. Scotland's first lighthouse was established here in the fifteenth century, or earlier, for ships entering the Firth of Forth. It was also a base of pirates and smugglers.

Maybole (South Ayrshire) 'Maiden's house'. *Maege* (old English) 'maiden, kinswoman'; *botl* (old English) 'house'. The oldest form known is Maybothel, from the late twelfth century.

Meall 'Humped hill', from Scottish Gaelic *meall*, 'humped or rounded hill.' A prefix to many mountain names, usually given to lower hills, around 3000ft/1000m, or less. In the southwest it is found scotticised into the form of Mill-, and sometimes Meowl-.

Mealfuarvounie (Highland) *Mayl-foor-voonie*. 'Hump of the cold mountains'. *Meall* (Scottish Gaelic) 'humped hill'; *fuar* (Scottish Gaelic) 'cold'; *mhonaidh* (Scottish Gaelic) 'of the mountain'. A distinctive mountain south of Inverness (2284ft/698m).

Mearns, The (Aberdeenshire, East Renfrewshire) *Merrns*. This name has been explained as 'the stewardship', and its Gaelic name is An mhaoirne, indicating an area administered by an officially appointed steward. But the terminal -s is not explained. The area of the Mearns covers a triangular fertile area south of Stonehaven, as far as the North Esk river, and east of the Highlands, corresponding to the eastern part of the former county of Kincardineshire. The Mearns district south of Glasgow has a river-named the Earn; and *magh* (Scottish Gaelic) 'plain', with the river-name, probably a pre-Celtic one based on the root-word -ar, indicating 'flowing water' (*see* Earn), have been proposed as a possible source here. However it is in Stewart country and the next parish is Stewarton (the surname Stewart means 'steward'). The two Mearns names may have different origins.

Meggat Water (Dumfries & Galloway; Borders) 'Boggy stream'. *Mig* (Brythonic) 'swamp'. Noted c. 1206 as Meggete.

Megginch (Perth & Kinross) Perhaps 'milk island', from *melg* (Old Gaelic) 'milk' (see Castlemilk) and *innis* (Scottish Gaelic) 'water meadow, island'. Earlier forms of the name include Melginch (c. 1200).

Meig, River (Highland) 'Boggy stream', from *mig* (Brythonic–Pictish) swamp.

Meigle (Perth & Kinross) 'Swampy field'. *Mig* (Brythonic–Pictish) 'swamp'; *dol* (Brythonic–Pictish) 'meadow'. Noted as Miggil, 1183. The district is rich in Pictish sculpted stones. Meigle Bay in North Ayrshire and Meigle Hill in the Borders have the same derivation.

Meikle Ferry (Highland) 'The great ferry'. *Meikle* (Scots) 'big', from Old Norse *mikil*. This ferry across the mouth of the Dornoch Firth, scene of a disastrous wreck in the nineteenth century, was replaced by a bridge in the later twentieth. The Gizzen Briggs sandflats here are Old Norse *gisnar*, 'leaky', and *brygga*, 'bridge'.

Meldrum (Aberdeenshire) The modern form of the name suggests 'mountain ridge'; *meall* (Scottish Gaelic) 'mountain'; *druim* (Scottish Gaelic) 'ridge', but early forms of the name, Melgedrom 1291, and Melkidrum 1296, make this improbable; the meaning of the prefix is uncertain, perhaps from the same origin as Megginch.

Melrose (Borders) 'Bare moor'. *Mailo* (Cumbric, cognate with

Gaelic *maol*) 'bare'; *ros* (Cumbric, cognate with Gaelic *ros*, 'wood, promontory') 'moor'. It was recorded as Mailros in a document of c. 700. The abbey here, founded in 1136, now a picturesque ruin showing some of the finest late Gothic architecture in Scotland, was the country's first Cistercian foundation; it has been improbably suggested that *maol* in the name refers to the bald heads of the tonsured monks.

Melsetter (Orkney) 'Farm of the grassy dunes'. *Melr* (Old Norse) 'grassy sand dune'; *saetr* (Old Norse) 'farm'.

Melvich (Highland) 'Bay of sea-bent dunes'. *Mealbhan* (Scottish Gaelic) 'sea-bent', from *melr* (Old Norse) 'bent grass, grassy dune'; *vik* (Old Norse) 'bay'. Melvaig, by Gairloch, has the same derivation.

Menstrie (Clackmannanshire) 'Hamlet in the plain'. *Maes* (Cumbric) 'open field, plain'; *tref* (Cumbric) 'settlement, hamlet'. Found as Mestryn in 1261.

Menteith, Lake of (Stirling) *Men-teeth.* 'Lowland of Menteith', from *leachd* (Scottish Gaelic) 'sloping ground'. The Gaelic form, Leachd Teàdhaich, scotticised as 'laich of Menteith', may explain the enduring insistence on referring to this loch as Scotland's only 'lake'. It lies within a natural basin surrounded by hills. Menteith is an ancient name; with Strathearn it was a province of Pictland. It derives as *moíne* (Scottish Gaelic) 'moor', or possibly from *mon*, a local Gaelic form of *monadh*, 'hill', with Teith (Celtic river-name). The Teith flows some way north of here, and neither into nor out of the lake, but documentary evidence shows its name was taken for a wide area of land around it. Early maps show Loch Monteith on the Laicht of Monteith, and records: Menetethe 1185; Mynynteth 1234; Monteath 1724.

Merchiston (Edinburgh) 'Merchion's farm'. *Merchiaun* (Cumbric personal name); *tun* (Old English) 'farmstead'. Now a district of Edinburgh. The inventor of logarithms, John Napier (1550–1617) lived here; his name is preserved in Napier University.

Merkland (Dumfries & Galloway; other regions) 'Land held for the rental of one merk'. Scots *merk*, 'mark', a unit of currency. A common locality name, especially in the south-west.

Merrick (Dumfries & Galloway) 'Pronged hill'. *Meurach* (Scottish Gaelic) 'pronged, branchy'. Merrick (2766ft/846m) is the highest point in the Galloway Forest. Noted as Maerach Hill on Blaeu's map, 1654.

Merse, The (Borders) The name of this fertile area watered by the Tweed and its tributaries comes from *maersc* (Old English) 'marsh', which came to mean 'low, flat land' in Scots. Noted in this form, 1560.

Methil (Fife) Perhaps 'boundary wood'. *Maid* (Cumbric) 'boundary'; *choille* (Scottish Gaelic) 'wood'. Alternatively, 'boggy wood', from *maoth* (Scottish Gaelic) 'bog'; or as one authority suggests, it may derive from *methl* (Old Norse) 'middle', signifying its location between Buckhaven and Leven. A record of 1250 shows Methkil. In the nineteenth- to twentieth-century heyday of the Fife coalfield, Methil was an important coal exporting harbour.

Methven (Perth & Kinross) 'Middle stone'. *Meddfaen* (Cumbric) 'middle stone, middle marker', as of a boundary. Noted as Methfen, 1211. In the early days of his kingship, Robert Bruce was defeated here by an English army, in 1306.

Midmar (Aberdeen) 'Bog of Mar'. *Mig* (Brythonic–Pictish) 'bog'; *Mar* (*see* Mar). Recorded as Migmarre, c. 1300.

Milngavie (East Dunbartonshire) *Mul-guy.* Perhaps 'windmill'. *Muilleann* (Scottish Gaelic) 'mill'; *gaoithe* (Scottish Gaelic) 'wind'. Windmills were unusual in Scotland, where water power was normally available. Alternatively, the origin of the name of this northern dormitory town for Glasgow may be derived: *Meal-na-gaoithe* (Scottish Gaelic) 'hill of the wind'. Noted on Blaeu's map, 1654, as Milguy.

Midlothian *See* Lothian.

Milleur Point (Dumfries & Galloway) 'Brown point', from Scottish Gaelic *maol*, 'rock-brow, promontory', and *odhar*, 'dun-coloured'.

Millport (North Ayrshire) This resort and port on the island of Cumbrae, in the Firth of Clyde, is named after the large grain mill that stood above the harbour when the town was originally developed in the first decade of the nineteenth century.

Milton (All regions) 'Place of the mill'. Often an English version of the original Baile a' Mhuíleann (Scottish Gaelic) 'place of the mill', found in anglicised form as Balavoulin.

Minard (Argyll & Bute) 'Small bay'. *Minni* (Old Norse) 'small'; *fjordr* (Old Norse) 'bay, loch'.

Minch, The (Highland, Western Isles) Possibly 'great headland(s)'. *Megin* (Old Norse) 'great'; *nes* (Old Norse) 'headland'. The name of this stormy stretch of sea between the northwest mainland of Scotland and the Outer Hebrides, separated into the Minch proper and the 'Little Minch', is almost certainly Scandinavian in origin. The cape in question could either be Cape Wrath, or the Butt of Lewis, or both. It is interesting that this name should have been preserved in anglicised form, as it was not used in Gaelic. The Gaelic name for the Minch is Cuan nan Orc, 'sea of whales'; for the Little Minch, Cuan Sgithe, 'sea of Skye'.

Mingary (Western Isles) Probably 'big garth'. *Mikla* (Old Norse) 'big', has become transposed to *mingil*; *gardr* (Old Norse) 'land between machair and moor'; adopted into Scottish Gaelic as *gearraidh.*

Mingulay (Western Isles) Probably 'big island'. *Mikla* (Old Norse) 'big', has become transposed to *mingil*; with *ey* (Old Norse) 'island'.

Minnigaff (Dumfries & Galloway) 'Hill of the smith', from *monadh* (Scottish Gaelic) 'hill'; and *a' gobhainn* (Scottish Gaelic) 'of the smith'. Recorded as Monygof, 1504. *See also* Challoch.

Mintlaw (Aberdeenshire) 'Mint hill'. *Mint* (the same word in Old English) was always an important herb; *law* (Scots from Old English *hlaew*) 'hill'. The Scots name indicates an origin in the fourteenth century or later; the village itself is relatively modern, one of the many established in the late eighteenth and early nineteenth centuries.

Moffat (Dumfries & Galloway) Possibly the place of the 'long plain', referring to the level ground between here and Annandale. *Magh* (Scottish Gaelic) 'plain'; *fada* (Scottish Gaelic) 'long'. Noted as Moffet, 1179. A fine statue of a Border ram in the main street testifies to the sheep-rearing importance of the area.

Moidart (Highland) Place of the 'muddy fiord'. *Moda* (Old Norse) 'mud'; *art* (Scottish Gaelic adaptation of Old Norse *fjordr*) 'sea-loch'. Recorded as Muddeward, 1292. This area of the West Highlands, between Ardnamurchan to the south and Morar to the north, takes its name from the shallow sea loch that stretches inland to Kinlochmoidart.

Monadhliath (Highland) *Mona-leea*. 'Grey mountains'. *Monadh* (Scottish Gaelic) 'mountain(s)'; *liath* (Scottish Gaelic) 'grey'. A wide, somewhat monotonous mountain massif of grey mica-schist rock, lying between upper Strathspey and the Great Glen, in which the Spey, Findhorn and Dulnain rivers rise. Its greatest height is Càrn Dearg (Scottish Gaelic) 'red cairn', 3100 ft/944m.

Monar, Loch (Highland) Its Gaelic name, Loch Mhonair, means 'loch of Monar', which has been tentatively explained as coming from a Pictish term related to Gaelic *monadh,* 'mountain', and indicating 'loch of the high ground'.

Moncrieff (Perth & Kinross) 'Wooded hill'. *Monadh* (Scottish Gaelic) 'mountain, hill'; *craoibh* (Scottish Gaelic) 'of the woods'. Recorded in 728 as Monad Croib, if it is indeed the site of the battle of that year between opposing Pictish factions.

Moniaive (Dumfries & Galloway) Possibly 'moor of crying'. *Moíne* (Scottish Gaelic) 'moor, peat bog'; *èibhe* (Scottish Gaelic) 'cry, death-cry'. Recorded in 1560 as Monyyife.

Monifieth (Dundee) 'Peat-bed of the bog'. *Moíne* (Scottish Gaelic)

'moor', peat bed'; *feithe* (Scottish Gaelic) 'bog'. Recorded as
Munifieth 1178. This residential town situated on the Firth of Tay
to the east of Dundee was largely developed in the nineteenth
century on a previously worked peat moss close to the shore.

Monklands (North Lanarkshire) 'The monks' lands'. This district
east of Glasgow and centred on the adjoining towns of Airdrie
and Coatbridge takes its name from the former parishes of Old
and New Monkland, a name which goes back to the twelfth
century, when King Malcolm IV granted lands here to the monks
of Newbattle Abbey near Dalkeith.

Montrose (Angus) 'The peat-moss of the promontory'. *Moíne*
(Scottish Gaelic) 'moor, peat bed'; *ros* (Scottish Gaelic) 'promontory'.
The name accurately describes this historic east coast town's
situation on a lowlying peninsula at the entrance to the tidal
Montrose Basin. The *t* in the name has been interpolated, as in
another Tayside name, Montroy, from *monadh* (Scottish Gaelic)
'mountain'; *ruadh* (Scottish Gaelic) 'red'. Records show Munros
c. 1200, Montrose 1296, Monros 1322, Montross 1480. The town
is notable for its links with a diversity of modern poets, Hugh
MacDiarmid, Edwin Muir, Helen B. Cruickshank, and Raymond
Vettese among them.

Monymusk (Aberdeenshire) 'Mucky peat bog'. Scottish Gaelic *moíne*,
'moor, peat bed'; *mosach* (Scottish Gaelic) 'foul.' Despite the name,
this was one of the earliest 'improved' agricultural estates in the
eighteenth century.

Monzie (Perth & Kinross) 'Corn plain'. *Magh* (Scottish Gaelic)
'plain'; *an*, 'of'; *eadha* (Scottish Gaelic) 'corn'. Recorded as
Mugheda, 1226. Moonzie in Fife has the same derivation.

Monzievaird (Perth & Kinross) Probably 'plain of the bards'. *Magh*
(Scottish Gaelic) 'plain'; *bhàrd* (Scottish Gaelic) 'bards'. Recorded
as Muithauard, c. 1200. Bards were held in great esteem and
frequently given grants of land: the Gaelic form *-bhaird*, 'bard's', is
often found incorporated in local names.

Moorfoot Hills (Midlothian) Moorfoot is 'moor place', from Old
Norse/Old English *mór*, 'moor', and *thweit*, 'place', with the sense
of a place cleared for grazing, from Old English *thwitan*, 'to cut';
another of the few instances of a 'thwaite' name in Scotland. Noted
as Morthwait, c. 1142.

Morangie (Highland) Perhaps 'the big meadows'; *mòr* (Scottish
Gaelic) 'big'; *innse* (Scottish Gaelic) 'water meadows'.

Morar (Highland) 'Big water'. *Mór* (Scottish Gaelic) 'big'; *dhobhar*
(Scottish Gaelic, from Brythonic) 'water'. Noted as Morderer,
c. 1292. This part of the west Highlands, between Knoydart to the

north and Moidart to the south, takes its name from the river that flows across the narrow isthmus between the loch and the sea. Its name was also given to the loch, which divides it into North and South Morar: the deepest inland water in Britain at over 1000ft (300m) below sea level – a depth not again reached for many miles out in the open sea.

Moray 'Sea settlement'. *Mori* (Old Gaelic name related to Brythonic–Pictish *mor-tref*, 'sea-home'). Noted in the *Pictish Chronicle*, c. 970, as Moreb; latinised into Moravia, 1124. The current administrative district and former county takes its name from the much larger ancient province and earldom of Moray, which also gave its name to the Moray Firth.

More, Ben (several locations) 'Big mountain'. *Beinn* (Scottish Gaelic) 'mountain'; *mòr* (Scottish Gaelic) 'big'. The best-known Ben More is probably that above Crianlarich (3853ft/1174m); others are often identified additionally by a district name, as in Ben More Assynt, Ben More Mull, etc.

More, Glen (Highland) 'Great glen'. *Gleann* (Scottish Gaelic) 'glen'; *mòr* (Scottish Gaelic) 'big'. It is known also as The Great Glen and Glen Albyn (Scottish Gaelic *Albainn*, 'of Scotland'). This major fault valley extends sixty-five miles (105km) across the width of Scotland, from the Moray Firth to Loch Linnhe, an arm of the Atlantic Ocean. An important communication and portage route from earliest times, its three lochs, Loch Ness, Loch Oich and Loch Lochy, were connected to each other and the sea in 1822 to form the Caledonian Canal.

Morebattle (Borders) 'Big house', possibly a hybrid formation of Scottish Gaelic *mòr*, 'big', and Old English *botl*, 'house', though it may be that Old English *mor*, 'moor' giving 'moor house', is more likely. Noted as Mereboda, 1116. The tower of the Kerrs was close to here.

Moriston, River and **Glen** (Highland) 'Big waterfalls'. *Mòr* (Scottish Gaelic) 'big'; *easain* (Scottish Gaelic) 'waterfalls'. Glen Moriston is well endowed with these. The *t* is a recent intrusion into the name; nineteenth century forms show Glen Morison. A battle was fought in Glen Mareisin, 728; probably the same location.

Mormond (Aberdeenshire) 'Big hill'. *Mór* (Scottish Gaelic) 'big'; *monadh* (Scottish Gaelic) 'hill'. Though not specially high, Mormond Hill (768ft/242m) stands out prominently in the Buchan landscape, well-known from the bothy ballad 'Fare ye weel, ye Mormond Braes'.

Morningside (Edinburgh) Perhaps 'Morgan's seat', derived in a similar way to Longmorn. The origin of the name of this pleasant

residential Edinburgh district, developed mainly in the nineteenth
century, is not entirely clear. There is another Morningside to the
east of Wishaw.

Mortlach (Moray) 'Big hill', from Scottish Gaelic *mòr,* 'big', and
tulach, 'hill'. Noted in 1157 as Murthilloch.

Morton (Dumfries & Galloway; Fife; Renfrewshire) 'Farm by the
moor'. *Muir* (Scots) 'moor'; *toun* (Scots) from Old English *tun,*
'farm'.

Morven (Aberdeenshire; Highland) 'Big hill'. Usually taken to be
a transposition of Ben More, from *mòr* (Scottish Gaelic) 'big';
and *beinn* (Scottish Gaelic) 'mountain'. However, if its source is
Brythonic–Pictish *morwen,* 'maiden' – and both Morvens are in
Pictland – it is more likely to be yet another of the many mountain
names which draw on the resemblance of the mountain's shape to
the female breast. Morven on the Ord of Caithness (2313ft/707m)
is close to another hill still called Maiden Pap.

Morvern (Argyll & Bute) 'Sea gap'. *Mor* (Old Gaelic) 'sea'; *bhearn*
(Scottish Gaelic) 'gap'. Noted in 1343 as Gawrmorwarne, with
the Scottish Gaelic prefix *garbh,* 'rough'. Christina of Garmoran
gave hospitality to the fugitive Robert Bruce, in 1307. This is
a triangular peninsula on the west Highland coast, lying south
of Ardnamurchan and bounded by the Sound of Mull and Loch
Linnhe. The 'sea gap' is possibly Loch Sunart, a long fiord that
penetrates along the north of this area, virtually cutting it off.

Mossgiel (East Ayrshire) 'Plain of the smallholding'. *Maes* (Cumbric)
'plain, open field'; *gafael* (Cumbric) 'holding'. This was one of
several places farmed by Robert Burns.

Motherwell (North Lanarkshire) 'The Mother's well'; Modyrwaile
in 1363. This former steel-making town in the Clyde valley to
the south-east of Glasgow takes its name from an ancient well
dedicated to the Virgin Mary, the site of which is today marked by
a plaque in Ladywell Road.

Moulin (Perth & Kinross) 'Bare hill'. *Maolinn* (Scottish Gaelic)
'bare round hill'. Found as Molin, 1207.

Moulinearn (Perth & Kinross) 'Mill by the alders', from *muileann*
(Scottish Gaelic) 'mill', and *fhearna* (Scottish Gaelic) 'alders'.

Mound, The (Highland) A nineteenth-century name, from the
embankment carrying the road and former Dornoch branch railway
line across the head of Loch Fleet.

Mount Vernon (Glasgow) This area of the city, once known as
Windyedge, is said to have been renamed by George Buchanan,
one of Glasgow's eighteenth-century 'tobacco lords', after the
Washington family's plantation in Virginia.

Mounth (Angus; Aberdeenshire; Perth & Kinross) 'The mountain(s)' from *monadh* (Scottish Gaelic) 'mountain'. This was the original Scots name of the mountains miscalled 'Grampians', recorded as Muneth, 1198.

Mousa (Shetland) This island name is of uncertain derivation, though *mose* (Old Norse) 'moss', has been hazarded, for 'mossy isle'.

Moy (Highland) 'The plain'. From *magh* (Scottish Gaelic) 'plain'. Loch Moy is the 'loch of the plain'. Noted as Muy, c. 1235. The centre of the Clan MacIntosh territory.

Moyle (Dumfries & Galloway) A name for the strait between the Mull of Galloway and Antrim, from Scottish Gaelic *maol*, 'bald, bare', referring to the coastal promontories (compare Minch). In Gaelic it is Sruth na Maoile, 'the Moyle stream'.

Muck (Highland) 'Pig island'. *Muc* (Scottish Gaelic) 'pig'. The reference is usually taken to pigs being kept here rather than a topographical or totemic feature of this small but fertile Inner Hebridean island.

Muckersie (Perth & Kinross) 'Pigs' bank'. *Muc* (Scottish Gaelic) 'pig'; *kerss* (Old Norse) 'low-lying river bank' – the source of Scots *carse*.

Muckhart (Clackmannanshire) 'Pig yard'. *Muc* (Scottish Gaelic) 'pig'; *gart* (Scottish Gaelic) 'yard, enclosure'. Noted as Mukard, 1250. Yetts of Muckhart, Scots *yetts,* 'gates' from Old English *geatan,* indicates the entrance to a narrow valley here.

Muckle Flugga (Shetland) 'Great cliffs'. *Micil* (Old Norse) 'great, big'; *fluga* (Old Norse) 'cliffs'. Once the most northerly inhabited point of Britain, this lighthouse-crowned rock is the outermost and highest of a group of sharp rocks or skerries to the north of the island of Unst. *See* Out Stack.

Muir of Ord (Highland) 'The moor of the rounded hill'. *Muir* (Scots version of Old English *mór*) 'moor'; *ord* (Scottish Gaelic) 'rounded hill'. The rounded hill is the western shoulder of the Black Isle; the moor the level ground on which the village, once the site of an important cattle market, is located. The Gaelic name is Am Blàr Dubh, 'at the black field'.

Muirkirk (East Ayrshire) 'Church on the moor'. *Muir* (Scots version of Old English *mor*) 'moor', *kirk* (Scots, from Old English *cirice*) 'church'.

Mulben (Moray) 'Bare hill'. *Maol* (Scottish Gaelic) 'bare, bald'; *beinn* (Scottish Gaelic) 'mountain'. Noted as Molben c. 1328.

Mull 'Bare headland', from Scottish Gaelic *maol,* with the sense of 'rocky brow'. A number of headlands bear this name, including the

Mull of Oa on Islay, the Mull of Galloway and the Mull of Kintyre.
These are on the West Coast, but there are also Mull Head on Papa
Westray in Orkney and Blue Mull on Unst in Shetland, deriving
from Old Norse *muli*, 'headland'.

Mull (Argyll & Bute) In Ptolemy's map of around AD 150, this island
is referred to as Maleos, sufficiently like the present name to make
a suggested Old Norse derivation improbable. This was 'island of
the headland' from *muli* (Old Norse) 'headland'. Other suggestions
have been made including *maol* (Scottish Gaelic) which can mean
'rocky brow' as well as 'bare summit'; and *meuilach* (Scottish
Gaelic) 'favoured one'. The Gaelic name today is Muile, or Eilean
Muileach. A Celtic source seems most likely, with *maol* or an
earlier form fitting the form of this many-caped island.

Mull of Kintyre *See* Kintyre

Mullardoch, Loch (Highland) 'Loch of the bare uplands'. *Loch*
(Scottish Gaelic) 'lake, loch'; *maol* (Scottish Gaelic) 'bare'; *àrdaich*,
from Scottish Gaelic *àrd,* 'height'; *-ach* locative suffix.

Munlochy (Highland) 'At the foot of the black goddess's stream'.
Bonn (Scottish Gaelic) 'foot'; *lòch* (Old Gaelic) 'black'; *dae* (Old
Gaelic, 'goddess', giving Scottish Gaelic *dia*). *See* Lochty; there
is also a stream on Benarty called the Moonlochty Burn. An
alternative derivation is *i mBun Locha* (Scottish Gaelic) 'at the foot
of the loch'. The loch is presumably Munlochy Bay, but almost
all similarly situated locations have the *kin* prefix, meaning 'head'.
The name is found in this form, 1328. Its Gaelic name now is Poll
Lochaidh, 'black mud'. There is also a Munlochy in Strathdearn,
south of Inverness.

Murrayfield (Edinburgh) This western suburb of Edinburgh, home
of Scotland's national rugby football ground, was named after
an eighteenth-century local landowner and advocate, Archibald
Murray.

Murthly (Perth & Kinross) 'Big hill'. *Mòr* (Scottish Gaelic) 'big';
tulach (Scottish Gaelic) 'hill'. Murthly is situated a few miles north
of Perth, on the Highland Line, just where the hills begin.

Musselburgh (East Lothian) 'Mussel town'. *Musle* (Old English)
'mussel'; *burh* (Old English) 'town'. This ancient burgh on the Firth
of Forth, immediately to the east of Edinburgh, acquired its name
over 800 years ago; documented in 1100 as Musleburge.

Muthil (Perth & Kinross) Perhaps 'pleasant, or gentle, place', from
maothail (Scottish Gaelic) 'soothing, tender'. Found as Mothel,
c. 1198.

N

Nairn (Highland) The name originally belonged to the river and is of pre-Celtic origin, deriving from a conjectured Indo-European root *ner-* with the sense of 'penetrating' or 'submerging', found in a number of European river-names. It was later applied to the town at its mouth, which was formerly the county town of Nairnshire. It was also at times known as Invernairn, Invernaren 1189, Narne 1583. The seventeenth-century 'Wardlaw Manuscript', written not far away, refers to it consistently as Narden, though the Gaelic form is Narrun. Its early twentieth-century atmosphere was captured in *Nairn in Darkness and Light* by David Thompson.

Naver, River, Loch, Strath (Highland) Noted on Ptolemy's map of c. AD 150 as Nabaros, the name derives from a pre-Celtic root which has been identified both as *nebh*, indicating 'water' (*see* Nevis), and *nabh*, indicating 'fog' or 'cloud'; with a typical Celtic *-ar* ending, indicating a river, as with Lugar, and the English River Tamar. This long Sutherland strath, once well-populated, was 'cleared' by the landowner in 1819.

Navitie (Fife; other areas) 'Holy place'. This locality, with Navitie Hill, just north of Ballingry, derives from Scottish Gaelic *neimheidh*, 'sacred or holy place', a term derived from Gaulish *nemeton*, meaning a place for ritual meetings. The sense was adopted into Christianity as 'land belonging to the church'. Navity on the Black Isle, noted as Navite, 1578, has the same derivation, as do numerous other local names, often with legends of saints or magic wells attached, including Nevie in Glen Livet and Dalnavie in Easter Ross. Navidale in east Sutherland shows how the Norse settlers absorbed the Gaelic term into a hybrid with Old Norse *dalr*, 'dale, valley'. A number of *nemeton* names may have been lost, including the important cult site Medionemeton, 'middle sanctuary', recorded in the seventh-century *Ravenna Cosmography* as being on the line of the Antonine Wall.

Nell, Loch (Argyll & Bute) 'Loch of the swans'. Loch (Scottish Gaelic) 'lake, loch,' *nan*, 'of the'; *eala* (Scottish Gaelic) 'swans'.

Ness From Old Norse *nes*, 'nose', in the sense of 'promontory', this word for a headland occurs at various points on the east coast and at many in the Northern isles, especially Shetland. On the Scottish mainland it is found mostly at major headlands – significant navigational points, like Fife Ness and Tarbat Ness, which served as landmarks to the Viking seamen. In Shetland it is the conventional term for a headland, though even here some are named 'Head' or 'Point' through Scots or English influence. The northernmost district of Lewis is Ness (*see* Butt of Lewis). But the Ness Glen of the River Doon in Ayrshire comes from Scottish Gaelic *an eas*, 'the waterfall'. *See also* Ness.

Ness, River, Loch (Highland) The name was originally that of the river; probably of pre-Celtic origin. In Adamnan's *Life of St Columba* it is referred to by the latinised *Nesa*. Its meaning is unknown, and it long predates any likelihood of being from Old Norse *nes*, 'cape.' In Gaelic it is Nis. Short but wide and prone to sudden floods, it flows from the loch into the Moray Firth at Inverness. Loch Ness (of 'Monster' fame), which stretches for some twenty-four miles (38km) down the Great Glen, more than 600ft (200m) deep, holds the largest volume of fresh water in the country. *See* Inverness.

Netherby (Dumfries & Galloway) 'Lower farm'. *Nedri* (Old Norse) 'lower'; *by* (Old Norse) 'farmstead'.

Nethy, River (Perth & Kinross; Highland) 'Shining stream'. *See* Abernethy.

Nevis, River, Ben, Loch (Highland) The name of the highest mountain in the British Isles, (4406ft/1343m), also of a river, glen and a sea-loch. Its origin is not definite; as with many other names, it was probably first that of the river, perhaps from the same pre-Celtic root form *nebh*, 'cloud', as has been suggested for Naver. A case has also been made for *nimheis* (Old Gaelic) 'venomous'. Many other unattested interpretations have been made, including: 'the awesome, the sky-high, the peak in the clouds', but until the nineteenth-century Ordnance Survey, Ben Macdhui was generally considered to be higher than Ben Nevis. The form Nevess is found from 1552. Its Gaelic form is Beinn Nibheis. It is notable that Loch Nevis is a long way from Ben Nevis, and must have acquired its name independently: another argument for the water-origin. There is a Knocknevis (Scottish Gaelic *cnoc*, 'hill') in Galloway, whose name may come from the nearby loch of Clatteringshaws (Old Norse *klettr*, 'cliff' with Scots *shaws*, 'woods').

New As a prefix it most often means 'new', but in local names it may have a different sense, as in Newmore in Ross-shire, from Scottish Gaelic *Neo'-mhór*, 'the great glebe'; the prefix a truncated form of *neimhidh*, 'church land'. *See* Navitie.

New Abbey (Dumfries & Galloway) This small town, near the mouth of the River Nith, is so named after the Cistercian abbey founded here in 1273 by Devorguilla Balliol, mother of Scotland's unfortunate King John, who is buried in front of the high altar with the heart of her dead husband. The latter is the basis of the romantic name 'Sweetheart Abbey', now commonly given to its ruins.

New Aberdour *See* Aberdour.

Newbattle (Midlothian) 'New building'. *Neowe* (Old English) 'new'; *botl* (Old English) 'house, dwelling'; the name dates from the foundation of the abbey in 1140. Noted as Niwe Bothla, 1141.

Newburgh (Fife; Aberdeenshire) 'New town'. *Neowe* (Old English) 'new'; *burh* (Old English) 'town'. Like many such 'new' places, these are now of some antiquity, the Fife one noted around 1130 as having an existence in the eighth century as Niwanbyrig.

Newcastleton (Borders) This little town stretching along the Hawick–Canonbie road in Liddesdale was established in 1793 by the third duke of Buccleuch, relocating the former Castleton, noted as Cassiltoun in 1275, a settlement around the castle which was destroyed by Cromwellian forces in the mid seventeenth century.

New Deer (Aberdeenshire) *See* Deer for derivation of the name. The parish of Deer was divided in two in the early seventeenth century, but the village of New Deer dates from 1805, when it was established by James Ferguson of Pitfour.

New Galloway (Dumfries & Galloway) This small royal burgh, at the head of Loch Ken, had its charter granted by King Charles I in 1629 to Sir John Gordon. Its name, first recorded as the New Town of Galloway in 1682, is probably a reference to the fact that the Gordon family already owned other properties in Galloway.

Newhaven (Edinburgh) 'New harbour'. The port, now part of the Edinburgh shore-front, was founded by King James IV in 1510 during his development of a Scottish navy, to provide a harbour for his ships.

Newington (Edinburgh) 'New place'. The name is first found around 1720; its form might be expected to be Newton. The *'ing'* element may have been interpolated on the model of other, older place-names in the vicinity.

New Lanark *See* Lanark

New Luce *See* Luce

New Machar (Aberdeenshire) 'New place of (Saint) Machar'. The name differentiates this site from the Aberdeen parish of Old Machar. Noted around 1300 as the church of St Machor or Machar, a pupil of Columbus, and patron saint of St Machar's Cathedral in Old Aberdeen.

New Pitsligo (Aberdeenshire) *See* Pitsligo for derivation of the name. This location dates from 1780, when it was founded by Sir William Forbes of Pitsligo.

Newport-on-Tay (Fife) This town on the south side of the Firth of Tay, directly across from Dundee, was established as a 'new' port in medieval times, with ferry connections until the construction of the road bridge in 1966.

New Scone *See* Scone for derivation of the name. This village was created in 1805, when the old village of Scone was demolished in order for the earl of Mansfield's park to be extended.

Newtongrange (Midlothian) This former coal-mining town south of Dalkeith was so called in contradistinction to the older grange of the nearby Newbattle Abbey, Prestongrange near Prestonpans.

Newtonmore (Highland) 'New town on the moor'. This village in upper Strathspey was virtually a late nineteenth-century creation of the Perth to Inverness railway and the tourist trade it brought. It is situated where the main route from Perth and the road from Lochaber via Loch Laggan converge.

Newton St Boswells *See* St Boswells

Newton Stewart (Dumfries & Galloway) This 'new town', on the right bank of the River Cree close to its estuary on Wigtown Bay, was established in 1671 by William Stewart, third son of the second earl of Galloway, who obtained a burgh charter from King Charles II. Such charters were important as burghal status conferred rights, like that to hold a market, or levy tolls.

Newtyle (Angus) This has been derived as 'New hill', from Scottish Gaelic *nuadh,* 'new', and *tulach,* 'hill'. In 1182 it was recorded as Neutyle. This Strathmore village was the terminus of one of Scotland's earliest railways, the Dundee & Newtyle, opened with horse traction in 1831. There is also Newtyle Forest in Moray, south of Forres.

Nick (Dumfries & Galloway) 'Pass, hill gap'. This appears to be a descriptive Scots term, found also in Middle English. Names such as Nick of the Balloch, in Carrick, suggest that it was applied when the sense of Gaelic place-names was lost in that region, since Balloch is Scottish Gaelic *bealach,* 'hill pass'.

Niddrie (Edinburgh) 'New house', or 'new farm'. *Newydd* (Cumbric) 'new'; *tref* (Cumbric) 'house'; 'farmstead'. Found as Nodref, c. 1249. There is also Niddry in West Lothian, with the same derivation.

Nigg (Highland; Aberdeen) 'On the bay'. *An uig* (Scottish Gaelic adaptation of the Old Norse *vik*) 'bay'. The Ross-shire village, which has greatly expanded in recent times as an oil rig construction site, has given the name back to Nigg Bay, and the same thing has happened with the other Nigg, just south of Aberdeen, noted c. 1250 as Nig. An alternative derivation is from Gaelic *'n eig,* 'the notch', and in both cases a notch or gully in the ground can be shown.

Nith (Dumfries & Galloway) 'Glistening stream', deriving from Cumbric *Nedd* (cognate with Nethy, also Neath in Wales and Nidd in England) meaning 'glistening' (Nedd in Assynt, Sutherland, An Nead in Gaelic, is perhaps Gaelic nead, 'hollow, nest'). The Novios river shown in Ptolemy's map c. 150 is in the approximate position of the Nith, but it seems unlikely that the names are related. It is noted as Nidd by Bede (731).

Nitshill (Glasgow) 'Nut hill.' *Nit* (Scots) 'nut.' Now a district of Glasgow.

Nochty (Aberdeenshire) 'Bare (place)'. *Nochdaidh* (Scottish Gaelic) 'naked'. The reference is to treelessness. The Water of Nochty is one of the head-streams of the Don.

Noltland (Orkney) 'Cattle land'. *Nauta* (Old Norse) 'cattle', giving Scots *nolt* or *nowt*.

North Berwick (East Lothian) North 'barley farmstead'. *Bere* (Old English) 'barley'; *wic* (Old English) 'farmstead'. This coastal resort on the Firth of Forth is set amidst the rich barley fields of East Lothian. The 'north' locative element may suggest that this name was borrowed from Berwick-upon-Tweed, presumably at an early date, or may simply serve to differentiate it from the larger town. It was recorded as Northberwyk in 1250. In 1590, a coven of witches from here was accused of plotting against King James VI. *See* Berwick-Upon-Tweed.

North Queensferry *See* Queensferry
North Ronaldsay *See* Ronaldsay
North Uist *See* Uist

Noss (Shetland; Highland) 'The nose'. *Nos* (Old Norse) 'nose'. This small uninhabited island, lying just off the far east side of Bressay from Lerwick, rises to a high snout in the spectacular cliffs of the Noup of Noss. Noss Head in Caithness has the same derivation.

Noup A very common name in Shetland toponymy, and also found in Orkney, as in Noup Head on Westray. From Old Norse *gnup*, 'peak'. It is also found in the form Neap, as in the North Neaps, on Yell.

Novar (Highland) Possibly 'Giant's house'. The Gaelic name is Taigh an Fhuamhair: *taigh* (Scottish Gaelic) 'house'; *an*, 'of'; *fhuamhair* (Scottish Gaelic) 'giant's', or 'champion's'. It is noted on Blaeu's map, 1654, as Tenuer. There are legends of Fingal's (Finn MacCool's) exploits in the locality.

O

Oa, Mull of (Argyll & Bute) 'Bare point of the cairn'. *Haugr* (Old Norse) 'cairn', giving Gaelic *Ho*; *maol* (Scottish Gaelic) 'brow of a rock, 'headland'.

Oakley (Fife) 'Oak-field', from oak and *ley* (Middle English and Scots) 'meadow'.

Oban (Argyll & Bute) 'Little bay'. *Ob* (Scottish Gaelic) 'bay' from Old Norse *hop*; *-an* (Scottish Gaelic diminutive suffix) 'little'. Its full Gaelic name is An t-Oban Latharnach, 'the little bay of Lorn'. The West Highland port, railhead and resort lies on a small sheltered bay off the Sound of Kerrera. It is the steamer port for the southernmost of the Outer Isles, Barra and South Uist, as well as several inner Hebridean routes.

Obbe (Western Isles) 'Bay'. *Ob* (Scottish Gaelic) 'bay', from Old Norse *hop*. *See* Leverburgh.

Ochil Hills (Clackmannanshire, Perth & Kinross) 'High hills'. *Ocel* (Cumbric) 'high'. The earliest references are to Cind Ochil in 700, Sliab Nochel 850, Oychellis 1461. The Ochils stretch some twenty-five miles (40km) from Stirling towards Perth, and rise steeply to over 2000ft/600m, in places. The battle of Sheriffmuir, in 1715, was fought on the Ochil slopes above Dunblane.

Ochiltree (East Ayrshire; West Lothian) 'High house'. *Ocel* (Cumbric) 'high'; *tref* (Cumbric), 'house, homestead'. Recorded as Okeltre, c. 1200.

Ochtertyre (Perth & Kinross) A scotticised form of Auchtertyre, 'upper land', from *uachdar* (Scottish Gaelic) 'upper'; *tiridh* (Scottish Gaelic) 'land'. Auchtertyre in Wester Ross, found as Wochtertory, 1495, has an identical meaning.

Ogilvie (Angus) Perhaps 'high plain', from *ocel* (Cumbric) 'high'; and *fa* (Cumbric) 'plain', related to Gaelic *magh*. Noted in 1205 as Ogilvin.

Ogle, Glen (Stirling) This steep, landslide-prone glen may derive its name from *ocel* (Cumbric) 'high'; but the Gaelic form, Oguil, does not correspond to this, and the derivation of the name, with the Angus Glen Ogil, remains uncertain.

Oich, River and **Loch** (Highland) 'Stream-place'. *Abha* (Scottish Gaelic) 'stream'; *ach* (Scottish Gaelic suffix) 'place'. Found in the present form 1769. The loch may have originally been *Loch Abha* (as in Awe). *See* Awe, Avoch.

Old Kilpatrick (West Dunbartonshire) 'Old place of St Patrick's church'. *Cill* (Scottish Gaelic) 'church'; *Padraig* (Scottish–Irish Gaelic personal name, from Latin *Patricius*, 'of noble birth'). Noted as Kylpatrick, 1233. Patrick, patron saint of Ireland (AD 387–458), according to one tradition, was born here. The village, situated on the north bank of the River Clyde, was formerly known simply as Kilpatrick, until the parish was split in 1649, since when it was prefixed first by 'West', and latterly by 'Old'.

Old Man of Hoy (Orkney) Perhaps 'High Rock of Hoy'; the Brythonic–Pictish *alt*, 'high', and *maen,* 'rock', anglicised via Old Norse into an apparently more meaningful form. If so, it is one of few pre-Norse names surviving in Orkney, which was a Pictish domain prior to the ninth century. This sea stack rises perpendicularly to over 450ft/138m. *See* Hoy. There is also the Old Man of Stoer, a similar sea-stack off the west coast of Sutherland.

Oldmeldrum (Aberdeenshire). *See* Meldrum. The 'Old' was added later when the former parish was divided.

Old Scone *See* Scone

Oldshoremore (Highland) The first two syllables are 'Asleif's Bay'. *Asleifar* (Old Norse personal name); *vik* (Old Norse) 'bay'. Asleif's Bay is mentioned in the *Orkneyinga Saga* (c. 1225). The Gaelic *mòr*, 'big', has been added in the post-Norse period to differentiate the place from nearby Oldshores.

Omoa (North Lanarkshire) This name was given to its locality, near Motherwell, by a local landowner, Captain John Dalrymple, who had fought in the capture of Omoa, in Honduras, in 1779. An ironworks was set up here in 1877.

Onich (Highland) 'Foamy place'. *Omhanaich* (Scottish Gaelic) 'of foam'.

Opinan (Highland) 'Place of bays'. *Obhain* (Scottish Gaelic) 'bays', from *hop* (Old Norse), 'sheltered bay', with diminutive *-an* (Scottish Gaelic) ending.

Oransay (Argyll & Bute) 'Oran's island', from Odhran (Irish Gaelic personal name), St Columba's colleague, and Old Norse *ey*, 'island'. Noted as Ornansay, 1549. There are numerous islands bearing forms of this name. *See* Oronsay.

Orbliston (Moray) This name has resisted clear derivation; the first part has been tentatively identified with *iorbull* (Scottish Gaelic) 'peaceful'; the form suggests a personal name with *-ton* (Scots) 'town, place'; but no document has yet been found to back this up.

Orchy, River and **Glen** (Argyll & Bute) An old Gaelic compound name, *Urcháidh,* 'woody stream place'. It has been seen as combining Scottish Gaelic *ar,* 'on, near', with Old Gaelic elements *cet* (as in Cumbric *coit*) indicating 'wood', and -*ia,* 'stream'.

Ord of Caithness (Highland) The hilly barrier between Caithness and Sutherland. *Ord* (Scottish Gaelic) 'round hill'. The Ord of Caithness was formerly known as the Mounth of Caithness, from *monadh* (Scottish Gaelic) 'mountain'. Its present form reflects its Gaelic name, an t-Ord Gallach. *See also* Caithness.

Orkney Possibly 'the Boar tribe's islands'. *Orc* (Celtic root mentioned in Latin texts of 320 BC) 'boar, pig'; noted in Old Irish as Insi-orc, 'islands of the pigs' (*uirc*); boars were prominent among the hieratic animals in Celtic beliefs. The name was recorded around 30 BC by the Greek geographer Strabo, from Pytheas's account of his voyage around Britain, and by the Romans in the first century AD as Orcades. This latter name is still occasionally used in a literary context. Ptolemy, c. 150, has Orkades; the *Pictish Chronicle*, c. 970, has Orkaneya; the islands were in the Pictish domain until around 875. The name was assimilated into Old Norse as *Orkneyjar,* meaning 'seal islands'. The Gaelic name is Arcaibh. The northern point of Shapinsay is known as the Ness of Ork.

Ormiston (East Lothian) 'Orm's farm'. *Ormr* (Old Norse proper name), *tun* (Old English) 'farmstead'. Found in this form in 1293, Ormiston is of historical interest as the first 'model village' in Scotland, set up here in 1731, which bankrupted its founder John Cockburn. There are other Ormistons in the Borders and Perth areas.

Oronsay (Argyll & Bute) 'Oran's isle'. *Odhrain* (Irish Gaelic personal name); *ey* (Old Norse) 'island'. This small island, separated from Colonsay to the north by a narrow tidal strand, was where, traditionally, St Columba first landed with St Oran. Its priory was founded by John, lord of the Isles, in 1360. *See* Oransay.

Orphir (Orkney) 'Tidal island'. Old Norse *orfiris,* composed of *or,* 'out of', and *fjara,* foreshore'.

Orrin, River and **Glen** (Highland) 'River of the chapel'. It seems that the name of the river comes from that of the church of Urray, *oifreann* (Scottish Gaelic), 'chapel, offering place', situated at its point of confluence with the Conon, recorded in 1440 as Inverafferayn. This may also have been a sacred site in pagan times. *See* Urray.

Orton (Moray) 'Edge of the hill'. *Oir* (Scottish Gaelic) 'edge'; *dhùin* (Scottish Gaelic) 'of the hill'. Noted as Urtene, 1542.

Otter Ferry (Argyll & Bute) 'Ferry of the reef'. *Oitir* (Scottish Gaelic) 'reef'. Noted as ly Ottyr, 1490.

Out Skerries (Shetland) 'Far out reefs'. *Ut* (Old Norse) 'far out, farthermost'; *skjaer* (Old Norse) 'rock, cliff'. This triangular shaped group of islands, some no more than rocks but with the two largest linked by a bridge and inhabited, forms the easternmost part of the Shetland archipelago; they lie five miles (8km) out from Whalsay.

Out Stack (Shetland) 'Far out rock'. *Ut* (Old Norse) 'far out, farthermost'; *stakkr* (Old Norse) 'steep-sided', often 'conical, detached rock'. This solitary outlying rock, just under half a mile (800m) north-east of Muckle Flugga, is the most northerly point of the British Isles.

Oxgangs (Edinburgh; other districts) This Scots name refers to an area of land that could be ploughed by an ox in a day. Oxgangs in Midlothian, originally a field name, now a district of south Edinburgh, is familiar to visitors as a bus terminus.

Oxnam (Borders) 'Ox farm'. *Oxenaham* (Old English) 'village of the oxen', noted c. 1150 as Oxanaham.

Oykel, River and **Strath** (Highland) This name has been taken as related to Ochil, from a Pictish word related to Cumbric *ocel* 'high'; perhaps with reference to its mountain source. Its connections, geographical and etymological, with the battle site between Norsemen and Scots, *Ekkjalsbakki* (Old Norse) 'Ekkjal's bank', of the *Orkneyinga Saga*, are no longer considered likely. It was noted as Okel, 1365.

P

Pabay (Western Isles) 'Priest's island'. *Papa* (Old Norse) 'priest'; *ey* (Old Norse) 'island'. Also Pabbay.

Padanaram (Angus) A Biblical name, home of Jacob (*Genesis*, 36:7) given in the seventeenth century. *See* Joppa.

Paisley (Renfrewshire) 'Pasture slope', from *pasgell* (Cumbric) 'pasture'; *llethr* (Cumbric) 'slope', cognate with Scottish Gaelic *leitir*, has been suggested as the most likely derivation. Recorded as Passeleth 1157, Paislay 1508. In medieval times best known for its abbey, it became an important textile town in the eighteenth century, source of the eastern-inspired 'Paisley pattern' used in the finely-woven Paisley shawl.

Panmure (Angus) 'Big hollow'. *Pant* (Brythonic–Pictish) 'hollow, dene', as in modern Welsh; *mawr* (Brythonic–Pictish) 'big'. Noted as Pannemore, 1286.

Papa Stour (Shetland) 'Great priest island'. *Papa* (Old Norse) 'priest'; *ey* (Old Norse) 'island'; *storr* (Old Norse) 'great'. The 'storr' here distinguishes this island from the many other Old Norse 'priest islands'; noted in 1229 as Papey Stora.

Paps of Jura (Argyll & Bute) The collective term for the three breast-shaped hills of Jura, recorded by Martin Martin in 1703, though none of them bears the Gaelic mountain-name *Mam* (breast).

Parbroath (Angus; Fife) This may be 'place of scrubby or mangy bushes' from *perth* (Brythonic–Pictish) 'thicket', and *brothaich* (Scottish Gaelic) 'mangy, scabby'. Noted as Partebrothoc, 1315.

Partan- From Scottish Gaelic *partan*, 'crab', this is a frequent element in local names on the east coast, from Partanhall near Burnmouth northwards.

Partick (Glasgow) 'Bushy place'. *Perth* (Cumbric) 'thicket'. Early records show Perdyec 1136, Pertheck 1158, Perthik 1362. This inner suburb of Glasgow lies on the north bank of the Clyde, which in pre-urban times no doubt was a bushy place. *Compare* Broomielaw.

Pathhead (Fife; Midlothian) 'Head of the steep track'. 'Path' from Scots *peth* indicates a footway up a steep slope or valley, and the locations of the numerous 'path' names confirm this. It is often found as a suffix in place-names, such as Redpath, Cockburnspath, etc. Pathhead is also found in Aberdeenshire, by St Cyrus, and East Ayrshire, across the river Nith from New Cumnock.

Patna (East Ayrshire) The name of an Indian city, transferred to this former mining village in 1810 by the local landowner, Provost

William Faulkner, who apparently had lived and made his fortune
in the Indian Patna. A number of other local names, like Vellore,
near Maddiston in Lothian, also indicate an Indian connection

Peebles (Borders) Place of 'sheilings'. Perhaps from *pebyll* (Cumbric)
'sheilings' or 'tents'. Noted as Pobles, c. 1124, Pebles c. 1126, this
market and former county town and resort on the upper Tweed
still lies in a sheep-grazing area, and this may have been a favoured
summer pasture in the past. *See* Galashiels.

Peffer *See* Strathpeffer

Pen The Cumbric word for 'head', equivalent to Gaelic *ceann,* is
found in many places, mostly south of the Forth–Clyde line, though
not in Galloway. It is often applied to hills.

Pencaitland (East Lothian) Possibly 'head of the wood enclosure'. *Pen*
(Cumbric) 'head, top of'; *coet* (Cumbric) 'wood'; *lann* (Cumbric)
'field, enclosure'. Found as Pencatlet, c. 1150. The description of a
pastoral village enclosed by woods remains valid today.

Penicuik (Midlothian) 'Hill of the cuckoo'. *Pen* (Cumbric) 'head,
hill'; *y* (Cumbric) 'the'; *cog* (Cumbric) 'cuckoo'. This small town
lies south of Edinburgh on the lower wooded slopes of the
Pentlands. Recorded as Penicok in 1250. The Scots word for
cuckoo, 'gowk', is found at Gowkley Moss, a mile north of the
town.

Penmanshiel (Borders) A hybrid name whose elements add up to
'pastureland at the head of stone', from *pen* (Cumbric) 'head';
maen (Cumbric) 'stone'. Compare Penmaenmawr ('great head of
stone'), in Wales. The Scots *-shiel* termination, indicating a summer
grazing place, is an addition from the post-Cumbric period.

Pennan (Aberdeenshire) 'Headland water'. *Pen* (Brythonic–Pictish)
'headland, hill'; *an* (Brythonic–Pictish) 'water, stream'. Normally
such a name would indicate a place 'at the head of a stream',
but here, in this small coastal village made famous in the film
Local Hero, the local burn flows into the sea off a steep headland,
beneath which nestle the former fishermen's cottages. A *pen-* name
is most unusual so far north; if Pictish, it is an almost unique
survival.

Penny This prefix generally indicates a place held on a penny rental,
though it may also stem from Brythonic *pen,* 'head'. In the north
of Lewis are Five Penny Borve and Five Penny Ness. 'Pennyland'
names in the south-west often have the prefix as Pin-, from the
Gaelic form (*see* Pinmore).

Pennyghael (Argyll & Bute) 'Pennyland of the Gael'. A pennyland
was an area held on a penny rental; this district of Mull was held
by Gaels as distinct from Galls, or non-Gaelic strangers.

Penpont (Dumfries & Galloway) 'Head, or end, of the bridge'. *Pen* (Cumbric) 'head'; *pont* (Cumbric) 'bridge'. The Cumbric name suggests a bridge of great antiquity, in this locality quite possibly a Roman one.

Pentland Firth (Highland; Orkney) 'Firth of Pictland'. *Pettr* (Old Norse) 'Picts'; *land* (Old Norse) 'land'; *fjordr* (Old Norse) 'sea inlet' or 'passage'. Noted as Pettlandsfjordr, c. 1100. The name of this stretch of sea between the north Caithness coast and the Orkney Islands, with its notorious tide-rips, really ought to be the Pictland Firth.

Pentland Hills (Midlothian) 'Hill-land'. *Pen* (Cumbric) 'hill'; *land* (Old English) 'tract of land'. Recorded as Pentlant, c. 1150. The name bears no relation to that of the Pentland Firth. The Cumbric source is attested in many other local names with the *pen-* prefix: Penicuik, Pencaitland etc.

Perth (Perth & Kinross) Place of the 'thicket'. *Perth* (Brythonic–Pictish) 'bush, thicket'. It was recorded as Pert in 1128. This ancient Royal burgh, favoured by several early kings of Scotland, was for several hundred years known as St Johnstoun, or St John's Toun of Perth, after the building of St John's Kirk in the twelfth century. The local football club is St Johnstone.

Peterculter (Aberdeen) 'Corner land of St Peter'. *Cuil* (Scottish Gaelic) 'corner'; *tìr* (Scottish Gaelic) 'land'. The 'Peter', referring to the dedicatee of its church, was added later to distinguish this satellite residential area of Aberdeen from the nearby village of Maryculter, hence its English form.

Peterhead (Aberdeenshire) 'St Peter's headland'. This major fishing – and one-time whaling – port was founded in 1593, taking its name from the large St Peter's Kirk built here in 1132 on the headland near to the mouth of the Ugie Water, and hence in the former parish of Inverugie. Noted in 1544 as Petyrheid, 1595 as Peterpolle, from Scots *poll* or *pow*, 'head'. Peterhead is notable for its pink granite.

Petty (Highland) 'Place of shares'. *Peiteach* (Scottish Gaelic from Brythonic–Pictish *pett*) 'of shares or portions'. Noted as Petin, c. 1250.

Pettycur (Fife) This location, at the point of land by Kinghorn (though the actual promontory name is the Pictish–Norse Rossness), has been construed as 'Portion at the high rental', from *pett* (Brythonic–Pictish) 'portion or piece of land', and *ocar* (Scottish Gaelic) 'usury, extortion'. An older form of the name is Petticur.

Philiphaugh (Borders) 'Shut-in valley'. *Ful* (Old English) 'closed'; *hop* (old English) 'hollow, valley'. Recorded in the thirteenth century as Fulhope. Scots *haugh,* indicating low ground by a stream, is a later addition. It was here that Montrose's campaign on behalf of Charles I was brought to an end by his defeat in 1645.

Pictavia The Latin name for the country of the Picts. In the mid-twelfth century, the *Book of Leinster* refers to the Pictish territory as Cruithentuath from Gaelic *cruithne,* 'Pict' and *tuath,* 'land-dwellers'.

Pierowall (Orkney) 'Little bay'. *Piril* (Old Norse) 'small', giving 'peerie' still in use today; and *vagr* (Old Norse) 'bay'.

Pinkie (East Lothian) 'Cé's height'. *Pen* (Cumbric) 'hill'. *Cé* (Cumbric personal name). Noted as Penke, c. 1260. A battle site, a mile south of Musselburgh, where the Scots were defeated by the English in 1547, during Henry VIII's 'Rough Wooing' of the child queen, Mary I.

Pinmore (South Ayrshire) 'Big penny-land'. *Peighinn* (Scottish Gaelic) 'Scots penny, denomination of land equal to a penny rental'; *mór* (Scottish Gaelic) 'great'.

Pinwherry (South Ayrshire) 'Pennyland of the copse'. *Peighinn* (Scottish Gaelic) 'Scots penny, denomination of land equal to a penny rental'; *an fhoithre* (Scottish Gaelic) 'of the copse'. Also found as Pinwherrie.

Pirnmill (North Ayrshire) 'Tree point'. *Prenn* (Cumbric) 'tree'; *maol* (Scottish Gaelic) 'brow of a rock, cape'.

Pit- This prefix, common on the eastern side of the country from Fife to south-east Sutherland, especially in Fife, Perthshire and Aberdeenshire, and found in only a handful of places elsewhere, comes from Brythonic–Pictish *pett,* meaning a portion of land (earliest record in *The Book of Deer,* c. 1150). This prefix is not found in other Celtic place-names and has been taken as a definite sign of Pictish origin. Modern research has noted that Pit- names are generally found on the best cultivable land. The suffix in most Pit- names is Gaelic, which scholars now take to imply that the *pit-* form was maintained since it had an administrative meaning that was not matched by any Gaelic word, and that Gaelic speakers may have formed Pit- names. Nevertheless, it also seems that in some instances an earlier Pit- may have been replaced by Scottish Gaelic *Baile* (*see* Bal-). *See also* Petty.

Pitagowan (Perth & Kinross) 'The smith's portion'. *Pett* (Brythonic–Pictish) 'portion' or 'piece of land'; *ghobhainn* (Scottish Gaelic) 'smith's.'

Pitblado (Fife) 'Portion of the corn-meal'. *Pett* (Brythonic–Pictish) 'portion' or 'piece of land,' *blatha* (Irish Gaelic) 'corn meal'.

Pitcairn (Fife) 'Portion of the cairn'. *Pett* (Brythonic–Pictish) 'portion' or 'piece of land', *càrn* (Scottish Gaelic) 'cairn'. Found as Peticarne, 1247.

Pitcalzean (Highland) 'Portion of the wood'. *Pett* (Brythonic–Pictish) 'portion' or 'piece of land'; *coillean* (Scottish Gaelic) 'of the wood'. The *z* here is a misreading of *y*.

Pitcaple (Aberdeenshire) 'Horse share'. *Pett* (Brythonic–Pictish) 'portion' or 'piece of land'; *capull* Scottish Gaelic) 'horse'.

Pitfour (Angus; Highland) 'Pasture share'. *Pett* (Brythonic–Pictish) 'portion' or 'piece of land'; *phúir* (Scottish Gaelic) 'pasture'. The Black Isle name is found as Pethfouyr, c. 1340.

Pitkeathly (Perth & Kinross) 'Cathalan's land'. *Pett* (Brythonic–Pictish) 'portion' or 'piece of land'; *Cathalan* (Irish Gaelic personal name: diminutive of Cathal). Found as Pethkathilin, c. 1225.

Pitkerrow (Perth & Kinross) 'Fourth part of land'. *Pett* (Brythonic–Pictish) 'portion' or 'piece of land'; *ceathramh* (Scottish Gaelic) 'fourth part'.

Pitlochry (Perth & Kinross) 'Piece of land by or with the stones'. *Pett* (Brythonic–Pictish) 'portion' or 'piece of land'; *cloichreach* (Scottish Gaelic) 'stones'. The 'stones' referred to here were almost certainly stepping stones across the River Tummel, by which the town, nowadays an important tourist resort, is located.

Pitmaduthy (Highland) 'MacDuff's portion'. *Pett* (Brythonic–Pictish) 'portion' or 'piece of land'; *mhic Dhuibh* (Scottish Gaelic) 'MacDuff's'.

Pitmilly (Fife) 'Portion of the mill.' *Pett* (Brythonic–Pictish) 'portion' or 'piece of land'; *muileann* (Scottish Gaelic) 'of the mill'.

Pitscottie (Fife) 'Portion of flowers'. *Pett* (Brythonic–Pictish) 'portion' or 'piece of land'; *sgothaich* (Scottish Gaelic) 'flowery'. Found as Petscoty, 1358.

Pitsligo (Aberdeenshire) 'Shelly portion'. Pett (Brythonic–Pictish) 'portion' or 'piece of land'; *sligeach* (Scottish Gaelic) 'shelly'. Found as Petsligach, 1426.

Pittencrieff (Fife) 'Portion of the tree'. *Pett* (Brythonic–Pictish) 'portion', or 'piece of land'; *chraoibhe* (Scottish Gaelic) 'of the trees'.

Pittendreich (Fife; West Lothian; Moray) 'Portion of the good aspect'. *Pett* (Brythonic–Pictish) 'portion' or 'piece of land'; *dreach* (Scottish Gaelic) 'aspect, beauty'. This is the most frequently-found Pit- name. Variant forms include Pittendrigh, Pendreich. The Lothian place is noted as Petyndreih, 1140.

Pittenweem (Fife) 'Place of the cave'. *Pett* (Brythonic–Pictish) 'piece of land, place'; *na* (Scottish Gaelic) 'of the'; *h-uamha* (Scottish Gaelic) 'cave'. Recorded in 1150 as Petnaweem. This East Neuk fishing port on the Firth of Forth has a cave, near the harbour, associated with St Fillan. *See* Wemyss.

Pittodrie (Aberdeen) 'Portion by the woodland'. *Pett* (Brythonic–Pictish) 'portion' or 'piece of land'; *fhodraidh* (Scottish Gaelic) 'by the wood'. The name is now synonymous with Aberdeen F.C.'s ground, though there is another Pittodrie in the Garioch area of Aberdeenshire.

Pityoulish, Loch (Highland) 'Loch at the portion of the fair station'. *Pett* (Brythonic–Pictish) 'portion', or 'piece of land', *gheall* (Scottish Gaelic) 'fair, bright'; *-ais* (Scottish Gaelic) 'stance, station', from *fas*, 'stance', indicating a drovers' stance.

Plean (Stirling) 'Flat land'. *Plen* (Cumbric) 'flat land'. Noted in 1215 as Plane.

Plockton (Highland) 'Town of the block'. *Ploc* (Scottish Gaelic) 'block, clod', with *-ton* (Scots) 'place'. Its Gaelic name is Am Ploc. This picturesque Wester Ross village is a favourite with artists.

Pluscarden (Moray) 'Place of thickets'. *Plas* (Brythonic–Pictish) 'place'; *cardden* (Brythonic–Pictish) 'thicket, brake'. Recorded in 1124 as Ploschardin. The site of a twelfth-century Valliscaulian abbey, which has been re-established and rebuilt in modern times.

Point A frequent name for a promontory in locations round the entire coast from Corsewall Point in Dumfries & Galloway to Point of Ness on Yell in Shetland (in this case the name is a hybrid Anglo–Norse doublet) and south again to Siccar Point in Lothian. Many 'Points' are likely to be map-makers' translations of Gaelic *Rudha*.

Pollokshaws (Glasgow) 'Pool by the thicket'. *Poll* (Cumbric) 'pool'; *-oc* (Cumbric diminutive suffix) 'little'; *sceaga* (Old English) 'wood'.

Pollok (Glasgow) 'Little pool'. *Poll* (Cumbric) 'pool'; *-oc* (Cumbric diminutive suffix) 'little'. Noted as Pullok, 1158. This south-western district of Glasgow, near the confluence of the Leven and White Cart Waters, is an area where there would have been many pools. The name also occurs in the adjoining districts of Pollokshaws and Pollokshields.

Polmont (Falkirk) 'Pool-hill'. *Poll* (Scottish Gaelic) 'pool, hollow'; *monadh* (Scottish Gaelic) 'hill, mountain'. Noted as Polmunth, 1319.

Polwarth (Borders) 'Paul's fields'. *Pol* (Old English personal name, a form of Paul); *worth* (Old English) 'field, enclosure'. This is one of a tiny number of *-worth* location names in Scotland. Found as Polwrth, c. 1200.

Pomona (Orkney) An alternative name for the Orkney Mainland,

first found in Fordun's *Chronicle*, c. 1380, and current until the
nineteenth century. Why the name of the Latin goddess of fruit
trees should have been attached to Orkney is not clear. It is not
used nowadays.

Poolewe (Highland) 'Pool of the (river) Ewe'. *Poll* (Scottish Gaelic)
'pool, hollow'; *iu* (Scottish Gaelic) river-name related to 'yew'. *See*
Kinlochewe.

Port Askaig *See* Askaig

Portavadie (Argyll & Bute) 'Beaching place of the dogs, or
foxes', from Scottish Gaelic *port,* 'harbour, beaching place', and
mhadhaidh, 'of dogs'. *See also* Lochmaddy.

Port Bannatyne (Argyll & Bute) This resort on the east coast of Bute
takes its name from the Bannatyne family who established their
seat at the nearby Kames Castle in the thirteenth century.

Port Charlotte (Argyll & Bute) This coastal settlement in south-
west Islay is named after Lady Charlotte, the mother of the Gaelic
scholar W. F. Campbell of Islay, who founded the village in 1828.

Port Ellen (Argyll & Bute) The main port of Islay, situated at the
south end of the island, is named after Lady Ellenor, wife of W. F.
Campbell, who founded the small town in 1821.

Port Elphinstone (Aberdeenshire) An inland location by Inverurie,
marking the terminus of a canal from Aberdeen, and named in the
early nineteenth century after Sir Robert Elphinstone.

Portessie (Moray) 'Port of the waterfall'. *Port* (Scottish Gaelic)
'harbour, beaching place'; *easach* (Scottish Gaelic) 'waterfall,
steeply falling stream'.

Port Glasgow (Inverclyde) This Lower Clyde industrial town was
developed by the municipality of Glasgow in the 1660s in order to
provide a deep-water port for the city's developing Atlantic trade.
It was for a time the main port for Glasgow until later dredging of
the River Clyde enabled bigger ships to come up to the city.

Portgower (Highland) This coastal hamlet, south of Helmsdale, was
built to house some of those evicted from the interior of Sutherland
in the nineteenth century; it is named from the duke of Sutherland's
family name, Leveson-Gower.

Portincaple (Argyll & Bute) 'Port of the horse'. *Port* (Scottish Gaelic)
'harbour, beaching-place'; *nan,* 'of the'; *chapuill* (Scottish Gaelic)
'horse'. Found as Portinkebillis c. 1350; also as Portinchapil, which
may indicate a false etymology based on 'chapel'.

Portknockie (Moray) 'Harbour by the little hill'. *Port* (Scottish
Gaelic) 'harbour'; *cnoc* (Scottish Gaelic) 'rounded hill'; *-ie*
(colloquial diminutive) 'little'. This small fishing port was founded
in 1677.

Portlethen (Aberdeenshire) 'Port of the slope'. *Port* (Scottish Gaelic) 'harbour, beaching ground'; *leathan* (Scottish Gaelic) 'slope'.

Portmahomack (Highland) 'Haven of (saint) Colman'. *Port* (Scottish Gaelic) 'harbour, beaching ground'; *mo*, 'my'; *Cholmáig* (Irish Gaelic) 'Colman's'. The name, borne by numerous Celtic saints, is derived from Latin *columba*, 'dove'. Noted as Portmachalmok, 1678. *See* Inchmahome.

Portnahaven (Argyll & Bute) 'Harbour of the river'. *Port* (Scottish Gaelic) 'harbour, beaching ground'; *na*, 'of'; *abhainn*, 'river'.

Portnalong (Western Isles) 'Port of the ships'. *Port* (Scottish Gaelic) 'harbour, beaching ground'; *nan*, 'of'; *long* (Scottish Gaelic) 'ship'.

Portobello (Edinburgh) The name of this seaside district of Edinburgh, a former independent burgh until amalgamated in 1896, comes from the name of a house built here by a sailor who had seen action at the battle of Puerto Bello in Panama in 1739. The name derives from Spanish, 'fine harbour', which is somewhat inappropriate here, as there is a fine sandy beach but no port.

Portpatrick (Dumfries & Galloway) 'Harbour of St Patrick'. *Port* (Scottish Gaelic) 'harbour'; *Padraig* (Irish Gaelic personal name, from Latin *Patricius,* 'nobly-born') patron saint of Ireland, to whom a chapel was dedicated here. Its harbour, founded in 1630, now silted up, was once the main packet port for Northern Ireland.

Portree (Highland) 'Harbour of the slope'. *Port* (Scottish Gaelic) 'harbour'; *ruigheadh* (Scottish Gaelic) 'of the slope'. The second element is often mistakenly thought to derive from *rí* (Scottish Gaelic) 'king', related to a royal visitation here by James V in 1540, though there appear to have been former names including Kiltarraglan, 'Talorcan's church', and Baile na h-Acarseid, 'anchorage village'. Portree is the main town of Skye.

Port Seton (East Lothian) 'Seton's harbour'. The Setons were a local landowning family who developed the harbour from the fifteenth century onwards, to export coal from their mines and salt from their salt-pans.

Portsoy (Aberdeenshire) 'Harbour of the warrior'. *Port* (Scottish Gaelic) 'harbour'; *saoi* (Scottish Gaelic) 'warrior'. This well-preserved historic port on the Moray Firth is a place of great antiquity, but there is no clue as to who might be the 'warrior' in its name.

Port William (Dumfries & Galloway) This small seaport and resort situated on Luce Bay southwest of Wigtown takes its name from Sir William Maxwell of Monrieth, who established the town here in 1770, one of hundreds of 'model villages' set up in that time of energetic 'improvement' and development.

Preston- As a prefix in numerous locality names, such as Prestonfield, it indicates a priest's or priests' holding, from *preost* (Old English) 'priest' and *tun* (Old English) 'village'.

Prestonpans (East Lothian) 'Priests' village by the salt-pans'. *Preost* (Old English) 'priest'; *tun* (Old English) 'village'; *-pans* (Scots) 'salt-pans'; the name refers to salt-panning here on the Firth of Forth by monks of Newbattle Abbey from the thirteenth century. Recorded as Saltprestoun 1587. Several notable battles were fought here, including Prince Charles Edward's defeat of government troops under Sir John Cope, in 1745.

Prestwick (South Ayrshire) 'Priests' farm'. *Preost* (Old English) 'priest'; *wic* (Old English) 'farm'. This resort town on the Ayrshire coas was originally, like Prestongrange near Prestonpans, an outlying farm of a religious house. Monkton ('monks' farmstead') is also a local name. The name was recorded as Prestwic in a document of 1170. Scotland's first international airport was established here, and it is still a centre of the aviation industry.

Q

Quanterness (Orkney) 'Bishop's point'. *Kantari* (Old Norse) 'bishop' (from 'Canterbury'); *nes* (Old Norse) 'cape, point'.

Quarff (Shetland) 'Shelter'. *Hvarf* (Old Norse) can mean 'shelter place' as well as 'turning' (*see* Cape Wrath).

Queensferry, North and **South** (Fife and Edinburgh) Both these towns, on respective sides of the Firth of Forth and lying underneath the latter-day rail and road bridges, share a name that commemorates Queen Margaret, wife of King Malcolm III of Scotland, who established a free ferry here for pilgrims on their way to St Andrews. Noted as Queneferie, c. 1295. The railway bridge was completed in 1890; the road bridge in 1974.

Quinag (Highland) *Koon-yak*. The name of this Sutherland mountain (2651ft/811m) has been compared to that of Cunningham in Ayrshire, with *cuinneag* (Scottish Gaelic) 'milk-pail' in mind, though any resemblance of shape is hard to detect. But other 'churn' names are known: *see* Chirnside. *Caoin* (Scottish Gaelic) 'fair, beautiful', has also been suggested. There is a Carn Chuinneag as a northern outlier of the Ben Wyvis massif.

Quinish (Western Isles) 'Cattle fold headland'. *Kví* (Old Norse) 'cattle-fold', *nes* (Old Norse) 'ness, headland'.

Quiraing (Highland) *Kwee-royng*. 'Crooked enclosure'. *Kví* (Old Norse) 'cattle-fold'; *rong* (Old Norse) 'crooked'. The fantastic pillar-like rock formations are the source of the name.

Quoich, River, Glen and **Loch** (Highland) Probably 'of the hollow'. *Cuach* (Scottish Gaelic; genitive *cuaich*) 'hollow of a hill'. The original name was given to the river. Names cognate with this are Queich in Aberdeenshire and Glen Quaich.

R

Raasay (Highland) 'Roe-deer ridge island'. *Rar* (Old Norse) 'roe deer'; *ass* (Old Norse) 'ridge'; *ey* (Old Norse) 'island'. This derivation is descriptive of this long ridge-formed island lying between Skye and the mainland; roe deer are still found here. Noted as Raasa 1263, a source of 1526 refers to Rairsay.

Rackwick (Orkney) 'Sea-wrack bay'. *Reka* (Old Norse) 'sea wrack, sea-weed'; *vik* (Old Norse) 'bay'. Found as Rekavik in the *Orkneyinga Saga*, c. 1225.

Rafford (Moray) 'High fort'. *Rath* (Scottish Gaelic) 'ring fort'; *àird* (Scottish Gaelic) 'high'. Noted as Raffart, c. 1700.

Raith (Fife) Probably 'Ring-fort'. *Rath* (Scottish Gaelic) 'ring-fort'. Noted as Rathe, c. 1320. This name is often used as a synonym for Kirkcaldy, whose football club is Raith Rovers.

Ranfurly (Renfrewshire) 'Portion of the farthing rental'. *Rann* (Scottish Gaelic) 'part, portion'; *feòirlinn* (Scottish Gaelic) 'farthing'.

Rankeilour (Fife) 'Portion by the clay stream'. *Rann* (Scottish Gaelic) 'part, portion'; *cìl* (Scottish Gaelic) 'red clay', *dobhar* (Brythonic–Gaelic) 'stream'. Noted as Rankeloch, 1293. Also found as Rankeillor.

Rannoch (Highland; Perth & Kinross; Argyll & Bute) 'Bracken'. *Raineach* (Scottish Gaelic) 'bracken fern'. This name forms part of several places in a wide area of the central Highlands: Rannoch Moor, Rannoch Forest, Loch Rannoch, etc. The original meaning probably only applied to the area around Loch Rannoch.

Ranza, River and **Loch** (North Ayrshire) 'Rowan tree river'. *Reynis* (Old Norse) 'rowan', *áa* (Old Norse) 'river'; the Norse names give a reminder that Arran was once part of the Vikings' island empire. Noted as Lockransay, 1433.

Ratagan (Highland) 'Little fort'; from *rath* (Scottish Gaelic) 'ring-fort', with the double diminutive suffixes -*ag* and *an*. This mountain gap over which the Glenelg road climbs is often known as Mam Ratagan, from the hills on either side, though one is a Ben and the other a Sgurr; Bealach ('pass') Ratagain is its Gaelic name.

Rattray (Perth & Kinross; Aberdeenshire) 'Homestead of the ring-fort'. *Rath* (Scottish Gaelic) 'ring-fort'; *tref* (Brythonic–Pictish) 'homestead'. Found as Rotrefe, 1291. The linguistic combination is intriguing. Rattray and Blairgowrie, on opposite sides of the

Ericht river, form a single urban unit, in the heart of a rich farming district, famous for its berry-fields, where the hybrid tayberry was developed. The same name occurs in Rattray Head, with Old Rattray inland, on the eastern coast of Buchan.

Reay (Highland) 'Ring-fort'. *Rath* (Scottish Gaelic) 'ring-shaped stone fort'. Noted as Ra, c. 1230. The Reay Forest, some distance west of the parish of Reay, was known in Gaelic as Dhùthaich Mhic Aoidh, 'Mackay's country', and presumably was given its name from being (until the nineteenth century) the territory of Mackay of Reay.

Reelick (Highland) 'Graveyard'. Found also as Reelig, Ruillick, from Scottish Gaelic *réilig*, 'churchyard'. Noted as The Relict, 1584.

Relugas (Moray) A complex name, likely to be a hybrid, with the first part perhaps *ruigh* (Scottish Gaelic) 'sheiling'; and the latter part perhaps cognate with Lugar and Luggie, an early Celtic stream name.

Rendall (Orkney) 'Valley of running water'. *Renna* (Old Norse) 'flow'; *dalr* (Old Norse) 'valley'.

Renfrew (Renfrewshire) 'Point of the current'. *Rhyn* (Cumbric) 'point'; *frwd* (Cumbric) 'current'. Records show Renifry 1128, Reinfrew 1158, Renfrew 1160. This old-established former county town is located west of Glasgow at the point at which the Clyde is joined by both the White and Black Cart rivers. In 1164, Somerled, lord of Argyll and ancestor of the lords of the Isles, was killed here whilst on a raid.

Renton (West Dunbartonshire; Borders) The Strathclyde industrial town, lying in the Vale of Leven to the north of Dumbarton, was named in 1782 by its founder, Jean Telfer Smollett (sister of the novelist Tobias Smollett), after her daughter-in-law, Cecilia Renton. The Borders name is much older, from *Regna* or *Regenhild* (Old English personal name); *ing*, (Old English possessive particle); *tun* (Old English) 'farm', recorded as Regninton from the eleventh century.

Restenneth (Angus) 'Moor of fire'. *Ros* (Brythonic–Pictish) 'moor'; *tened* (Brythonic–Pictish) 'of fire'. Recorded as Rostinoth, c. 1150. This was a religious centre in Pictish times, the site of a priory. Also spelt Restennet, Restinnot.

Reston (Borders) 'Rhys's place'. *Rhys* (Cumbric personal name); *tun* (Old English) 'settlement, farm'. Rhys was a princely name, likely to have stuck long after the fading of the Cumbric speech from the district.

Rhiconich (Highland) 'Mossy grazings'. *Ruighe* (Scottish Gaelic) 'sheiling, summer grazing'; *chóinnich* (Scottish Gaelic) 'mossy'.

Rhu (Argyll & Bute) 'Cape, headland'. *Rudha* (Scottish Gaelic) 'cape'. There is a very distinct promontory jutting into the Gareloch here. *Rhu* and *Rudha* prefix many names up the West Coast. *See* Rudha.

Rhum *See* Rum

Rhynd (Perth & Kinross; Aberdeenshire; Highland) 'Point of land'. Scottish Gaelic *rinn*, 'tail' or 'point of land'. The Perth location, where the Earn joins the Tay, was noted as Rindalgros, 'point of the spit', 1147; the latter part was later lost.

Rhynie (Aberdeenshire; Highland) The Aberdeenshire name, found as Ryny, c. 1230, is 'division or portion of land', from Scottish Gaelic *roinnean*, a diminutive of *roinn*, 'share, portion of land'. The Ross-shire name, Gaelic Ràthan, is from *rathan*, 'small fort' (found as Rathne, 1529).

Riccarton (Borders; East Ayrshire) 'Richard's place'. *Riccart* (Old English personal name), *tun* (Old English) 'settlement, farm'. Riccarton in the Southern Uplands was once reachable only by railway; a remote moorland junction on the 'Waverley' route between Edinburgh and Carlisle, which was closed in 1969. The name is found in various other localities, sometimes as Rickarton. The Kilmarnock one is named after Sir Richard Wallace, an uncle of William Wallace.

Rinnes, Ben (Moray) Perhaps 'promontory hill'. *Beinn* (Scottish Gaelic) 'mountain', and *rinn* (Scottish Gaelic) 'promontory, point'; alternatively 'hill of the shares', from *roinn* (Scottish Gaelic) 'division'. In Gaelic it is Beinn Rinneis. Most 'rinns' names are coastal but this mountain (2755ft/842m) is well inland. *See* Rinns of Galloway.

Rinns of Galloway (Dumfries & Galloway) Probably 'promontories'. *Rinn* (Scottish Gaelic) 'point, promontory'. Two other Gaelic words have also been suggested as the source, *rann*, 'part, portion', but also in some places 'promontory'; and *roinn*, 'share, portion', a word certainly used in demarcation of farmland. Noted 1460 as le Rynnys. Also spelt Rhinns, Rhynns.

Rinns of Islay (Argyll & Bute) Whilst the same derivation as for the Rinns of Galloway seems quite possible, this has also been taken to be from *rann* (Scottish Gaelic) 'division', but also 'promontory' in some districts. It is highly noticeable that the Rinns of Islay and of Galloway are peninsular locations, though the plural form, compared with Rhind, suggests the land-portion source.

Risk (Dumfries & Galloway) 'Marsh, bog'. *Riasg* (Scottish Gaelic) 'morass'. One of the many words used to define boggy terrain. It is also found in other regions, and cognate forms include Reisk and Ruskie (this, with Ruskich, is from the related *riasgach,* 'boggy place').

Robroyston (Glasgow) 'Robert's place'. Noted as Roberstoun in the sixteenth century. This area of Glasgow has nothing to do with Rob Roy MacGregor.

Rockall (Western Isles) 'Bare island in the stormy sea'. *Rok* (Old Norse) 'stormy sea'; *kollr* (Old Norse) 'bald head'. This derivation, as suggested by one authority, aptly describes this uninhabited and remote isolated rock that rises to only 63ft (19m) above sea level and lies some 186 miles (300km) west of St Kilda. It was only in 1972 that Rockall was formally annexed to Scotland.

Rodil (Western Isles) Perhaps 'roe deer valley'. *Rá* (Old Norse) 'roe'; *dalr* (Old Norse) 'valley'. Noted as Roadilla, 1580. Raadil might be expected; *see* Raasay. The old church of St Clement here has some fine carving, notably on the tomb of Alasdair Crotach, seventh chief of MacLeod. The name is sometimes found as Rodel.

Rogart (Highland) 'Red enclosure'. *Raudr* (Old Norse) 'red, reddish'; *gardr* (Old Norse) 'enclosure, garth'. Noted as Rothegorth, c. 1230.

Rogie, Falls of (Highland) 'Deep cleft'. *Ro* (Scottish Gaelic prefix of intensity) *agaidh* (Scottish Gaelic) 'cleft, narrow pass'. There is a fine cascade on the River Blackwater here. Other Rogie burns have a similar derivation.

Rohallion (Perth & Kinross) 'Ring-fort of the Caledonians'. *Ràth* (Scottish Gaelic) 'ring-fort'; *chaileainn* (Scottish Gaelic) 'of the Caledonians'. The name was presumably bestowed by the eastward-migrating Scots, encountering settlements of the Picts. *See* Dunkeld.

Romanno (Borders) 'Fort of the monk'. *Rath* (Scottish Gaelic) 'ring-fort'; *manaich* (Scottish Gaelic) 'of the monk'. Noted as Rothmanaic, c. 1160. At Romanno Bridge, two gypsy tribes, Faas and Shaws, fought a pitched battle in 1677.

Rona (Highland; Western Isles) 'Rough rocky island'. *Hraun* (Old Norse) 'rough, rocky'; *ey* (Old Norse) 'island'. The uninhabited island, just north of Raasay, was a den of pirates in the sixteenth century but its pirate harbour, 'Port nan Robaireann', is no longer on the map. It is sometimes referred to as South Rona to distinguish it from North Rona, in the Atlantic Ocean, forty-eight miles (75km) north-west of Lewis, where the eighth-century hermit St Ronan lived and died. His name, from *rónan* (Scottish Gaelic) 'little seal', has sometimes been supposed to correspond with that of the island, but the island is more likely to share the same derivation as South Rona. There is also a small hilly island called Ronay on the east of North Uist.

Ronaldsay, North (Orkney) 'Ringan's isle'. *Ringan* (Old Norse form of Ninian) *ey* (Old Norse) 'island'. Recorded as Rinarsey in *Orkneyinga Saga*, c. 1225. This island, the most northerly and one of the smallest in the Orkney archipelago, is far away from South Ronaldsay, with which it appears to share a basic name element only by coincidence. It indicates how far north in Pictish territory the missionary work of St Ninian and his followers extended.

Ronaldsay, South (Orkney) 'Rognvaldr's isle'. *Rognvaldr* (Old Norse personal name) equivalent to *Raghnall* (Scottish Gaelic) or 'Ronald' (Scots); *ey* (Old Norse) 'island', recorded as Rognvalsey in the Norse sagas. South Ronaldsay is connected to Burray, which is in turn joined on to the Mainland of Orkney by the Churchill Barrier, a causeway built as a World War II defence, closing off entrances to Scapa Flow.

Rose This element, prefixing a number of names, can be from Scottish Gaelic *ros* or from Brythonic–Pictish and Cumbric *ros*, both with the meanings of 'promontory, wood', or sometimes, especially in Cumbric, 'moor'. The Rose- names are more often Brythonic in origin, while Ross- names tend to be Gaelic.

Rosehaugh (Highland) 'Bank of the wood'. *Ros* (Scottish Gaelic) 'wood; *haugh* (Scots) 'bank of land'.

Rosehearty (Aberdeenshire) 'The point, or wood, of *Abhartach*' (Old Gaelic personal name), prefixed by *ros* (Scottish Gaelic) 'point', or 'wood'. Found as Rossawarty, 1508. The coastal position of this fishing port might suggest the former sense here.

Rosemarkie (Highland) 'Promontory, or moor, of the horse'. *Ros* (Scottish Gaelic) 'promontory, moor'; *marc* (Scottish Gaelic) 'horse, steed'. Just inland is Drummarkie, 'ridge of the horse'. Noted as Rosmarkensis, 'of Rosemarkie', 1128. This Black Isle village lies inland of the promontory known as Chanonry Point, which juts into the Moray Firth; the adjoining town is Fortrose. Rosemarket in Pembrokeshire, another ancient site, shows an Old Welsh form of the same prefix, though the suffix has been derived from Old French *marché*, 'market'. Rosemarkie was the site of an important monastery of the Celtic Church, though the name may suggest an earlier animal cult. Here Coinneach Odhar, the 'Brahan Seer' was, according to legend, burned to death around 1577.

Roslin (Midlothian) 'Holly moor'. *Ros* (Cumbric) 'moor'; *celyn* (Cumbric) 'holly'. Recorded as Roskelyn, c. 1240. This former mining village lies on the north bank of the North Esk river, close to the fourteenth-century Rosslyn Castle and its famous collegiate chapel of 1446, with much elaborate and highly symbolic stone-carving.

Rosneath (Argyll & Bute) 'Point of the sanctuary'. *Ros* (Scottish Gaelic) 'promontory', *neimhidh* (Scottish Gaelic) 'of the holy place'. Noted simply as Neveth, c. 1199, Rosneth 1225. The spelling Roseneath is still found. *See* Navitie.

Ross (Highland; Argyll & Bute; Dumfries & Galloway) Earlier forms of this name are found both in the Brythonic languages and in Gaelic. Brythonic *ros* or *rhos* means 'promontory' or 'moor'; Gaelic *ros* can mean both 'promontory' and 'wood'. The name of the Highland district and former county is generally taken to mean 'promontory', Scottish Gaelic *ros,* from its long eastern peninsulas. It has also been suggested that *ros* here is a form of Scottish Gaelic *riasg*, 'moor'. The alternative Gaelic *ros*, 'wood', might equally be appropriate here. This ancient territorial name, grouped with Moray as one of the seven provinces of Pictland, referred only to the eastern side, which became 'Easter Ross' when the county of Ross was formed. The locations of the Ross of Mull and the several Ross names on the western tip of Kirkcudbright Bay also suggest the Gaelic 'promontory' meaning.

Rosque, Loch (Highland) 'Loch of the Crossing, or Pass'. *Loch* (Scottish Gaelic) 'lake, loch'; *chroisg* (Scottish Gaelic) 'crossing'. The loch lies where two routes from the west converge on Achnasheen.

Rosyth (Fife) The name may be a hybrid, combining *ros* (Scottish Gaelic) 'promontory', with *hide* (Old English) 'landing place'. 'Headland of the arrows', *saighead* (Scottish Gaelic) 'arrow' has also been suggested; not an improbable source if there were suitable trees growing, or a specialist workshop. Noted as Rossyth, c. 1130. This town on the Forth, close to Dunfermline, is an important naval dockyard.

Rothes (Moray) 'Ring fort'. *Rath* (Scottish Gaelic) 'ring fort'. This small town, situated south-east of Elgin, is the location of a thirteenth-century castle, on the site of an earlier fortification. Found as Rothes, 1238.

Rothesay (Argyll & Bute) 'Rotha's isle'. *Rotha* (Old Norse personal name); *ey* (Old Norse) 'island'. The name is found as Rothersay, 1321; it originally referred to Rothesay Castle, which is still surrounded by a moat, and was extended to the town, whose Gaelic name is Baile Bhòid, 'town of Bute'. Rothesay is the chief town of Bute. Its dukedom was the appanage of the heir to the Scottish crown. Now a resort town, its growth was due to industry; the first large water-powered cloth mill was built here in 1779.

Rothiemurchus (Highland) 'Muirgus's fort'. *Rath* (Scottish Gaelic) 'ring fort', later developing the sense of 'fortified house'; *Muirgus*

(Old Gaelic personal name). Recorded as Rathmorchus, 1226. The Rothiemurchus Forest still has many stands of the native Scots Pine. This was the territory of Clan Grant.

Rousay (Orkney) 'Hrolfr's island'. *Hrolfr* (Old Norse personal name – adaptation of Old German *Hrodulf*) 'renown-wolf'; *ey* (Old Norse) 'island'. The name of the island was documented in 1260 as Hrolfsey.

Rowardennan (Stirling) 'Eunan's high promontory'. *Rudha* (Scottish Gaelic) 'cape, promontory'; *àird* (Scottish Gaelic) 'height'; *Eonain* (Scottish Gaelic personal name) 'of Eunan'.

Roxburgh (Borders) 'Hroc's fortified dwelling'. *Hroc* (Old English personal name) 'rook'; *burh* (Old English) 'fortified dwelling, castle'. Recorded as Rokisburc in 1127. This name presumably replaced an unrecorded Cumbric name. Once an important royal burgh, one of Scotland's oldest, it is now a small village with a mound to show the site of its great castle, the scene of James II's accidental death during the siege of 1460.

Roy, River and **Glen** (Highland) 'Red River'. *Ruaidh* (Scottish Gaelic) 'red'. The Roy is not notably red but it may be a figurative name. Glen Roy's distinctive terraces, the 'parallel roads', were believed to be the work of giants until nineteenth-century geologists showed they were caused by glacial lakes.

Rubha *Roo-a*. 'Point of land, headland'. The conventional Scottish Gaelic term for a promontory, also found in the older form *Rudha*. Most frequent on the west coast of the mainland and on the inner isles from Arran northwards, it is rare on the north and east coasts.

Rubislaw (Aberdeen) 'Rubie's Hill'. *Rubie* (Scots diminutive of Reuben); *law* (Scots) 'hill'. This district of Aberdeen is the site of great granite quarries.

Ruchil (Perth & Kinross; Glasgow) The Tayside Ruchil is 'red flood'; *ruadh* (Scottish Gaelic) 'red'; *thuil* (Scottish Gaelic) 'flooding stream'. The Glasgow district name is 'red wood', with the second part being *choille* (Scottish Gaelic) 'wood'. It is sometimes found as Ruchill.

Rudha *See* Rubha

Rum (Highand) Perhaps 'spacious (island)'. *Rùm* (Scottish Gaelic) 'room, space'. But a pre-Celtic origin has also been suggested for the name. The *h* in the alternative spelling, 'Rhum' was inserted by its early twentieth-century owner, Sir George Bullough, a Lancashire textile magnate. Recorded as Ruim in 677.

Rutherford (Borders) 'Ford of the horned cattle'. *Hrythera* (Old English) 'horned cattle'; *ford* as in modern English. Found in this form 1215.

Rutherglen (South Lanarkshire) 'Red valley'. *Ruadh* (Scottish Gaelic) 'red'; *gleann* (Scottish Gaelic) 'glen, valley'. The form Ruthirglen is found in 1153. This industrial town is situated south-east of Glasgow in the Clyde valley where reddish coloured soils are to be found.

Ruthven (Highland; Perth & Kinross) *Rivven*. 'Red river', from Scottish Gaelic *ruadh* 'red'; and *abhainn*, 'river'. The stream at Ruthven, Inverness-shire, is said to be reddish coloured from mineral ore. The prominent ruin of Ruthven Barracks, by Kingussie, were destroyed by Jacobites in 1746. Huntingtower, west of Perth, was once known as Ruthven Castle, and there is another Ruthven close to Airlie in Angus.

Ruthwell (Dumfries & Galloway) 'Well of the Holy Cross', from *róde* (Old English) 'cross, rood'; and English 'well'. The cross, one of the finest carved Celtic crosses, is still to be seen there. In this village the world's first savings bank was established by the local minister, Henry Duncan, in 1810.

Ryan, Loch (Dumfries & Galloway) 'Of the chief', is a possible derivation for the name of this south-western sea-loch, noted on Ptolemy's map of c. AD 150 as Rerigonios Kolpos (Greek 'gulf'); with Cumbric *rigon*, 'chief', cognate with Welsh *rhion*.

S

Saddell (Argyll & Bute) This old abbey site in Kintyre is referred to as Sagadul, 1203, perhaps from *sag* (Old Norse) 'saw'; and *dalr* (Old Norse) 'valley, dale'; a place for sawing timber.

St Abb's Head (Borders) Named after Aebba, the first prioress of Coldingham, and sister of the seventh-century King Oswald of Northumbria. Many capes on the eastern coast are named 'Head', Scots *heid*, from Old Norse *hofud* or, as more likely here, Old English *heafod*.

St Andrews (Fife) This historic town and international headquarters of golf is named after its cathedral, dedicated to Scotland's patron saint. But it has had several names in its time. Prior to its elevation as a Christian cult centre, which happened during the ninth century, it was Mucros, 'wood, or point, of the pigs'. A hill here was known as Ceannrighmonaigh, 'top of the king's mound' (*Annals of Tighernach*), changed to Cillrighmonaidh with the foundation of the church and monastery (Scottish Gaelic *cill),* which later became Chilrimunt, c. 1139, then Kilrymont. The *righ* element (*see* Portree) has also been read as 'slope'. According to legend it was St Regulus, or Rule, who brought the relics of St Andrew (Greek Andreas, Scots Androis, hence the terminal -s: an apostrophe here is a solecism) here from Greece, and the town was known in Gaelic as Baile Reuil (Scottish Gaelic) 'town of Rule'. It became the ecclesiastical capital of Scotland until the Reformation, and the country's first university was founded here by Bishop Wardlaw in 1411.

St Boswells (Borders) The town is named after St Boisil, the seventh-century abbot of Melrose and friend of St Cuthbert. The -wells part is from Norman French -*vil* or *ville*, 'town'. Nearby is the later-established Newtown St Boswells, the administrative headquarters for the Borders region.

St Cyrus (Angus) 'Church dedicated to St Cyricus'. Another form of the name is Ecclesgreig, from a conjectured Brythonic–Pictish *egles*, 'church', deriving from Latin *ecclesia* and perhaps borrowed via Cumbric *egles;* and *Girig* (Pictish–Scottish personal name): 'Girig's church'. Found as Eglesgreig, 1243 The church here was dedicated by Girig, a ninth-century king of the Scots and Picts, to St Cyricus.

St Fillans (Perth & Kinross) 'Place dedicated to St Fillan'. *Faolán* (Irish Gaelic proper name) literally 'Little Wolf', was the name of sixteen saints, but this was the prime one in early Scotland, the successor to St Mund as abbot in the monastery of the Holy Loch, and who died in 777. The decorated hook end, or *coigreach*, of his crozier is still preserved as one of the country's most ancient and venerable relics. The village lies in Strathfillan, recorded as Strathfulane, 1317, 'Fillan's strath'. Killilan in Wester Ross is *cill* (Scottish Gaelic) 'church', *Fhaolain*, 'Fillan's'.

St Fort (Fife) 'Sand ford'. The name is noted as being Sandfurde in 1449. In the seventeenth century it is recorded as Santford, and this form of spelling appears to have driven the name into its present misleading form. There are still sand-pits in the vicinity.

St Kilda (Western Isles) The remote group of steep Atlantic islands, lying thirty-five miles (56km) northwest of North Uist, is not named after a St Kilda – no saint of this name is known. The name Skildar is found in a document of 1540, but it appears to have related to some islands closer offshore: it is Old Norse *skildir*, 'shields', suitable for low-lying rather than spiry islands. A sixteenth-century map-maker's mistake transferred the name to the remoter archipelago. Thus the name is 'wrong' on two counts. Another suggested source of the name as *kelda* (Old Norse) 'well', is based on the fact that the landing place on Hirta, the main island, is in Gaelic Tobar Childa, which in the post-Norse era may have been misunderstood as 'Kilda's well', though it simply means 'well' in both languages. But it does not explain the Sk- element. The Gaelic name of the island group was and is *Hirt*, now applied in English only to the main island, as Hirta. The islands, inhabited for many centuries despite their remoteness, were finally evacuated in 1930. *See* Hirta.

St Margaret's Hope (Orkney) 'St Margaret's Bay'. *Hop* (Old Norse) 'bay, hollow place'.

St Monans (Fife) This small harbour town in the 'East Neuk' of Fife was once believed to be named after St Ninian, but is now thought to bear the name of St Monan, the sixth-century bishop of Clonfert in Ireland, to whom its handsome thirteenth-century Auld Kirk, on the very edge of the sea, is dedicated. Noted as Sanct Monanis, 1565, the name was later spelt as St Monance, until the twentieth century.

St Ninian's Isle (Shetland) The missionary activities of St Ninian of Whithorn or his followers along the east coast have left traces in local names all the way to this most northerly one, linked by a tombolo to the south-west Mainland, where a Pictish treasure-trove was found in 1958. Perhaps because of the island's small size, its name escaped the alteration undergone by North Ronaldsay.

St Rollox (Glasgow) 'St Roche'. A chapel to St Roche was set up here in 1502. In the nineteenth and early twentieth centuries this district was at the centre of Glasgow's railway engineering industry.

St Vigeans (Angus) Perhaps a form of St Féchín, an Irish saint whose death is recorded in the mid seventh century. In the Pictish heartland, St Vigeans has a superb collection of Pictish sculpted stones.

Salen (Argyll & Bute) 'Inlet'. *An* (Scottish Gaelic) 'the'; *sailein* (Scottish Gaelic) 'little inlet of the sea'.

Saline (Fife) 'Salt pit'. In 1613 the name is recorded as Sawling.

Salisbury Crags (Edinburgh) The curiously English name of these Edinburgh crags has been ascribed to the earl of Salisbury who accompanied Edward III of England to Scotland in 1335, and who played a substantial part in diplomatic negotiation with his reluctant hosts. It was not a tourist visit, but perhaps the earl took time off to scale them.

Saltburn (Highland) The name, from Scottish Gaelic Alltan an y-Saluinn, with identical meaning, has been explained as a hiding-place for salt, when duty was payable on imported salt.

Saltcoats (North Ayrshire) Place of the 'salt huts'. *Salt* refers to the process of saline extraction by boiling it out in great iron pans (*see* Prestonpans); *cots* (Scots) 'cottages, huts'. Noted as Saltcotes, 1548. The name of this town and resort on the Firth of Clyde derives from the salt-works established here in the sixteenth century in the reign of James V.

Saltoun (Midlothian) Recorded in 1140 as Saulestoun, and in 1250 as Sawilton, it records a personal name, perhaps Savile, with the Scots -*ton* suffix, from Old English *tun,* 'farmstead'. This Lothian district was made famous by an early eighteenth-century proprietor, Andrew Fletcher, a leading opponent of union with England.

Sanday (Orkney) 'Sand island', from *sand* (Old Norse) 'sand', and *ey* (Old Norse) 'island'. Found in this form 1369.

Sanquhar (Dumfries & Galloway) 'Old fort'. *Sean* (Scottish Gaelic) 'old'; *caer* (Cumbric) 'fort'. Recorded as Sanchar c. 1150. An ancient earthwork known as the 'Sean Caer' is on a hillock just north of the town; there are numerous other early fortifications in the neighbourhood.

Sauchieburn (West Lothian) 'Burn by the willows'. *Saileach* (Scottish Gaelic) 'willow'; *burn* (Scots) 'stream'. Here in 1488 James IV's rebel army fought his father, James III, who was assassinated in a house nearby. There is also a Sauchieburn in Aberdeenshire, south of Fettercairn.

Sauchiehall (Glasgow) 'Willow haugh'. *Saileach* (Scottish Gaelic) 'willow'; *haugh* (Scots) 'water meadow, sloping bank'.

Saughton (Edinburgh) 'Place by the willows'. *Saileach* (Scottish Gaelic) 'willow'; *tun* (Old English) 'settlement'; giving the Sots place termination *-ton*. A western district of Edinburgh, with a large prison.

Scalloway (Shetland) 'Bay of the huts'. *Skali* (Old Norse) 'huts'; *vagr* (Old Norse) 'bay'. This port and former main settlement of Shetland, six miles (10km) west of Lerwick, derives its name from the temporary huts or booths the Viking people erected here by the bay when attending the annual 'Lawting', or open assembly, held at nearby Tingwall. Scalloway remained Shetland's capital until the early 1600s.

Scalpay (Western Isles, Orkney) 'Ship isle'. *Skálp* (Old Norse) 'skiff, ship'; *ey* (Old Norse) 'island'. Scalpay in Orkney is different: 'ship isthmus': the suffix being from *eidh* (Old Norse) 'isthmus'.

Scapa Flow (Orkney) Probably 'Sea-flood bay of the boat isthmus'. *Skálp* (Old Norse) 'boat'; *eidh* (Old Norse) 'isthmus'; *floa* (Old Norse) 'flood'. This vast, almost circular bay is surrounded by a chain of islands, separated by narrow channels, some of which have been blocked by the 'Churchill barrier' causeways of World War II. It was used as a major naval base in both world wars. Here the German High Seas Fleet was scuttled by its crews in 1919.

Scarba (Argyll & Bute) 'Cormorant island'. *Skarfr* (Old Norse) 'cormorant'; *ey* (Old Norse) 'island'. Skarfskerry has the same derivation, with *skjaer* (Old Norse) 'rock'.

Scarinish (Argyll & Bute) 'Seagull point'. *Skári* (Old Norse) 'young seagull'; *nes* (Old Norse) 'point, headland'. In the north of Scotland, 'scorrie' is still used to refer to seagulls.

Scarp (Western Isles) 'Cliff island'. *Skarpr* (Old Norse) 'steep-faced'.

Scavaig, River and **Loch** (Highland) The derivation of the first part of this Skye name is unclear, though it has been linked to an Old Norse root *ska*, 'scrape'. The suffix is *vik* (Old Norse) 'bay'. It may be an old river-name with *-vaig* back-formed on to it.

Schiehallion (Perth & Kinross) Perhaps 'maiden's pap', from *sine* (Scottish Gaelic) 'breast', and *chailean* (Scottish Gaelic) 'girl's'. But it has also been related to *sithich* (Scottish Gaelic) 'fairy'; *chailleainn* (Scottish Gaelic) 'of the Caledonians', with the notion of it being a 'fairy hill' (*see also* Ben Ledi). Noted as Schachalzean, 1642; a conspicuous isolated mountain (3554ft/1087m), of apparently near perfect conical shape when seen from the north-west, it retains a certain mystical quality for many people. *See* Rohallion.

Sciennes (Edinburgh) A corrupt form of 'Siena'; the name refers to the former monastery of St Catherine of Siena in this part of Edinburgh, once outside the walls; recorded in the sixteenth century as Shenis.

Scone (Perth & Kinross) 'Mound'. *Sgonn* (Scottish Gaelic) 'mound, lump'. The reference here is to the Mote Hill, an ancient ritual site of Scottish kings. It was recorded as Sgoinde in 1020. In the early nineteenth century the name of this location became Old Scone, when its residents were transferred to New Scone a mile to the east. Likely to have been a sacred site from prehistoric times, Scone became a Christian foundation under the Picts, and the *Lia Fail,* or 'Stone of Destiny' of the Scots was brought here some time in the ninth century after the Norsemen overran Iona. It became the crowning-place of the kings of Scots. The abbey was refounded by Alexander I in 1114.

Scoraig (Highland) 'Bay of the gully'. *Sguvr* (Old Norse) 'rift, gully'; *aig* (Scottish Gaelic form of Old Norse *vik*) 'bay'. This crofting township on the peninsula between Loch Broom and Little Loch Broom is one of the few inhabited places on the mainland with no road access.

Scotia 'Scotland'. A latinised form of 'land of the Scots', originally applicable to Ireland, then to medieval Scotland, and nowadays used in a poetic, antiquarian or fanciful sense for Scotland.

Scotland 'Land of the Scots'. The original Scots (*Scoti* in Latin) were Gaelic-speaking immigrants from northern Ireland, who in the fifth and sixth centuries settled in the south-west of what was then Caledonia or Pictavia, the Latin names for northern Scotland. By the mid tenth century the name Scotia had replaced the latter. 'Scot' was legendarily supposed to derive from an ancestress Scota, daughter of an Egyptian pharaoh; the actual derivation is obscure. Scotland, with its Anglian suffix -*land*, is probably a name awarded from outside, by the Anglian population of Northumbria and Lothian; in Gaelic the name was and remains Alba. *See* Alba, Caledonia, Scotia.

Scotsburn (Highland) The name of this Easter Ross crofting district may be a Scots rendering of *Allt* (Scottish Gaelic) 'stream'; *nan,* 'of'; *Albannaich* (Scottish Gaelic) 'the Scots'; and so may denote a Gaelic translation of a Pictish name, indicating the site of a battle or a land-division between Picts and Gaelic-speaking Scots; there are similar names in Moray and Sutherland.

Scotscalder (Highland) 'Calder of the Scots' (see Calder). Nearby there was a Norn Calder, both noted in 1538, as Scottiscaldar, Nornecaldar; originally demarcating land held by those of Scots and Norse extraction in this once Norse region on the border of Sutherland and Caithness.

Scotstarvit (Fife) This hybrid name indicates 'Scot's bull place'. *Tarbh* (Scottish Gaelic) 'bull'; *ait* (Scottish Gaelic suffix) indicating place. The *Scot-* prefix may come from the land-owner's name, which was Scot (or vice versa) or perhaps goes back to the thirteenth- and fourteenth-century encroachment of Scots speech into this once Gaelic-speaking region. Just south of Cupar there is a spread of 'bull' names on each side of Tarvit Hill.

Scourie (Highland) 'Place of the wood'. *Skógr* (Old Norse) 'wood'. The Gaelic name is Sgobhairidh.

Scrabster (Highland) 'Rocky farmstead'. *Skjaere* (Old Norse) 'rocks'; *bolstadr* (Old Norse) 'farmstead'. A personal name or nickname, Skara, has also been suggested for the prefix. In the *Orkneyinga Saga* (c. 1225) it is Ská-ra-bólstadr. It is the ferry-port for Orkney, with frequent sailings to Stromness.

Seaforth, Loch (Western Isles) 'Loch of the salt-lagoon-firth'. This apparently tautological name is explained by the semi-landlocked part of the loch, *saer* (Old Norse) 'salt lake', with *fjordr* (Old Norse) 'firth, fiord'. Gaelic 'loch' was added in the post-Norse era. This area of Lewis, once the land of the MacLeods, became Mackenzie territory and gave its name to the Mackenzie earldom of Seaforth.

Seil (Argyll & Bute) 'Seal Island'. *Seil* (Old Norse) 'seal'; the Gaelic name, Saoil, has the same meaning.

Selkirk (Borders) 'Church by the hall'. *Sele* (Old English) 'hall, manor house'; *cirice* (Old English) 'church', becoming Scots 'kirk'. This woollen-manufacturing town on the Yarrow Water was recorded as Selechirche in 1124.

Sgùrr This Gaelic term for a 'high, sharp-pointed hill' is often found as the prefix of a hill-name, especially in the West Highlands and Skye.

Sgùrr Alasdair (Highland) 'Alexander's peak'. *Sgùrr* (Scottish Gaelic) 'high, pointed hill'; *Alasdair* (Scottish Gaelic personal name) 'Alexander'. The Skye peak (3309ft/1011m) is named after the nineteenth-century Gaelic scholar Alexander Nicholson, its first recorded climber in 1873. Previously it was Sgùrr nan Gillean ('the lad's peak').

Shandon (Argyll & Bute) 'Old fort'. *Sean* (Scottish Gaelic) 'old'; *dùn* (Scottish Gaelic) 'fort'.

Shandwick (Highland) 'Sand bay'. *Sand* (Old Norse) 'sand'; *vik* (Old Norse) 'bay'. There is a wide sandy bay here, overlooked by the 'Shandwick Stone': a finely-carved standing stone of Pictish origin.

Shanter (South Ayrshire) 'Old land'. This Ayrshire name, made famous by Robert Burns's poem 'Tam o' Shanter', comes from *sean* (Scottish Gaelic) 'old', and *tìr* (Scottish Gaelic) 'land'; probably by comparison with 'new land' taken into cultivation from the moors.

Shapinsay (Orkney) 'Hjalpand's island'. *Hjalpand* (Old Norse personal name); *ey* (Old Norse) 'island'. Noted in the *Orkneyinga Saga* (c. 1225) as Hjalpandisay.

Shaw Found in many localities, and meaning 'wood', it may derive from Old English *sceaga* or Old Norse *skógr*, 'wood'. It is also often found in the plural form, Shaws.

Shawbost (Western Isles) 'sea-lake-farm'. *Sjá* (Old Norse) 'lake partly open to the sea'; *bolstadr* (Old Norse) 'farmstead'.

Shawfield (Glasgow) 'Wood field'. *Shaw* (Scots) 'wood' from *sceaga* (Old English) 'thicket, wood'.

Shee, Glen (Perth & Kinross) 'Fairy glen', or 'glen of peace'. *Gleann* (Scottish Gaelic) 'valley, glen'; *sìth* (Scottish Gaelic) meaning both 'fairy' or 'spirit', or 'peace'. The river coming down Glen Shee is the Blackwater, and perhaps this is another 'black goddess' stream (*see* Lochty); after joining with the Ardle it becomes the Ericht. There is another Glen Shee, north-west of Perth.

Shetland Perhaps 'Hilt land'. The Old Norse name was 'Hjaltland'. *Hjalt* (Old Norse) 'hilt of a sword' or 'dagger'; *land* (Old Norse) 'land'. The reference could be to the long, narrow outline of the archipelago as appreciated by the early Viking navigators. While the first *l* was dropped, the initial *Hj* was mutated to *Sh*, and in some areas by the Gaelic mutation to *Z*, giving the alternative spelling of Zetland. The derivation is a conjectural one. The Norse form is still preserved in the diminutive 'Sheltie', referring to the Shetland breed of pony. The oldest recorded Gaelic name is Innse Cat, 'islands of Cat' (*see* Caithness), latterly it is Sealtainn.

Shettleston (Glasgow) Originally noted in a Latin document of 1170 as 'the vill or villa of Seadna's daughter'. *Villa* (Latin 'house, place'; perhaps here equivalent to Gaelic *baile*); *inghine* (Scottish Gaelic) 'of a daughter'; *Seadna* (Scottish Gaelic personal name). The form Inienchedin is found in 1186. By 1515 *villa* was translated into Scots *-tun*, 'township', as Schedilstoune.

Shiant Isles (Argyll & Bute) 'Holy islands'. *Na-Eileanan* (Scottish Gaelic) 'the islands', *Sianta* (Scottish Gaelic) 'holy'. In pre-Viking times, these islands were inhabited by Christian hermits.

Shiel, River, Loch and **Glen** (Highland) Probably 'flowing water', from a Pictish word stemming from the continental Celtic root-form *sal*, 'flowing'. Gaelic *seileach*, 'willow' stems from the same source. The battle of Glenshiel in Kintail marked the end of the

1719 Jacobite Rising; Sgùrr na' Spainnteach, 'Spaniards' peak', commemorates the Spanish troops who fought on the Jacobite side. Loch Shiel is in Moidart, well to the south.

Shieldaig (Highland) 'Herring bay'. *Sild* (Old Norse) 'herring, sild'; *aig* (Gaelic form of Old Norse *vik*) 'bay'. Its Gaelic form is Sìldeag.

Shin, River and **Loch** (Highland) From a pre-Celtic root-word *sinn*, indicative of flowing water, and also the source of Irish 'Shannon'. Recorded in 1595 as Shyn. The Shin is a notably fast-flowing river, famous for its falls and its salmon leaps.

Shira, Glen (Stirling) 'Lasting river'. *Sìorabh* (Scottish Gaelic) 'lasting river', indicating a stream that flows all year. Noted as Shyro, 1572. This glen above Loch Fyne was the sanctuary of Rob Roy MacGregor's family during his time as an outlaw.

Shiskine (North Ayrshire) 'Marshy place'. *Sescenn* (Scottish Gaelic) 'marsh'. Noted as Cescen, c. 1250.

Shotts (North Lanarkshire) Place of 'steep slopes'. *Sceots* (Scottish Gaelic) 'steep slopes'. This former mining town lies on a high undulating plateau that forms part of the watershed between the Forth and Clyde river basins. *See* Kirk o' Shotts.

Shuna (Argyll & Bute) 'Sighting place', which seems to be derived from *sjón* (Old Norse) 'sight'. The isle of Shona has the same probable derivation.

Sidlaw Hills (Perth & Kinross; Angus) Perhaps 'pasture hills', from *saetr* (Old Norse) 'shieling, hill pasture', and *hlaew* (Old English) 'hill'. 'Hills of seats' has also been suggested, with the first syllable from *suidhe* (Scottish Gaelic) 'seat', often used in association with the name of a holy man. In either case 'hills' is a linguistically unnecessary later addition.

Sinclairtown (Fife) This suburb of Kirkcaldy is named after the Sinclair family who lived in the nearby Dysart House.

Sionnascaig, Loch (Highland) A hybrid name, with the addition of Scottish Gaelic 'loch' to an Old Norse form incorporating *sjónar*, 'observation, look-out', and *skiki,* 'strip of land'. Ordnance Survey cartographers rendered the gaelicised form into Loch Skinaskink.

Skara Brae (Orkney) 'Bank by the shore'. *Skari* (Old Norse) 'shore'; *brae* (Scots) 'bank'. This describes the situation of this remarkable Neolithic village (3100–2450 BC) which was preserved by the high bank of sand behind the shore at Skaill (Old Norse *skali*, 'shieling') Bay, that covered it until its excavation in 1850.

Skelbo (Highland) 'Shelly farm'. *Skel* (Old Norse) 'shell'; *bol* (Old Norse, abbreviated form of *bolstadr*) 'farm'. Noted as Scelbol, 1214, Scellebol c. 1300.

Skelmorlie (North Ayrshire) 'Scealdamer's meadow'. *Scealdamer*

(Old English personal name); *ley* (Scots) 'meadow'. Noted as Skelmorley, c. 1400.

Skene, Loch (Aberdeenshire; Dumfries & Galloway) Perhaps 'loch of bushes', from *loch* (Scottish Gaelic) 'lake, loch', and *sgeachan* (Scottish Gaelic) 'of bushes' or 'of hawthorns'. The Aberdeenshire loch is known as Loch of Skene, found in this form 1318. Loch Skene, source of the 'Grey Mare's Tail', is also found as Skeen.

Skerryvore (Western Isles) 'Great skerry'. *Skjaer* (Old Norse) 'sharp rock'; giving *sgeir* (Scottish Gaelic) 'reef'; with *mhòr* (Scottish Gaelic) 'big'. The beautiful lighthouse here, twenty-five miles west of Mull, was built by Alan Stevenson in 1844 and refurbished after a fire in 1959.

Skibo (Highland) This has been derived as 'barn place, granary', from Scottish Gaelic *sgiobal* 'granary'. But with Norse Embo and Skelbo close by, 'Skithi's farm' has also been suggested from *Skithi* (Old Norse personal name) and *bol* (Old Norse abbreviated form of *bolstadr*) 'farm'. Recorded as Schytheboll, 1275.

Skipness (Argyll & Bute) 'Ships' headland'. *Skipa* (Old Norse) 'ship'; *nes* (Old Norse) 'headland'. Recorded as Schepehinch, c. 1250, Skipnish 1260. The castle here on the elbow of Kintyre, controlling the northern entrance to Kilbrannan Sound, was a strategic point in medieval times.

Skye (Highland) Perhaps 'Winged Isle'. *Sgiathach* (Scottish Gaelic) 'winged'. The reference appears to be to the shape of the island, with its many peninsulas. It is noted by Ptolemy, c. AD 150, as Ski or Skitis; and as *Scia* in Adamnan's *Life of St Columba* (c. 700). The familiar Gaelic name is *Eilean a'Cheo*, 'isle of mist'. It is the largest of the Inner Hebrides, and since 1992 has been joined to the mainland by a bridge over Kyle Akin.

Slamannan (Falkirk) 'Hill of Mannan'. Manau was the Cumbric name of the area at the head of the Firth of Forth, cognate with the (Isle of) Man. The prefix is *sliabh* (Scottish Gaelic) 'hill'; but was originally *mynnyd* (Cumbric) 'hill'. The form in 1250 was Slethmanin. *See* Clackmannan.

Slapin, Loch (Highland) The derivation of this Skye sea-loch may be from *slappi* (Old Norse) 'lump-fish'; though if so the attenuated -*fjord* ending found in other Norse Skye loch-names, like Snizort or Scavaig, has gone completely.

Sleat (Highland) 'Level place', presumably by comparison with other parts of Skye, from Old Norse *sletta*, 'level area'. Found as Slate, c. 1400. This area name, the territory of the Macdonalds, has also been derived from Gaelic *sliabh*, 'slope' (*see* Sliabh).

Sliabh 'Mountain, moor, slope' are the chief meanings of this

Scottish Gaelic term, with different force in different locations. In the Inner Hebrides where the 'mountain' meaning prevails, it has been taken to show the naming of topographical features by the incoming Dalriadan Scots, at an earlier date than the 'moor' and 'slope' forms. In the Highlands and Islands it is usually found in names retaining the Gaelic form, but the fact that it seems to be the source of the local Slew- hill-names of western Galloway has suggested an early Scots colony there, prior to the one founded c. 500 in Argyll.

Sligachan (Highland) 'Shelly place'. *Sligeach* (Scottish Gaelic) 'abounding in shells'; *-an* (Scottish Gaelic diminutive termination). The village is familiar to climbers and walkers heading for the Cuillin Hills on Skye.

Smoo Cave (Highland) 'The hiding place'. *Smuga* (Old Norse) 'hiding place'. The name of a vast sea cavern eaten into the limestone cliffs near Durness in north-west Sutherland.

Snab Point (West Lothian) 'Point, apex', from *snáp-r* (Old Norse) 'apex'; with English 'point' a later addition.

Snizort, Loch (Highland) This Skye name may come from *Sneisfjordr* (Old Norse) 'split firth'; but *Sneasfjordr* (Old Norse) 'snow firth', has also been suggested. Noted in 1501 as Snesfurd. The form of the inner loch, divided by the Aird, supports the former explanation.

Soay (Western Isles) 'Sheep island'. *Sautha* (Old Norse) 'sheep'; *ey* (Old Norse) 'island'. The name of Soay in the St Kilda group is preserved in the Soay breed of sheep, but there are numerous other Soays. *See also* Fair Isle.

Solway Firth (Dumfries & Galloway) 'Firth of the muddy ford'. *Sol* (Old Norse) 'mud'; *vath* (Old Norse) 'ford'; *fjordr* (Old Norse) 'fiord, firth, estuary'. It was recorded as Sulewad in a document of 1229. The shallow Solway, stretching far inland between Cumbria and Galloway, was always a problem to cross with its mud-banks and swift tides. In Old Welsh poetry it is referred to as the *echwydd*, 'tidal flow'.

Sorbie (Dumfries & Galloway) 'Bog settlement'. *Saur* (Old Norse) 'bog, mud'; *by* (Old Norse) 'settlement'. Noted on Blaeu's map, 1645, as Soirbuy. Soroba, by Oban in Argyll, has the same source, and there is another Sorbie in East Fife.

Sound From Old Norse *sund*, 'strait'; perhaps once indicating a swimmable strait, this is the common term for the seaway between two islands or between an island and the mainland, throughout the Northern and Western Isles. In the Western Isles the form is as in Sound of Harris; in the Northen Isles the parts are often combined, as in Baltasound.

South Queensferry *See* Queensferry, North and South
South Ronaldsay *See* Ronaldsay, South
South Uist *See* Uist, North and South
Soutra (Borders) 'Homestead with the wide view'. *Sulw* (Cumbric) 'broad view'; *tref* (Cumbric) 'homestead'. Noted c. 1160 as Soltre.
Spean, River and **Glen** *See* Spey
Spey, River (Highland; Moray) The derivation of the name of Scotland's swiftest river is not clear. 'Hawthorn river' has been suggested, from a word cognate with *yspyddad* (Brythonic) 'hawthorn'; as has a link with the pre-Celtic root form *squeas*, 'vomit, gush'. On Ptolemy's map of c. AD 150 it appears as Tvesis; the form Spey is found in 1451. The Spean, which rises close to the Spey, is seen as a diminutive form of the same name, with the -*an* (Scottish Gaelic) diminutive ending.
Spidean (Highland) This name is found applied to mountain features or sub-peaks in the northern Highlands; Scottish Gaelic *spidean* refers to a game similar to pitch-and-toss, with a *spid* or stick. The Gaelic root *spid* however means 'spite, malice'.
Spinningdale (Highland) Although a spinning mill was set up here in the eighteenth century, the name long predates it and is noted as Spanigidill in 1464. An origin has been suggested in *spong* (Old Norse) 'spangle, speckle', with *dalr* (Old Norse) 'valley, dale'. There is also Spango Hill in the Southern Uplands, perhaps with the same derivation.
Spittal (Moray; Highland) 'Refuge'. *Spideal* (Scottish Gaelic) 'refuge, hospital'. Spittals tend to be on remote hill passes, like Spittal of Glen Shee. *See* Dalnaspidal.
Sprouston (Borders) 'Sprow's farmstead'. *Sprow* (Old English personal name); *tun* (Old English) 'enclosure', later 'homestead', leading to Scots *toun*. Noted as Sprostana, 1124.
Spynie (Moray) 'Hawthorn place', from a conjectured *spiathan* (Scottish Gaelic) 'thorn', cognate with *yspyddad* (Brythonic–Pictish) 'hawthorn' (*see* Spey). Recorded as Spyny, c. 1220. Spynie was the site of a cathedral before the headquarters of the see of Moray was moved to Elgin in 1224; Spynie Palace remained the bishop's residence until the Reformation.
Stack Polly (Highland) 'Mountain of the river Pollaidh'. *Stac* (Scottish Gaelic) 'steep rock'; *Pollaidh* (Scottish Gaelic) 'pools, holes', designating the river that flows to the north side of the mountain (2009ft/614m) in the Inverpolly Nature Reserve. The comparison between its spiky summit and a parrot's crest is purely a joke.
Staffa (Argyll & Bute) 'Pillar island'. *Stafr* (Old Norse) 'staff, rod,

pillar'; *ey* (Old Norse) 'island'. The name reflects the vertical columns of basaltic rock found on this small uninhabited island lying to the west of Mull. Staffin in Skye has the same derivation. *See also* Fingal's Cave.

Stake, Hill of (Renfrewshire) Perhaps from *stac* (Scottish Gaelic) 'steep rock', or *stakkr* (Old Norse) 'steep'. This is the highest point in Renfrewshire, at 1712ft/521m.

Stanley (Perth & Kinross) The name was given around 1700 in honour of Lady Amelia Stanley, when she became marchioness of Atholl.

Start Point (Orkney) This headland on Sanday is named from Old Norse *stertr*, 'tail'. Start Point in South Devon at the other end of the British Isles is from the cognate Old English *steort*.

Stenhousemuir (Falkirk) 'Moorland by the stone house'. *Stan* (Old English) 'stone'; *hus* (Old English) 'house'; *mór* (Old English) 'moor'. The meaning in this order rather than the other way round, i.e. of the 'stone house on the moor', is clearly the case as the final element was added only in the seventeenth century. It was recorded in 1200 as Stan House and in 1601 as Stenhous. There are numerous Stenhouses still found as local names.

Stenness (Orkney) 'Headland of stones'. *Stein* (Old Norse) 'stone'; *nes* (Old Norse) 'headland'. The reference is probably to the standing stones on this site, already ancient when the Norsemen reached Orkney.

Stepps (North Lanarkshire) 'Wooden road'. *Stap, stepp* (Scots) 'stave'. The reference is to a roadway made with wooden staves laid parallel, sometimes called a 'corduroy road'.

Stewartry (Dumfries & Galloway) The contemporary name of the administrative district set up in 1975 records the former judicial stewardship by the earls of Douglas over the 'stewartry' or stewardship, of Kirkcudbright. *See* Mearns.

Stirling Possibly 'land enclosure by the stream'. *Sruth* (Scottish Gaelic) 'stream'; *lann* (Scottish Gaelic) 'land enclosure'. This fits the site, by the meanders of the River Forth, but remains a conjecture. A Cumbric source from *ystre,* 'dwelling', and *Felin* (personal name) has also been proposed. It was recorded as Strivlin 1124, Estriuelin c. 1250, Striviling 1445, Sterling 1470. The location referred to by Bede (731) as Urbs Giudi has been linked to Stirling by some scholars. Stirling Castle was for centuries Scotland's principal stronghold, secure on its precipitous rock and strategically placed in the narrow centre of the country; the fight for it was the immediate cause of the Battle of Bannockburn (1314), and the Stewart child kings, and Queen Mary, grew up in its protection.

The national monument to William Wallace looks across to it from the Abbey Craig on the north side. The town, now a university and light industry centre, has also given its name to a unitary local authority.

Stobinian (Stirling) The name of this distinctive mountain (3827ft/ 1165m) has been subjected to different explanations. Its original Gaelic name appears to have been Am Binnein, 'the peak', with *Stob,* which also means peak, a late addition, perhaps because of numerous other Stob- mountains in the vicinity. Despite the flat-looking shape of the summit, the Gaelic form seems unlikely to stem from *innean* (Scottish Gaelic) 'anvil'. *See* Inneans.

Stobo (Borders) 'Hollow of stumps'. *Stub* (Old English) 'stump'; *how* (Old English giving Scots howe) 'hollow'. The name is noted in the twelfth century as Stoboc.

Stockbridge (Edinburgh) 'Bridge of tree-trunks', from Old English *stocc,* 'tree-trunk', and *brycg,* 'bridge'. Stockbriggs in Lanarkshire has the same derivation.

Stonehaven (Aberdeenshire) Possibly 'stony landing place'. *Stan* (Old English) 'stone'; *hyth* (Old English) 'landing place'. Recorded in documents as Stanehyve 1587, Steanhyve 1629, which would suggest that the above derivation is more probable than the alternative Old Norse *steinn,* 'stone', and *hofn,* 'harbour'. This east coast fishing port, former county town of Kincardineshire, is also the market centre for a large landward area.

Stormont (Perth & Kinross) 'Moor of the stepping-stones'. *Stair* (Scottish Gaelic) 'stepping-stones'; *monadh* (Scottish Gaelic) 'mountain, moor'. Older forms include Starmonth in 1374. The name of this Perthshire district between the Tay and the Ardle–Ericht strath is also found as Stormonth.

Stornoway (Western Isles) Possibly 'Steering Bay'. *Stjorn* (Old Norse) 'steering'; *vagr* (Old Norse) 'bay'. The exact sense of this designation remains uncertain, and other possibilities include 'star bay' from Old Norse *stjorna,* 'star'. Recorded as Stornochway in 1511. The main port and town of Lewis, and administrative headquarters of the Western Isles authority. Loch Stornoway in Argyll would seem to have a similar derivation.

Stow (Borders) 'Place'. *Stow* (Old English) 'place, town'. It is unusual to find it on its own with no other defining word.

Stracathro (Angus) 'Strath of the fort'. *Srath* (Scottish Gaelic) 'broad valley'; *cathraich* (Scottish Gaelic) 'of the fort'. Found in 1212 as Stracatherac. The loss of the terminal -*th* is more often found in Ireland, as in Strabane ('white strath'), though *see* Strathaven.

Strachan (Aberdeenshire) 'River valley'. *Srath* (Scottish Gaelic) 'broad valley'; *eithin* (Old Gaelic) 'of the river'. The pronunciation was 'Strawn', though it is often nowadays pronounced as it is spelt.

Strachur (Argyll & Bute) 'Twisting valley'. *Srath* (Scottish Gaelic) 'wide valley'; *cor* (Scottish Gaelic) 'twist, bend'. Recorded as Strachore, 1368.

Straiton (South Ayrshire; Midlothian) 'Place on the Roman road'. *Straet* (Old English from Latin *strata*) 'road'; *tun* (Old English) 'farmstead, settlement'. There was considerable Roman military activity in this area in the second century AD. Straiton Hill and North and South Straiton in north-east Fife are also by a Roman route to the Tay ferry-point. Straiton in the southern suburbs of Edinburgh is noted as Stratone, 1296.

Stranraer (Dumfries & Galloway) *Stran-raar.* 'Place of the fat peninsula'. *Sron* (Scottish Gaelic) 'nose, peninsula'; *reamhar* (Scottish Gaelic) 'fat, thick'. This description appears to be a reference to the location at the foot of the thicker of the two arms of the Rinns of Galloway. The latter part of the name occurs again in Barraer Fell, not far away, *barr* (Scottish Gaelic) 'crest', *reamhar* (Scottish Gaelic); 'fat, of great rotundity'; and *fell* (Scots, from Old Norse *fjall*) 'hill'. Stranraer is the railhead and main ferry-port for Northern Ireland.

Strath From *srath,* which has slightly different meanings in Irish and Scottish Gaelic. The Irish sense, of level land by a lake-shore, is rarely found in Scotland (*see* Gartney), and the conventional Scottish Gaelic sense is that of a wide valley between hills, with a level or gently sloping floor, traversed by a river, and in most cases named after the river. *See* Glen.

Strathallan *See* Allan

Strathaven (South Lanarkshire) *Strayven.* 'Wide valley of the Avon'. *Srath* (Scottish Gaelic) 'wide valley'; *abhainn* (Scottish Gaelic) 'river'. Noted as Straithawane, 1552. Here the terminal -th has been lost in speech but preserved in the spelling. The river flowing through this small town south of Hamilton is the tautologous Avon Water (*see* Avon).

Strathbungo (Glasgow) 'Mungo's strath'. *Srath* (Scottish Gaelic) 'wide valley'; *Mhungo* (Scottish Gaelic nickname) 'Mungo's'. It was the pet-name, meaning 'dear one', for St Kentigern.

Strathclyde (South Lanarkshire) 'Wide valley of the cleansing stream'. *Srath* (Scottish Gaelic) 'wide valley'; *Cloid* (Cumbric river-name) 'cleansing one'. Recorded as Straecled, 875. This was from 1975 to 1994 the largest local authority area in Britain. The name of Strathclyde has always been linked with the old Cumbric-speaking kingdom whose capital was on Dumbarton Rock. *See* Clyde.

Strathconon *See* Conon

Strathdon *See* Don

Strathearn *See* Earn

Strathfarrar *See* Farrar

Strathkinness (Fife) 'Strath of the water-head'. *Srath* (Scottish Gaelic) 'wide valley'; *cinn* (Scottish Gaelic) 'at the head of', *eas* (Scottish Gaelic) 'water, waterfall'. The short strath of the Kinness Burn has no notable waterfall today; the village of the same name is situated high on its northern flank. Noted as Stradkines, 1144.

Strathmiglo (Fife) 'Strath of the bog-loch'. *Srath* (Scottish Gaelic) 'wide valley'; *mig* (Brythonic–Pictish) 'bog'; *loch* (Scottish Gaelic) 'lake, loch'.

Strathmore (Perth & Kinross; Angus) 'The great wide valley'. *Srath* (Scottish Gaelic) 'wide valley'; *mór* (Scottish Gaelic) 'big, great'. The wide and fertile valley that lies between the southern edge of the Mounth and the Sidlaw Hills.

Strathpeffer (Highland) 'Wide valley of the shining stream'. *Srath* (Scottish Gaelic) 'wide valley'; *pevr* (Brythonic–Pictish) 'radiant one'. Noted as Strathpeffir, 1350. Set above the valley of the Peffery Water, west of Dingwall, it was developed in the nineteenth century as a spa resort, drawing on the chalybeate springs that rise here. The *pevr* form is found again in Innerpeffray (Perthshire) 'mouth of the shining stream', and it has been noted that the Silverburn stream in Aberdeenshire was recorded as Peferyn, 1247. There are also cognate Brittonic names, such as Peover, in Cheshire, England.

Strathspey *See* Spey. The dance and common-time music known as the 'strathspey', first recorded in 1653, presumably had its origin here.

Strathtay *See* Tay

Strathy (Highland) 'Of the strath'. *Srath* (Scottish Gaelic) 'wide valley'; with *-ach* (Scottish Gaelic) ending denoting place. This Sutherland crofting township stretches along the valley.

Strathyre (Stirling) Probably derived like Strachur, as 'twisty strath.' *See* Strachur.

Strawfrank (South Lanarkshire) 'Valley of the French'. *Srath* (Scottish Gaelic) 'wide valley'; *frangaich* (Scottish Gaelic) 'of the French', a reference to incoming landholders in medieval times. Noted as Strafrank in 1528.

Strelitz (Perth & Kinross) This wholly German name was given in honour of Queen Charlotte, wife of King George III, to a village on the site of Whiteley Farm, set up in the late eighteenth century for veteran soldiers. Charlotte was the daughter of the ruler of Mecklenburg–Strelitz.

Striven, Loch (Argyll & Bute) 'Loch of the point'. *Loch* (Scottish Gaelic) 'lake, loch'; *sroighean* (Scottish Gaelic) 'of the nose or point'; referring to the promontory between it and the Kyles of Bute. Recorded as Lochstryne, 1400.

Stroma (Highland) 'In the current', from Old Norse *straumr,* 'current, stream'. Recorded in 1150 as Straumsey (Old Norse *ey,* 'island'). Stroma lies in the middle of the Pentland Firth tide-race.

Strome Ferry (Highland) 'Ferry of the channel'. *Straumr* (Old Norse) 'current, stream'. The ferry has been superseded by a road to the South side of Loch Carron.

Stromness (Orkney) 'The headland of the current'. *Straumr* (Old Norse) 'sea current'; *nes* (Old Norse) 'headland'. This describes the situation of this fishing port and second town of Orkney. The headland at the end of the settlement rounds on to the Sound of Hoy. Records show it as Straumness in 1150. An earlier alternative name was Hamnavoe, meaning 'harbour on the bay', and this is often used to refer to the place in the writings of George Mackay Brown (1921–1996) who lived here. *Compare* Hamnavoe (Shetland).

Stronachlachar (Stirling) 'The mason's point'. *Srón* (Scottish Gaelic) 'point, nose'; *a'* 'of'; *chlachair* (Scottish Gaelic) 'the mason's'.

Strone (Argyll & Bute; Stirling; Highland) 'nose, point', from *srón* (Scottish Gaelic) 'nose'. Strone by Dunoon is noted in 1240 as Strohon. A descriptive name for a headland or crag. Stron- or Sron- are often found as prefixes in other names. The spelling Stroan is often found in the south-west; Stroan Loch in Dumfriesshire has an alluvial 'nose'.

Stronlarig (Stirling) 'Point of the beaten path'. *Srón* (Scottish Gaelic) 'point, nose'; *lairig* (Scottish Gaelic) 'pass, beaten path'.

Stronsay (Orkney) 'Star island', from Old Norse *stjorna,* 'star', and *ey,* 'island'. Noted as Stiornsay, 1150.

Strontian (Highland) 'Promontory of the beacon'. *Srón* (Scottish Gaelic) 'promontory'; *teine* (Scottish Gaelic) 'beacon'. The mineral strontium, first discovered near here in 1790, is named after this Loch Sunart village.

Succoth (Aberdeenshire; Argyll & Bute; other areas) 'The snout', meaning a point of ground between two converging streams, from Scottish Gaelic *socach,* 'snout'. There is also Succothmore, 'big snout', near Strachur.

Sullom Voe (Shetland) 'The gannets' fiord'. *Sulan* (Old Norse) 'gannets', giving Scots *solan; vagr* (Old Norse) 'bay, sea inlet'. This deep sheltered inlet has housed a major North Sea oil terminal since the 1970s.

Struan (Perth & Kinross; Highland) This place name has two forms, both connected with streams. Struan in Atholl is 'stream place'; *Srùthán* (Scottish Gaelic) 'current place, stream place'; Struan in Skye is An Sruthán (Scottish Gaelic) 'the little stream'.

Struy (Highland; Perth & Kinross) 'Stream place'. Scottish Gaelic *sruth,* stream, with *-ach* suffix denoting place; *sruthaigh* is its locative form. At Struy in Inverness-shire the rivers Glass and Farrar meet, and there are rivers or large streams at the other locations, usually spelt as Struie, including those above Ardgay in Ross-shire, at the Ord of Caithness, and near Forgandenny in Perthshire.

Suie (Clackmannan; Aberdeenshire; Highland) 'Seat', from Scottish Gaelic *suidhe,* 'seat, resting-place', often with the sense of having been a holy person's seat. This is an often-found name in hilly districts.

Suilven (Highland) Perhaps 'sun mountain'. *Sul* (Old Scottish Gaelic) 'sun'; *bheinn* (Scottish Gaelic) 'mountain'. However, the Gaelic name of Suilven is Beinn Buidhe (Scottish Gaelic) 'yellow'; its steep face looks directly to the setting sun. The derivation of the first part of the name from *súlr* (Old Norse) 'pillar' has also been suggested, as it suits the shape of the mountain (2399ft/733m) as seen from the sea.

Sumburgh (Shetland) Probably 'Sweyn's stronghold'. *Sweyn* (Old Norse personal name); *borgr* (Old Norse) 'fort, stronghold'. A prehistoric armoury was discovered here. The name of this southern headland of Shetland, and of the busy airport nearby, was recorded as Swynbrocht in 1506.

Summer Isles (Highland) These now uninhabited islands off the coast of Coigach, Wester Ross, are so called because they were used by crofters for summer grazing. The name is a direct translation of Gaelic Na h-Eileanan Samhraidh.

Sunart, Loch (Highland) 'Sweyn's fjord'. *Sweyn* (Old Norse personal name), *fjordr* (Old Norse) 'sea inlet, firth'. Recorded as Swynwort, 1372.

Sutherland (Highland) 'Southern territory'. *Suthr* (Old Norse) 'south'; *land* (Old Norse) 'territory'. Recorded as Suthernelande, c. 1250. This present-day administrative district and former county was named by Norsemen coming from further North. Today, Orkney and Shetland still refer to the Scottish mainland as 'the South'. The Gaelic name is *Cataibh*, from the old Pictish name *Cat*, comprising Caithness and eastern Sutherland.

Sutors of Cromarty (Highland) The two headlands of the Cromarty Firth are known in Gaelic as na Sùdraichean, 'the tanners', and the association of sound and meaning has produced the Scots form *Sutors*, 'cobblers'; recorded as the Sowteris, 1593. There is also a Souter Head just south of Aberdeen, and again adjacent to a Nigg Bay.

Swanbister (Orkney) 'Sweyn's farm'. *Sweyn* (Old Norse personal name); *bolstadr* (Old Norse) 'farmstead'.

Swanton (Borders) 'Suen's place'. *Suen* (Old English personal name); *tun* (Old English) 'settlement, place'.

Symbister (Shetland) The full meaning of the name of the fishing port and main settlement on the island of Whalsay remains obscure. The first part may be a Norse personal name. The second element is Old Norse *bolstadr*, 'farmstead'; a frequent suffix in Northern Isles place-names.

Symington (South Lanarkshire) 'Simon's farm'. *Symon* (Old English personal name); *tun* (Old English) 'farmstead'. The Simon was Simon Lockhart; the name noted around 1179, as Villa Symonis Lockard. As well as the Symington in the Clyde valley, there is another further west, near Troon in South Ayrshire.

T

Tain (Highland) 'Water'. This ancient Royal burgh, on the south shore of the Dornoch Firth, stands at the mouth of a small river, the Tain Water. The name has been ascribed to a pre-Celtic root form indicating 'river' or 'water'. Similar river-names also ascribed to the same root are Teign in Devon, and Tyne in Northumberland and Lothian; there is also Tain l'Hermitage in south-east France. Modern Gaelic *tain* means 'water'. It is recorded as Tene 1226, Tayne 1375, Thane 1483. Despite its proximity to long sandspits, these older forms do not correspond to Old Norse *taing*, 'spit of land'. The Gaelic name is however Baile Dhubhthaich, 'Duthac's Town', from the church of St Duthac here, a medieval pilgrimage place.

Taing This very common name along the Orkney and Shetland coasts is from Old Norse *thang*, indicating a low headland or spit.

Talisker (Highland) 'Sloping rock'. *T-hallr* (Old Norse) 'sloping'; *skjaer* (Old Norse) 'rock'.

Talla (Borders) 'The brow'. *Talg* (Cumbric) 'front, brow'.

Tanera (Highland) 'Harbour isle'. *t-h-fnar* (Old Norse) 'harbour'; *ey* (Old Norse) 'isle'. There are two Taneras in the Summer Isles, differentiated as *Mór*, 'big', and *Beag*, 'small'.

Tankerness (Orkney) 'Tancred's cape'. *Tancred* (Old Norse, and Norman, personal name) *nes* (Old Norse) 'headland, cape'.

Tantallon (East Lothian) 'High-fronted fort'. *Din* (Brythonic) 'fort'; *talgan* (Cumbric) 'of the high front, or brow'.

Taransay (Western Isles) 'Isle of (Saint) Taran'. *Taran* (Pictish personal name); *ey* (Old Norse) 'island'.

Tarbat Ness (Highland) 'Cape of the isthmus'. *Tairbeart* (Scottish Gaelic) 'isthmus, portage point'; *nes* (Old Norse) 'cape, headland'. Noted c. 1226 as Arterbert, with Scottish Gaelic *ard*, 'high'. The Gaelic name is Rubha Thairbeirt.

Tarbert (Argyll & Bute; Western Isles) 'Place of the isthmus'. *Tairbeart* (Scottish Gaelic) 'isthmus, portage point'. Tarbet by Loch Lomond is recorded as Tarbart, 1392. Tarbert on Loch Fyne is Tairpirt Boetter, 'facing Bute', 711. The ancient practice of portage, the dragging of boats and contents from sea to sea across narrow necks of land, is commemorated in the many places of this name or a similar form (e.g. Tarbat, Tarbet). As a consequence there are numerous Loch Tarberts, usually differentiated as East and

West, because of the southwest-northeast grain of the Scottish landscape.

Tarbet (Argyll & Bute) *See* Tarbert.

Tarff (Highland; Perth & Kinross; Dumfries & Galloway) 'Bull stream, bull place'. *Tarbh* (Scottish Gaelic) 'bull'. This frequently found name also takes the form Tarves and Tarvie; it is a reminder both of the commercial and mythological importance of the bull in the Celtic world. In association with a river it may indicate a tutelary spirit.

Tarland (Aberdeenshire) 'Bull's enclosure', from *tarbh* (Scottish Gaelic) 'bull', and *lann* (Scottish Gaelic) 'field, enclosure'. Noted as Tarualund, 1183. The Gaelic form of the name is Tarbhlann.

Tarradale (Highland) 'Bull's dale'. From Old Norse *tarfr,* 'bull', and *dalr,* 'dale'.

Tarskavaig (Highland) Suggested as 'Cod bay'. *Thorskr* (Old Norse) 'cod'; *vaig* (from Old Norse *vik*) 'bay'. An alternative derivation is from *Tar* (Scottish Gaelic prefix) 'across from'; and the name may mean 'across from Scavaig'. This sense may have been 'grafted' on to the Norse name after the decline of Norse speech in Skye. *See* Scavaig.

Tay, River, Strath, Loch, Firth (Perth & Kinross) Scotland's longest river, noted in the first century AD by Tacitus as Taus, and by Ptolemy, around AD 150, as Tava. It flows 120 miles (192km) mainly eastwards through Loch Tay and on into the North Sea by way of the Firth of Tay. The name, cognate with the Taw in Devon, England, may derive from a conjectured Brythonic Tausa, meaning 'silent one' or 'strong one' – aspects of the river's controlling deity – or simply 'flowing' (see also Teith). The Tay has the greatest volume of water of any river on the British mainland, is a major salmon river, and is famous for its pearl fisheries: here the largest freshwater pearl found in Scotland, 'Wee Willie', was harvested in 1967.

Tayinloan (Argyll & Bute) *Tie-in-loan.* 'House in the meadow'. *Taigh* (Scottish Gaelic) 'house'; *an*, 'of the'; *lón* (Scottish Gaelic) 'meadow'.

Taymouth (Perth & Kinross) Not at the estuary of the Tay, but where the river flows out of Loch Tay, thus mouth of the loch rather than that of the river. The first lime trees in Scotland were planted in the castle grounds here, in 1664.

Taynuilt (Argyll & Bute) *Tie-noolt.* 'House by the stream'. *Taigh* (Scottish Gaelic) 'house'; *an*, 'of the'; *-uillt* (Scottish Gaelic) 'of the stream'.

Tayport (Fife) This town lies on the southern side of the Firth of Tay, opposite Broughty Ferry, with which it had long-serving ferry links prior to the rail and road bridges being built nearby. The current name dates only from 1888; before then this port was successively called Scotscraig, South Ferry, Portincraig, Ferryport-on-Craig and South Craig, all these names having a reference either to its ferry across the Tay or to the crag on which the town is situated.

Tayvallich (Argyll & Bute) *Tie-vy-allich*. 'House in the pass'. *Taigh* (Scottish Gaelic) 'house'; *bhealaich* (Scottish Gaelic) 'of the hill pass'.

Teith, River (Stirling) Another ancient river-name whose origins are unclear, but which is presumed to stem from the same pre-Celtic, or possibly non-Indo-European, root element *tau*, 'flowing, melting', as Tay, Teviot. *See* Menteith.

Templand (Aberdeenshire; Dumfries & Galloway) 'Temple-land', indicating land once belonging to the Knights Templar; the place-name Temple (Lothian and elsewhere) has the same sense. These names were bestowed in the post-Gaelic-speaking era, south of the Highlands; Gaelic *teampull* ('temple, church') names in the Hebrides simply indicate a church.

Tents Muir (Fife) 'Moor of the fort'. Its origin has been suggested as a hybrid: *dinas* (Brythonic–Pictish) 'fort'; with the later addition of *muir* (Scots) 'moor'. Tents Muir is now largely forested, but evidence of prehistoric sites has been found.

Teviot, River (Borders) As with so many river-names, its origin goes far back into unrecorded history; it has been conjectured as linked to a pre-Celtic root form *tau*, 'flowing, melting' (*see* Teith). Noted c. 600 as Teiwi, c. 1160 Teuiot. It appears to be cognate with Welsh and Cornish river-names like Teifi and Tavy.

Texa (Argyll & Bute) 'Bird cherry island'. The name of this small island off Islay, referred to as Tisgay in Dean Monro's account of the Western Isles, 1549, has been construed as *t-heggs* (Old Norse) 'bird cherry'; *ey* (Old Norse) 'island'.

Threipland (Aberdeenshire; South Lanarkshire) 'Debateable land'. *Threap* (Middle English and Scots) 'scold, dispute'; and 'land'. A tract of ground at one time under disputed ownership.

Throsk (Stirling) 'House on the river'. *Tref* (Cumbric) 'dwelling'; *usc* (Cumbric, related to Gaelic *uisge*) 'river, water'. Noted as Threske, 1246. The situation of Throsk is right by the River Forth, south of Stirling.

Thundergay (North Ayrshire) 'Backside to the wind', from Scottish Gaelic *tòn*, 'backside'; *ri gaoith*, 'to the wind', presumably a comment on the Arran site's exposure. There is also Tunregaith in South Ayrshire, and Timothy Pont's 1645 map shows a Tonreghe near Whithorn.

Thurso (Highland) 'Bull's river'. *Thjor-s* (Old Norse) 'bull's'; *aa* (Old Norse) 'river'. It was recorded as Thorsa in a document of 1152, and this still accords with local pronunciation. The origin may be pre-Norse, since Ptolemy's name for the neighbouring headland, Tarvedum (c. AD 150) suggests a conjectured Brythonic *tarvo-dubron,* 'bull-water', and later Norse speakers perhaps made a false relation to the god-name Thor. This market town on the north Caithness coast takes the name of the salmon river on whose estuary it stands. The spacious town plan was laid out in the late eighteenth century by Sir John Sinclair of Ulbster.

Thwaite (Dumfries & Galloway) 'Meadow', or 'clearing', from Old Norse *thveit,* 'clearing'. This and other Norse names in the area indicate colonisation in the tenth century from the Viking kingdom centred on York. A common name in England but unusual in Scotland (but *see* Twatt).

Tibbermore (Perth & Kinross) 'Big well' or 'Mary's well'. *Tobar* (Scottish Gaelic) 'well'; with either *mór* (Scottish Gaelic) 'great', or *Mhoire* (Scottish Gaelic) 'Mary's'. Recorded as Tubermore, c. 1200. Also found as Tippermuir. *See* Tobermory.

Tighnabruaich (Argyll & Bute) *Tie-na-brooach.* 'House of the bank'. *Taigh* (Scottish Gaelic) 'house'; *na* (Scottish Gaelic) 'of the'; *bruaich* (Scottish Gaelic) 'bank'. This small resort, developed in the nineteenth century, is situated where originally a solitary house stood on the high ground overlooking the western arm of the Kyles of Bute.

Tilt, River and **Glen** (Perth & Kinross) In Gaelic Abhainn, 'river' Teilte, whose derivation is unclear; it may be from an Old Gaelic personal name.

Tillicoultry (Clackmannanshire) 'Hill-slope in the back land'. *Tulach* (Scottish Gaelic) 'hill, hill-slope'; *cul* (Scottish Gaelic) 'back'; *tìr* (Scottish Gaelic) 'land'. Recorded as Tulycultri, 1195. This former coal-mining town lies at the base of the Ochil Hills.

Tillienaught (Aberdeenshire) 'Bare hill'. *Tulach* (Scottish Gaelic) 'hill, hill slope'; *nochd* (Scottish Gaelic) 'bare'.

Timsgarry (Western Isles) 'Tumi's garth'; from *Tuma* (Old Norse personal name) 'Thomas's'; *gardr* (Old Norse) 'enclosure'.

Tinto (South Lanarkshire) 'Beacon hill'. *Teine* (Scottish Gaelic) 'fire, beacon'; *ach* (Scottish Gaelic suffix denoting place). Noted as Tintou, c. 1315, but into the nineteenth century it was known as Tintock. Tinto (2320ft/709m) is visible for many miles around.

Tiree (Argyll & Bute) Possibly 'land of corn'. *Tìr* (Scottish Gaelic) 'land'; *eadha* (Scottish Gaelic) 'corn'. This low-lying, fertile island was renowned for its high productivity of grain crops. However, the Old Irish personal name _Ith_ has also been suggested as the source of the latter part, giving 'Ith's land'. Early forms include Tir Iath, sixth century, Terra Ethica, c. 700, Tiryad, 1343.

Tobermory (Argyll & Bute) 'Mary's well'. _Tobar_ (Scottish Gaelic) 'well'; _Moire_ (Scottish Gaelic) 'Mary's'. Noted as Tibbirmore, 1540. The main town on the Island of Mull, developed in the eighteenth century by the British Fisheries Society, it is named after a well dedicated to the Virgin Mary, still to be found nearby.

Tolsta (Western Isles) Perhaps 'Toli's stead', or 'hollow stead'; _Tolu_ (Old Norse personal name); _stadr_ (Old Norse) 'farmstead'. If 'hollow' it would be a mutation of the first letter from an _h_ to _t_, from an original _hol_ (Old Norse) 'low, hollow'.

Tom- As a prefix to place-names, it generally means 'hill' or 'knoll', from Scottish Gaelic _tom_, 'hill'; but in some Western areas and the Western Isles, it also has the meaning of 'copse'.

Tomatin (Highland) 'Juniper hill'. _Tom_ (Scottish Gaelic) 'hill', knoll', _aitionn_ (Scottish Gaelic) 'juniper'.

Tomdhu (Highland) 'Black hill'. _Tom_ (Scottish Gaelic) 'hill'; _dubh_ (Scottish Gaelic) 'black'. Tomdow (Grampian) is of the same origin.

Tomintoul (Moray) 'Little hill of the barn'. _Tom_ (Scottish Gaelic) 'hill'; _an t-sabhail_ (Scottish Gaelic) 'of the barn'. This village stands at an elevation of 1100ft (340m) on a small plateau, and is one of several places in the central Highlands with the prefix _Tom_ in their name.

Tomnahurich (Highland) 'Little hill of the yew wood'. _Tom_ (Scottish Gaelic) 'hill, knoll'; _na_, 'of the'; _Iubhraich_ (Scottish Gaelic) 'yew wood'. This hill outside Inverness, now a cemetery, was reputed to have been the home of a fairy tribe.

Tongland (Dumfries & Galloway) 'Tongue-shaped piece of land', from Old English _tunge_, 'tongue', cognate with Old Norse _tunga;_ and Old English _land_. Noted as Tuncgeland, c. 1150. The fifteenth century alchemist and would-be flyer, Damian, was titular abbot of Tongland.

Tongue (Highland) 'Tongue or spit of land'. _Tunga_ (Old Norse) 'tongue (of land)'. Tongue in Sutherland, noted as Toung, 1542, Toung in Orkney and Shetland, Tong or Tunga in Lewis, and Teangue in Skye all share the same derivation.

Tore (Highland) 'Bleaching place'. The name of this village in the centre of the Black Isle has sometimes been construed as Gaelic _torr_, 'hill', but the Gaelic name is _an Todhar_, 'the bleaching place'. _See_ Balintore.

Torlundy (Highland) 'Mound of the boggy place'. _Torr_ (Scottish

Gaelic) 'mound'; *lud* (Brythonic–Pictish, giving Scottish Gaelic *lodan*) 'muddy, boggy'.

Tornapress (Highland) 'Farmstead of the copses'. *Treabhar* (Scottish Gaelic) 'farmstead'; *nam*, 'of the'; *preas* (Scottish Gaelic) 'copses'. This name, now given to the formidable hill on the Applecross road, originally related to a farm at the foot.

Torness (East Lothian; Highland; Shetland) In Lothian, 'mound of the headland'. *Torr* (Scottish Gaelic) 'mound, hill'; *nes* (Old Norse) 'headland'. Torness near Inverness may be *Torr nan eas* (Scottish Gaelic) 'mound of the stream or waterfall'. Tor Ness in Shetland may have a similar derivation to Thurso, as 'bull head'. The Lothian site, east of Edinburgh, is now dominated by a nuclear power station.

Torphichen (West Lothian) Although 'hill of magpies' – *Torr* (Scottish Gaelic) 'mound, hill'; *phigheainn* (Scottish Gaelic) 'of magpies' – seems to fit, it has been pointed out that *pigheann* is a late Gaelic borrowing from Middle English, and hence unlikely to form the second element in the name. Found as Thorfechin, 1165. Torfichen Hill in the Moorfoots seems to share the name.

Torphins (Aberdeenshire) 'White mount'. *Torr* (Scottish Gaelic) 'mound, hill'; *fionn* (Scottish Gaelic) 'white, fair'. Its terminal *-s* may indicate a plural in the original Gaelic name. Torphin in south Edinburgh shows a singular form, with the same derivation.

Torran (Argyll & Bute; Highland) Scottish Gaelic *torran*, 'little hill', is the most likely derivation for the hamlet names from Loch Awe, Raasay and Easter Ross, but the name of the Torran Rocks off Mull has been linked to Scottish Gaelic *torrunn*, 'thunder', also found in the Irish River Torand.

Torridon (Highland) The name of this mountainous region remains unexplained. The first part may be *torr* (Scottish Gaelic) 'hill(s)', but a meaning based on the Irish Gaelic verb *tairbhert,* 'transfer' (related to Tarbert) has also been suggested, on the supposition that Glen Torridon was a portage route from the head of Upper Loch Torridon to Loch Maree. In 1464 it was recorded as Torvirtane.

Torrin (Highland) This Skye name probably has the same derivation as Torran.

Torrisdale (Highland) 'Thor's dale'. *Thoris* (Old Norse, genitive form of proper name *Thorir*); *dalr* (Old Norse) 'valley'. Thorir derives from Thor, the Norse thunder god. Recorded as Glentoresdale, c. 1251.

Torry (Aberdeen) 'Hilly place'. *Torr* (Scottish Gaelic) 'hill'; *aidh* (Scottish Gaelic suffix denoting place). Torry, noted in this form 1350, is now part of Aberdeen city.

Touch Hills *See* Tough

Tough (Aberdeenshire) 'Hills' or 'hilly place'. *Tulach* (Scottish Gaelic) 'hill, ridge'. Recorded as Tulluch, c. 1550, Towch 1605. The Touch Hills to the south of Flanders Moss, recorded 1329 as Tulch, have the same derivation.

Town Yetholm *See* Yetholm

Trabrown (Scottish Borders) 'Place on the hill', from Cumbric *tref,* 'place, settlement'; *yr,* 'of the'; *bryn,* 'hill'.

Tradeston (Glasgow) This Glasgow district was developed as a residential area around 1790 by the Glasgow Trades House, a guild of merchants.

Trailtrow (Dumfries & Galloway) 'House of the cup-bearer', from *tref* (Cumbric) 'house, homestead' and *trulliad* (Cumbric) 'cup-bearer'. Noted around 1124 as Trevertrold. The name suggests a property given to a royal official.

Tranent (East Lothian) Apparently 'village by the valley'. *Tref* (Cumbric) 'settlement'; *yr neint* (Cumbric) 'by the valley'. The form Trauernent is found c. 1127. This former coal-mining town sits on a ridge of rising ground above the valley of the River Esk.

Traprain (East Lothian) 'Homestead of the tree'. *Tref* (Cumbric) 'homestead'; *pren* (Cumbric) 'tree'. Traprain Law has the addition of *law* (Scots) 'hill'. In the first and second centuries AD it was the main stronghold of the Votadini tribe.

Traquair (Borders) 'Homestead on the river Quair'. *Tref* (Cumbric) 'homestead'; the river-name is probably from *vedra* (Cumbric) 'clear one'; and is cognate with Weir. Older forms of Traquair include Treverquyrd in 1124. Traquair House is claimed to be the longest-inhabited house in Scotland.

Trearne (Renfrewshire) 'House among the sloes', from Cumbric *tref,* 'house', and *àirne,* 'the sloe trees'. This rather obscure quarry site east of Beith has one of the rare unaltered Tre- prefixed names in Scotland; only a handful compared to the many in Wales and Cornwall, and all attached to very minor localities; another is in the Pictish area, Trelong by St Cyrus, from *tref* and *long,* 'ship': 'boat-house'.

Treig, River and **Loch** (Highland) 'Place of desolation'. *Treig* (Scottish Gaelic) 'desolation' has been taken as the origin of this name; the landscape is undoubtedly a wild one, but the derivation remains provisional.

Trool, Loch and **Glen** (Dumfries & Galloway) 'Loch of the stream'. *Loch* (Scottish Gaelic) 'lake, loch'; *an t-,* 'of the'; *sruthail* (Scottish Gaelic) 'stream'.

Troon (South Ayrshire) 'Headland'. *Trwyn* (Cumbric) 'headland, point'. Alternatively, this name has been derived by some as: *an t-sron* (Scottish Gaelic) 'nose, point'. Either way, the name is apt. Recorded as le Trone in 1371. This resort and port, on the Firth of Clyde, is built around a distinct promontory. The same root name is found in Duntrune, Argyll, 'fort on the headland'.

Trossachs, The (Stirling) Apparently 'the cross-hills', from a Cumbric word cognate with Welsh *trawsfynydd*, 'cross-hill', rendered into Gaelic form in modern times as Na Trosaichean. *Tros* (Old Welsh) signifies 'across'. The name applies to the countryside of transverse wooded ridges and lochs between Loch Achray and Loch Katrine, with Aberfoyle as its main centre. Formerly part of the Cumbric-speaking kingdom of Strathclyde, it has later historical links with the Clan MacGregor, and is the main scene of Sir Walter Scott's *Rob Roy. See* Ardrossan.

Trotternish (Highland) 'Thrond's Headland'. *Throndar* (Old Norse personal name); *nes* (Old Norse) 'headland'; recorded as Trouternish, 1309, Tronternesse in the mid sixteenth century. With Minginish and Vaternish, one of the three main divisions of the Isle of Skye.

Truim, River and **Glen** (Highland) 'Of the elder trees'. *Trom* (Scottish Gaelic) 'elder tree'. Glen Tromie has a similar derivation.

Tulla, River and **Loch** (Perth & Kinross) The scotticised form might suggest Scottish Gaelic *tulach,* 'hill', but the Gaelic name is Toilbhe, of uncertain origin.

Tullibardine (Perth & Kinross) 'Hill of warning'. *Tulach* (Scottish Gaelic) 'hill slope'; *bàrdainn* (Scottish Gaelic) 'warning'. The reference is to a signal beacon. Noted as Tulibarden, 1234.

Tullibody (Clackmannanshire) 'Hill of the hut'. *Tulach* (Scottish Gaelic) 'hill, hill slope'; *bothaich* (Scottish Gaelic) 'of the hut'. Some older forms had the prefix *Dun-*, perhaps through Cumbric influence: Dunbodeuin, 1147. Now an industrial and residential village to the west of Alloa.

Tulloch (Highland; Perth & Kinross) 'Hill slope'. *Tulach* (Scottish Gaelic) 'hill, hill slope'. This is a frequent local and farm name, and an often-disguised element in many names; *see* Tillicoultry.

Tullochgorum (Angus) 'Greenish hill'. *Tulach* (Scottish Gaelic) 'hill, hill slope'; *gorm* (Scottish Gaelic) 'blue-green'. John Skinner's famous poem of this name (he was the episcopalian parson here for much of the eighteenth century) has given it a degree of fame. There is also Tullochgorm near Minard in Argyll & Bute.

Tullybelton (Perth & Kinross) 'Beltane hill'. *Tulach* (Scottish Gaelic) 'hill, hill slope'; *Bealtainn* (Scottish Gaelic) 'Beltane', the Celtic May feast, when ritual fires were lit on conspicuous hilltops.

Tullymet (Perth & Kinross) 'Fertile hill'. *Tulach* (Scottish Gaelic) 'hill, hill slope'; *meith* (Scottish Gaelic) 'fertile'. Recorded as Tulichmet, c. 1200.

Tullynessle (Aberdeenshire) 'Hill of spells'. *Tulach* (Scottish Gaelic) 'hill'; *an,* 'of'; *eoisle,* 'the charm, or spell'. Recorded as Tulynestyn, c. 1300. This seems to be an alternative version of Esslemont, in the same region.

Tummel, River, Strath and **Loch** (Highland) 'Dark river'. *Teimheil* (Scottish Gaelic) 'dark'. Like many other river-names, it may be older than this suggests, from a pre-Celtic form that contains the same meaning and the same root-element, shared with English Teme.

Tundergarth (Dumfries & Galloway) Though the suffix may be Scottish Gaelic *gart,* 'enclosure', the name's early thirteenth-century form of Thonergayth also makes possible the same derivation as Thundergay.

Turnberry (South Ayrshire) The ending has been taken as *borgar* (Old Norse) 'fort'; but the first part has yet to be satisfactorily explained. Noted as Turnebiri, c. 1200. The site of a luxury hotel and golfing resort, established originally by the Glasgow & South-Western Railway.

Turin (Angus) 'Little hill', from Scottish Gaelic *torran*: *torr* ('hill') with diminutive suffix *-an*. A site of pre-Pictish fortifications.

Turnhouse (Edinburgh) The name is found at Turnhouse Hill in the Pentlands, west of Penicuik, and at the site of Edinburgh Airport. A possible derivation is 'hill of the spectre', from *torr* (Scottish Gaelic) 'hill'; *na,* 'of'; *fhuathais* (Scottish Gaelic) 'of the spectre'.

Turret, River and **Glen** (Highland; Perth & Kinross) 'Little dry stream', from Scottish Gaelic *tur,* 'dry', and *that,* a suffix indicating 'small'. The reference is to a stream that dries out in summer.

Turriff (Aberdeenshire) Possibly 'hill of anguish'. *Torr* (Scottish Gaelic) 'hill'; *bruid* (Scottish Gaelic) 'anguish' or 'a stab'. This is a name in which the second element may have changed, and as such its exact derivation remains uncertain. Records show Turbruad, in the *Book of Deer* c. 1000, Turrech 1300, Turreff 1500. A small agricultural market town at the heart of a wide farming district, featuring, as 'Turra', in a number of the area's famous bothy ballads.

Tuskerbuster (Orkney) Tusherbist. 'Peat-cutter's farm'. *Torf* (Old Norse) 'peat'; *skeri* (Old Norse) 'cutter'; *bolstadr* (Old Norse) 'farmstead.' It was an earl of Orkney, Einar, who was said to have given his countrymen the idea of burning peat, and received the name 'Torf-Einar'.

Twatt (Orkney) 'Clearing, settlement'. *Thveit* (Old Norse) 'clearing, meadow', cognate with English 'thwaite'.

Tweed (Borders) A river-name of uncertain derivation. It may stem from the same root as Tay and Tyne, in being derived from the Brythonic root form *tau* or *teu*, indicating 'strong, silent', or 'flowing'. This in turn has been linked to the Sanskrit *tavas*, meaning 'surging' or 'powerful'. The name was recorded in an early text of around 700 as Tuuide. This famous salmon river, which rises at Tweed Well, north of Moffat, and flows eastwards across Tweedsmuir to enter the North Sea at Berwick-upon-Tweed, marks for part of its course the Border between England and Scotland. Its name was transferred to the woollen cloth made in the area by a London clerk's misreading of the Scots *tweel*, 'twill' (first noted in 1847).

Tyndrum (Argyll & Bute) 'House on the ridge'. *Taigh* (Scottish Gaelic) 'house'; *an*, 'on the'; *druim* (Scottish Gaelic) 'ridge'.

Tyne, River (East Lothian) This river-name remains of obscure origin, probably from a pre-Celtic root, cognate with Tain and Tay.

Tyninghame (East Lothian) 'Village of the dwellers by the Tyne'. *Tyn* (see Tyne); *inga* (Old English) 'of the people'; *ham* (Old English) 'settlement, village'.

U

Uamh, Loch nan (Highland) 'Loch of the Cave'. *Loch* (Scottish Gaelic) 'lake, loch'; *nan*, 'of'; *uamh* (Scottish Gaelic) 'cave'. This was where Prince Charles Edward Stewart's vessel dropped anchor in July 1745, and from where he was rescued in August 1746, a cairn marks the spot.

Uddingston (South Lanarkshire) 'Oda's people's farmstead'. *Oda* (Old English personal name); *inga* (Old English) 'of the people'; *tun* (Old English) 'farmstead'. Curiously, an early form of 1296 is recorded as Odistoun, just 'Oda's farmstead'. There is also Uddington in the same district, two miles north-east of Douglas.

Udny (Aberdeenshire) 'Streams'. *Alltan* (Scottish Gaelic) 'streams'; with *-ait* (Scottish Gaelic suffix denoting place). Around 1400 it was recorded as Uldeny.

Ugie, River (Aberdeenshire) 'Stream of nooks and corners', from *ùigeach* (Scottish Gaelic) 'nook, hollow'. The South Ugie Water, especially, is a very twisty stream.

Uig (Highland; Argyll & Bute; Western Isles) 'Bay'. *Uig,* a Gaelic form of *vik* (Old Norse) 'bay'. The Skye village on Loch Snizort is the island's main port for onward ferry crossings to the Western Isles, and lies on the only really sheltered deep-water bay on this part of its coast. There are other Uigs on Loch Dunvegan in Skye, at the head of the Holy Loch, and on the west coast of Lewis.

Uist, North and **South** (Western Isles) 'An abode'. *I-vist* (Old Norse) 'in-dwelling'. The latter is the literal meaning traditionally ascribed to the basic name of these two Outer Hebridean islands, separated by the intervening Benbecula. It was recorded in 1282 as Iuist and in the fourteenth century as Ywest. The modern Gaelic form is Uibhist, and the meaning of the name appears to correspond with that of Lewis.

Ulbster (Highland) 'Ulf's farm', from Old Norse personal name *Ulfa* (signifying wolf-like), and *bolstadr,* 'farmstead'. The suffix is a compressed form of the -bister names of Orkney, as with numerous other northern mainland places, like Lybster. Recorded as Ulbister, 1538.

Ullapool (Highland) 'Olaf's settlement'. *Olaf* (Old Norse personal name); *bol* (Old Norse mutated form of *bolstadr*) 'farmstead, settlement'. Recorded in 1610 as Ullabill. The harbour was developed in 1788 by the British Fisheries Society to encourage the herring industry. It is the car-ferry-port for Stornoway, in Lewis.

Ulva (Argyll & Bute) 'Ulf's island'. *Ulfa* (Old Norse personal name or nickname) 'Wolf'; *ey* (Old Norse) 'island'. Recorded in 1473 as Ulway.

Unapool (Highland) 'Uni's farm'. *Uni* (Old Norse personal name); *bol* (from Old Norse *bolstadr* 'farmstead, settlement'). *See* Eriboll.

Unst (Shetland) 'Eagles' nest'. *Orn* (Old Norse) 'eagle'; *nyst* (Old Norse) 'nest'. This, the most northerly of Shetland's main islands, is still the home of many rare birds. Its name was recorded in a document of around 1200 as Ornyst.

Urie (Aberdeenshire) Perhaps 'place of the yews'. *Iubharach* (Scottish Gaelic) 'of yews'; though a derivation from Scottish Gaelic *uar*, 'landslip, water-spout', may also be possible, with the often-found river-name suffix *-aidh*. A further suggestion is *uidhre*, genitive of *odhar*, 'drab, grey-coloured'. There are two Uries in Aberdeenshire, the tributary of the Don noted in 1185 as Oury. In Glen Ury, by Stonehaven, an alternative spelling is found.

Urquhart (Highland) 'Woodside'. *Air* (Brythonic–Pictish) 'on, upon'; *cardden* (Brythonic–Pictish) 'thicket, wood'. Adamnan's *Life of St Columba*, c. 700, records the name as Airchardan; the Urquhart form is found from 1340. In Gaelic it is Urchardainn. A parish and district to the west of Loch Ness. The strategic fortress of Urquhart Castle, razed in the seventeenth century, was built to control passage through the Great Glen.

Urr, River (Dumfries & Galloway) Another river-name from remote antiquity, ascribed to a pre-Celtic origin. Intriguingly, it has been compared to Basque *ur*, 'water', but it would be rash to draw conclusions from this. Recorded c. 1280 as Urrer.

Urrard (Perth & Kinross) 'Fore-headland', from Scottish Gaelic *air*, 'on, upon'; *àirde*, 'height'. The rocky point where the rivers Garry and Tummel meet.

Urray (Highland) This name has been derived as 'remade fort'. *Air* (Scottish Gaelic) 'on'; *rath* (Scottish Gaelic) 'ring fort', with the notion of a fortification set up on top of an earlier one. Noted as Vrray, 1546. The presence of a church here gave its name to the River Orrin.

Uyea (Shetland) Two islands bear this name, a small one off Yell and a larger off Unst. It comes from Old Norse *öyja*, 'island'.

V

Vatersay (Western Isles) Perhaps 'Glove island'. *Vottr-s* (Old Norse) 'glove's'; *ey* (Old Norse) 'island', though the significance is not clear. Recorded as Vatersa, 1580. The Gaelic form is Bhatarsaigh. A small island to the south of Barra, and linked to it by a causeway.

Venue, Ben (Stirling) 'Little mountain'. *Beinn* (Scottish Gaelic) 'mountain'; *mheanbh* (Scottish Gaelic) 'small'. Noted as Benivenow, 1794. The name of this mountain (2386ft/730m) is given perhaps by comparison with nearby Ben Lomond.

Vennachar, Loch (Stirling) 'Horned loch'. Although 'Loch of the fair valley', from *loch* (Scottish Gaelic) 'lake, loch'; *bhana* (Scottish Gaelic) 'fair'; *choire* (Scottish Gaelic) 'of the mountain hollow, or corrie', has been put forward, an older form of the name is Banquhar, c. 1375, and the Gaelic form is Loch Bheannchair, making it cognate with Banchory, from Scottish Gaelic *beannchar*, horn-shaped (incorporating the elements *beann*, 'horn' and *cor*, 'situation, setting'). The loch's gently curving shape is the source of the name. *See* Banchory.

Voe (Shetland) 'Bay'. *Vagr* (Old Norse) 'bay', normally a long indented inlet, as often found in Shetland. Several Shetland Mainland settlements at the head of voes take this name, or incorporate it as an element.

Voil, Loch (Stirling) Perhaps 'lively', from *beò* (Scottish Gaelic) 'life, breath'. The Gaelic name is Loch Bheothail.

Vorlich, Ben (Stirling, Perth & Kinross) 'Mountain of the sea-bag'. *Beinn* (Scottish Gaelic) 'mountain'; *muir* (Scottish Gaelic) 'sea'; *bolc* (Scottish Gaelic) 'bag'. The reference to a bag-like bay in the adjacent loch has been accepted in the case of Ben Vorlich (Loch Lomond, 3088ft/944m), noted on Blaeu's map in 1645 as Benvouirlyg, but disputed in that of Ben Vorlich (Loch Earn, 3231ft/988m), which has also been linked to a hypothetical Old Gaelic personal name, *Murlag*.

Vrackie, Ben (Perth & Kinross) 'Speckled mountain'. *Beinn* (Scottish Gaelic) 'mountain'; *bhreachaidh* (Scottish Gaelic) 'speckled'. This mountain (2760ft/844m) dominates the northern view from Pitlochry. Ben Bhraggie, above Golspie in Sutherland, has the same derivation.

W

Walkerburn (Borders) 'Waulker's stream'. *Waulker* (Scots, from Old English *walcere*) 'fuller of cloth'; *burna* (Old English) 'stream', giving Scots 'burn'. This small town on the River Tweed developed around a woollen mill in 1854, but the name suggests cloth working from a much earlier date.

Walls (Orkney; Shetland) 'Bays', from Old Norse *vágar*, 'bays'. Walls at the south of Hoy is noted as Vagaland in the *Orkneyinga Saga*, c. 1225.

Wallyford (Midlothian) *Wallee* is an old Scots term for 'spring' or 'marshy spring', and this may be the origin of the name, though there is a Scots adjective *wally*, with the sense of 'beautiful, fine', and this place-name could also be a descriptive one, effectively meaning 'good ford'.

Wamphray (Dumfries & Galloway) Perhaps 'cave of the offerings'. *Uamh* (Scottish Gaelic) 'cave'; *aifrionn* (Scottish Gaelic) 'place of offerings, chapel'. Recorded as Vamphray, 1275.

Wanlockhead (Dumfries & Galloway) Stream-head of the 'white flat stone'. *Gwyn* (Cumbric) 'white'; *llech* (Cumbric) 'flat stone'. The name may have been first that of the Wanlock Water, with the English *-head* suffix added at a much later date to denote the position of the village at the head of the stream; recorded as Wenlec, 1563. The former mining village, 1380ft/425m up in the Lowther Hills (the highest in Scotland), now a 'heritage site' has, like its near neighbour Leadhills, been involved in mineral extraction, especially lead, gold and silver, since before the Roman invasion.

Ward Hill (Orkney; Shetland) 'Sentry hill'. Old Norse *vardr*, 'watch, guard'. Ward Hill on Hoy, 1577ft/480m, is the highest point in Orkney. There are numerous Ward Hills in Shetland especially, sometimes spelt as Vord.

Wardlaw (Highland) 'Sentry hill'. The meaning is the same as that of Ward Hill, but the derivation is from the cognate Old English *weard*, 'guard, watch', and Old English *hlaew*, 'hill'. This location, west of Inverness, has one of the oldest English names in the north, noted 1210 as Wardelaue. Among other forms of the name is Wairdlaw in West Lothian. For the Gaelic equivalent *see* Fare, Hill of.

Waterbeck (Dumfries & Galloway) This village name, on a stream of the same name, appears to be a rare example in Scotland of 'beck' from Old Norse *bekkr*, 'stream', with *vatn* (Old Norse) 'water'. But nearby is Torbeck Hill (Scottish Gaelic *torr*, 'hill', and *beag*, 'small'); the juxtaposition is interesting.

Waterloo A number of locations, like those east of Wishaw, in North Lanarkshire, and adjoining Bankfoot in Perthshire, and on the Isle of Skye, have this name in commemoration of the battle of Waterloo in 1815.

Waternish (Highland) 'Water headland'. *Vatn* (Old Norse) 'water'; *nes* (Old Norse) 'headland'. Noted as Watternes, 1501. With Minginish and Trotternish, one of the three main divisions of the island of Skye.

Watten (Highland) 'Water, lake'. *Vatn* (Old Norse) 'water'. The locality, west of Wick, takes its name from its loch, now inevitably known as Loch Watten. Noted as Watne, 1230. There is another Loch Watten on Egilsay in Orkney.

Wauchope (Dumfries & Galloway) 'Den of strangers'. *Walc* (Old English) 'stranger, foreigner'; *hop* (Old English) 'hollow place'. Noted as Walchope, 1214.

Weem (Perth & Kinross) 'Cave'. *Uamh* (Scottish Gaelic) 'cave'.

Wemyss (Fife; North Ayrshire) *Weems*. 'Caves'. *Uamh* (Scottish Gaelic) 'cave'. In the case of both East Wemyss and West Wemyss on the Firth of Forth, noted as Wemys 1239; and Wemyss Bay on the Firth of Clyde, there are many coastal caves to be found in their raised-beach cliff locations. The same name is found in Port Wemyss on Islay.

Western Isles This name, Na h-Eileanan an Iar in Gaelic, given official recognition as the 'Island Authority' created in 1975, is a long-standing alternative term for the Outer Hebrides; the westernmost archipelago of 200-plus islands that stretches for 130 miles (200km) in a crescent off the north-west mainland of Scotland, from Lewis to Barra Head.

Wester This typically Scottish form of 'west' is from Old Norse *vest-r*, 'west', seen in many area and local names. *See* Easter.

Wester Ross *See* Ross

West Lothian *See* Lothian

Westray (Orkney) 'West island'. *Vestr* (Old Norse) 'west'; *ey* (Old Norse) 'island'; found as Westray in the *Orkneyinga Saga*, c. 1225. Although this island is not the most westerly of the group, apparently it was perceived as such by the Vikings since their compass cardinal points were set at a 45° difference from present-day bearings.

Whalsay (Shetland) 'Whale's island'. *Hval-s* (Old Norse) 'whale's'; *ey* (Old Norse) 'island'; Hvalsey in the *Orkneyinga Saga*, c. 1225.

The meaning here may relate to the whale-like shape of the island, but more likely to the presence of whales, or the practice of hunting them.

Whitburn (West Lothian) 'White stream'. *Hwit* (Old English) 'white'; *burna* (Old English) 'stream'. This Anglian form gave Scots 'burn', which continued in use here whereas 'brook' largely replaced it in England. Recorded in 1296 as Whiteburne.

Whithorn (Dumfries & Galloway) 'White house'. *Hwit* (Old English) 'white'; *erne* (Old English) 'house'. Called Candida Casa (Latin 'white house') on its foundation in AD 397 by St Ninian, and noted as Hwitan Aerne c. 890, this was an important religious centre for many centuries.

Whiten Head (Highland) 'White cape'. *Hvítr* (Old Norse) 'white'. The Gaelic name is a literal translation, An ceann gheal. The reference may be to breaking waves on this exposed north-western headland.

Whiting Bay (North Ayrshire) The name appears to be quite literal, 'bay of the whitings'.

Wick (Highland) 'Bay'. *Vik* (Old Norse) 'bay'. The fishing port, former county town of Caithness, takes its name from the narrow bay on which it stands. It was recorded as Vik in 1140, Weke in 1455. The northern terminus of the Highland Railway, it was one of the world's busiest herring ports up to the 1950s. Its Gaelic name is *Inbhir-Uig*, 'river-mouth bay'. *See* Uig.

Wigtown (Dumfries & Galloway) 'Wicga's farm'. *Wicga* (Old English personal name); *tun* (Old English) 'farm'. This derivation is the same as for Wigton (Cumbria) across the Solway Firth. Recorded as Wigeton in 1266. This small town was also the county town of the former Wigtownshire; it is now a mecca for book collectors.

Winchburgh (West Lothian) 'Winca's fort'. *Winca* (Old English personal name); *burh* (Old English) 'fortified place'. Recorded as Wynchburch, 1375.

Windygates (Fife) 'Windy gap'. *Geat* (Old English) 'gate' became Scots *yett,* also with the meaning of hill pass or gap, as in Yetts of Muckhart. Although an old form Windeyetts is recorded, the g- form has been preserved here. There is a Windy Yet on the Cunningham moors in Ayrshire

Wishaw (North Lanarkshire) Probably 'Willow wood'. *Withig* (Old English) 'willow'; *sceaga* (Old English) 'wood' giving Scots *shaw.* Such a description of this industrial town, south-east of Motherwell, is still evident in the wooded banks of the South Calder Water, on which it stands. The same name, with the same derivation, is found in Warwickshire, England.

Wormit (Fife) 'Wormwood'. *Wormit* is the Scots word for 'wormwood', and here presumably refers to a plantation of trees. Recorded as Wormet, 1440.

Wrath, Cape (Highland) 'Turning point'. Cape (English from Latin *caput*, 'head', via Old French *cap*) 'promontory, headland'; *hverfa* (Old Norse) 'to turn'. Recorded as Wraith, 1583. Despite the seemingly apt suggestion of storms, the derivation of this name, the only Cape among so many Heads, Rubhas, Points, Mulls and Nesses, lies in the location of this point around which Viking seamen changed course on the route between Scandinavia and western Scotland. The name of the district between here and Durness, the Parph, preserves a Gaelic form of the Norse name.

Wyvis, Ben (Highland) 'Majestic mountain'. *Beinn* (Scottish Gaelic) 'mountain'; *Uais* (Scottish Gaelic) 'noble, majestic', a shortened form of *uasal*, 'proud'. *Fhuathais* (Scottish Gaelic) 'of the bogle or goblin', has also been suggested, though the commanding position of the mountain (3433ft/1050m) makes the first meaning more probable. It was noted as Weyes in 1608.

Y

Yarrow, River (Borders) 'Rough (river)', from *garw* (Cumbric) 'rough'. Recorded as Gierua, c. 1120. This secluded river, flowing from St Mary's Loch, has been a subject for numerous poets, including William Wordsworth (twice), but the classic Yarrow poem is the anonymous 'Willie's Rare', with its tragic ending: 'She sought him high, she sought him low, She sought him near and far, O. Syne in the cleaving of a craig, She found him drooned in Yarrow.'

Yell (Shetland) 'Barren place'. *Geldr* (Old Norse) 'barren'. This old Viking name remains descriptive of Shetland's second largest island, lying between Mainland and Unst. In the *Orkneyinga Saga* of c. 1225 the name was recorded as Ala; and in later documents as Jala; Jella and Yella.

Yester (East Lothian) 'House, dwelling'. *Ystre* (Cumbric) 'dwelling'.

Yetholm (Borders) 'Village of the pass'. *Geat* (Old English) 'gate, gap', become Scots *yett*; *ham* (Old English) 'village'. This ancient 'gateway' settlement, situated in the Cheviot Hills just north of the border between Scotland and England, is split into Kirk Yetholm and Town Yetholm, on opposite banks of the Bowmont Water. Old Norse *holmr*, 'island', including 'river island', would seem to be the source of the suffix, but early records show the *ham* form: Gatha'n c. 800, Jetham 1233, Kirkyethame c. 1420. Kirk Yetholm marks the end of the road and the first place in Scotland for walkers coming north along the Pennine Way. For centuries it has been the chief settlement of the Scottish gypsies.

Yetts of Muckhart *See* Muckhart

Yoker (Glasgow) 'Low ground'. *Iochdar* (Scottish Gaelic) 'low-lying ground'. Found in this form 1505. There was a ferry here across the Clyde.

Ythan, River (Aberdeenshire) 'Talking stream'. *Iaith* (Brythonic–Pictish) 'language, talk'; with the *-on* ending found in many stream-names, deriving from a hypothetical early Celtic form *-ona*, indicating 'water'. Found in 1373 as Ethoyn, 1477 Ithane.

Z

Zetland *See* Shetland

Bibliography

Books

Black, George F., *The Surnames of Scotland* New York, 1946
Cameron, Kenneth, *English Place Names* London, 1961
Dauzat, Albert, *La Toponymie Française* Paris, 1971
Dingwall, C. H., *Ardler: A Village History*. Dundee, 1988
Drummond, Peter, *Scottish Hill and Mountain Names* Edinburgh, 1991
Dwelly, Edward, *Illustrated Gaelic–English Dictionary*, second edition, 1920, reprinted Glasgow, 1973
Ekwall, E. *English River-names* Oxford, 1928
Forbes, A. R., *Place Names of Skye* Paisley, 1923
Gelling, Margaret, *Place-Names in the Landscape* London, 1984
Jackson, Kenneth, *Language and History in Early Britain* Edinburgh, 1953
Johnston, James B., *Place-Names of Scotland*, 3rd edition London, 1934
Joyce, P. W. *Irish Names and Places* Dublin, 1871
MacBain, Alexander, *Place Names: Highlands and Islands of Scotland* Stirling, 1922
Macdonald, A., *Place Names of West Lothian* Edinburgh, 1941
Nicolaisen, W. F. H. *Scottish Place-Names, Their Study & Significance* London, 1976
Nicolaisen, W. F. H. *The Picts and Their Place-Names* Rosemarkie, 1996
Maxwell, H., *Scottish Land-Names* Edinburgh, 1894
The Oxford English Dictionary Oxford, 1983
Reaney, P. H., *The Origin of English Place Names* London, 1960
Room. A., *Concise Dictionary of Modern Place-Names in Great Britain and Ireland* Oxford, 1983
Stewart, John, *Shetland Place Names* Lerwick, 1987
Wainwright, F. T. (ed.) *The Problem of the Picts* Edinburgh, 1955
Wainwright, F. T., *Archaeology, Place Names and History* London, 1962

Watson, W. J., *Place-Names of Ross & Cromarty* 1904, reprinted
    Inverness, 1976
Watson, W. J. *History of the Celtic Place-Names of Scotland*
    Edinburgh, 1926

Journals

Review of Scottish Studies
Scottish Historical Review
Scottish Place Names Society Newsletter
Transactions of the Gaelic Society of Inverness

List of Place-names Noted Outside the Alphabetical Sequence

Please refer to the bracketed entries for
information on these place-names

Add, River (Dunadd)
Aikiehill (Deer)
Altnaharrie (Altnaharra)
Ardkinglas (Kinglass)
Ardlair (Ardle)
Ardler (Ardle)
Ardullie (Ardelve)

Balconie (Evanton)
Balgay (Balgie)
Barraer (Stranraer)
Berry, The (Berriedale)
Black Rock (Kiltearn)
Boddin (Boddam)
Bonjedward (Jedburgh)
Braes of Balquhidder
  (Balquhidder)
Branderburgh (Lossiemouth)
Braoin, Loch (Broom)
Buck, The (Cabrach)
Bucksburn (Buckie)
Buddon (Boddam)

Cairnsmore of Carsphairn
  (Carsphairn)
Callater (Calder)
Camaslongart (Longart)
Campbelltown (Ardersier)
Cassley, Glen (Cassillis)
Clunes (Cluanie)
Cockburnspath (Pathhead)
Conglass, River (Kinglass)
Cononsyth (Conon, Kilsyth)

Cornie Burn (Abercorn)
Coulin, River (Cuillin)
Crook of Alves (Crook of
  Devon)

Dalginross (Dalcross)
Dàl Riada (Dal-)
Dhu Heartach (Hirta)
Dorb, Loch an (Dava)
Dorback (Dava)
Drungan (Dron)
Duncryne (Gartocharn)
Duntrune (Troon)
Durris (Durrisdeer)

Edinbanchory (Edin-)
Erichdie (Ericht)
Ethie (Eathie)

Fhada, Benn (Attow, Ben)
Faithlie (Fraserburgh)
Fechlin (E)
Fitty, Loch (Footdee)
Five Sisters of Kintail (Attow, Ben)
Fowlis (Foulis)

Gairney (Cleish)
Glenluie (Lui, Ben)
Gourdon (Gordon)
Grannda, Allt (Kiltearn)

Haamer (Hamar)
Harstane (Hare Law)

Heisker (Hasker)
Hogganfield Loch (Barlinnie)

Inverlochy (Fort William)

Kilberry (Berriedale)
Kilchomain (Fort Augustus)
Kilcreggan (Gourock)
Kilillan (St Fillans)
Kinglassie (Kinglass)
Kinnell (Kinnoul)
Kintocher (Duntocher)
Kippendavie (Kippen)
Kirkettle (Kingskettle)
Kirkgunzeon (Kilwinning)
Kirkliston (Ingliston)
Knocknevis (Nevis)

Lednock, River (Comrie)
Loan (Loanhead)
Lonbain (Loanhead)
Lungard, Loch (Longart)

Millig (Helensburgh)
Montroy (Montrose)
Morrich More (Lovat)
Myot Hill (Dumyat)

Navidale (Navitie)
Nedd (Nith)
Nethy (Abernethy)
Newhall (Hailes)

New Lanark (Lanark)
Newstead (Eildon)

Osnaburgh (Dairsie)

Parph (Wrath, Cape)
Port Errol (Errol)

Redpath (Pathhead)
Redpoint (Butt of Lewis)
Reisk (Risk)
Ruskie (Risk)

Shona (Shuna)
Skaill Bay (Skara Brae)
Skarfskerry (Scarba)
Soroba (Sorbie)
Spango Hill (Spinningdale)
Stinchar, River (Ballantrae)
Sudreys (Hebrides)

Tarves (Tarff)
Tarvie (Tarff)
Tarvit (Scotstarvit)
Tingwall (Dingwall)
Trabrown (Traprain)
Trowglen (Knapp)

Ullie, River (Helmsdale)
Urlar Burn (Aberfeldy)

Vord Hill (Ward Hill)